The Life & Times of Lafayette Head

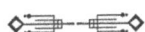

Early Pioneer of Southwest Colorado

BY CYNTHIA S. BECKER AND P. DAVID SMITH

"As a resident of Colorado, he preceded the pioneers.
He was here to welcome them when they came."
   Rocky Mountain News, March 10, 1897

WESTERN REFLECTIONS PUBLISHING COMPANY®
Lake City, Colorado

© Copyright 2019
Cynthia S. Becker and P. David Smith
All rights reserved in whole or in part

ISBN 978-1-937851-36-1

First Edition
Printed in the United States

Cover and Text Design by Laurie Casselberry
Laurie Goralka Design

Western Reflections Publishing Company
P. O. Box 1149
951 N. Highway 149
Lake City, Colorado 81235
www.westernreflectionspublishing.com
(970) 944-0110

Cover: "Conejos," *Harper's Weekly*, May, 1876
Portrait Insert: Head family portrait, Courtesy of Luther Bean Museum, Adams State University.

This book is dedicated to a very special friend, Marty Priest, without whose help this book and several others would not have been possible. Thank you for always being there.

A Tribute to Cynthia Becker

I first met Cynthia Becker in 2002 when she called me about a book she was writing on Chipeta, Ute Chief Ouray's faithful companion. She had read my book on Chief Ouray and was hoping I could give her some additional leads in her research. It so happened that I was also writing a book on Chipeta at that same time, and after several long telephone conversations, we decided to collaborate on the book. I soon learned that Cynthia was a very detailed and careful researcher, and that our writing styles blended together well.

Over the next year and a half, we passed our manuscript back and forth with each of us adding or questioning items in the book. Sometimes this required waiting for Cynthia to return from national natural disasters, as she was then a member of a Federal Emergency Management Agency's response team. Over the course of a year and a half, we produced a book that both of us were very proud of and which was well received by the general public. *Chipeta: Queen of the Utes* went on to win several literary awards, including an EVVY, and we gave book signings and lectures on Chipeta—Cynthia on the Eastern Slope and I on the Western Slope of Colorado.

A few years later, Cynthia decided to change course and write mainly historical Colorado juvenile books. Her first such book was a retelling of Chipeta's story for a younger audience, and then she produced five educational library-marketed books. In 2009 her book *Chipeta: Ute Peacemaker* was a finalist for the prestigious WILLA award in the Children and Young Adult Fiction and Non-fiction category. Cynthia also wrote numerous articles for magazines and newspapers that included *The New York Times*, *The Saturday Evening Post*, and *Learning Through History*.

Several years ago, Cynthia contacted Western Reflections Publishing Company about publishing a juvenile book she had written about Lafayette Head. Unfortunately we had to decline, as our audience consists mainly of adults. Then I heard nothing more until early 2017, when Cynthia's husband, David, contacted Western Reflections Publishing to let me know that she had passed away after a battle with a very aggressive cancer. He also asked if we would be interested in publishing her almost finished juvenile book. After reading the book and having several discussions with David, I agreed to do additional research, rewrite the book for adults, and have Western Reflections Publishing Company publish it as an adult biography of Lafayette Head. David Becker was also quick to agree to share Cynthia's research material on Lafayette Head with me, and it did not surprise me when I found her research to be very detailed. What follows is the finished product, but Cynthia deserves major credit for this book and also for the significant contribution she made to further Colorado history, especially among young people. She will be missed.

P. David Smith
Co-author and Publisher at Western Reflections Publishing Company

Cynthia S. Becker

Preface

One of the problems in researching and writing a book on the life of Lafayette Head has been that although Head was a major figure of his time, the history of his life is considerably confused and many aspects are missing. Head was a very humble man, but sometimes seemed to give himself a little more credit than he deserved, even though he had many great accomplishments during his life. This will be the first definitive book on his life, and we have tried hard to make it as accurate as possible, but in some cases it will be necessary to relate the most likely account of a detail of his life and those of his friends.

Even Lafayette's name is somewhat confusing. In his youth, the short form of the name "Lafayette" was usually "Fayette" or "Fate," but other nicknames for Lafayette included "Lafe, Lave, Fay, and Laffie." Cynthia chose to refer to him as "Lafe" (rhymes with "safe"), as his relatives evidently called him by that nickname; but I have usually preferred the more formal title "Lafayette." We will use both first names in this book. Lafe also often appears in Mexican-American historical records as "Raphael Cabeza." "*Cabeza*" means "head" in Spanish, but no one has yet to explain where the name "Raphael" came from. Perhaps it was a pet name that his wife Martina first used for Lafayette, as she was a very young widow with one (possibly two) children when he married her, and "Raphael" is one of the guardian angels of the Catholic Church.

Throughout his adult life, most Americans referred to Lafe as "Major Head." His official U.S. military service record from 1846-47 lists him as a private; however, he was later, in 1855, voted in by his comrades to fill an empty Second Lieutenant's position in the Colorado Mounted Volunteers, and that was only for the last month of his service. In an article in *Ranch and Range* magazine, "Mrs. Piedad Sisneros" (Lafe's granddaughter) writes that he was "created a Major in the Colorado Territorial Army" and that he "served with distinction in the brief but bloody Indian War of 1847." This is probably a reference to Lafe fighting as a U.S. soldier in the New

Mexico Pueblo Revolt of 1847, but Colorado did not become a territory of the United States until 1861. In an October 12, 1924 letter to D. W. Working of Fort Collins, Colorado, Lafe's great granddaughter, Evangeline Hill, wrote of another possibility; but this time, an honorary title.

> In 1861 he (Lafayette Head) kept the Indians and the Mexicans from taking the part of the enemies of the Union. For his services the government commissioned him a Major of the Colorado Volunteers. The Diary of the Jesuit Residence (explained later) supports this version, noting (in 1861) that "Lafe was made a Major in the Colorado Volunteers. It was an honorary title for keeping the Indians loyal to the Union during the Civil War." [1]

A few historians have written that Lafayette Head served in Price's Missouri Confederate Regiment during the Civil War, and that his title of "Major" may have come from that service. However his name does not appear on the Regiment's official roster during that time; and, as documented by his great-granddaughter, during this period of his life he was well-occupied as an Indian Agent trying to keep the Native Americans and the Mexican-Americans who still held a grudge against the United States peaceful toward the Union in Colorado. Although a considerable number of Colorado men supported the Confederacy, almost all of Lafe's personal friends (and evidently Lafayette himself) supported the Union, as did the Government of the Territory of Colorado.

We have come to believe that his title of "Major" was honorary, given to him by the Colorado Mounted Volunteers for his help in the Civil War in controlling the Native Americans, but it was a title often used. His highest official rank in regular military service was in the Colorado Mounted Volunteers as a Second Lieutenant. This one point alone shows the confusion that occurred in relating Lafayette Head's or Raphael Cabeza's life.

It is possible that a few Mexican-Americans may think some of the statements in this book to be incorrect or even hostile or racist. This problem might be brought on, at least in part, by the fact that Lafe was both greatly loved and hated by different people during his lifetime. Some of his contemporaries called him ignorant, others called him extremely smart. Some felt he was a crook, others thought him completely trustworthy. When we have noticed a conflict of opinion, we have tried to present both sides, unless it was obvious to us that one side was correct. Either way, we apologize if anyone is offended by statements we believe to be factual, or which might be contained in quoted material that may well show the bias of the time that existed towards Mexican-Americans. As an example, we have chosen the word "Mexican-American" instead of many other choices that could have been used, because most of Lafe's contemporaries were Mexican nationals who had chosen to become Americans in their adulthood after the end of the Mexican-American War. Lafe was so firmly entrenched in the Mexican-American community that many people of the time and some later historians believed he was of Mexican descent. He was not, and in fact grew up in Missouri and as a child or young adult was friends with such American heroes as the Daniel Boone family and Kit Carson. Another example of racial bias against Mexican-Americans is shown today in the designated area of central southern Colorado called simply "Southern Colorado," which is a euphemism for "Mexican-American Colorado," and which is an area that only covers a portion of the geographic southern Colorado.

We believe that it is important that Lafayette Head's life and the life of his chosen people, the Mexican-Americans of south central Colorado, be more recognized in the annals of Colorado history. Lafayette Head's achievements are many. The grit and toil of the Mexican, Spanish, and later Mexican-American people was, and still is, commendable, and should not be ignored in American and Colorado history. Our main reason for writing this book is to once again bring their history to the forefront of the general public and acknowledge their achievements in Colorado and American history.

Acknowledgements
(from Cynthia Becker's notes)

Numerous people assisted me in research for this book. In particular, Mary Mitchell at the Missouri State Archives; Carol Wendt, Sandra Romero Cordova, and Felix Gallegos of the Conejos County Clerk's Office; Cat Olance of the Luther Bean Museum in Alamosa, Colorado; Mary, Reference Librarian at Adams State University; Sarah Lillis at the Colorado State University Archives; Gerald Cook, Jesuit Archives and Special Collections, Regis University Library; and Dennis Northcott, Library and Research Center, Missouri History Museum. The Divas Critique Group read every chapter (of the preliminary juvenile version of the book) and offered many helpful suggestions. Special thanks to my husband, David, with the eagle-eye for the misspelled words, punctuation errors, and strange sentence structure. And thanks to Sinatra, the Siamese cat, who shared the chair while I typed.

Note from Publisher: To those who Cynthia had not yet included in her notes we apologize, as we know there were many more.

Acknowledgments
(from P. David)

First and foremost, I have to thank my spouse Jan for her proofreading and editing skills, helping me to decipher handwritten notes and letters, computer help, and for putting up with endless hours of my being absent while working on all my books. Many thanks also to my bilingual daughter, Tricia, for helping me with some of the Spanish words and phrases I have encountered. Although Cynthia discovered a lot of research material on Lafayette Head, I have relied on the book, *The San Luis Valley, Land of the Six-Armed Cross, Second Edition* by Virginia McConnell Simmons to help make decisions of what versions of Lafayette Head's life are probably correct, as well as it being the best overall history of the San Luis Valley. Tawney Becker of the Luther Bean Museum at Adams State University was very helpful in finding information and photographs about the Head family donated to that museum by Head's great-granddaughter, Evangeline Hill. Also thanks to Sheryl Smith for checking footnotes and dates in the book, for help in trying to get my footnotes straightened out, and for proofreading. And finally, thanks to Marley, my Shih Tsu dog, who kept me company on the Navajo rug on the floor of my office on many long nights while I was researching or writing.

Table of Contents

Preface vii
Acknowledgements xi
Chapter 1 Lafayette Head—A Forgotten Colorado Pioneer and Hero (1825—1897) 1
Chapter 2 Boyhood in Missouri (1825-1846) 16
Chapter 3 Soldier in the Mexican-American War and the Pueblo Revolt (1846-1847) 28
Chapter 4 Businessman and Lawman in New Mexico (1848-1854) . . 57
Chapter 5 A Home in the San Luis Valley and the Ute War of 1855 (1854-1855) 78
Chapter 6 Conejos, Fort Garland, Indians, and the '59ers (1855-1859) 110
Chapter 7 Colorado Territory, San Juan Excitement, The Utes, and the Civil War in Colorado (1860-1862) 132
Chapter 8 Family Man, the Utes, and an Exciting Trip from Washington City (1863-1864) 164
Chapter 9 Otto Mears, New Mexico Slavery, and Starving Utes (1864-1866) 182
Chapter 10 The Kit Carson Treaty of 1868 and Saguache (1866-1870) 206
Chapter 11 Friend of the Fathers (1857-1897) 230
Chapter 12 The San Juans and a Political Leader Once Again (1870-1875) 247
Chapter 13 Colorado Statehood, "The Utes Must Go," and Mormons (1876-1880) 275
Chapter 14 Piedad, Grandfather, and More Mysteries (1881-1897) . . 307
Epilogue 322
Endnotes 324
Bibliography 330
Index 342

CHAPTER ONE

Lafayette Head—A Forgotten Colorado Pioneer and Hero
(1825-1897)

*The plain man is the basic clod
from which we grow the demigod;
and in the average man is curled
the hero stuff that rules the world.*
                        Sam Walter Foss

The State of Colorado has been home to many amazing men, but recent history has generally not included Lafayette Head as one of them. Head was a man whose worth was recognized by his American and Mexican-American peers in the last half of the nineteenth century and also by the Ute Indians; but his legacy has mainly been forgotten, and occasionally even wrongfully tarnished. Today he is a man who is almost unknown in Colorado history. If he is known, it is usually for only one or two of his many achievements. For years this author must sadly admit that he only knew Head was a Ute Indian Agent stationed in Conejos, Colorado, in the San Luis Valley. However, his achievements went far beyond that position, which he handled with amazing dignity and honor toward the Native Americans for nine years—longer than any other early Ute Agent served.

Lafayette Head was born on the Missouri frontier, which at the time of his birth was just east of the Missouri River. The members of his family were originally from Great Britain but were true American pioneers and were good friends of better known neighbors like Daniel Boone and his children, the family of Kit Carson, and William Becknell, who was later known as the "Father of the Santa Fe Trail." The Head family made a home on the Missouri frontier in the early nineteenth century, fought the local Native Americans, and constantly risked their lives in a true wilderness. "Lafe," as he was called by his family, ran away from home at age sixteen. The reason may have been a romance with which his family did not agree or it could have been spurred by several long conversations he had with Kit

CHAPTER 1

Carson, who was visiting his family near the Head homestead when Lafe was sixteen. Lafe's family felt Carson inspired the boy to seek excitement, as Carson had done at the same age.

In 1848, at the age of twenty-one, Head came to Santa Fe, then in the Mexican Province of New Mexico, as a private in the United States' "Army of the West." When the Mexican-American War broke out in 1846, Head had quickly joined the Missouri Mounted Volunteers of the U.S. Army. The

This photograph of Lafayette Head was taken about 1876, when he was about fifty years old and had just been elected Lieutenant Governor of Colorado at the peak of his political career.

Photo courtesy of Luther Bean Museum, Adams State University.

Americans conquered most of New Mexico Province, including its capital of Santa Fe, without a shot being fired; but just a few months later, Lafe was a participant in several savage fights to put down "The Pueblo Uprising," also called the "Taos Revolt," a rebellion of over 1,000 armed Mexicans and Pueblo Indians who resented the cowardice of New Mexican Governor Don Manuel Armijo, who had retreated to Chihuahua, Mexico, without having ordered his army to fire a single shot in defense of their province. Lafe was wounded in several of the ensuing battles to put down the Pueblo Revolt, spent several months recovering from his wounds, and was then mustered out of the Army. However Lafe was so enamored with New Mexican life and its people that he decided to stay in Santa Fe.

Head worked for a Santa Fe shopkeeper and soon became fluent in Spanish. Within a year, he moved about sixty miles northwest to Abiqui, New Mexico, near the Chama River, where he ran his own trading post. His clients were the local residents, travelers of the Old Spanish Trail, and the Ute and Jicarilla Apache, who visited Abiqui often to trade furs and horses for American-manufactured items like cooking pots and utensils, goods such as sugar and tobacco, and especially guns, ammunition, and knives. Abiqui and Taos had been favorite wintering spots for American mountain men, fur traders, and trappers in southwest Colorado in the early 1800s; and a few of them still lived in the area. Lafe was used to Indians being around his native home in Missouri and soon met many of the Utes and Apache. About 1850 (the exact date is unknown as their marriage license has never been found) he married Martina Cisneros (also spelled Sisneros), a widow with two children (possibly one was an "adopted" slave) from a prominent Mexican family.

The early records are very confusing or even missing for Abiqui and the area covered by Arriba County as well as Taos County. When Mexico won its independence from Spain in 1821, New Mexico was generally divided into two areas—"Rio Arriba" or "Upper River" and "Rio Abajo" or "Lower River." The river referred to was the Rio Grande and the dividing line was a little north of Santa Fe.[2] Lafe seems to have been appointed a special U.S. Marshal for Arriba County with Tierra Amarilla as the county seat in 1848 or 1849 and was also the Arriba County tax collector at the time. In 1852 New Mexico became a territory of the United States and Rio Arriba was one of the new territory's first nine counties. From 1851 to 1853, Lafe was a Deputy U.S. Marshal and the Arriba County Sheriff, but he was responsible for a slightly different territory.

Lafe also made what proved to be a life changing decision when he became a member of the Santa Fe Masonic Lodge, where he made many

CHAPTER 1

important political and business contacts. In 1852, thanks to his Masonic friend Kit Carson, Lafayette Head was made a Special Agent for the Utes at Abiqui. He further served as a Sub-Agent for the Jicarilla Apache, the Southern Utes, and the Tabeguache Utes during the early 1850s. Lafe's connections to his fellow Masons became very important to him throughout his life.

In 1854 Lafe led a large group of settlers (a total of about 150, but split into two groups that were taken at different times) from the Chama River Valley to the very fertile, but unsettled, San Luis Valley. There he founded the Town of Conejos in 1855, which was then in New Mexico Territory, but in just six years would be in Colorado Territory. At Conejos, Lafe and Martina were instrumental in forming one of the first churches in the San Luis Valley and helped construct the first church building that still exists (although only parts of it) in Colorado—Our Lady of Guadalupe. He became very active in the Catholic Church and became good friends with the priests and bishops of the area, including New Mexico's Bishop Juan Lamy of *Death Comes to the Archbishop* fame.

Conejos quickly became one of the largest and most successful of the San Luis Valley settlements, and Lafayette built a small home that doubled as a fort when the settlement was attacked by Utes and Jicarilla Apaches. After 600 years of occupation, the Utes considered the San Luis Valley to be their land, and there was often conflict between the two cultures. Lafe was usually successful at calming matters down with both the Native Americans and the Whites. After a general Ute and Jicarilla Apache uprising in December 1855, he joined the New Mexico Mounted Volunteers, and he became close friends with many of the famous mountain men who had stayed in New Mexico after the fur trade had basically disappeared. This included the military leaders of the New Mexico Volunteers, Kit Carson, Ceran St. Vrain, Albert Pfeiffer, and many others who became lifelong friends.

Within a few years, Lafayette had become very popular throughout central southern New Mexico and was elected to the New Mexico Territorial legislature. He was the only Anglo elected at that time and served three one-year terms (1856-1858), the last year of which he was made President of the New Mexico Territorial Senate.

In 1859, at the suggestion of Kit Carson, Lafe was made a Tabeguache Ute Agent (sometimes joined by the Jicarilla Apache), and in 1860 Conejos was chosen to be the site for the Tabeguache Ute sub-Agency. In 1861 Lafayette became the head Tabeguache Ute Indian Agent at Conejos. The Ute Indians consisted of seven bands at this time. Besides the Tabeguache,

Lafe was back in Missouri with his entire immediate living family in April 1859, or in May of 1863. Left to right, his mother Margaret Heard Head, his younger sister Bartena Head (later Gray), his older sister Eliza (later Downing), and Lafayette.

Courtesy of the Luther Bean Museum, Adams State University, Gift of Gwendolyn Hill, #1975.10.1l.

CHAPTER 1

the Capote, Mouache, and Weeminuche bands were assigned to the Taos Agency with Kit Carson as Agent. The other three Ute Bands lived far enough to the north that no consideration was given to them at this time. Head eventually learned the difficult Ute language, became an official Ute translator, and successfully negotiated many small and large conflicts between the tribes and American settlers. In time, he accompanied the Utes to Washington for several peace treaties and became very close friends with Ute Chief Ouray and his wife Chipeta, as well as many of the other Ute chiefs and braves.

The Utes at first disliked Lafe as their Agent because they thought he was responsible for their annuities not arriving on time, and perhaps even stealing from them, and they were starving as the game they used for food was being killed by the hordes of newly arrived Americans. The problem was that Lafe was not yet fluent in the Ute language and had been furnished with a Ute translator who, unbelievably, could not speak their language. Kit Carson suggested Ouray, then just a young Ute who could also speak Spanish, as a new translator. With Ouray's help, the Utes soon learned that Lafe had no control over their supplies (or money to buy supplies) not being sent, and that Lafe was often feeding them his own food supplies until their food arrived from "The Great White Father." Lafe also helped the Utes try to understand the confusion that was going on around them and helped them figure out the best actions to take. Early on, he and Kit Carson counseled the Utes for the need to go to a reservation on the western slope of Colorado, but it would be almost a decade before the Utes agreed to do so.

Lafe was honest with the Utes and was quick to tell the U.S. government when the Utes had been lied to or cheated by other Americans. Lafe also made it clear to the U.S. government when it was Native Americans other than the Utes that were killing, robbing, or committing atrocities initially blamed on the Utes. Head was fair with the Utes, and they soon found they could believe what he told them, even during times when they were constantly being lied to by the U.S. government. After complaints were made by civilians, Carson and Head were usually able to make the military understand why the Utes were stealing cattle and food. They were starving because of the actions of the then Territorial and U.S. Government officials in not getting food to the Utes—sometimes because of ineptness, but many times on purpose.

During the Civil War, Head was credited with keeping the Colorado Native Americans at peace during a time when the Confederates were encouraging them to revolt and attack the people of Colorado Territory, most of whom had sided with the Union. Head ended his Tabeguache

Agent's position in 1869, after the Utes were moved from the San Luis Valley to western Colorado. Head helped to negotiate the treaty for their removal, and with Kit Carson's help convinced the Utes that the treaty would be good for them, as it moved them away from White settlers to what was then considered a remote part of Colorado; and, for the first time, the treaty actually defined specific lands as the property of the Utes. It also opened all of Colorado east of the Continental Divide to legal White settlement; most of which territory, however, was already occupied by them. Lafe had grown to love the San Luis Valley and did not want to leave, but Indian Agents were then by law required to live with the tribe to which they were assigned. Lafe decided to resign as Agent, although he had already been appointed to another two-year term. However he remained an official interpreter and adviser to the United States on Ute affairs for many more years.

In 1874 Lafayette was elected a member of the Tenth Colorado Territorial Senate and was a delegate to the State of Colorado Constitutional Convention. In 1876 he was elected the first Lieutenant Governor of the State of Colorado (and thereby President of the Colorado Senate) after being the runner-up candidate for the Republicans for the State of Colorado's first governor.

After Lafe and Martina had moved to the San Luis Valley in 1854, they quickly became very prominent in the Mexican-American community

The Colorado Capitol Building shortly after it was finished.

From postcard in author's collection.

and were called by the titles of "Don" and "Doña"—terms saved for much respected residents. Lafe became a very successful grain farmer and sheep rancher; and he built several of the first flour mills in the San Luis Valley (which also qualified as the first in Colorado). In addition, Head had a #2 Priority water right on the Conejos River and what would be one of the earliest irrigation ditches in all of the future Colorado. In 1858-1859, the years in which some consider the first Colorado pioneers to have arrived, Lafe and his friends, both Anglos and Mexican-Americans, had already lived in the San Luis Valley for five years and in the area for eleven years. Some of the '59ers were foolish enough to walk to the Pike's Peak area with only the supplies they carried on their backs, and it was Lafe and his Mexican-American friends who supplied the hordes of Americans that arrived in 1859-1860 with much of their food, work animals, and other supplies that were badly needed.

Lafe gained his high position in the Mexican-American community not through wealth or power, but through respect and caring. He helped take care of the poor and the hungry, often inviting them to come to his house to eat. He was quick to loan his equipment and animals to those who needed them. He was a major contributor to his church, often supplying large amounts of food (especially flour and meat) as a gift for the church's priests. He helped the new Mexican-American citizens to learn the American way of life—matters like voting and laws based on British common law rather than Spanish codes—and he acted as an English translator when the new Americans needed to communicate with authorities who could only speak English. He and Martina were godparents for many of the Conejos children, and Lafe was instrumental in providing the children of Conejos with one of the finest schools in Colorado. Lafe was a true Spanish "patron," in the most favorable sense of the word.

Head helped to build several of the first roads, bridges, and ferries in the San Luis Valley. He was postmaster of Conejos and belonged to many Colorado political, business, and economic organizations. He helped Otto Mears, as well as many other "pioneers," start their businesses in future Colorado and was always a friend to the early territorial pioneers whom he met. Lafe was to build a log fort immediately after arriving at the Conejos site. As soon as his adobe home fort was ready for occupation, he moved out of his original fort, but allowed settlers who came after him to use it for free as a home until they built their own, and to use it as a fort if they needed protection from marauding Native Americans. As stated in a later magazine interview with his granddaughter, Piedad Nelson:

> He knew not the limits of hospitality and seldom was his house
> free from a dozen or more of his friends, as he was favorably
> known by almost everybody throughout Colorado and New
> Mexico, and he never enjoyed life so much as when he had a
> company of his friends around the fireplace.[3]

Lafe could not have children, although his wife Martina had a natural child (possibly two) when they married. Lafe adopted her child José. Even this is questionable as no child named José appears in the 1850 or 1860 census (there is a Cresencio Sisneros, age sixteen, in the 1860 census) in Lafe's home, but there was no official ceremony for adoption at the time. Then over the years, they adopted over a dozen orphaned Mexican or Native American children, but Lafayette was later threatened with criminal action when U.S. authorities claimed he was keeping the children as slaves. He was not, and later proved to U.S. officials that all of the orphans still at his home were taken in when they were abandoned, about to be killed, or were being sold by Native Americans. Head also had Navajo slaves that were treated harsher than the other slaves, but they were all released before the Emancipation Proclamation made slavery illegal. Before this time, slavery of Indians was accepted in New Mexico, even by the Catholic Church. Navajos were taken as slaves so often that one historian estimated that seventy percent of all Navajo families had lost at least one family member to slave traders. Many of Head's "adopted" children took the Head name and lived with him and Martina until well into adulthood, although all were free to leave after they were able to take care of themselves—usually when they were about fifteen or when they married. This was a custom the Spanish and later Mexicans had followed for centuries and was thought of as an act of grace.

When the Mormons settled in the San Luis Valley, Lafayette became their friend and was later honored for what he did for them. At a time when the Mormons were being discriminated against, he welcomed them to the San Luis Valley and loaned the Mormons animals and equipment to plow and plant crops. He also helped by supplying them with food for several years until they learned how to successfully farm in the dry climate of the San Luis Valley using proven irrigation techniques.

Lafe represented Colorado at the Republican National Convention in 1880 in Chicago, although after his stint as Colorado's first Lieutenant Governor, he was basically content to retire to his ranch and enjoy life with his many friends. He was famous throughout his forty years in the San Luis Valley for the hospitality that he always offered strangers and travelers at

CHAPTER 1

his Conejos home. One friend said that none of Lafe's friends got within a 100 miles of his house without knowing they needed to pay him a visit. On the other hand, if a total stranger needed help, Lafe was always there to lend a hand.

Ranch and Range magazine called Lafayette Head "perhaps the most prominent man who figured in the early history of New Mexico and Colorado," and noted that "he was a warm friend of Governor Gilpin, Governor Routt, Bent, Kit Carson, Dick Wooten (sic), Maxwell, and many others whose names are familiar in frontier history."[4]

However, as mentioned earlier, even with all that he accomplished for Colorado in both the private and public sectors, Lafayette Head seems today to be no more than a footnote in most Colorado history books, becoming more and more forgotten as time goes by. This trend started soon after he died in 1897. When the Colorado capitol building was being finished during the late 1890s, it was decided that the capitol dome would contain sixteen stained glass portraits, a "Hall of Fame" of noteworthy Colorado pioneers. Although Head was immediately nominated along with seventy-six other pioneers, he did not make the final cut. Most knowledgeable people knew he should have been included and were greatly upset when he did not receive the honor. Many of those who did get their portraits in the dome (completed in 1899, two years after Lafe's death) were Lafe's close friends and colleagues. Many others were men and women who, with the passage of time, have been found to not deserve the honor half as much as Lafe. There are several whose portraits are in the dome merely because they were rich and/or powerful, not because they helped Colorado grow.

Even Otto Mears, who was on the committee to pick the sixteen pioneers but was not a finalist, wrote:

> *The idea of the Board seems to be to put in this gallery the portraits of anybody who drove an ox wagon across the plains in '59.... Some of the selections have been good, but there are some names already on the list which should not be there.* [5]

It is noteworthy that Chief Ouray was the second person picked for the list, Kit Carson the third, and that even the notorious Governors William Gilpin and John Evans were numbers eight and nine. All of these men were good friends of Lafayette Head.

Lafayette Head was not a perfect man, but he was a good man—a very good man who did much for Colorado and New Mexico. He probably did more for Colorado's Mexican-American community than any Anglo before or after him. Lafayette Head had all the credentials of a hero, so why has he not received more attention? Why has Head been overlooked in today's Colorado history books?

One reason was that Lafayette Head was a very modest man who did not like to be in the spotlight. He often let others, like Otto Mears, take the credit for something he had done or made possible. It must be remembered that Lafe lived at a time when wealth and power were everything. Capitalism was running rampant. Greed was usually used to gain power and wealth, and often it was looked upon as honorable to use whatever means necessary to make a dollar. Those means included lying, cheating, disrespect, bad behavior, corruption, and many other questionable traits. Lafayette Head was not that type of man. Lafe lived well economically, but he was also humble and shared his wealth with those in need.

Another reason Lafe might have been overlooked was that he was a solid and revered member of the Mexican-American community—a group that received very little recognition for its role as the earliest of the European settlers in America's Southwest and for their achievements and contributions to early Colorado. Even the Spanish colonials overlooked the pioneering achievements of their people in the Province of New Mexico, giving most of the honor or praise to the inept Spanish aristocrats who ran the province.

> *As the years passed, official (Spanish) reports increasingly characterized the settlers as "rustic," "uncouth," and "obstinate": a measure of the growing cultural gap between the administrators and the administered, both Indians and Hispanic.*[6]

If the cavalry came to the rescue in Colorado or New Mexico in the decade after 1848, it would be composed almost entirely of Mexican-Americans. It was Mexican-Americans who grew the food the citizens of Colorado Territory needed. If a new settlement was built in the future South-Central Colorado, it was built almost entirely by Mexican-Americans. It was mainly Mexican-Americans who traveled eastward to the U.S. on the historic Santa Fe Trail, and it was they who helped build and maintain the first railroad lines, bridges, and other means of transportation. And, perhaps most importantly, after the Mexican-American War ended, almost all Mexicans in New Mexico Territory wanted to become U.S. citizens. A ready work force was already present.

New Mexico Territory's first delegate to the U.S. House of Representatives, an Anglo, Richard Weightman, had this to say about the territory's citizens in 1852:

CHAPTER 1

> *I have never met in any part of the United States people more hospitable, more law-abiding, more kind, more generous, more desirous of improvement, more desirous that a general system of education be established among them, more desirous that the many and not the few should govern, more apprehensive of the tendency of power to steal from the many for the few, more desirous of seeing in their own idiom the Declaration of Independence, the Constitution of the United States... Among them I have met men of incorruptible integrity, of honor, refinement, intelligence, and information.*[7]

Perhaps this quote is just a little too flattering, but Weightman was writing to try to counter a point of view that was much too negative toward the Mexican-Americans. The first Americans to visit New Mexico Province, basically fur trappers and traders, did not see the Spanish or Mexican communities in a negative light. They found them to be friendly, helpful, and easy-going without the "hang-ups" of many of the more "civilized" American citizens of the time. Many of these early Americans married Spanish or Mexican women and stayed to enjoy the exciting and inviting life of the Province of New Mexico in the first half of the nineteenth century. They were followed by the soldiers of the "Army of the West" that occupied New Mexico during the Mexican-American War. The attitudes of the soldiers seemed to be a direct result of their cultural background and place of origin. Those soldiers with eastern U.S. backgrounds tended to see the Mexicans as "lazy," "simple," "stupid," or even "savages." Those who were from the frontier of the United States (from the Appalachians to the Mississippi River) or recent immigrants tended to see the New Mexico community with excitement and pleasure.

The negative attitude of many easterners probably explains the delay (and failure in many cases) of the United States to recognize Spanish and Mexican land grants for many years after the end of the Mexican-American War (and then only partially), even though these grants under Article 10 of the Treaty of Guadalupe-Hidalgo were to be examined by U.S. authorities, and, if found to be legal under Mexican law, were to be honored by the United States. Article 10 of the Treaty of Guadalupe Hidalgo was struck by the U.S. Senate before they ratified the treaty. The Mexican Grants were mostly ratified, but with many limiting conditions. A continuation of this attitude toward the Hispanic community probably explains the reason that New Mexico was not made a state until 1912, more than sixty years after it became a territory. Only recently in historic terms have several books been written about the discrimination suffered by early day Hispanics from many Americans and the failure to document their well-deserved place in Colorado history. One of the best of these books is *Enduring Legacies: Ethnic Histories and Culture of Colorado*, edited by Auturo Aldama, and published by The University of Colorado Press. Another is *Los Primeros Pobladores: Hispanic Americans of the Ute Frontier* by Frances Leon Swadesh, published by The University of Notre Dame Press; a third is *The Hispanic Contribution to the State of Colorado* by Jose' de Onis, published by Westview Press of Boulder, Colorado; and a fourth is *Manifest Destiny, The Making of the Mexican-American Race* by Laura E. Gómez published by NYU Press. All are academic tomes that give considerable space to the problem, but which have probably not been read by many members of the general American public outside the Mexican-American community.

Yet another reason for the lapse in historical recognition for the early Mexican-American communities and their leaders, including Lafayette Head, was that they were generally Roman Catholic (and in the San Luis Valley also often Penitentes, a matter which we will discuss later) at a time when anti-Catholic discrimination was at its greatest in the United States. There was also an anti-immigrant bias present, mainly because many immigrants were Catholic or could not speak English. This bias obviously continues up to present day, but usually included violence in Lafe's time. White settlers in the Territory and State of Colorado, as opposed to the Territory of New Mexico, tended to think of Mexican-Americans as immigrants, even though they or their ancestors may have lived on their land for decades or even centuries before any Americans came west.

Perhaps the saddest reason that Lafayette Head's accomplishments have not been acknowledged in recent Colorado history is the Ute Indians and the Mexican-American people were Lafe's friends and were the two races of people he mainly lived among. The Utes, as most Native-Americans, were ignored by the Whites, many of whom debated at that time if they were even human or of some other species. The Whites badly mistreated them; but at the time, with Manifest Destiny leading the way, White-Anglo Protestants simply looked the other way and ignored what happened to America's natives. Although there were efforts at assimilating Native Americans into White society, these were usually feeble and soon abandoned for the policy of putting them away somewhere from the rest of American society, where they could be ignored and forgotten on their reservations. Even the Indian movements of the late nineteenth century and early twentieth century did not stop this isolationist policy. Only in recent times has this attitude changed, and only to a small extent.

CHAPTER 1

The same occurred with the Mexican-American community in "Southern Colorado." The Mexican-American communities of Texas, New Mexico, Arizona, and California (the other populated areas lost by Mexico in the Mexican-American War) have not only been allowed to keep their culture, but it is often celebrated by the Whites. Mexican-Americans are recognized as being the original culture of at least major parts of these states, while it is not in all parts of Colorado. The Mexican-Americans who pioneered Colorado are simply a forgotten people, especially in the San Luis Valley, which is the poorest area of all of Colorado. The ghettos of the metropolitan areas of Colorado are not forgotten, but those of the San Luis Valley and around Pueblo and Trinidad are. The San Luis Valley is still strongly agricultural (81% of land is agricultural or grazing). About half of the population of the San Luis Valley is Hispanic, and there is a 37.5 percent poverty rate, mostly Hispanic.

So perhaps the reason Lafe has been forgotten and ignored is because he lived his good life and did his humanitarian deeds in an area where most of the people belonged to and still belong to cultural communities that the rest of Colorado and the United States wanted to (and in some places still want to) ignore and forget. It is our desire that this book may in some way help spread awareness of the important role played by Mexican-Americans and the Ute Indians in Colorado's past and present. It must also be noted that even in his time Lafe's history was often biased because of the traditions and accepted practices of his day. Hopefully this book will set the record straight and bring light to the life of a great pioneer, humanitarian, and hero and provide Lafayette Head the credit that he most justly deserves.

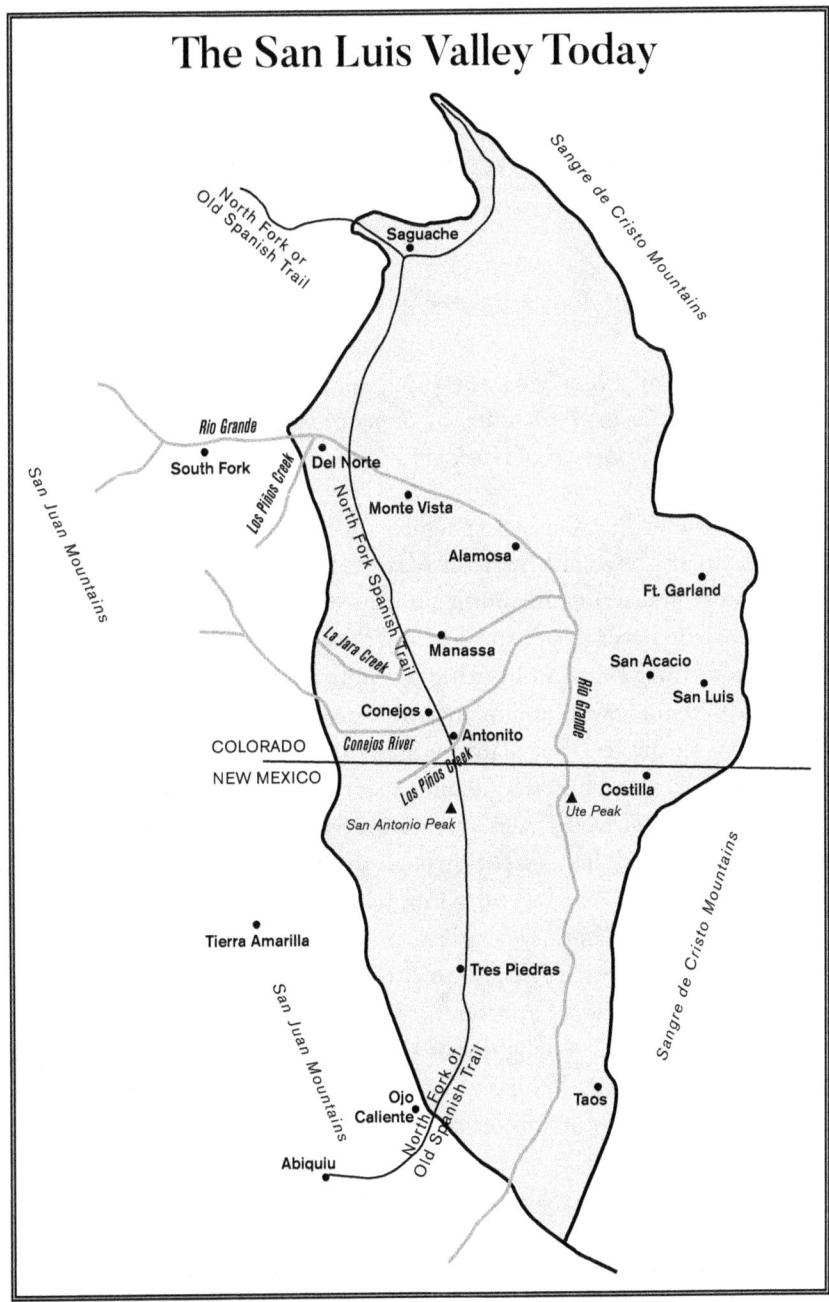

Map showing selected historic spots mentioned in this book in the San Luis Valley in 2019. (Not to scale)

Western Reflections Publishing Co. Map.

CHAPTER TWO

Boyhood in Missouri
(1825-1846)

> "Thursday 7th of June 1804. Set out early...to the mouth of a creek Called big monitu.... Some buffalo signs...."
> Journal of Lewis and Clark, 25th day of expedition

Lafayette Head probably first sighted Indians through a gun slit in the walls of his boyhood home in Missouri. The shrieks and cries of the painted warriors circling his home on wild-eyed horses were said to haunt his dreams. He never forgot the *zing* and *thwap* of Native American arrows loosed from their bows and hitting the house he lived in as a boy; but it would be 900 miles away and many years later before he fought back against Native Americans and eventually became their Indian Agent and friend.

Lafayette's grandfather, William Head, was a pioneer settler who had arrived in central Missouri from Virginia in 1811, just seven years after explorers Lewis and Clark had passed through the area and before Missouri was even a territory. William was born in England, moved to the United States, lived in Washington County, Virginia, and served in the Revolutionary War before he and his brother Moses came to Howard County, Missouri, with a group of Revolutionary War veterans. Lafe's grandfather William had married Elizabeth Heard, a daughter of the Heard family, which had come to Virginia with William. William Head's son (later Lafe's father), Alfred R. Head, was born in Virginia and also came west to Missouri with his parents. The Heads had decided to settle on land being offered for free by the U.S. government to veterans of the American Revolution, and it was where William planned to farm and trap for the rest of his life.

After the Heads and their fellow veterans had picked their land, but before they could finish their log houses, the veterans were summoned to duty again—this time it was the War of 1812, which was a confrontation started by Great Britain inciting Native Americans to go on the warpath. The British hope was that the Native Americans, with British assistance,

Boyhood in Missouri

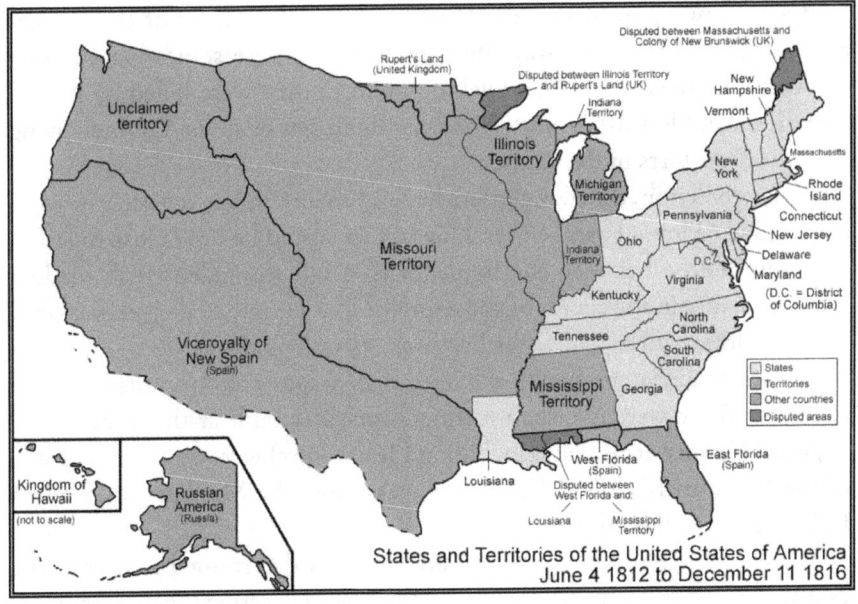

Missouri Territory in 1812 had been created out of the Louisiana Purchase, but Spain could have legally contested this claim as its sale to France contained a provision that the property had to be sold back to Spain.

Courtesy of Wikipedia.

would drive the American settlers from the northern territory of the United States. Alfred Head served as a private in the War of 1812 alongside his father William, who served as Captain of the 3rd Regiment, County of St. Charles, Missouri. After the war ended, William and Alfred were released from the army, and they finally settled on the land they had picked in Missouri. In 1812, to avoid confusion with the new Louisiana, which had just been formed out of the old Louisiana Purchase, Missouri had become a huge territory that covered much of the western part of today's Continental United States.

When William Head, his son, and his friends returned from the war, Missouri was still a very wild place—the true frontier of the United States. Many of the Native Americans who had been stirred up by the British were still on the warpath. Missouri had long been occupied by many different Native Americans tribes—Winnebago, Pottawatomie, Kickapoo, Sac (Sauks), Fox, and Iowa; and now the Cheyenne, Crows, and Arikarees (Rees) were also sometimes in the area. The land along the Missouri River was getting crowded, and the Americans were unwanted intruders; so, the Native Americans set out to get rid of the people building homes on their land and plowing up the earth. They tried to kill as many of the settlers as possible and to scare away the rest, and they were somewhat successful. Between 1812 and 1814, twelve American men were killed by Native Americans in Howard County, Missouri alone, out of about 112 men living in the various forts in the county.

For protection, the new settlers banded their families together in what were called "Home Forts." Several log homes would be built close together and were fenced between the homes with a tall stockade, which made a tight enclosure in the center of the complex that in time of danger was used for the horses, cattle, and other livestock, as well as the settlers—much as wagon trains did later when they circled their wagons on the trails in Indian territory. There were five such forts or stockades built at this time in the Howard County area. Four (including Head's Fort) were on the north side of the Missouri River and Cole's Fort was across the Missouri River and a little to the south on the prairie.

The Americans coming to this area were as determined to stay as the Native Americans were to run them out. The new settlers were war-hardened pioneers and well-armed, and they included men like Lindsey Carson (father of Kit Carson); Daniel Boone and two of his sons (Nathan and Daniel Morgan Boone); and William Becknell, later known as the "Father of the Santa Fe Trail."

The area west of the Mississippi River (including today's State of Missouri) was still considered Spanish Territory (at least by the Spanish), but the Louisiana Purchase gave Americans a somewhat questionable right to this land. Prior to the arrival of the Heads and their fellow veterans, the Daniel Boone family had already lived in that part of Missouri for almost a decade. Since 1809, the Missouri Fur Company had been going up the Missouri River in boats with their fur trappers and traders, and they passed through or very close to the land where the new settlers decided to make their home.

Daniel Morgan Boone (not to be confused with his famous father), was the first Boone to set foot in today's Missouri and was a famous frontiersman in his own right. He had been sent by his father to check with the Spanish Lieutenant Governor about homesteading, and he was given a land grant near present-day Defiance and Matson, Missouri. The Spanish officials also told him that if his famous father would come, he would also be given a land grant; and his father not only came, but he brought other settlers with him. Daniel Morgan Boone built a double log house on his new property about 1800 and his parents lived there with him for a number of years. The senior Daniel Boone is often recognized as the founder of the

Boyhood in Missouri

"Western Movement" in the United States, and it was in this type of environment that Lafayette Head would be raised.

Lafe's grandfather, William Head, and William's good friend Price Arnold, with the help of their older sons, built what they called "Head's Fort" in a curve on the east side of a bend of Moniteau Creek.

> ... about two miles north of Rocheport and about two miles south of where the old St. Charles road, and about a half mile west of the Boone line... It was located at a spring of never failing water. [8]

Two miles to the south of Head's Fort, Moniteau Creek flowed into the Missouri River. Head's Fort was about four miles from the later settlement of New Rocheport, Missouri. Head's Fort had gun slots cut out of the fort's log walls and was well prepared for an Indian attack. Local leaders were chosen to take charge of the forts in case of attacks and were given the unofficial title of "Captain," although that was also his War of 1812 rank. William Head was also the leader of his fort and was sometimes referred to as "Captain Head."

Head's Fort sat between two major transportation routes for people heading west or going back east. One was the Missouri River and the other

Although this home fort was built by Lewis and Clark, it is a good example of what "Head's" Fort must have looked like.

Oregonencyclopedia.org.

was a trail called "Boone's Lick Trace," located about a mile and a half from Head's Fort. Since Head's Fort sat between those two well-traveled routes, Lafe met many people who were passing through while going to a new life in the West. In 1816, the town of Franklin, Missouri (named after Benjamin Franklin), had been located near where Boone's Lick Trace ended at the Missouri River. The town was made the county seat of Howard County in 1817; and, by 1818, Franklin had a newspaper, 120 homes, thirteen stores, four taverns, two blacksmiths, and two steam-powered lumber mills. Franklin also had a post office and a courthouse with a jail.

William Becknell had settled in the Boone's Lick area in 1812 at the same time as the Heads and the Arnolds. Franklin would become one of the early jumping off points, if not **the** jumping off point, for the Santa Fe Trail. The population in Missouri along the trail boomed from 500 back in

Map showing the United States and Mexico about 1830. The Adams-Onis Treaty created the boundary between Mexico and Oregon Territories, which was claimed by both Great Britain and the United States. Note there were only two Mexican Provinces in what is now the United States.

Map courtesy of Wikipedia.

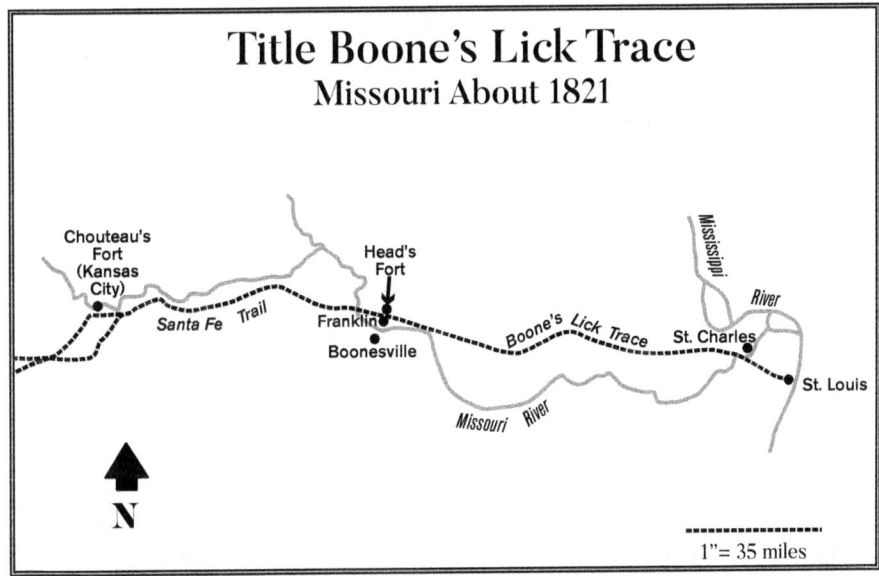

The eastern end of Boone's Lick Trace near St. Louis was used after 1764 by fur trappers. By 1805 it was also being used by settlers to Franklin, and it connected with the Santa Fe Trail in 1821 near Chouteau's Fort (now Kansas City, Missouri), and became one of the main routes to Mexico.

Western Reflections Publishing Co. Map.

1812 to 15,000 in 1821 due in part to the opening of the new country of Mexico to Americans.

The winter of 1825-26 had a heavy snowfall in the Rockies that caused the Missouri River to flood. It was said that it "carved off much of the town of Franklin," but "New Franklin" was soon built on high ground two and a half miles away. Franklin was also a port on the Missouri River opposite Booneville in Cooper County, and steamboats delivered passengers and supplies to both of those towns, many of the passengers intending to go to the West. Certainly with such a strong westward migration going on around Lafe's home, Lafe would have been influenced at an early age to eventually head west himself.

For many years Boone's Lick Trace was the only land route leading into Franklin from the east—its name being reflective of pioneer and even pre-pioneer times.

> Boone's Lick Trace was "the Grandad of all trans-Mississippi trails to the West," especially after the War of 1812 when most of the Indians were driven out of the area.[9]

CHAPTER 2

A "trace" was an Indian trail used by Native Americans and later by trappers, who in this case were going west after 1764, when St. Louis became a fur trading center. The older Daniel Boone first used the east end of the trace in 1797. The trail would be used from the time when he and others had been lured by the promise of free land for settlers until the time of the railroads in the 1890s. In 1800, many people, including the older Daniel Boone's family, settled along the eastern beginning of the trail, which is now followed west fairly closely by Interstate 70. The two Boone brothers had traveled further down the trail and located a "salt spring" about 100 miles west of the Boone family home in 1805, and it was later misnamed a "salt lick" by others, and the name stuck. The Boone brothers employed several men to boil salt from the water; and, after their personal use, there was enough salt to sell the remainder along the trail and along the Missouri River all the way to St. Louis. The traffic of the Boone brothers over the trail permanently established the route on which the towns of Booneville, Rocheport, Arrow Rock, and Franklin were located.

In the early 1800s, Lafayette's father, Alfred Head, was a surveyor by trade, who supplemented his income with farming. Lafe's mother, Margaret Heard, was born May 30, 1802 in Kentucky. She was one of eight children of John Heard and Jane Stephenson Heard. After her father died, Margaret, her mother, and all her brothers and sisters moved to Boone County, Missouri, in 1818. Lafayette's parents both came from large families that lived together after the Heards moved to Head's Fort.

Life in this part of Missouri did have some civilization and the settlers' lives were not spent just waiting for Indian attacks. There was school for the children, religious services, and all the regular household chores, especially preparing and preserving food. The men had their crops planted just outside of the fort where they could quickly get to the safety of the stockade and shoot at the attacking Indians; and there was good hunting and fishing in the deep woods of Howard County.

In 1821, after Mexico had gained its freedom from Spain under the Treaty of Cordova, several men from Howard County (including William Becknell) had gone to Santa Fe to trade, as Mexico (as opposed to Spain) was now welcoming Americans. It was at this time that the American trappers were also at their peak in the future Colorado and New Mexico.

Lafayette Head's grandfather, William Head, died in 1824; and Lafayette was born just a few months later at Head's Fort (also called "Fort Head") on April 19, 1825. It was less than five years after Missouri had gained its statehood on August 10, 1821—the only state at the time that was entirely west of the Mississippi River. Lafe lived with his extended family on the far western edge of "civilization" for over sixteen years.

During Lafe's childhood,

> *Missouri was an almost unbroken wilderness, and the county was full of wild game which furnished meat in abundance to the settlers. There were large droves of wild turkey, elk, deer, and bear, and as soon as a cabin was ready for occupancy the men folks turned their attention to hunting and fishing. The range was good and the stock kept fat on the luxuriant grasses, while nuts and berries of all kinds furnished ample food for every species of animal.*[10]

Alfred and Margaret Head gave their new son his unusual French first name following a custom quite popular at the time of naming children after heroes of the day. "Lafayette" was named for the well-known Frenchman–Marie-Joseph-Paul-Yves-Roche-Gilbert, Marquis du Motier de La Fayette, who fought for the Americans in the American Revolution. The Marquis de Lafayette was enough of a Revolutionary War hero that the seven acre park directly north of the White House is still named for him. The reason for choosing the name was probably that just four months before Lafayette's birth, the Marquis de Lafayette returned to visit America and his stops included the nearby county seat of Fayette, Missouri, which had been named for him by William Head and the other Revolutionary War veterans.

Lafayette was just five years old when his father, Alfred, died in 1830. Young Lafe fortunately had his large extended family living close around him and grew up surrounded by uncles, aunts, and cousins. Lafayette also had an older sister, Eliza Jane, and a younger sister, Barthena. Eliza Jane was born in 1821 and Barthena was born in 1827.

Lafe's many uncles helped to ease the pain of not having a father or a grandfather present in his early years. As he grew older, his uncles included him in the work done by their own sons, so he could learn how to farm. He tended cattle and built up his physique while plowing behind a horse, cutting hay with a scythe, and planting fields by hand. It was hot, sweaty, and tiring work. For recreation, Lafe enjoyed fishing in the many nearby streams, and he eventually used his deceased father's shotgun to hunt wild turkey, deer, elk, and bear in the wooded Missouri hills. His granddaughter said many years later that Lafe became a dead shot with "unerring aim." He also trapped beaver and river otters for their pelts, which brought him a good price from the fur traders passing through on Boone's Lick Trace. Lafe grew into a tall, lanky boy with dark hair. He was said to be "calm and straight spoken," and he made friends easily.

CHAPTER 2

Unlike many of her neighbors, Margaret Head, Lafe's mother, could read and write, and she schooled her children at home from books she had brought with her when her family had moved west from Kentucky. She taught her children to read and also to write with a flourishing cursive handwriting that included plenty of loops and curving lines. Under his mother's watchful eye, Lafe received a good education and developed an elegant penmanship that in his later life many people greatly admired. Later on, Lafe also received a limited public school education, such as it was, at a Missouri "common school."

Lafe's older sister, Eliza Jane, later described their mother, Margaret, as a "prudent, plain, practical, (and) kindhearted woman." However Margaret was strict, and Eliza Jane said "once she made up her mind, no amount of arguing would change it."

Despite Lafayette Head being born to a wilderness family in Missouri, his mother taught him how to read and write well. In later life many people commented on his writing.

Letter courtesy of J. M. Francisco Papers, Colorado State University Archives.

> (Mother) recognized the serious obligations of life in all daily matters, and strove to discharge them with unshrinking and conscientious fidelity.... Once her opinion was formed, it was seldom changed by argument. [11]

Eliza Jane spoke from experience. At age fifteen, she had fallen in love with a man she had met at a revival. Nathan Downing was twenty-five and wanted to marry her. Margaret refused to give her permission; but that did not stop Eliza, who evidently was just as strong-willed as her mother. She eloped with Nathan, a Cumberland Presbyterian minister, on March 16, 1836, and the couple settled over a hundred miles away in Hannibal, Missouri. Later they moved east to Illinois, and they had moved to Virginia by 1850. Barthena Head, Lafe's younger sister, married J. Thomas Gray in 1850 and lived in Virginia most of her life, although by 1900 she was living with her son, John T. Gray, in Henry County, Missouri. She died March 9, 1917.

Lafe was sixteen when his mother remarried. John Arnold, his new stepfather, was a man Lafe knew well. When Arnold's first wife, a sister of Lafe's father, died, Arnold married Margaret in 1841 and a year later Jesse Arnold, Lafe's half-brother, was born. Jesse Arnold was the only child of John Arnold and Margaret (Heard) Head Arnold.

To a backwoods boy like Lafe, the town of Franklin, Missouri, must have been a strange and wonderful place. The town had so many homes scattered along its dirt streets that Lafe probably could not imagine there were enough people in the area to fill all those houses. He must have wandered wide-eyed through the dozen little frontier stores in Franklin that sold food, clothes, and tools—much of it to be traded by mountain men to the Native Americans in the West for furs. Many of Franklin's citizens heard trappers' stories, as the town was an American trapper home base for renewing supplies and touching in with civilization.

In 1841, Kit Carson, a neighbor's son, came back home to Franklin to visit. Kit was born December 24, 1809 in Kentucky, but was brought by his father Lindsey Carson to the Boone's Lick area of Howard County in 1810 when Kit was only one year old. The Carson and Boone families were good friends, and the Carsons settled on the grant given to Daniel Morgan Boone by the Spanish. In 1826, at age sixteen, Kit had decided to seek adventure in the Wild West that he had heard so much about from the men who came to the saddle maker's shop where he had been apprenticed at age fourteen. It was a job he hated. He ran away and hired on to herd cattle with a wagon train going west on the Santa Fe Trail. By 1841, he had already spent many

CHAPTER 2

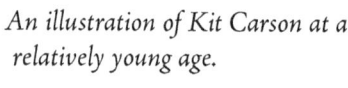

An illustration of Kit Carson at a relatively young age.

From Clamp, *Echoes from the Rocky Mountains*.

years in the Rocky Mountains, trapped in the Sangre de Cristo and San Juan Mountains, traveled all over the West, and fought Indians on many occasions. Carson therefore knew the San Luis Valley and the future Colorado well, but he had yet to be recognized for his skill and trustworthiness outside the mountain man community. News of Kit's return to Franklin spread quickly. He was on his way to take his four-year-old daughter, Adaline, whose mother was Kit's deceased Arapaho wife, Waa-Nibe (Singing Grass), to St. Louis to live with his sister and be educated back East. Adaline was Carson's only child by his first wife.

Besides the tales told by other travelers, Lafe would have certainly sat and listened to Kit's tales of adventure in the Rocky Mountains, and Kit already had many exciting stories to tell. Several months later, during his return trip to the Rockies, Carson would meet explorer John C. Fremont on a paddle wheeler on the Mississippi and Missouri Rivers and would sign on as Fremont's guide to South Pass, with other area's to be explored along the way. The trip would make Carson famous, and within a few more years he would become a good friend of Lafe in New Mexico Territory. In the meanwhile, Lafe stayed awash in Western Expansion and Manifest Destiny politics in Missouri.

Whether it was a result of Kit's tales or those told by others, the prevailing political climate, problems with his stepfather, or a broken heart, according to his family, Lafe ran away from home not long after Carson's visit. Lafe later said the reason was that he was in love with a young girl, but neither her parents nor Lafe's would give them permission to marry. Some authors have written that his romance was with a cousin. Lafe would not go back to his boyhood home to visit his mother until 1859 or 1861.

Boyhood in Missouri

On May 11, 1846, the United States declared war with Mexico. President James K. Polk called for 50,000 volunteer soldiers to fight in the war, and three companies of volunteers were quickly formed in Missouri. Many more men soon followed, especially from Missouri, including Lafe.

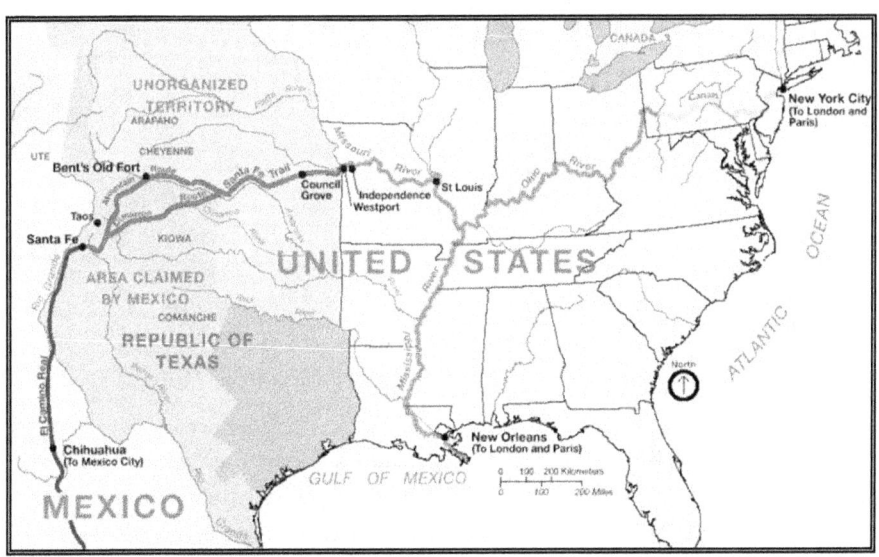

U. S., Mexico, and Texas in 1845, a year before the Mexican-American War and also showing Native-American territory near today's Colorado.

From santafeselection.com.

CHAPTER THREE

Soldier in the Mexican-American War and the Pueblo Revolt
(1846-1847)

News is received here that...Colonel Price, who has command of the Malitia (sic) from the States, will be in soon, he is now within a few miles of the city.
Diary of Susan Shelby Magoffin, Santa Fe, 1846

For a half a century before Lafayette Head was born, events had been occurring in Spanish, Mexican, and American politics that would greatly affect his future. About 1770, Spain had ended its expansion and exploration to the north of Taos in the Province of New Mexico. The country had considerable problems back in Europe and was quickly going broke. By 1800, both Spain and the United States viewed the Great Plains and the Rockies as a desolate buffer zone that would keep their citizens apart. However by 1840, the appearance of the Doctrine of Manifest Destiny, the Western Expansion Movements, reports of valuable minerals being discovered in today's Southwest, and the successful revolt of Texas from Mexico had caused many Americans to want to expand the United States all the way west to the Pacific Ocean. The first step in this direction had been the Louisiana Purchase and the creation of the Missouri Territory, but this territory ended at the Continental Divide.

In the Adams-Onis Treaty, signed in 1819, but not in effect until 1821, New Spain gave up its rights to the territory basically north of the Sabine River at its mouth and then along the Red River west to the 100th Meridian, then north to the Arkansas River and west to its headwaters, then north to the 42nd Parallel and west along the 42nd Parallel to the Pacific (then known as the "South Sea"). However, the United States still had not reached the Pacific Ocean, as Mexico still owned California in the south, and Oregon Territory was still claimed by both the U.S. and Great Britain in the north. Mexico won its independence from Spain shortly after the Adams-Onis Treaty, and the Treaty of Cordoba was signed in 1821.

Senator Thomas Hart Benton of Missouri was in the forefront of the expansionist movements. In 1842, he sponsored a $30,000 appropriation to survey and map the major trails over the Rocky Mountains, and in the same year James K. Polk ran for President on an expansionist platform. In 1846, just shortly before the start of the Mexican-American War, the U.S. agreed with Britain that the 49th Parallel would be the common boundary with British North America, and the U.S. finally had undisputed territory to the Pacific. Now it turned its desires for more land toward the south and the relatively new and weak country of Mexico.

Mexico had been noticing the preparation for growth by the United States; but it was a very poor country with an ill-equipped army, so it could do very little about it. One action it did take in the 1830s and 1840s was to award almost 200 land grants, several of them for millions of acres, in the hopes that private Mexican citizens (including Americans who had become naturalized Mexicans) might help defend their country from Native Americans and the Americans. However, the grants came too late, efforts to settle were too feeble, the Indians became even more hostile and well-armed, and the Americans were too enamored with their new expansionist policies.

By the beginning of 1846, when Lafe was twenty-one years old, it was obvious that the United States would enter into a war with Mexico. When Texas had gained its independence from Mexico ten years earlier in 1836, the United States and many European nations had quickly recognized the new country of the Republic of Texas. However Mexico refused to do so unless Texas would agree to never seek annexation by the United States. Texas would not agree; and it continuously claimed that under the terms of Santa Anna's surrender to Texas, its country extended all the way to the headwaters of the Rio Grande at the Continental Divide in today's Colorado. Most Texas citizens wanted statehood, but Texas was not immediately admitted as a state because of the then ongoing U.S. slavery issue. Texas would obviously be a slave state, and it was reserving the right to split into as many as five states, which would have given the slave states major power in the U.S. Congress.

Annexation proceedings for Texas had been considered as early as 1844 by the United States, even though Mexico threatened war if Texas was annexed. Annexation proceedings were formally begun by the U.S. Congress on March 1, 1845, and Texas was formally admitted to the

CHAPTER 3

Union in December, 1845. In order to protect Texas from Mexico, General Zachary Taylor with a U.S. Army of 3,500 men had quickly been moved to near the mouth of the Rio Grande River; and the Mexican Army moved to the immediate south of the river, preparing to invade Texas. On April 24, 1846, Mexican General Mariano Aristo communicated to Taylor that he considered the United States and Mexico at war and, on the same day, a party of American dragoons were attacked and sixteen U.S. soldiers were killed. The Americans considered that action as a declaration of war against the United States, and on May 13, 1846 the U.S. Congress officially declared war against Mexico. President James Polk's authorization of the enrollment of 50,000 volunteers to serve one year in the military was an example of how quickly the United States government felt it could win the war.

The battle line with Mexico would spread over almost 2,000 miles from the Gulf of Mexico to the Pacific Ocean; and, in the West, Brevet General Stephen Watts Kearny was chosen to lead what would be called the "Army of the West," while Taylor commanded the troops along the huge border in Texas. Kearny was a good choice to lead the Army of the West. An American unit on horseback called "Rangers" had guarded some of the American wagon trains from hostile Indians on the Santa Fe Trail after 1829; and after 1833, U.S. "dragoons" had occasionally ventured out on to the plains to "impress the Native Americans so as to keep them peaceful." Kearny had trained dragoon units, and then for several years commanded the first cavalry unit. He had gone over the Oregon Trail as far as South Pass in Wyoming with five companies of dragoons in 1845 to council with the Sioux about not attacking wagon trains going to Oregon. Then he went south to Bent's Fort and back east to Fort Leavenworth.

Kearny's regular army men would be some of the first U.S. troops to see service in a war while mounted on horses, as he had one unit of cavalry and three units of dragoons under his command. The main difference between the two units was that dragoons were taught to ride their horses into battle and then quickly dismount to fight. Cavalry were men who were taught to fight with a sword or a gun while still mounted on their horses. Congress was able to discern that a mounted force, whether dragoons or cavalry, was a good way to fight in the arid and sparsely inhabited (except for Native Americans) Southwest and northern Mexico.

Missouri Governor John C. Edwards had within weeks of the declaration of war (in May of 1846) called for men from his state to join in the fight. Enlistment records show that Lafayette Head volunteered on August 5, 1846, and was inducted into Company D of the 2nd Regiment of Missouri Mounted Volunteers, which required him to enroll for a little more than a year—from August 1846 to October 1847. The First Regiment of Missouri Mounted Volunteers had already met on June 18, 1846, and elected their field officers for the Mexican campaign. A. W. Doniphan was elected Colonel, C. F. Ruff as Lieutenant Colonel, and William Gilpin as Major.

Because of the large number of troops he would have with him, Kearny chose to go to Santa Fe by way of the Mountain Branch of the Santa Fe Trail. It was a longer trip, but there was more water along that route than on the Cimarron Cut Off, and he planned to make Bent's Fort on the Mountain Branch one of his bases of operations in the West.

Doniphan, acting as an advance guard, left Fort Leavenworth several days before Kearny, who moved out with the U.S. regular troops as the rear guard on June 29. Kearny left with two batteries of artillery, three squadrons of dragoons, one regiment of cavalry, and two companies of infantry, totaling 1,657 men. It was 564 miles from Fort Leavenworth to Bent's Fort. The Second Regiment of the Missouri Mounted Volunteers that Lafe had joined would leave a little later than Kearny under the command of then Colonel Sterling Price. The Mormon Battalion and the Third Regiment of Mounted Missouri Volunteers would eventually follow Price and be a part of Kearny's Army of the West. Like many Army volunteers of the time, Lafe may have used his own horse and may have needed to bring his own gun to ride West following Kearny.

Part of Kearny's force was the Mormon Battalion which had been formed at a time when the Mormons were trying to convince the U.S. of

U. S. Cavalry Officer by Frederick Remington.

CHAPTER 3

The Mexican-American War Mounted Missouri Volunteers, of which Lafe was a member, had no uniforms and only sometimes were supplied weapons, but would have looked something like this soldier.

From Twitchell, *The Conquest of Santa Fe, New Mexico, 1846.*

their loyalty to the country so as to gain help in their movement to the West. Most of the Mormon soldiers' pay, which was paid in advance, went into the church coffers to help other Mormon civilians travel west to avoid persecution. The Mormon Battalion contained about 550 volunteers who signed up for about a year.

Kearny had left with a huge supply and ammunition train of 1,500 wagons that were pulled by nearly 2,500 oxen and 4,000 mules. Kearny's wagons were loaded with tons and tons of supplies that were meant to last his entire army for at least a year. A dozen slow oxen pulled each of Kearny's cannons and many of the heavier loaded wagons. Oxen could only travel about ten to twelve miles per day, and herders followed them driving extra horses, mules, and oxen to replace the animals that died along the way. Kearny realized that certain units within his huge army and supply train would travel at slower rates of speed than other units, so before he left with the main force, he had started sending out caravans of supplies and equipment almost every day from the first of June. Each caravan was accompanied by a few regular troops. He ordered an artillery battalion of 100 men to be sent out early on June 13 since the oxen that had to pull the heavy cannons would make them the slowest group; but the artillery battalion had to wait at Fort Leavenworth for their cannons to arrive. The topographical engineers left on June 27 to mark the trail, so no one got lost. All of the different units were told to meet at Bent's Fort on August 1. By July 30, Kearny was at Bent's Fort (still barely in U.S. territory on the north side of the Arkansas River) with, amazingly, all his army and equipment present. Interestingly, the two companies of infantry made it to Bent's Fort the fastest.

Susan Magoffin, who wrote *Down the Santa Fe Trail and Into Mexico*, was already at Bent's Fort with her husband, James Magoffin, who had evidently been hired by the United States to help secretly convince (and if necessary bribe) Mexican officials to not resist the American army. She wrote that the fort and its surrounding area was so overflowing with men that it "seems the whole world is coming with him (Kearny)."[12] She and her group waited to fall in behind the supply wagons that followed the soldiers toward Santa Fe.

Even though Kearny had already left Bent's Fort, Colonel Sterling Price and the Second Regiment of Missouri Mounted Volunteers were still at Fort Leavenworth and excited to leave on the adventure ahead. They were said to be "in high spirits" when they left Fort Leavenworth on August 5. They sang patriotic songs and boasted that they would win the war before the year's end. Little did they realize the extremes of boredom and danger that immediately lay before them; but there was not yet any threat from Mexican soldiers in New Mexico. However, conditions for traveling to New Mexico were not ideal for Lafe and his companions, as it was mid-summer. The heat was staggering and the high humidity from summer thunderstorms was described as being "as thick as gauze."

The Army of the West led by General Stephen Watts Kearney, included regular army, volunteers, infantry, cavalry, and dragoons. Only the artillery is not shown in this drawing.

From Twitchell, *The Conquest of Santa Fe, New Mexico, 1846.*

CHAPTER 3

Lafe's leader, Colonel Price, was an interesting man. Later in the war he was promoted to brigadier general; and, after the Mexican-American War ended, he was elected Governor of Missouri in 1852, but four years later he retired to his Missouri farm. Later he was elected President of the Missouri Convention held to determine if the state would secede from the Union. He supported the Union, but also was a strong advocate of State's Rights. The Missouri Convention decided to stay in the Union, but soon thereafter Union volunteer troops entered Missouri and killed at least twenty-eight Confederate sympathizers at Camp Jackson. Price then raised an army of Missouri volunteers to prevent outside interference in the state, and eventually he fought for the Confederacy. Price lost most of the battles he participated in during the Civil War; and, when the war ended, he and many of his men went to Mexico rather than surrender. Eventually he came back to the United States and died penniless. Price was supposedly related by marriage to Lafayette Head's extended family through Price's wife Martha (whose maiden name was Head and married Price in Randolph, Missouri in 1833), but other details are not known.

Like Kearny, Price's regiment began the trip of over 800 miles from Missouri to Santa Fe on the Santa Fe Trail in two detachments—a forward and a rear guard. Two days out of Leavenworth, Lafe had his first view of what Army explorer Stephen H. Long in 1820 had called "The Great American Desert," but which we now call "The Great Plains." Lafayette would have seen it as an endless prairie stretching westward until it met the sky, but eventually the Rocky Mountains were visible from over 100 miles away. The grass was often waist high, providing plenty of food for the horses and oxen; but Lafe would have seen only a few trees to use for firewood, and drinking water would have been limited. It must have been like a different world for the young man who had lived all his life in the thick, humid forests of Missouri.

Price's men, although not hampered with a huge supply train, did not make much better time than Kearny because of the extremely rutted condition of the trail caused by Kearny's heavy wagons and cannons and the oxen pulling them. The men dripped sweat in the late summer heat. Thunderstorms rolled across the prairie, bringing some relief; but the sweaty men were then often chilled to the bone by the strong wind hitting their wet clothes. Rain turned the trail into mud, and swarms of mosquitoes often attacked the men and animals at night. More than anything else on the trip, the men hated the mosquitoes.

The soldiers' food was the same almost every day—biscuits, beans, sowbelly (salt-cured bacon), and coffee were the standard trail rations. Lafe often ate cold food when firewood could not be found. Near where the trail met the Arkansas River, about 250 miles west from Fort Leavenworth, they spotted buffalo herds for the first time. From a distance, the shifting mass of animals was said to look like a rippling black lake. A team of men rode out to hunt, and the whole regiment feasted on fresh meat that night.

When he had arrived at Bent's Fort on July 30, General Kearny dispatched Lieutenant James De Courtney and twenty men to Taos, New Mexico. There were many Americans living in Taos, and he wanted to know what the general sentiment of its citizens was towards Americans. Then on July 31, Kearny, who was still in U.S. territory on the north side of the Arkansas River, issued a proclamation before entering Mexico. He announced, in part, that he was entering the Province of New Mexico "seeking union with and ameliorating the conditions of its inhabitants." This proclamation also indicated that the United States would only be claiming territory to the Rio Grande River, although this limitation was never mentioned again. On August 2, Captain Phillip St. George Cooke was sent from Bent's Fort to Santa Fe with a written proclamation from Kearny that was basically the same as the one he had read two days earlier. By August 9, Cooke was in Las Vegas, New Mexico.

Kearny's main group left Bent's Fort on the afternoon of August 2 and crossed Raton Pass three days later on August 6. De Courtney reported back to Kearny along the trail to Santa Fe on August 11, and he brought

When General Kearney got to Las Vegas, New Mexico Province on August 15, 1846, he stopped to climb to the roof of one of the towns' government buildings to issue a proclamation that it was now part of the United States.

From Twitchell, *The Conquest of Santa Fe, New Mexico, 1846.*

CHAPTER 3

prisoners taken in Taos who gave exaggerated reports that the Pueblo and Ute Indians would all fight the United States. On August 14, Kearny received the following official message from the Provincial Governor and General of the New Mexico Army Don Manuel Armijo:

> You have notified me that you intend to take possession of the country I govern. The people of the country have risen en masse in my defense. If you take the country, it will be because you prove the strongest in battle. I suggest to you to stop at Sapello and I will march to Las Vegas (New Mexico) and we will meet and negotiate on the plains between them. [13]

Kearny was already at the Sapello River when he received the message, and instead of stopping, he and his men galloped into the Las Vegas plaza at 8 a.m. the next day. He suggested to the local officials that they go to the top of a building to give an announcement that he was there to "free" the New Mexicans. Before he left Las Vegas, Kearny was told that the Mexican Army was waiting for him just outside the town, but an American scouting party found no one there.

When Cooke had passed through Las Vegas, New Mexico, on August 9, he had also been welcomed peacefully. He quickly went on to Santa Fe where, on August 12, 1846, he met with Provincial Governor Armijo, who declined to surrender. Included with Captain Cooke's men was Susan Magoffin's husband James, who had been a U.S. trader with merchants in Chihuahua and Santa Fe for many years and who knew many of the "important" people in those towns. Cooke was to try to see if he could negotiate a peaceful surrender of New Mexico Province. On that same day, Magoffin had a "secret meeting" with Armijo and other Mexican officials, but he evidently had no success in convincing them not to fight. While Kearny was still in Las Vegas, Armijo had met with his officers and many of them, including his local military commander, Colonel Diego Archuleta, said they did not want to fight. Whether Magoffin's bribes were taken by Armijo or Archuleta is unknown; although Magoffin later asked the U.S. to reimburse him for bribes he made in Chihuahua, but no bribes were mentioned as being made in Santa Fe. Several letters that were written at the time state "inducements were offered Armijo and Colonel Archuleta," but whether they took them was not mentioned. Later Armijo sent a message to Kearny stating again that he would fight the Americans, that he had assembled 4,000 men to fight, and that he was "willing to sacrifice his life and all his interests in defense of his country." Meanwhile, Americans in Santa Fe were going to Armijo urging him not to fight.

On August 14, Armijo ordered a defensive position set up at Apache Canyon, a short distance east of Santa Fe, but when he arrived at the spot himself, he ultimately decided not to fight. He instead ordered his soldiers to go home, and he and seventy-five to 100 of his dragoons retreated to Chihuahua, dragging all the Mexican cannons with them. However Armijo soon abandoned the cannons (presumably because they were slowing him down), which were discovered by American soldiers and later brought to Santa Fe.

On August 15, Kearny was notified that he was now a brigadier general. As Kearny marched toward Santa Fe, reports still reached him that Armijo had a large army (historians estimate it to have been anywhere between 2,000 and 6,000 men) waiting for him.

Armijo's decision not to fight was probably made on the basis that the United States Army, although a smaller force of men, was better armed, trained, and experienced than most of his men. Some of Armijo's men, mainly unpaid Pueblo Indian volunteers or civilian militias, were armed only with bows and arrows. Armijo's decision was probably further based on the major conflicts still going on among his officers about whether to fight or not.

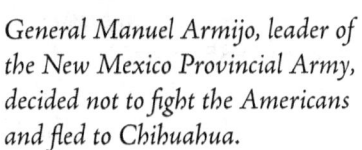

General Manuel Armijo, leader of the New Mexico Provincial Army, decided not to fight the Americans and fled to Chihuahua.

From Twitchell, *The Conquest of Santa Fe, New Mexico, 1846.*

While approaching the city, Kearny encountered a messenger who brought a letter from New Mexico Province Lieutenant Governor Juan Vigil stating that no one would fight his entry into Santa Fe. By 6 p.m. on August 18, Kearny was in the Palace of the Governors, refreshments were served, and the American flag was hoisted over the palace. A thirteen cannon salute was made from the future spot of Fort Marcy overlooking the city. On August 19, Kearny assumed his duties as military governor, ordered a fort built at Santa Fe, and said he wanted the flag in the fort to be hung on "a tall flagstaff... spine upon spine towards the heavens and bearing the American banner...." His orders were followed and " Old (Mexican) men were said to have walked sixty miles to see the flag."[14] After Santa Fe was taken without a shot, Magoffin went to

Chihuahua to try to convince the Mexicans there to surrender, but instead he was arrested for attempted bribery and spent the rest of the war in jail.

Back in Santa Fe, Kearny also read a proclamation on August 19, 1846, stating that the Mexican people of New Mexico Provence were now citizens of the United States. This was not the case, and President Polk repudiated the statement in December, as only the U.S. Congress could take such an action. On August 20, Kearny again addressed the people of Santa Fe. He said that he had arrived to protect and not to harm them and tried to assure them they would benefit from the takeover by the Americans. Afterwards, Lieutenant Governor Vigil spoke, saying that it was not up to his people to decide his nation's boundaries; but he told the Americans:

> *Do not find it strange if there has been no manifestation of joy and enthusiasm in Seeing this city occupied by your military forces. To us the power of the Mexican Republic is dead.*[15]

Kearny issued yet another proclamation on August 22. Obviously he had heard of discord among the Mexican people, so he announced that he had a large force with him and had an equally strong force following him (the Mormon Battalion and the 2nd and 3rd Regiments of Missouri Mounted Volunteers). He stated that he had more troops than necessary to put down any opposition, and that it "would be but folly or madness for any dissatisfied or disconnected persons to think of resisting him."[16]

A month later, on September 22, "Kearny's Code," New Mexico's first set of American laws, was issued. They were complete enough that they were used until 1885. It was based on a combination of Mexican and American law, but instituted a Bill of Rights protecting individual rights that the Mexicans had never had. The Code was good enough that it remained New Mexico's basic law with only a few amendments when New Mexico became a territory, and many of its provisions are still contained today in New Mexico's state laws.

Before he left Santa Fe, Kearny established a civil government with Charles Bent as Governor. Bent, like Kearny, was worried about the general unrest of New Mexico's citizens and realized that part of the problem was that:

> *There is a great want of discipline and subordination among the troops here.... I shall use every means to impress on the commander the necessity of a more rigid care with regard to the treatment of the inhabitants. He must conciliate and not exasperate.* [17]

On the same day, September 22, 1846, Kearny was ordered by President Polk to conquer California, which at the time had a much smaller population than New Mexico. Kearny decided to take 300 1st Dragoons with him and the Mormon Battalion would follow him after they arrived in Santa Fe. Colonel Doniphan and his men were to stay in Santa Fe until Colonel Price arrived. A battalion of Doniphan's infantry and artillery were also to permanently stay in Santa Fe during the war to protect that city, while the main force would proceed south to Mexico City.

On September 25, Kearny and 300 troops left Santa Fe, even though Price and his men had not quite yet arrived. Kearny and his men headed south along the Rio Grande River and then planned to go overland to California. At Socorro, New Mexico, Kearny met Kit Carson, who had just come from John Fremont's group in California. Carson incorrectly informed Kearny that California had already been surrendered to the United States represented by John Fremont; so Kearny left 200 of his men in New Mexico and enlisted Carson to lead him and 100 dragoons to California.

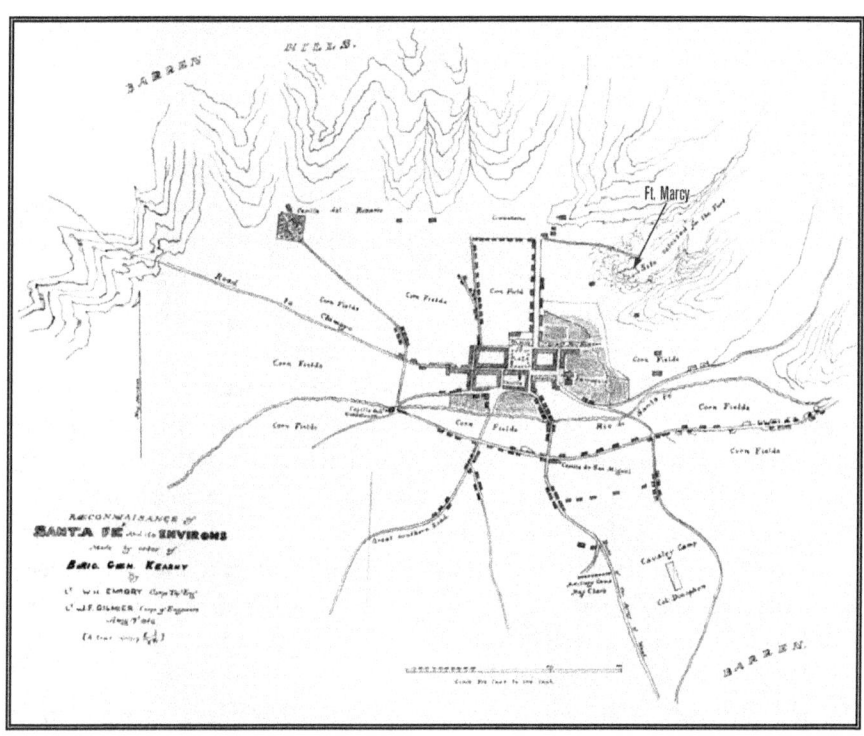

Santa Fe at the time of being occupied showing proposed spot for Ft. Marcy.

Courtesy historicsantafe.org.

CHAPTER 3

Kearny's group reached California in early December and learned the Mexicans in California had, in fact, not surrendered. Kearny lost his first skirmish with the Mexicans and was twice wounded, but then joined forces with General Robert F. Stockton and took San Diego and Los Angeles. Kearny and John Fremont came into conflict over who should be appointed Governor of California, but Kearny was backed by the generals in Washington and Fremont ended up being court martialed and resigned from the army. Kearny went to Mexico City after that city surrendered, and he served as military governor from March 1, 1847 to June 1, 1847, when he caught malaria and died after returning to the United States on October 31, 1848.

Like Kearny's main force, most wagon trains on the Santa Fe Trail took the longer, but safer fork of the Santa Fe Trail that went west to Bent's Fort. It was called "The Mountain Branch," as from Bent's Fort, the trail turned south and went over Raton Pass in the Raton Mountains. The 800 mile main trail from Fort Leavenworth to Santa Fe normally took about seventy-five days.

However, Colonel Sterling Price and his soldiers, including Lafe, were in a hurry. After more than a month on the trail, the men were eager for action, so Price took the Cimarron Cutoff, which shortened the route by 100 miles (8 to 10 days travel), but was prone to the hardships of Indian ambushes and lack of water at the time of year he crossed it. A few Indian skirmishes gave Price's men something to brag about, but they mainly needed water for their animals. Fortunately, Price's group found enough water along the way and made it to Santa Fe around the first week of October, traveling from Fort Leavenworth in about fifty-three days without seeing any Mexican soldiers. Lafe was now in New Mexico for the first time.

When the volunteer Mormon Battalion left Fort Leavenworth in mid-August, they also had followed the Cimarron Route but, after passing into New Mexico, met stiff resistance from both Mexicans and Native Americans. Reinforcements under the command of Colonel Price were sent to help them, and Lafe may have been with Price at this time. When the Mormon Battalion arrived in Santa Fe later in October, it was put under the leadership of Captain Phillip St. George Cooke, and soon headed for California to join up with General Kearny.

While the Mexican-American War was going on, the Utes and Jicarilla Apache took the opportunity to continue raiding New Mexico settlers and small towns. They were merely responding to more and more settlers coming on to their homelands, as the number of New Mexico residents had almost doubled during this time, mainly because of Land Grants. William

Gilpin, who fifteen years later would become the first territorial governor of Colorado, was stationed by Doniphan at Abiqui with troops to quell local uprisings and to meet with the Utes and Navajo and try to keep them peaceful. Since the U.S. now had control of all of New Mexico, an 1846 treaty was made by the United States with the Mouache Utes, as well as an agreement with the Navajo. The U.S. agreed to defend and protect the Mouache in the areas east and north of Taos. However, Ute raids continued in other areas. The Utes eventually said they would stay peaceful, and the Americans agreed to leave the Utes alone, except to pass through their land or build military posts and agencies to protect the Utes from their enemies.

In October of 1846, Major Gilpin was out again chasing more marauding Native Americans, this time a formidable group of Navajo along the San Juan River who were evidently testing the strength and resolve of the Americans. In addition to his troops, Gilpin took sixty-five Mexicans as guides and "general utility men" (probably a euphemism for servants). He went north along the Chama River from Abiqui and then west through the lower San Juan Mountains to bypass his enemy. Although Kearny had conquered New Mexico without a shot, Gilpin did not have such an easy task. It was a very cold and harsh winter, and deep snows already blanketed the mountains and foothills. The Navajos finally made peace; but by this time Gilpin had traveled almost 750 miles, half the Americans' horses had given out, and half of Gilpin's men were therefore on foot. It is noteworthy to point out that Gilpin later stated he or his men spotted numerous "blossoms of gold and silver" in the southern San Juan Mountains during the entire time he was out; and, for years afterwards he preached to anyone who would listen about the great possibilities of mineral wealth in the San Juan Mountains. He was talking mainly of the La Plata Mountains, a subgroup of the southwestern San Juan Mountains that proved to be very rich; but a small amount of gold was also found along several other rivers of the southern San Juan Mountains. Later, Gilpin would send men to

General Sterling Price was the leader of Lafe's Company during the Mexican-American War.

Twitchell, The Conquest of Santa Fe, New Mexico, 1846.

CHAPTER 3

prospect in the northern and eastern San Juan Mountains and placer mine near the headwaters of the southern San Juan River, but they would not have much luck.

Meanwhile, upon his arrival in Santa Fe, Colonel Price and his command were left to guard all of New Mexico, but especially Santa Fe. Although Kearny had moved into present-day New Mexico and seized Santa Fe on August 18, 1846, there still were a substantial number of Mexicans and Pueblo Indians in New Mexico in October who felt their Mexican Provincial Governor was a coward and had betrayed them by not fighting. Kearny had ordered Colonel Alexander Doniphan to guard Santa Fe until Colonel Price arrived, and then Doniphan was to head south to Chihuahua, Mexico.

Enroute to Chihuahua, however, Doniphan was delayed along the way because he was given orders to first put down yet another Navajo uprising along the lower Rio Grande near today's Las Cruces, New Mexico. When approached by Doniphan's force, the Navajo said they recognized the Americans' superiority and would be peaceful, but they could not understand why they could not raid the Mexicans, who both they and the Americans were fighting at the time. Doniphan had to explain, as best he could, that the Mexicans they were attacking were now Americans and should be left alone.

After Doniphan left along El Camino Royal, Price and his men, including Lafe, were to stay in Santa Fe to keep order and to guard the city, a duty which included building a large fort.

General Kearny had ordered Fort Marcy built the day after he arrived in Santa Fe. He sent two engineers to look for a site for the fort, specifying a good defensive site as top priority. Within days of their arrival, the American soldiers under Colonel Price started building the fort on a hilltop 650 yards from the plaza. The spot picked for Fort Marcy had a clear view in every direction over the whole valley. It was the first United States Army fort in the American Southwest, and the only real fort in the Southwest until Fort Union was built eight years later in 1854.

Fort Marcy, named for Secretary of War William L. Marcy, was not meant so much to defend against the Mexican Army, as it was meant to be a place of retreat and protection for the American civilians and soldiers in the event of a rebellion by the Mexican locals. It was to be a safe place to stay until reinforcements could arrive. Originally the fort was intended to garrison 280 men in barracks; but instead, the existing Mexican barracks near the plaza were used with some additional buildings constructed there, including a hospital. The soldiers' descriptions of the Mexican barracks were not kind. The nearby Governor's Palace, was now occupied by the American officials and authorities.

Besides protection, the fort was meant to serve as a symbol to Santa Fe citizens of the might and domination of the Americans. To this end, the captured Mexican cannons that Armijo had tried to drag away were used for the fort. American soldiers and hired Mexican men did the work of building the five-foot-thick adobe walls that were nine-feet high and which formed an irregular hexagon (many called it a starburst pattern) that followed the terrain. On the immediate outside, the fort was surrounded by a five foot deep ditch, which effectually made the walls fourteen feet tall. Inside were log structures used to store gunpowder and supplies. Lafe spent much of his initial six weeks in Santa Fe working on the fort, but most of the really hard labor, such as making and transporting the adobe bricks, was probably left to the Mexicans.

The fort was big enough to hold 1,000 people, but no living quarters were ever built inside the walls. A few limited living quarters were built directly outside the fort for the guards who kept watch over the ammunition and supplies stored inside; but almost all of the soldiers, including Lafe and the mounted men's horses, were housed behind the buildings on the north side of the main Santa Fe plaza. This central location was actually more pleasant for the American soldiers.

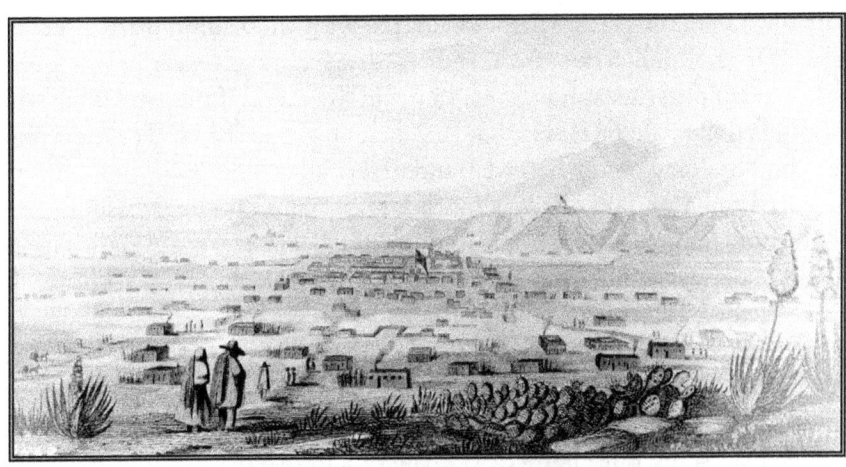

A drawing of the City of Santa Fe from a distance in 1846 by Lt. J. W. Abert. Note the huge American flag flying on the mesa right of center in the background as well as another in the central plaza.

U. S. National Archives.

CHAPTER 3

Unfortunately, the expected rebellion feared by General Kearny and New Mexico Governor Charles Bent that caused Fort Marcy to be built did happen, but it occurred sixty miles away in Taos and not in Santa Fe; so Fort Marcy never saw any real action. Fort Marcy was abandoned in August of 1868, but after 1853 the name "Fort Marcy" was usually applied to the troops' barracks behind the Palace of the Governors. Marian Russell, author of *Land of Enchantment: Memoirs of Marian Russell Along the Santa Fe Trail*, wrote that Fort Marcy was used as "kind of a burial ground" after it was abandoned. On September 30, 1887, a tourist, Mrs. Tassie Wilson, found $2,300 in Spanish silver coins buried in the walls of the decaying fort, and the resulting rush to dig for more treasure destroyed most of what was left of its standing walls.

Soon after their October arrival, Lafe and some of the other soldiers in the Second Missouri Mounted Volunteers settled into life in Santa Fe. The town of Santa Fe de San Francisco (the City of Holy Faith of St. Francis) was named after the Franciscan fathers, who arrived early in its history to convert the natives to Christianity. Santa Fe was like no other town the American soldiers, and especially Lafe, had ever seen. Most houses were adobe, basically the same color as the surrounding hills from which their adobe bricks were made. The dirt streets rambled through the hills, interspersed with vegetable gardens and corn patches surrounded by small wooden jackal (stick) fences. Chickens and goats wandered freely, and burros were much more numerous than horses or mules. The roofs of the town's buildings were flat and covered with adobe mud plastered over sturdy logs. Wooden doors swung on leather hinges and were held in place by wooden pegs. Most houses had no windows; and if they did, they had shutters that could be closed, but they had no glass. The bells of five Santa Fe churches rang on the hour day and night.[18]

The town of Santa Fe was much larger than Franklin, Missouri, and Lafe must have been very impressed, although some of the American soldiers, especially some from the East, saw the Spanish town as a hovel. It is nestled among the foothills of the usually snow-covered mountains to the north of Santa Fe, as the town was at the extreme southern end of the Sangre de Cristo Range at an elevation of about 7,000 feet. It had "about twenty-five stores, a printing shop, many saloons, two tailor shops, two shoemaker stalls, one apothecary, a bakery, and two blacksmiths."[19]

The center of town was a large open plaza. A long building called the "Palacio" stood on the north side of the square. Before the war, the Palacio, now called the "Palace of the Governors," had been filled with government officials and their voluminous records, as Santa Fe had been the capital of the Province of New Mexico for over two centuries. After the Americans took Santa Fe, many of these records were used to start fires or to light the cigars of the American officers. The fronts of the public buildings had covered walkways, called *"portales,"* for protection from the sun, rain, or snow. On market day, the plaza would be alive with people—both Mexican and Native Americans—who were mainly buying vegetables, bread, and wood for cooking and heating.

The forefathers of the Pueblo people who were at the plaza had lived in pueblos spread along the Rio Grande River for up to 800 years, although pueblos were sometimes abandoned and later resettled. The Pueblo people had been integrated into Spanish culture over a 250 year period and were very peaceful as opposed to warring Native American tribes surrounding Santa Fe—the Ute and Apache in the mountains to the north and west, the Navajo to the south and west, and the Comanches on the prairies to the east. The Pueblo Indians grew crops, raised sheep for wool and food, made pots and blankets, and traded their goods in the plaza market.

The Utes had been at peace much more often than any of these other tribes, and the Utes claimed they only attacked Spanish settlements when desperate for food or horses. The main reason the Utes were more peaceful was they did not have a culture like the Plains Indians that glorified war. Later in the mid-1700s the Spanish had even allied with the Utes in battles against the Comanche and Navajo.

A diversified picture of Santa Fe and its inhabitants emerges from writings of the time. Josiah Gregg in his book *Commerce on the Prairies* gives us a good description of the town of Santa Fe:

> *Its situation is twelve or fifteen miles east of the Rio del Norte (the Rio Grande River).... The population of the city itself but little exceeds 3,000; yet, including several surrounding villages which are embraced in its corporate jurisdiction, it amounts to 6,000 souls.... The only attempt at anything like architectural compactness and precision consists in four tiers of buildings, whose fronts are shaded with a fringe of portales or corredores of the rudest possible description. They stand around the public square and comprise the Palacio, or Governor's House, the Customs House, the Barracks (with which is connected the fearful Calabozo), the Casa Consistorial of the Alcaldes, the Capilla de los Soldados or Military Chapel, besides several private residences as well as most of the shops of the American traders.*[20]

CHAPTER 3

Lieutenant James Albert of the Army Topographical Corps of Engineers, who had arrived in Santa Fe with General Kearny, attended a Catholic service in Santa Fe and found the women sitting on the dirt floor on the right side of the church. He joined the men, who were standing on the left side. He also attended a dance called a "fandango" in Spanish. The women, he said "were wrapped in splendid *rebozos* and sat along the walls rolling corn husk cigarettes." When dressed up, the Mexican men at Santa Fe wore fancy shirts, short jackets, and tight pants. Their high-heel boots were usually fitted with silver spurs. Most men wore a brightly striped blanket over one shoulder and a sombrero with a very tall, pointed crown. When working, the Mexican men wore simple off-white, roughly woven clothes. The women of Santa Fe usually wore low-cut blouses and their skirts were short as compared to American women. At a time when many American women were embarrassed to show their ankles, many of the Mexican women were barefoot. Most American men felt the Mexican women very attractive and pleasant compared to American women. One American, Albert Richardson, in *Beyond the Mississippi* wrote:

> *(Mexican women) …are uniformly tender and self-sacrificing, ready to divide their last crust with the hungry, and deny*

Cigarette smoking and barefoot señoritas were a surprise to the American soldiers, who also found them very attractive and friendly.

Author's collection.

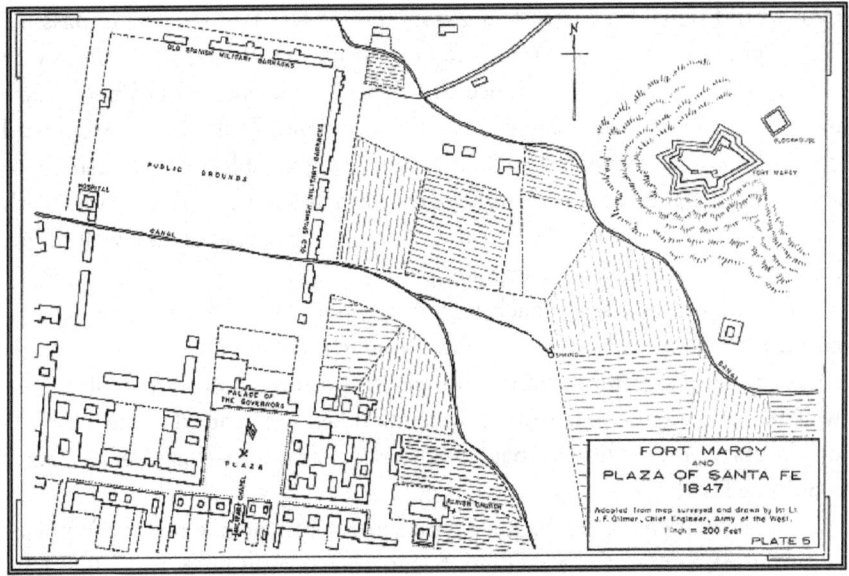

Fort Marcy is the irregular shape in the upper right corner. The fort was built in 1846 for protection from possible Mexican retribution and no barracks were ever built in the fort. Instead the soldiers were quartered in the old Mexican barracks that are in the upper left and that area was later called Fort Marcy.

Drawing by Lt. J. F. Gilmer, U.S. National Archives.

themselves every comfort to nurse the sick and minister to the wretched.[21]

Another man added, "Many (Mexican women) had pleasant features, and all displayed the sparkling eyes of their race." Many of the Americans, probably because of the Mexican women's low cut blouses and short skirts, felt that Mexican women were "loose." This attitude was fortified by the fact that many drank alcohol, smoked cigarettes, and showed affection easily; but there were probably no more prostitutes in Santa Fe than in any large town back East. However Richardson wrote:

Chasity is practically unknown among them, but they present all the other distinctive virtues of their sex.[22]

Richardson also noted that there were only one or two "American" ladies in Santa Fe. One ceremony among the "nicer Mexican women" caught Lafe's attention on a particular afternoon. Young men strolled in a circle around the plaza, and young women circled in the opposite direction, facing the men. A

CHAPTER 3

man would signal his interest in a woman by a word or a glance in passing. She might encourage him with a nod or a smile, which was his invitation to look for her at the evening dance. An American woman would never have done such a thing! Dancing was a passion in Santa Fe. Richardson pointed out "There were three or four 'fandangos' (lively couple's dances, usually to a guitar) in Santa Fe every night; the Mexicans always participated with wonderful zest."[23] He described the dancing as "somewhat like waltzing… but more complicated and confusing."

The arrival of a stagecoach was a big event since Santa Fe was so isolated. Drivers would circle the plaza and whip their horses to full speed so as to make a grand entrance. Shouts and often pistol shots would help welcome the stagecoach. Town people would gather around to see who was on the stage, and all hoped that some of the mail and packages on the stage would be for them.

After living in Santa Fe for a while, and with the newness of the place wearing off, some of the soldiers began to list grievances that they had, such as the dust in the air, lice in their bedding, or sharp goat head thorns that stuck to their pant legs; and many Americans quickly became tired of Mexican cuisine. Lafe had never known any climate other than the damp and muggy river bottoms in Missouri. The dry air probably made him feel energized, but it also meant his lips chapped and he was often thirsty. It was a fascinating place for a young man from the Missouri backwoods.

One problem for many Americans was that Santa Fe citizens were generally Roman Catholics; and there was only one Protestant church at this time (which had no building or land) in the entire city, perhaps led by the Army chaplain. As mentioned, the people of Santa Fe played their church bells on the hour, which also annoyed many of the Americans. Other Americans did not like the decorations on the Catholic Cathedral in the Santa Fe plaza. It was a huge adobe building with "effigies of the Savior and the Virgin" on the outside, and "lurid paintings of Christ's suffering on Calvary decorating its walls."[24] Many Americans wrote home that they were living among pagans.

Anti-Catholic attitudes had been brought to the American colonies by British Protestants and were continued as part of an anti-immigrant (many of them Catholics) sentiment that hit its peak in the middle of the nineteenth century. Immigrants from Ireland, Italy, and Poland were especially met with such prejudice, and Mexican-Americans were to join them after the Mexican-American War made so many of them U.S. citizens. In the eastern United States the anti-Catholic bias sometimes even turned to mob violence and the burning of Catholic property. Unfortunately, many of the

U.S. soldiers in New Mexico had come from such cultures; but, as matters turned out, Lafe, and many other "backwoods" soldiers not only accepted Catholicism but became Catholic.

Meanwhile the Mexicans and Pueblo Indians of New Mexico were getting more and more upset that their province had been handed over to the Americans without a fight. This attitude was not helped by the fact that many of the American soldiers treated the Mexicans and Pueblo Indians as inferior and stupid. The Mexican locals also blamed the U.S. Army for bringing a measles epidemic to Santa Fe. Adding to these wounds, the Mexican political leaders and officials had been replaced with mainly Americans, and the Mexicans wanted their jobs back. Besides all the other problems, the Mexicans feared their land titles might be taken away from them by the Americans and that American sympathizers would prosper in their businesses at Santa Fe and Taos at the expense of Mexican businessmen. It was a dangerous situation made more dangerous by the fact that there were 50,000 Mexicans and 17,000 Pueblo Indians in New Mexico, while only about 500 American soldiers and about 300 American citizens remained in the area.

Fears of revolt previously expressed by Charles Bent, the American Civil Governor of New Mexico, and General Kearny were to become reality. Plans for a revolt against the Americans had started as early as October, 1846. Originally the Pueblo Indians planned the rebellion to take place at Christmas, but their plans were discovered by the Americans. However, rather than give up the idea after its discovery, the rebellion was simply postponed. James Magoffin later reported from Chihuahua, Mexico, that former Provincial Governor, General Don Manuel Armijo, was at this time trying to start a rebellion back in New Mexico to try to regain some of his lost honor and as revenge for his "being forced to leave."

Governor Bent owned Bent's Fort on the North Branch of the Santa Fe Trail with his brother William. Governor Bent had married a woman from a prominent Mexican family and had chosen to live in Taos instead of Santa Fe where his office was located; while William Bent lived in and ran Bent's Fort on the Arkansas River. As mentioned, the first Pueblo rebellion, which did not happen, was planned for Christmas Day in Santa Fe. Governor Bent had arrested seven of the revolt's conspirators and the matter was basically forgotten, but the threat was still very present.

On January 14, 1847, Governor Bent left his office in Santa Fe to help his family move from Taos to the capital city, where they could retreat to Fort Marcy if necessary and where there was a much larger American community. When Bent got to Taos, his friends urged him to immediately

CHAPTER 3

leave with his family for Santa Fe. However, Bent paid little attention to what his friends were saying. In the early hours of the morning of January 19, a mob composed mainly of Pueblo Indians formed and marched on Bent's home. Governor Bent had received a warning that night that a mob was forming and would be coming to his house, but he insisted he would go out to meet them. He had lived in Taos for twenty years, and he felt comfortable doing so.

Hispanic Pablo Montoya and Pueblo Indian Thomasito Romero led what came to be called the "Taos Rebellion" or the "Pueblo Revolt." Romero went with the Pueblo Indians to Bent's house and shot Bent with a rifle through his locked door. The mob then broke open the door, shot Bent full of arrows, and scalped him in front of his family. Somehow Bent, age 52, survived all of this, but was killed shortly afterwards. Bent's wife, Ignacia; her sister, Josepha Carson (Kit Carson's wife); three of their children; Mrs. Thomas Boggs; and a Mexican servant woman barely escaped. They were able to break through the adobe common wall of their homes into the house of their neighbor, and all escaped out the back. Later Bent's home was burned. Other Americans were not so lucky. A lawyer from Ohio, who was visiting Taos, had his eyes burned out before he died.

The next day, 500 Hispanics and Native Americans attacked Simon Turley's mill and distillery near Arroyo Hondo, just eight miles northwest of Taos. Local mountain man Charles Autobees saw the mob coming and raced to Santa Fe to get help from the military under General Price. After a battle at Turley's Mill that lasted several days, the mob killed all of the ten men still there. That same day, Hispanic insurgents killed seven American traders who were simply unlucky enough to be going to Turley's Mill and Taos to sell furs and buy Taos Lightning. They had just passed through the settlement of Mora at the time. One of them, a mountain man named Head, was supposed to be a distant relative of Lafe.

According to Arizona Historian Marshall Trimble, Taos Lightning is a particularly spicy brand of whiskey concocted by mountain man Peg-Leg Smith and partners in 1824. From the early 1830s until his death in 1847, Simeon Turley, grew and milled wheat just north of Taos, then sold the brew.

News of the attack on Bent and the other Americans reached Santa Fe three days later on January 23. Lafe was among the 400 Missouri Mounted Volunteers and seventy-nine other volunteers (mostly American mountain men living in the area) who immediately set out for Taos under the leadership of Colonel Price. Lieutenant Colonel Willock stayed in Santa Fe with the rest of the U.S. force to guard that town. Price wrote to his superiors:

It appears to be the object of the insurrectionists to put to death every American and every Mexican who has accepted office under the American government.[25]

Travel was slow as the group had to pull supply wagons and cannons through deep snow and the temperature dropped to below freezing every night. At La Cañada, 180 men, including Lafe, fought a much larger group of 600 to 700 hostile Mexicans and Pueblo Indians, who were intending to march on Santa Fe. In the Battle of La Cañada on January 24, 1847, the insurgents were hiding on both sides of a canyon, as well as being in a forest with many large boulders on a steep slope. Price in his official report stated

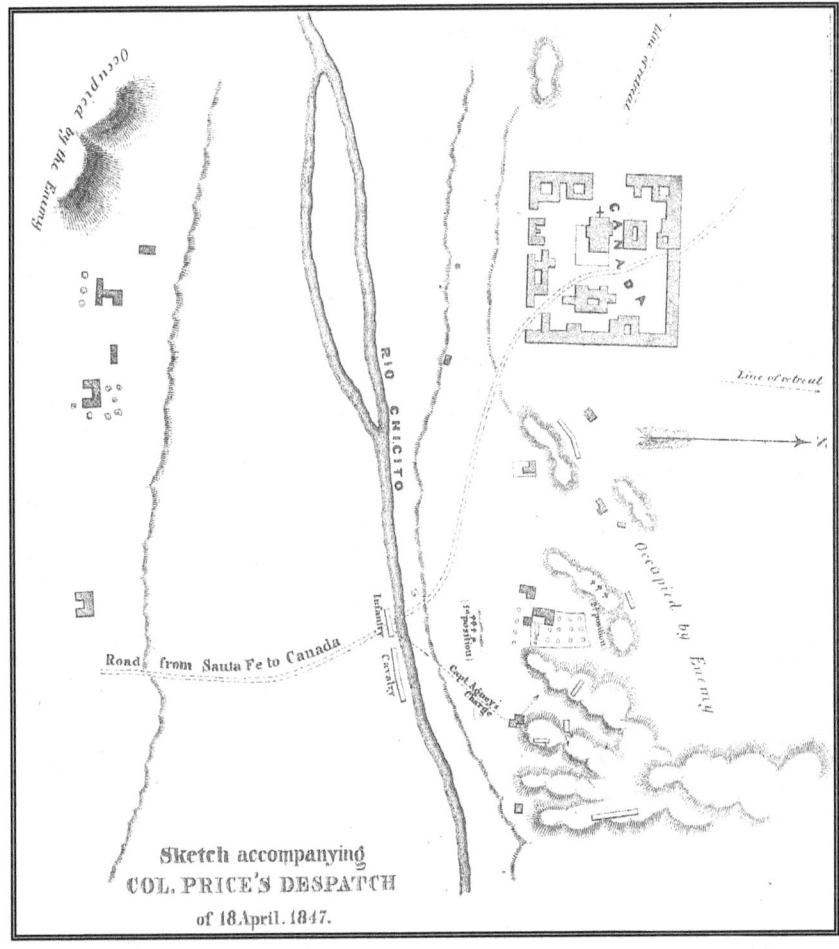

Colonel Price's report contained this drawing of the Battle of La Canada and the surrounding terrain.

Courtesy of Wikipedia.

that the Americans flanked them on both sides; and Price, who was using four mounted howitzers, had his artillery fire on the three fort-like houses that some of the rebels were using for cover at the base of one side of the canyon. Then he split his force, so one group could protect his wagon train three miles to the rear. Price and his other men overtook the men in the houses and then charged up the hill to engage the other rebels. Price wrote in his official report that "in a few minutes my troops had dislodged the enemy at all points, and they were flying in every direction."[26]

After routing the enemy, Lafe was in a group of two companies of soldiers led by Colonel Ceran St. Vrain and Captain Burgoin that went on toward Taos; but they had another skirmish at El Embudo Pass along the way. On January 29, without hesitating, the Americans moved through both sides of a narrow canyon, forcing another 600 to 700 insurgents waiting for them there to move back to the town of El Embudo. Price reported that the Americans quickly flanked the town and, as their main body moved in, the insurgents raised a white flag. There was also another battle at Mora, in which Lafe did not take part, where a force led by Captains Israel Hendley and Jesse Morin defeated the insurgents in that area, while Price and his men were engaged in the Battles at La Cañada and Embudo. The entire American force regrouped on January 31 and spent February 1 and 2 tramping through deep snow in the hills above Taos. Many of the men received frostbite, as they were packing down the snow for the artillery that was following, and they had to use extreme exertion to break and pack the trail.

About 9 p.m. the night of February 2, Pablo Montoya came to the American camp and began talking with the soldiers. It did not take long for the Americans to realize that he was only trying to determine the number of men and the types of weapons at their camp, and they took him captive. The next day, February 3, the U.S. troops marched unopposed through the town of Taos to the nearby Taos Pueblo, and a battle started with the rebels. Soon the rebels moved to the Pueblo's church (Mission San Geronimo de Taos). The Native Americans and Mexicans evidently thought the Americans would not attack a church; and, at first, the Americans did simply surround the building.

Lafe later said he was on picket duty with other men at this time, keeping guard that night at the back of the church so that the insurgents could not escape, and he received two or three bullet wounds at that time, as well as a possible saber cut across his head from insurgents trying to escape at night. Different historians say Lafe was wounded in different places, but only Lafe mentions the saber wound and only once.[27] Toward the morning of February 4, the soldiers moved closer and using their bayonets chopped a hole in the side of the adobe church. The American soldiers were under fire the entire time and several were killed. The Americans threw hand grenades (which started fires) and shot off cannons loaded with shrapnel. Then the Americans switched their six pound cannon to fire grape shot, and the cannon was moved closer and closer, firing into a hole in the church's wall that was getting bigger. They continued to fire their cannons directly into the interior, filling the church with smoke, and killing about 150 rebels. The next morning they captured 400 more rebels and a formal surrender was made. Hundreds of Pueblo people were wounded in the attack. About fifty more rebels were killed fleeing out the back of the church where Lafe was located. Only two or three escaped in that manner, and only seven Americans were killed in the entire Taos attack. After Taos, there were small skirmishes at Red River Canyon and Las Vegas, as well as another small skirmish at Taos; but by mid-February the revolt was totally under control.

After a summary trial, six of the captives were hung for treason and murder. Montoya, the suspected spy, had been quickly tried at a "drum-head court," where he was sentenced to hang and was duly executed the day after the victory. The next day, some more of the rebels were summarily shot. Then after a trial, fifteen more Mexican men were found guilty and executed. All in all, twenty-eight Mexican or Pueblo men were eventually executed. One was hung for treason even though the United States had not yet granted citizenship to the Mexicans, as the war was still raging. Donaciano Vigil was made Acting American Civil Governor of New Mexico until the

The Church of the Taos Pueblo was where the Americans basically ended the Pueblo Revolt by the killing or wounding of hundreds of the Taos Pueblo Indians who revolted during the Pueblo Rebellion.

Photo Courtesy of Wikipedia.

signing of the Treaty of Guadalupe-Hidalgo. Some forty years later, when Lafe gave his account of the "Taos Revolt," he simply said:

> "I was promoted to the rank of Major (sic), and in Colonel Price's command, left to garrison the place (Santa Fe)." Lafe removed his hat and showed a large scar on his head. "I got that at the siege of Taos, (plus) two or three bullet wounds that for years afterwards crippled me quite badly. I have overcome them now, and the government is paying me eight dollars a month for these tokens of loyalty."[28]

There are discrepancies in Lafe's interview, which was conducted when he was an old man. Some historians say Lafe was wounded in the hand, some say he was wounded in the foot, his granddaughter said it was in the leg, some say both; but neither the military's records nor anyone other than Lafe mentions that he was promoted from a Private to a Major at this time.

The rest of Lafe's one year military career was quiet, as he must have spent several months in the hospital recovering from his wounds. He was discharged in Santa Fe on September 17, 1847. Santa Fe had changed dramatically in the year since Lafe's arrival. *The Santa Fe Republican* reported:

> *The merchants have fitted up large and convenient rooms in place of small and crowded ones, and the doors, windows and other marks of improvement.... The ruins of old houses, which were scattered all over town, have given place to new and better built ones, and as fast as workmen and materials can be procured, new buildings are going up. Not a street in the place presents the appearance it did this time one year ago, and if things continue in one more year, the whole appearance of the city will be changed.*[29]

It should be noted that when the Army of the West in New Mexico, now under the command of Colonel Sterling Price, put down the 1847 Taos Revolt, President James K. Polk promoted Price to brigadier general on July 20 of that year. That same month, Brigadier General Price was named military governor of Chihuahua.

The Mexican-American War ended on February 2, 1848, with the signing of the Treaty of Guadalupe-Hidalgo, which was ratified by the United States Congress on March 10. However, Brigadier General Price led 300 men from his Army of the West in the Battle of Santa Cruz de Rosales on March 16, 1848, defeating a Mexican force three times his size. Many historians cite this battle as the last battle of the war, even though it took place

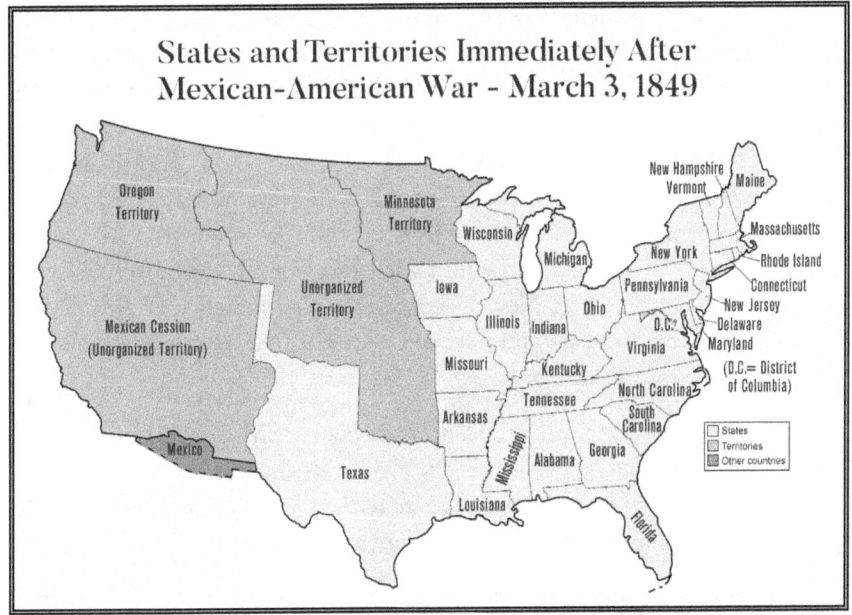

Oregon became a territory and Texas a state before the Mexican-American War. With the New Mexican territory gained, the United States had more than doubled in size in only five years.

Western Reflections Publishing Co. Map.

days after the Treaty of Guadalupe Hidalgo had been ratified. Although reprimanded by Secretary of War William L. Marcy and ordered to return with his army to New Mexico, Price was not punished. He was honorably discharged on November 25, 1848, and returned to Missouri a hero.

With the Mexican American War over, the Treaty of Guadalupe-Hidalgo resulted in an immense amount of land (although much of it was unsettled) being purchased by the United States from Mexico for $15 million and the assumption of about $3 million in debts. The U.S. had recently settled the "Oregon Dispute" with Great Britain, and there had been the annexation of Texas; so after the Mexican-American War ended, the United States was close to its present boundary. It was a huge chunk of land ready to be settled and explored, and it was filled with many natural resources. The Gadsden Purchase from Mexico and a few boundary adjustments on the Canada border were all that remained to arrive at the present boundaries of the continental United States.

Within the Treaty of Guadalupe-Hidalgo, Mexico finally recognized Texas as part of the United States, but the U.S. Senate struck a provision (Article 10) that all Mexican Land Grants would be recognized by the United States. The treaty did say that the United States would protect Mexican property rights, which led to many future court cases. Basically, if grants were never occupied or controlled, they went back into the public domain. New Mexico residents, if they wanted, could become U.S. citizens or they could move to Mexico. All but about 1,000 Mexican citizens chose to become U.S. citizens and the 1,000 who left were mainly Mexican officials or aristocracy. Mexican-American citizens were considered "white" by the terms of the treaty and could vote. It was not, however, until 1850 that the U.S. established New Mexico Territory which contained all of New Mexico and Arizona and part of Colorado. The 1850 census showed 61,547 people in the territory.

> The American frontier no longer ended at the Mississippi River. The addition of one million, two hundred thousand square miles had almost doubled the size of the United States. There was a lot of new territory to explore and settle.[30]

Following the Mexican-American War, the Ute, Navajo, and Jicarilla Apache raids increased, and by July, 1848 a major force guided by mountain man Old Bill Williams had chased the Jicarilla Apache into the San Juan Mountains. They were joined there by Utes and a fierce battle occurred near Cumbres Pass. Thirty-seven Native Americans and two soldiers were killed in the battle.

Native American disdain for and hostility toward Mexican settlers in particular was noted in 1847 when George Frederick Ruxton reported that when he passed through Rio Colorado (now called Questa), the Indians told him they tolerated the presence of the Mexican peons "for the sole purpose of having at their command a stock of grain and a herd of mules and horses, which they make no scruples of helping themselves to, whenever they required a remount or a supply of farinaceous food."[31]

CHAPTER FOUR

Businessman and Lawman in New Mexico
(1848-1854)

Lafayette Head was an energetic merchant in Abiqui and a Special Agent for the Jicarilla Apache and Utes.

Virginia Simmons

Lafe decided not to return to Missouri after he was discharged from the Army in September of 1847. Up to that point, he had learned to speak only a little Spanish, but from the time of his discharge until the end of the Mexican-American War (about a year), he took a clerk's job with a Santa Fe merchant. His new job enabled him to greatly improve his Spanish, learn how to run a mercantile dealing with Mexican-Americans and Native Americans, and save some money. The Mexican-American people and their easy-going way of life appealed to him, and they soon called him "Raphael Cabeza." "Cabeza" is the Spanish word for "head;" however, there is no equivalent in Spanish for "Lafayette." How he got the Spanish name "Raphael" is unknown, but it may have had something to do with his conversion to Catholicism and his Baptism and Confirmation in the Catholic Church, which he did in order to marry his future wife Martina; or perhaps it was a pet name she had for him. Raphael is an archangel of the Catholic Church associated with physical and emotional healing, and the name means "God Heals" in Hebrew. Perhaps the name, if a pet name given by Martina, was the result of her feeling that God had sent Raphael (Lafe) to help heal her wounds from her first husband's death and to help her with her two (one) children.

The end of the Mexican-American War in 1848, and the discovery of gold in California near the end of that year marked the beginning of the movement of Americans into the Far West. In the summer of 1848 alone, 3,000 wagons, 12,000 people, and 50,000 head of livestock traveled over at least some part of the Santa Fe Trail. Most of these people went on to travel the Oregon or California Trails to the north of Bent's Fort, but a few

CHAPTER 4

The church in Santa Fe was one block east of the plaza. Although the current La Fonda Inn was not built until 1922, it was built on the site of this La Fonda ("fonda" means "inn" in Spanish).

Grafton, *The American West*.

Americans made their way southwest to Santa Fe or went west through the San Luis Valley. From Santa Fe, most travelers continued on to California on the southern (the main branch) of the Old Spanish Trail, which began at Abiqui, New Mexico, about sixty miles northwest of Santa Fe. Some travelers took the North Branch of the Old Spanish Trail, which began in the San Luis Valley of today's Colorado and tied back into the southern branch near today's Green River, Utah. On September 9, 1850, New Mexico adopted a constitution and was made a territory that was much bigger than the present state.

With the increased movement of Americans westward, the Utes became upset that so many outsiders were now coming to the far southern portion of what they rightly considered their land. Small skirmishes continued with the aggressor being both the U.S. and the Utes. In 1849, Lieutenant J. H. Whitley discovered a camp of fifty Ute lodges near today's Red River, New Mexico, attacked them, and then fought off others who came to aid their fellow Utes. A few Utes were killed, but many more were wounded and a chief's son and some of the Ute women were taken captive. Then that same summer, the Utes attacked settlements outside Las Vegas, New Mexico.

The Utes and Jicarilla Apaches also attacked a small wagon train on the Santa Fe Trail, killed the men with the wagon train, and took a woman and her daughter as hostages.

In February of 1849, Lafe gave up his clerk's job in Santa Fe and left that town. He had bought a stock of general merchandise and moved north to the town of Abiqui, which had for decades been a "jumping off point" for trappers, slave dealers, and traders going into what would become today's Colorado or traveling to California over the Old Spanish Trail. Lafe was moving into a part of New Mexico inhabited by many Native Americans, mainly Utes and Jicarilla Apaches. This was "Rio Arriba" or "Upper River," an area north of what might even loosely be called "civilization." There were no roads, few stores (really just small trading posts), and only an occasional white man (usually trappers or traders) that passed through the area.

However, in 1849, the Spanish community of Abiqui was already located near the Chama River about sixty miles northwest of Santa Fe as the crow flies. It was founded in the eighteenth century on the ruins of a Tewa Pueblo that was established in the thirteenth century and abandoned in the sixteenth century, probably due to an extended drought or to overuse of the local natural resources. The area is still referred to as "P'efu" by the

Dr. J. S. Newberry made this drawing of the Abiqui area from a sketch by the U. S. John N. Macomb Expedition of 1859. Abiqui is in the canyon below Abiqui Peak.

Thayer, *Marvels of the West*.

Tewa; but the Tewa had a second name for the area, "Avenshu," which the Spanish pronounced as "Abiqui."

By 1730, a few Spanish settlers were moving north into the southern Chama Valley, as it was very fertile; and, by 1744, about twenty Spanish families were living a few miles south of today's Abiqui, and they called their settlement by that name. Unfortunately, the area they initially moved to had to be often abandoned because of Ute and Comanche raids; so, in 1750, the Spanish authorities mandated that the settlement be moved to Abiqui's present site, which is on a bluff a few miles away and much more defendable. The name of the old settlement was kept for the new location. The Native American attacks unfortunately continued; and, in 1754, the Spanish community land grant of "Abiqui" was made to thirty-four genizaro families. Genizaros were Native Americans who served as household servants, shepherds, nannies, or in other trusted positions for the Spanish and had been freed by their owners.

Many genizaros were of mixed Spanish and Pueblo Indian blood, and they usually had been raised as Christians. Genizaros generally were considered a part of the extended family of their Spanish, Mexican, and American owners. By 1800, almost one-third of the population of New Mexico was genizaros or their descendants. Most were set free by the choice of their owners, but some because they had complained to the authorities of mistreatment and were freed by the government. They and their families were allowed to settle on Mexican and Spanish land grants as "buffer communities" from Native American attacks. Genizaros included Navajo, Pawnee, Apache, Kiowa Apache, Comanche, Ute, or Piute, and genizaros and their descendants were at the bottom of the Spanish and Mexican economic and social ladder.

By the late 1700s and early 1800s, a tenuous peace had been made by the Spanish with the Ute and Comanche, and more settlers and ranchers moved into the Chama River and lower Rio Grande areas. The Spanish government's hope was that by moving genizaros to Abiqui these often educated people would have their own land and would serve as their own defenders, instead of depending on the very small and insufficient local Spanish Army to protect them. That hope was so strong that when Mexico gained its freedom from Spain, one of the first acts of the New Mexican government was to give the right to their provincial governors to give grants of large amounts of land to these loyal and subservient citizens. In the 1830s and 1840s, Mexican Provincial Governor Don Miguel Armijo gave away a staggering amount of land through over 200 land grants; and, all told, Spanish and Mexican governors gave away over nine million acres of land.

After 1830, Abiqui became a major Mexican trading partner with California on the east end of the Old Spanish Trail, with Native Americans and mountain men often visiting the town. Abiqui was third in trading in New Mexico Province in the 1830s and 1840s, behind only Santa Fe and Taos. Some of the Native Americans dealt with the same Mexican traders for decades, and a bond was established between the two groups in the nineteenth century; although as more and more Mexicans moved further north along the Chama and Rio Grande Rivers, tensions began to grow between the Utes and the Mexicans.

During the last half of the eighteenth century and the first half of the nineteenth century, the Utes had progressed from a very poor people to a relatively well-off culture, mainly because they were one of the first of the Native American tribes to gain the horse. They had changed their small family hunter-gatherer groups into larger "bands" that were still very nomadic, moving with the seasons to different areas that their people knew contained food at that time of year. These larger groups were also now necessary in times of war against other Native Americans who were being pushed west by the Americans. The Utes had by this time extended their hunting grounds for hundreds of miles into the Great Plains, where they had found the buffalo, which they killed for their hides and their meat.

However with the large Mexican Land Grants being made, Ute land was being encroached upon from the south by Mexicans, and also from the east by Native American Plains tribes (Arapaho, Cheyenne, Comanche, and Kiowa). In 1846, the Americans joined the crowd. For a few years the Americans lived somewhat peacefully with the Utes, as the Americans were recognized as better warriors and better armed than the Mexicans, and they had many desirable items to trade. However, as more and more American settlers moved into the Utes' traditional territory, the Utes' interest shifted from trading to raiding to get what they wanted. By this time, it was an activity they had carried on with other Indian tribes for over a hundred years. The focus of their raids was basically to obtain food and horses; and their participation in actual wars shifted mainly to the other Native American groups that were moving into traditional Ute territory on the plains.

In September of 1844, over 1,000 Utes had come to Abiqui to express their grievances about Mexican soldiers attacking their peaceful camps to the north of that town. The Mexican soldiers often had trouble telling one tribe from another and usually attacked any and all Native Americans they saw. Unfortunately, this time they attacked friendly Utes. Nothing came out of the Abiqui meeting, but six chiefs and 108 warriors went on to Santa Fe to address the same grievances to Governor Mariano Martinez. The talks

CHAPTER 4

ended with the killing of eight Utes. The Utes called it an ambush. Martinez said the Utes started the fight. Utes throughout what would become southern Colorado and northern New Mexico went on a rampage, killing all but one man at Antoine Robidoux's trading post on the Uncompahgre River near present-day Delta, as well as many settlers in the lower Chama and San Luis Valley. The anger of the Utes and other Native Americans had continued after American troops arrived in New Mexico in 1846.

It was into this atmosphere of recent tension that Lafe moved, obtained a license as a Native American trader, and opened a small trading post at Abiqui that served the local Mexican people and the various Native Americans, mainly Utes, who traveled through the area. Lafe's trading post was said to be a "hive of people of mixed race and tribes," speaking many different languages.

Procedures for a trading license with the Native Americans were first instituted on November 21, 1849 by James Calhoun, New Mexico Superintendent of Indian Affairs. They included provisions that a trader had to be a U.S. citizen with good character references and needed to post a bond not to exceed $5,000 and signed by one or more sureties. Trade in firearms, powder, lead or other munitions of war was prohibited, but were often still sold. The applicant had to name the specific tribe(s) he would trade with and could not trade with other tribes. About 1852 another regulation was passed that the local military could not buy their food and supplies directly from local traders. These regulations hampered Lafe's trade with all but the Mexican-Americans, who were mostly very poor, and the new regulations probably made him start thinking about another line of work. Lafe had sold or traded his goods at a decent profit and was now well-accepted and liked in the community. Most importantly, in Abiqui, Lafe found a pretty, young widow— Marina Martina Martinez Sisneros.

There is much confusion and mystery surrounding Martina and her children (if any) and the date of her marriage to Lafe. This includes Martina's age, full name, and date of birth. Most records, including the Head Family Research Center, state she was born November 24, 1839, but this makes her only eleven years old with a three year old child when she married Lafe. Some sources write she was born in 1829 or 1830; which makes her twenty-one or so at the time of her marriage, and this does align with her death on November 18, 1888 at age fifty-six. Her tombstone however notes that she was born in 1839, making her a few days short of forty-eight when she died. The 1850 federal census shows her as age eighteen, making her date of birth in 1832, but it also indicates there were no children in the Head household, and we know she had at least one child with her.

When Marina Martina Martinez (her name according to *the Diaries of the Jesuit Fathers*) and Lafe met is unknown, but her family lived in the Abiqui/Servilleta area, and she was living with Head in Abiqui and using his last name in 1850 (census records). They were also living in Servilleta by 1852 (possibly even as early as immediately after the census in 1850). The earliest date given for their co-habitation was by the granddaughter Piedad as 1847, shortly after Lafe got out of the army; but Lafe did not move to the Abiqui area (where Martina lived) until about 1849. So the year 1850 seems therefore to be a good guess on their marriage date. Martinez was almost certainly Martina's maiden name, but further information is very confusing. Martina is identified in various written records as Maria Juanita, Maria Juana, Juanita, or just M.J. and, as mentioned, a footnote to the Jesuit diary states that her full maiden name was Marina Martina Martinez (pg. 17n). Her full name might have been Maria Juanita Sisneros (first marriage and sometimes spelled Cisneros) Head. Historian Frank Hall writes that Lafe married eighteen-year-old Maria Juana de la Cruz Martinez in 1851. However, according to a letter from her descendant Evangeline Hill to Colorado State University, Lafe married Maria Juanita Martinez in 1847 and historian Mark Thompson also speculates that Lafe could have married Martina as early as 1847. Piedad, Lafe's granddaughter, also stated in her *Ranch and Range* article that the date was 1847.

The 1850 U.S. Federal census shows "Raphael Head" living in Abiqui with an eighteen year old named "Marta" living with him with no children, but does not indicate they were married. Many historians and later records indicate that Martina had one child (José Sisneros); and that if there was a second child in her household, it was probably an Indian slave. Another mystery is that no child named José is indicated in the 1850 or 1860 census; although a Cresenio Sisneros, age 16, is. It is possible that Lafe and Martina lived together for several years before officially marrying, or perhaps they declared they were married by common law. However a common law marriage is unlikely, as Lafe was evidently baptized in the Catholic Church so that he could marry Martina. Lafe called his wife by the pet name "Martina" (the feminine form of "Martin" in English) and treated her boy, José Cresencio Sisneros (the name of Martina's first husband), as his own son. Martina would be Lafe's lifelong companion and helper until she died in middle age on November 18, 1888.

In the meanwhile, Lafe and Martina were living among basically hostile Utes, who the American government wanted to be farmers. In February of 1849, Lieutenant Colonel John Washington, military commander for New Mexico had written:

CHAPTER 4

> *The period has arrived when they (the Native Americans) must restrain themselves within the present limits and cultivate the earth for an honest livelihood, or be destroyed.*[32]

Although the U.S. government had begun military campaigns against the Native Americans in New Mexico less than a month after their arrival in the area, James S. Calhoun, Indian Affairs Superintendent for the Territory of New Mexico, had deep concerns for the Native Americans in his territory. He suggested Native Americans should have civilian not the traditional military Agents, who he considered too hostile.

One major event that occurred in December 1849, just shortly after Lafe moved to Abiqui, was the making of the first official peace treaty between the United States and the Utes. The 1849 Calhoun Treaty at Abiqui confirmed the 1846 agreement, plus the Utes were promised food supplies to replace the game that was being killed by Mexican-Americans and Anglos. The United States agreed in the 1849 treaty that an Agency for the Utes would be opened in the town of Taos the next year (it was, but it was not funded for several more years), and the Utes agreed to recognize the sovereignty of the United States (obviously, as events showed, they had no idea what this meant). The Utes also agreed not to depart from their "accustomed territory" (although no boundaries were given), unless they were given specific permission to leave (this they never followed). The Utes further agreed to a perpetual peace (the peace only lasted a few days), to abide by all laws of the United States (but they had no idea what those laws were), and to allow military posts (which they came to hate) and Indian Agencies to be built on their land. The treaty stated that a fixed boundary for Ute land would be established later after it was determined where they could "live, farm, build homes and such other industrious pursuits as will promote their happiness and prosperity."[33]

An Agency for the Utes was established in Taos in 1850, but funding was not provided until 1851 with John Greiner as Agent. No survey was ever made for their land, and after only a few days the Utes raided the U.S. troops near Abiqui. Perhaps the problem of the continuing Ute raids was that the Utes were used to making agreements only for their small family groups. James Calhoun in a letter of January 31, 1850, blamed the problems with the Navajo and Utes on some local Abiqui traders, which probably did not include Lafe as he had just obtained his license.

> *Abiqui has long been the headquarters of a very mischievous band of traders with the Navajos and Utes with these Indians; and that they caused the outbreak mentioned, I entertain not the slightest doubt.*[34]

Twenty-eight Utes signed the treaty. James Calhoun arranged for the treaty and represented the United States, so it is generally called the "Calhoun Treaty." The unstated purpose of the conference from the U.S. point of view was simply to assure the Utes that the Americans were friendly, so as to keep them peaceful while the U.S was fighting the Navajo and Apache. "After the twenty-eight Ute leaders expressed their utter aversion to labor,"[35] Calhoun, without authority to do so, promised that the United States would help take care of the Utes to the amount of $5,000 a year in goods." Because of lack of funding this did not occur. It was an inauspicious beginning to the Ute-American relationship.

Meanwhile Lafe's popularity among the general community of Abiqui settlers increased greatly. Abiqui was in Rio Arriba County, whose early records are very incomplete; but in 1847 or 1848, Lafe had evidently been appointed Deputy or Assistant U.S. Marshal under Richard Dallum or John G. Jones for the Third Judicial District (there were no counties formed yet) in the northern part of the future New Mexico Territory. It was a job that included trying to stop any type of violence on the frontier—Native American, Mexican-American, or White. Lafe was further listed in the state records as a "county tax collector," which may have given him a reason to become an Assistant or Deputy U.S. Marshal, in an effort to show he had some official authority.

When the Mexican-American War had ended, some former U.S. soldiers had seen an opportunity in the Southwest; and, like Lafayette Head, did not return to the East. They brought with them familiar social organizations, and the Grand Lodge of Missouri chartered Montezuma Masonic Lodge #109 in Santa Fe on May 8, 1851, and it opened August 12, 1851. Lafe joined the Santa Fe Lodge on December 13, 1851, just shortly after it was chartered; and he would be made a Master Mason on January 1, 1853.

Americans were still few in number in the early American New Mexico Territory, and the Masons were one of the few social centers available to them. Scores of American military, politicians, and commercial leaders joined the Santa Fe Lodge, and for nine years it was the only Masonic Lodge in the Territory of New Mexico. Most of its early members were from Missouri. The Lodge not only offered a social life, but also mutual protection, as well as providing political and business opportunities. To make their meeting place feel more like back East, they brought wagonloads of furniture from Missouri. Scores of leaders in the military, commercial, and public life (some of them nationally famed) became Masons. Except for saloons and gambling halls, there was no other place to socialize.

CHAPTER 4

> On August 12, 1851 Montezuma No. 109 was established, and for eleven years was the only active lodge in New Mexico. Some of the early leading men in the New Mexico Territory joined Freemasonry at the new lodge in Santa Fe, including Lafayette Head, prominent merchant, U.S. Marshall, and later to be the first Lieutenant Governor of Colorado; famed trapper and scout Kit Carson; and Ceran St. Vrain, founder of the Santa Fe Gazette newspaper.[36]

Another very important reason for joining the Masons was that for a while after the Mexican-American War ended there was no Protestant church in Santa Fe (only a military chaplain), and as only Catholics could be buried in the Catholic cemeteries, there was therefore no cemetery in Santa Fe where Protestants could be buried. The Montezuma Masonic Lodge and the International Order of Odd Fellows (IOOF) established the first Protestant cemetery in New Mexico and would handle most of the Anglo and Protestant burials there for many years to come. Later, the Bent Masonic Lodge was formed at Taos, making it easier for Taos area members such as Carson, Head, Albert Pfeiffer, Ceran St. Vrain, and others to attend Lodge meetings until it closed in the 1870s.

Lafe already knew Kit Carson well, as he came from the Franklin, Missouri area, both men served in the "Army of the West," and Carson spent a lot of time in Santa Fe, Abiqui, and Taos when Lafe was there (although these were fairly large towns, the Anglo populations were small). Kit Carson became a Lodge brother three years after Lafe was inducted. Many of the members of this Lodge went on to become business and/or political leaders in the future territories and states of Colorado and New Mexico, and Lafe's Lodge connections greatly enhanced his future business and political opportunities. Although he had only lived in Santa Fe for a year or two, he remained a member of the Santa Fe Lodge for almost thirty years, at which time he switched his membership to the Alamosa Masonic Lodge.

On September 9, 1850, the United States had created the State of California, and the Territories of Utah and New Mexico. Nine counties were created in New Mexico, and William Lane was appointed the Territorial Governor. The first New Mexico territorial legislature was formed in 1851, but it was two more years before Lafe got into politics. He was the only non-Hispanic in the New Mexico Territorial legislature. Such elections and appointments throughout his life show how well-liked and respected Lafe was from the age of twenty-seven on.

Businessman and Lawman in New Mexico

Lafe and Martina moved to Servilleta (near Ojo Caliente), and he was appointed Sheriff of the new Rio Arriba County authorized by the new territory of New Mexico on February 20, 1852. Head would have done well with his trading post at Abiqui during this time except he made the mistake of many beginning merchants and issued credit too freely to his neighbors. Eventually these sums totaled about $15,000 and, evidently rather than try to do something to collect the money, he decided to change professions. After talking with friends, including some members of Martina's family who were part owners or heirs of the Conejos Land Grant, he decided in 1852 to move to the Servilleta near Ojo Caliente, so as to be nearer the San Luis Valley and Kit Carson in Taos. He was also checking out the ranching and agricultural possibilities of the Conejos Grant for the Martinez family. The previous sheriff, Pedro Salazar, had been removed from office after serving only four months. The local citizens elected Lafe to serve the remainder of Salazar's two-year term that ended on October 1853; then he was reelected for two more years as Rio Arriba Sheriff, making a total of three

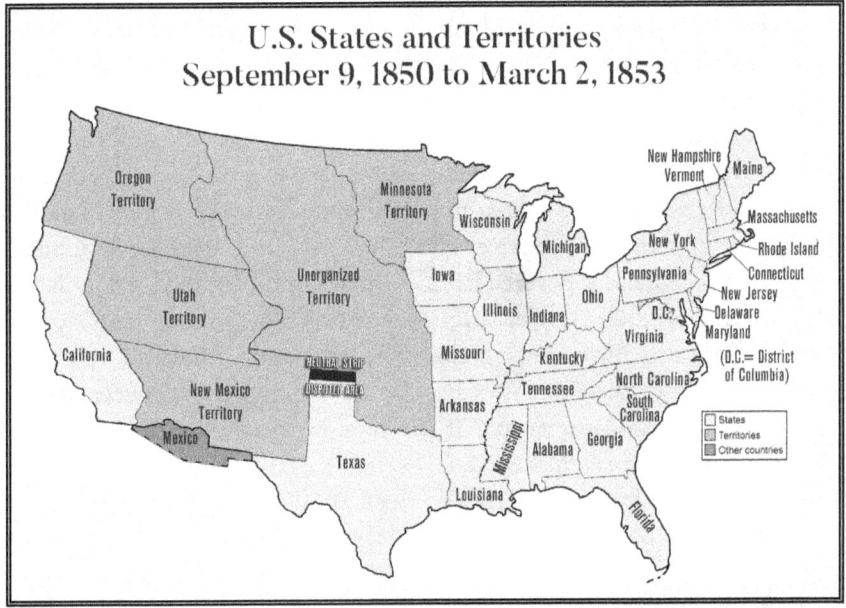

When New Mexico and Utah became territories, they originally included Nevada and Arizona as shown on this map. However there was also "The Notch" in New Mexico's northeast corner that kept the southern part of the future Colorado in New Mexico.

Western Reflections Publishing Co. Map.

CHAPTER 4

years that he served as such. Lafe performed his duties of law enforcer and tax collector well, as his Deputy U.S. Marshal's job territory was the same as the Sheriff's position. In 1852, he was appointed Special Agent for the Utes and Apache at Abiqui since Greiner was not even present there, and Head was elected one of the five representatives to the New Mexico Third Territorial House (although his name was spelled "La Fayette Head") that same year, starting his service for Rio Arriba County in December, 1853. Head had at age twenty-six become "the man to go to," and he had a distinct advantage in being bilingual in a territory where English was a foreign language to the vast majority of the residents.

The New Mexico Territorial legislature met in Santa Fe in the 250 year old Palace of the Governors. Most members were farmers and ranchers, so their legislative work began on the first Monday of January, and they usually met for about fifty days. They conducted all their business in Spanish. However, bills that were passed were translated into English, and the official record included copies of bills in both languages. After serving for only one year in the New Mexico legislature, Lafe did not run for the next three years because of his efforts in getting the Conejos Grant recognized and the town of Conejos established; but he would run again in 1856 with even more success in the New Mexico Senate.

The original Arriba County was huge—for a while it ran in a narrow strip from the Rio Grande River west to the New Mexico-California state line, as New Mexico then included the area that is now Arizona. As mentioned, before 1851 all the area north of Santa Fe was referred to as Rio Arriba or ("upper river"), the river being the Rio Grande. Rio Arriba County was now formed and it covered 26,237 square miles and had a population of more than 10,000 people. After New Mexico became a territory, only Taos County was further north than Arriba County. However, in practical terms, most of the citizens of Rio Arriba County lived between Abiqui and Taos, with very few people at the time in the San Luis Valley or in the mountainous areas to the west. The western end of Rio Arriba County ran through Ute Indian Territory to the California border, an area which would be totally unsettled by Americans for twenty more years. It should be noted that it did not hurt Lafe's chances for winning the election as Arriba County Sheriff, being one of the few white men living in the area. Mexican-Americans tended not to vote at the time, as democracy was new to them.

In the 1800s, there were several other Servilletas not too far from Conejos, which makes the town's history confusing. The later road leaving Conejos to the north to Fort Garland from Guadalupe/Conejos passed through an area called Servilleta, where there were nineteen citizens still

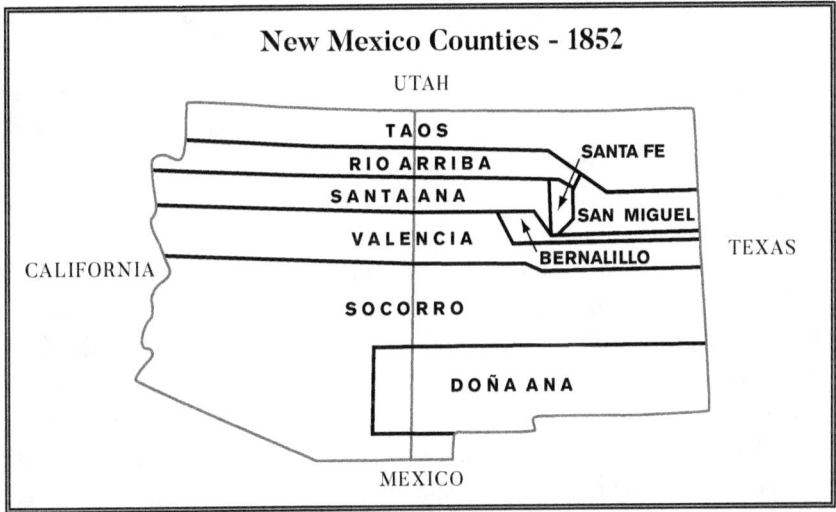

When New Mexico became U. S. Territory in 1850 it was divided into three large counties, Rio Arriba at the top, Rio Abajo at the middle, and Doña Ana at the bottom By 1852 it had ten counties and looked like this map. Lafe was to move into Taos County when he moved to the San Luis Valley.

Western Reflections Publishing Co. Map.

living in 1879, and that Servilleta was still on an 1882 map, but was said to be abandoned at the time. Another Servilleta was near Tierra Amarilla, and another (possibly the one Lafe and his group first used as a fort in the San Luis Valley) was said to be five or six miles downstream (northeast) from the future settlement of Conejos. Besides the Servilleta that Lafe and Martina moved from (10 miles South of Tres Piedra and near Ojo Caliente), some historians feel that the Servilleta fort was in existence by 1852, was so named, and had a long ditch running to it or the future Guadalupe site by 1854.

As promised in the 1849 Calhoun Treaty, the U.S. government had opened an Agency for the Utes at Taos in 1850, but the United States Congress had not appropriated any funds for the Agency. In early 1851, a little more than a year after the signing of the Calhoun Treaty, John Greiner was appointed Agent for the Ute tribe (and possibly the Jicarilla Apache) with their Agency to be located at Taos, but they still had not received any funding. At this time there was still very little actually being done by the United States government for any of the Native Americans who were being displaced throughout the United States. In 1853, forty Ute families, who were living on the Culebra and Costilla Rivers in the San Luis Valley, were found to be eating pine and aspen bark, because they were hungry and there was no game in the area. As bad as this sounds, the inside portion of the bark was scrapped out and produced a mealy substance that the Utes had used for centuries as an emergency food ration. That same year (1853) funding was finally given to the Ute Agency at Taos, and Kit Carson was appointed to replace Greiner as Agent. It was a position Carson would hold for eight years.

In 1852, Governor James Calhoun had died on the Santa Fe Trail, and William Carr was appointed the new territorial governor by United States President Millard Fillmore, a veteran of the Mexican-American War. Carr took his office after a new law that automatically made the governor of any state or territory the Superintendent of Indian Affairs for his territory. Carr soon fired the Indian Agent for the Jicarilla Apache and replaced him with Michael Steck, who had been the sub-Agent for the Abiqui Indian Agency. This created a vacancy at Taos; and Steck, a Masonic Lodge brother, recommended Lafe as a Sub-Agent to Kit Carson. It was easy to sell Governor Carr on a fellow Missouri man and Mason. Lafe took over his new duties as Sub-Agent on June 5, 1853, and served about a year in that position. On July 1, 1853 he visited Governor Carr's Santa Fe office and reported, "Jicarilla all well and behaving the same and their fields doing very well."[37] Apparently, they did not require or desire a lot of attention, and Lafe still worked the final four months of his term as Rio Arriba Sheriff.

Unfortunately, there is considerable confusion about the appointments of Colorado and New Mexico Indian Agents from 1849 to 1863, and especially the "Special Agents," who were usually appointed to help the actual head Agents with their assigned Native Americans when they were located some distance from their Agency. Before 1863 and the first attempt to get the Utes to a reservation, it is hard to tell who the Ute Agents were, where they were located, and whether any given official was an Agent, Sub-Agent or Special Agent. Agents were originally military officers, then civilians appointed by the territory's or state's governor. Sometimes the appointments were not recorded or were recorded improperly. In addition, special agents or sub-Agents were sometimes appointed for only a specific purpose or a specific territory without a record of the limitation. Lafe was referred to in different reports during the 1850s by all three titles, but he definitely became the official head Tabeguache Agent in 1859, with his Agency moved to Conejos in 1860.

"Special Agents" seem to have been sometimes chosen and/or appointed at the whim of the local Indian Agent, who was in charge of the whole tribe, but they may have been a "Special Agent" only for the purpose of performing a specific duty or an assignment to a specific small band of a tribe. Sub-Agents were appointed by the U.S. and worked under the Agent, being in charge when the Agent was gone. Lafe was to serve as both the regular Agent and as a Special Agent for the Apache and the Tabeguache, as well as Head Agent of the Utes at different times in his life. During the 1850s, only four of the Ute bands needed attention—the Mouache, Capote, Weeminuche, and Tabeguache. The Weeminuche band, which bordered the Tabeguache to the south and west along the southern border of the San Juans, was supposed to have an Agency, but the Weeminuche were very individualistic and wanted no part of being controlled in any way by the Americans. The rest of the Ute bands were too far to the north to have much interaction with the Americans at this time. Plans were, however, already being made that all seven of the Ute bands would be consolidated on a reservation somewhere in the Colorado mountains, as that area was not good ranch or farm land and was therefore not desired by American settlers. The Uintah, White River, and Yampa comprised the Northern Utes and the Capote, Mouache, and Weeminuche made up the Southern Utes. The dividing line was generally accepted as the Gunnison River, and the Tabeguache band roamed on both sides of the river and in the San Luis Valley. Any of the seven bands could safely travel in any of the other Utes territory.

David Merriweather replaced William Carr and became New Mexico's first non-military governor in 1853. Carson was actually his choice to replace the Taos Agent, as John Greiner did not relate well to the Native Americans and Kit understood them by this time. (Carson had been an avid hater of Native Americans in his early career, killing every Indian he saw; but he had greatly changed his attitude over the years.) By 1853, the Native Americans respected Carson and knew that he was sympathetic to their problems and was absolutely fair with them. Continuous Navajo, Apache, and Ute raids for food and other plunder, coupled with the government's failed promises to deliver food and other supplies to the New Mexico Native Americans, had caused Kit Carson to decide to retire from government service in 1852 to live on a ranch on the Maxwell Grant with his friend and fellow mountain man Ceran St. Vrain. However Carson had soon learned he was not ready to retire and quickly accepted the December 1853 appointment as the U.S. Indian Agent in Taos, with Abiqui being a sub-Agency.

When the Tabeguache Utes heard of rations being issued to the Capote and Mouache, they also came to Taos and asked for food. Kit Carson immediately suggested to the government that an Agency be established for them closer to Tabeguache territory than Taos, but it would be several years before his suggestion was acted upon.

CHAPTER 4

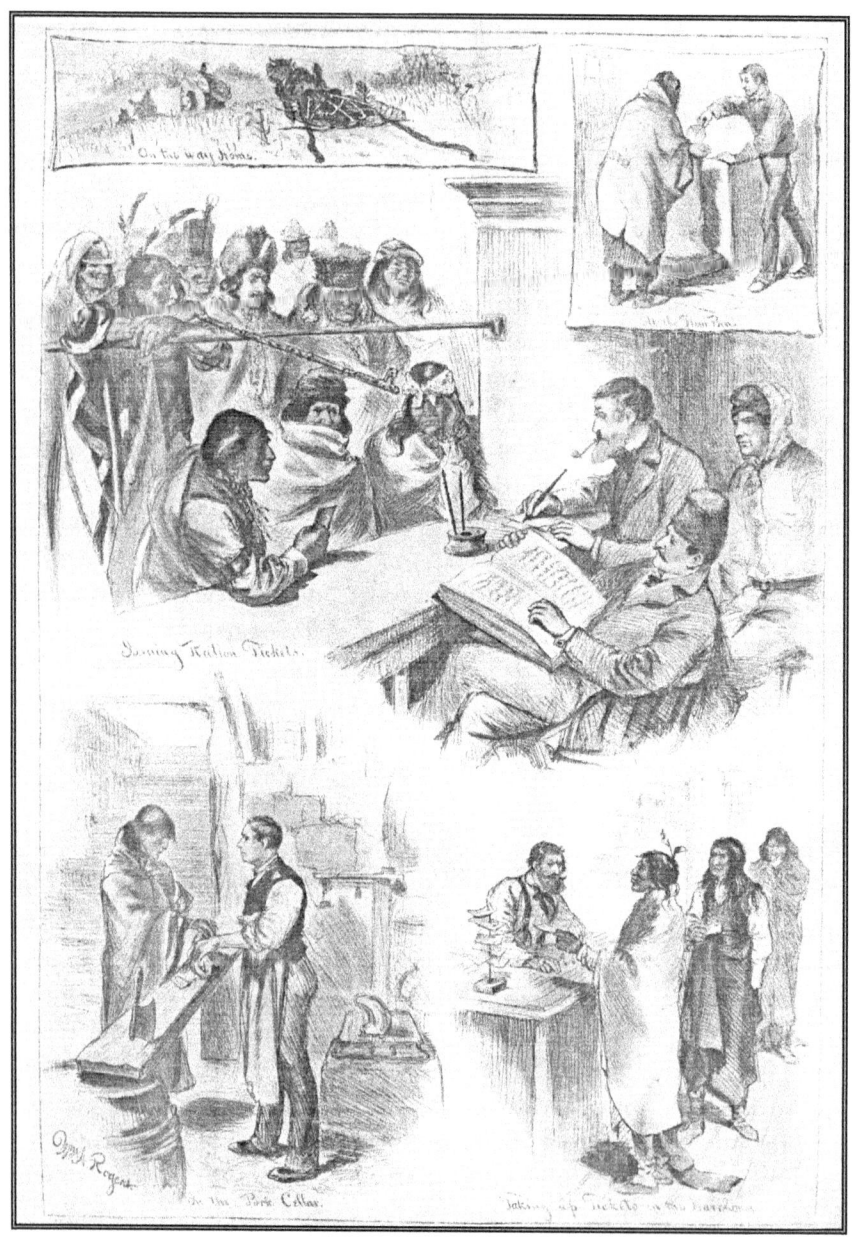

When Native American Agencies were established and they got rations, U. S. officials tried to keep tabs on which individual Indians had received their rations.

Source: *Harpers Weekly* April 5, 1879.

The amount of food and supplies finally given the Native Americans at this time was very limited. An 1853 list of supplies delivered to the Utes and the Jicarilla Apache, and meant to serve several thousand people for up to six months, was for 40 fanegas of wheat (grain was measured by the Spanish *fanega*, which was 1.6 bushels), 96 fanegas of corn, 10 fanegas of corn meal, 3 fanegas of peas, 1 beef, 15 pounds of lead, 4 canisters of powder, 3 plugs of tobacco, and eight dollars' worth of fodder (course food meant for horses or cattle). The receipt of the order was witnessed on June 3, 1853, by Lafayette Head and Joré Auti Manranam, but Lafe identified himself as "Acting Agent for the Jicarilla and Ute Indians."

Although the Jicarilla Agency was originally established in Abiqui, during this time the Jicarilla Apache and the Mouache Utes were usually east of the Rio Grande. These two tribes were closely related by marriage and disposition. Once the Cheyenne and Arapahoe had received horses and arms, they had ranged to the west and became the Ute's bitter enemies, so much so that the Utes could no longer hunt very far on to the Plains.

After New Mexico Territory (which included what would become extreme southern Colorado) was established in 1850, the first serious actions had been taken to provide security for its citizens from the Native Americans. Besides Fort Marcy in Santa Fe, in 1851, the U.S. built Fort Union fifty-five miles northwest of Santa Fe near the western junction of the Mountain Branch of the Santa Fe Trail and the Cimarron Cutoff. It served as a depot for troop supplies coming in on either route, and it got most of the New Mexico troops out of Santa Fe, thus avoiding conflicts with the town's citizens. The American troops seemed to always get drunk and cause some type of trouble when in town, so it was a policy at the time throughout the United States to build U.S. Army forts outside of populated areas.

By the mid-1800s, the army was getting tired of spending large amounts of time and money chasing Native Americans through their own land after they raided American settlements for food that the U.S. government had not given them as required. Even the Secretary of War Charles M. Conrad suggested to Congress in 1852:

> *The newly acquired Territory of New Mexico is so remote and inaccessible, and holds so little inducement to emigrants, that the struggle between the two races (Indians and Whites) is destined, in all probabilities, to continue there long after it shall have ceased in every other portion of the continent.... Would it not be better to induce the inhabitants to abandon a country which seems hardly fit for the habitation of civilized man....*[38]

CHAPTER 4

This attitude by the military was, of course, bitterly resented by the citizens of New Mexico Territory. Congress accepted the position of the residents and built three new forts to protect future settlements in the northern part of New Mexico Territory. On March 30, 1852, military orders were issued to authorize the first of these three forts and it would be built in the San Luis Valley; Fort Massachusetts would be the furthest north of the three. The first actual settlement in San Luis Valley had been on the Sangre de Cristo Grant in 1849, just south of today's Colorado-New Mexico border. It was called "Costilla." The settlement was built far enough south and close enough to Taos to be reasonably safe from Native Americans. The next settlement built in the valley was San Luis, built in the spring of 1851. It is probable that the new settlers of San Luis had heard the news that a military fort would be built on the Sangre de Cristo Grant to protect settlers in the San Luis Valley and travelers on Sangre de Christo and La Veta Passes. Other new settlements on the east side of the Rio Grande followed and all were fairly close (about a half day's hard ride away) to where the fort would be built.

When the United States built Fort Massachusetts near the western base of La Veta and Sangre de Cristo Passes in 1852, it was meant to protect the 200 or so settlers already in the San Luis Valley at that time. It was the first U.S. Army fort and the only symbol of American civilization (except perhaps Bent's Fort) in what is today's Colorado. Fort Massachusetts was authorized in March, 1852 and was ready for occupancy just months later. There were soon 150 soldiers building walls for the new fort, using large pine logs that were ten feet high picketed on three sides and horizontal logs on the fourth side. The fort was officially established on June 22, 1852. It included officer quarters and soldiers' barracks, a laundry, kitchen, blacksmith shop, and a hospital.

Originally the infantry was chosen to man the fort, and they had left from Fort Leavenworth in the late summer of 1851; however, they encountered early snows in the Sangre de Cristo Mountains and were forced to build temporary quarters on the east side of the range. They crossed over to the San Luis Valley in the spring of 1852. Fort Massachusetts was given first priority by the United States because of the Indian troubles that were plaguing the San Luis Valley; but, unfortunately, many of the Mexican-Americans felt the main reason the fort was built was to establish a very visible American military presence in the valley as a warning for them not to rebel.

Major George A. Blake, the fort's first commander, selected the site of the fort on Utah Creek (now called Ute Creek). Virtually every commander who followed Blake felt he had made a mistake. The site was too far off the main trails over the Sangre de Cristo Mountains and was in a swampy, unhealthy area. It was also not easily defended, as it was surrounded on three sides by steep hills. In the summer of 1853, Lieutenant Edward F. Beale was at Fort Massachusetts to get provisions and he noted another reason the fort was built in the wrong place:

> (It) is too far removed from the general track of Indians to be of much service in protecting the settlements from attack in the San Luis Valley....A post established at the (north) head of the Valley of San Luis would be much more effective in keeping marauders in check.[39]

Fort Massachusetts was 320 feet long and 270 feet wide and was located at the southern base of 14,345 foot high (fifth highest in Colorado) Mt. Blanca. San Luis was about twenty-five miles south of the fort, with Taos about eighty miles and Santa Fe about 130 miles. The original infantry garrison was soon switched to both infantry and cavalry because of the large distances in the territory to be covered by the fort's soldiers. The First Dragoons and H Company of the U.S. Infantry ended up finishing the stockade at Fort Massachusetts on June 22, 1852.

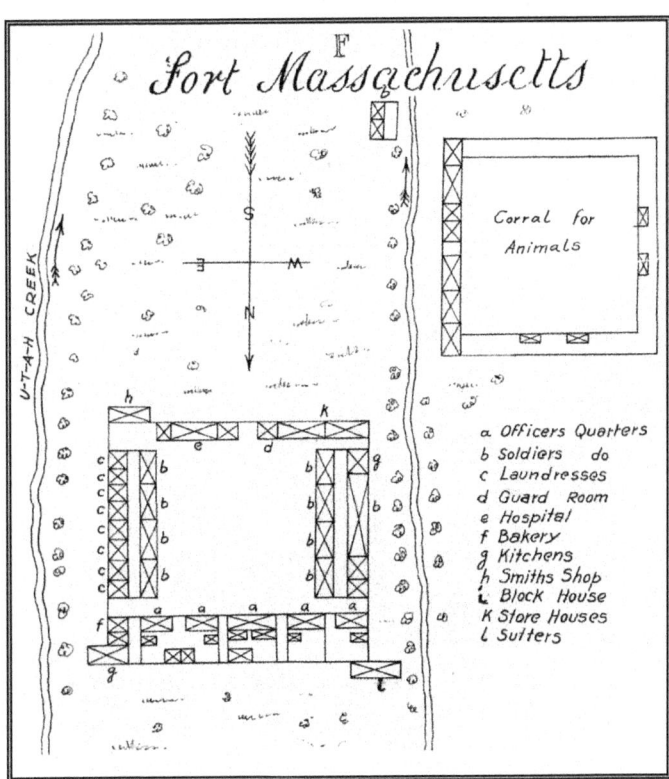

This sketch was made of Fort Massachusetts about 1853 and sent to superiors in Washington.

U. S. National Archives.

CHAPTER 4

Lafe must have welcomed the military's presence in the valley, as it would certainly help him keep law and order. At this time Lafe worked out of the Sheriff's office in the small settlement of Servilleta,[40] and he supervised only a few deputies throughout the huge county. Servilleta means "Flat Plain" or "napkin" in Spanish, but it is also one of the commemorative titles often given the Virgin Mary in Spanish.

With his Deputy U.S. Marshal and Sheriff's duties, Lafe was surely in the San Luis Valley many times before he moved there in September of 1854, and very probably he had seen much of the valley of the Conejos River. However, we have written proof that he was officially at the Conejos River in September 1854, when a Jicarilla chief called "Chacon" met with the Governor of New Mexico Territory David Merriweather and the new Commander of Fort Union near Santa Fe. Chacon said his people were not involved in recent Jicarilla attacks on New Mexican settlers and offered to bring in the Native Americans who were responsible. He said it might take a month for him to do so and asked for help feeding his hungry people in the meantime. Merriweather asked Lafe as Special Agent for the Jicarilla Apache to purchase and deliver 40 fenagas of corn to Chacon's people, who were camped in or near the future town of Conejos on the Conejos River. Lafe did as instructed and reported back to Merriweather that the

This drawing of the exterior of Fort Massachusetts was also sent to Washington in 1853. The edge of the stables is seen at left.

U. S. National Archives.

Jicarilla had insulted and threatened him when he delivered the corn. He also reported that there were at least 100 lodges (each lodge could hold two or three warriors with as many as a dozen dependents) in the camp. This number was far more Jicarilla than Chacon had reported to the governor. Lafe warned that instead of wanting peace, the Jicarilla band near the future Conejos were very likely gathering for a "Trojan Horse" raid.

Unfortunately, the settlers who moved into the San Luis Valley after 1850 had more to worry about than the Native Americans. The threat came from land grants given by Spain and Mexico to their citizens. As mentioned, the Treaty of Guadalupe-Hidalgo stated that Mexican property rights would be recognized by the United States. The entire southern half of the San Luis Valley, as well as much of the nearby mountains on both sides, was covered by several of these grants. However, the grants were only valid if their original conditions were met. This left an important question—was there any land that the new settlers in the fertile southern San Luis Valley could legally settle on in the 1850s?

CHAPTER FIVE

A Home in the San Luis Valley and the Ute War of 1855
(1854-1855)

The flat mountain valley... was 40-60 miles wide and 100 miles long.... The State of Connecticut could have fit on the valley floor.

From *Dry Land and Water: San Luis Valley*
by Paul R. Baumann

In 1854, when Lafe moved from Servilleta to the San Luis Valley (usually referred to as simply "El Valle" or "The Valley" by its residents), it was a fairly well-known area, but not well-settled. History records that a few attempts by different non-Native American settlers had been made to locate there; but the Utes and Jicarilla Apache defended the valley aggressively, as it was one of their favorite locations, especially for hunting. The Spanish had even sent military expeditions to try to push the Utes out of the valley, but they never were successful, even though the nearby settlement of Taos was first occupied by the Spanish as a town in 1780. After that the south end of the San Luis Valley was sometimes called the "Taos Valley," as it is separated from the rest of the San Luis Valley by high hills but only one true mountain (San Antonio). Because of the Ute threat, the Spaniards and later the Mexicans contented themselves with sending shepherds and their flocks to the San Luis Valley during the summer, as it was known for its thick, rich grass; and the Utes tolerated them as long as they built no permanent structures.

Since most development throughout the Territory of New Mexico had occurred along the sides of the Rio Grande River, it was only logical for New Mexican expansion to continue at this time to the north along the same river. However this section of the Rio Grande River itself was a problem. Not only did the river run much deeper, faster, and wider than it does today, because of irrigation water currently being taken out, but the Rio Grande Gorge, a steep 850 foot deep chasm, totally blocked most travelers from crossing the Rio Grande River for about twenty miles, from ten to

A Home in the San Luis Valley and the Ute War of 1855

twenty miles south of today's Alamosa to south of Taos. As Josiah Gregg wrote in 1851 in his book *Commerce on the Prairie*:

> *New Mexico possesses but few of those natural advantages, which are necessary to anything like a rapid progress.... (The Rio Grande River) opposite Taos, especially for an uninterrupted distance of nearly fifteen miles, it runs pent up in a deep cañon, through which it rushes in rapid torrents. This frightful chasm is absolutely impassable.... The river is only known*

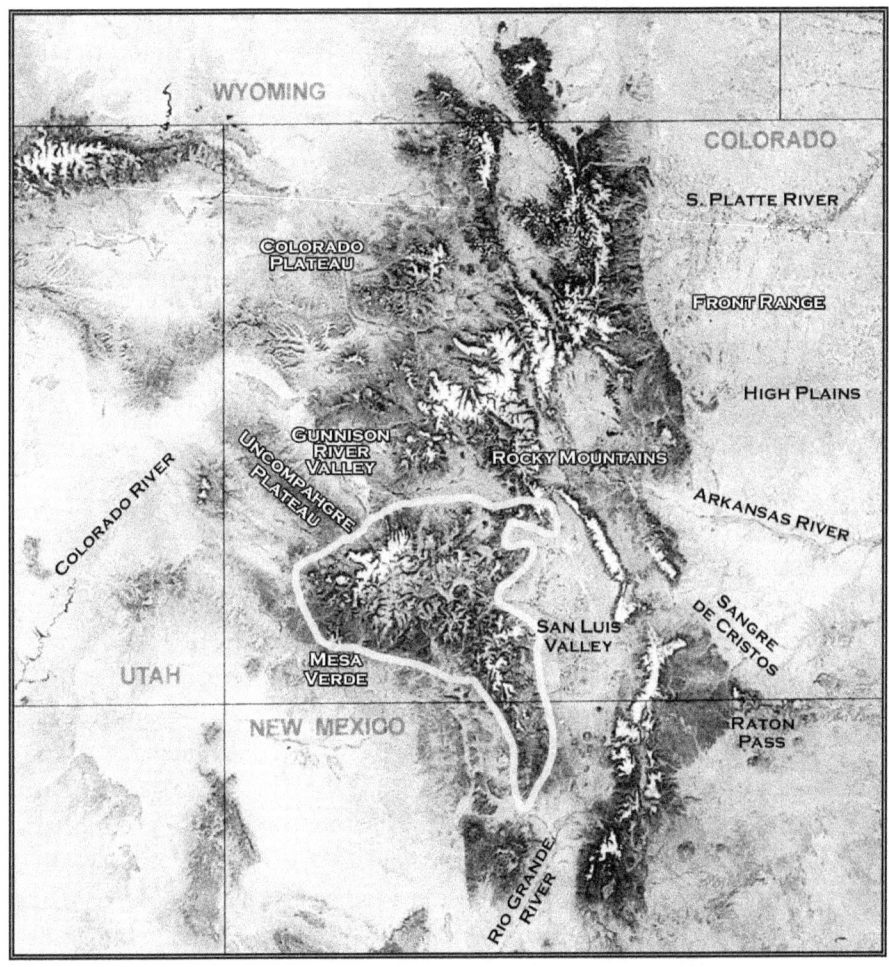

This NASA satellite photograph shows how the San Luis Valley is virtually surrounded by tall mountains as well as the other mountain ranges and parks in Colorado.

Adapted from Nasa Earth Observation by Western Reflections Publishing Co.

CHAPTER 5

> to the inhabitants of Northern Mexico as Rio del Norte, or North River, because it descends from that direction; yet in its passage southward, it is in places called Rio Grande, on account of its extent; but the name of Rio Bravo (Bold or Rapid River), so often given to it on maps, is seldom if ever heard among the people....[41]

The barriers of the river and its gorge effectively split the southern portion of the San Luis Valley into two parts, and settlers from Taos, which is located to the east of the Rio Grande, usually ventured north through the San Luis Valley on the east side of the gorge. Fort Massachusetts' trail to Taos was also along the east side of the river and gorge, so travelers usually went this way when going from the Front Range of today's Colorado to Taos or Santa Fe. Therefore the first attempts of settlement of the San Luis Valley were on the east side of the Rio Grande River.

The San Luis Valley floor covers about 8,200 square miles and is surrounded on all sides by mountains except for small portions at its southern end. The San Juan Mountains to its west and the Sangre de Cristo to its east are by far the highest barriers—some of these mountains being over 14,000 feet. The San Antonio Mountains at the south are mainly high hills except for San Antonio Mountain itself, which is 10,890 feet. At the north end of the valley are higher mountains often called the "Sawatch Range," but which are geologically a part of the San Juan Mountains.

Before 1830, the Utes seemed to be generally peaceful toward travelers, visitors, and even military units passing through the San Luis Valley, and most of the valley's streams and many of the surrounding mountains had Spanish names by 1800. However, the Utes were adamant—this was their land and they would not allow anyone else to permanently settle in the San Luis Valley. Despite the Ute stance, Mexican-Americans preparing to move into the San Luis Valley in the early 1850s intended to coexist with the Utes, as they had in much of New Mexico for generations; however that had been Spanish and not Ute occupied land for hundreds of years. Still, many of the San Luis Valley's first settlers had the very different mentality that they could live in peace with the Utes rather than the later "The Utes Must Go or Be Exterminated!" attitude of most of the Americans.

The Old Spanish Trail is not nearly as well known as the Santa Fe Trail, but since about 1830 it was a somewhat well-traveled route from Abiqui, New Mexico, to Monterrey, California. The trail was first used by mountain men, then later became a preferred route for explorers and

A Home in the San Luis Valley and the Ute War of 1855

the military, and eventually was used by settlers going to trade or live in California. It was not a single trail, but rather many different branches or shortcuts. It allowed New Mexican traders to take sheep, wool, and blankets to California to trade for fine horses and mules, which were brought back to Santa Fe merchants, who usually sent them on up the Santa Fe Trail to Missouri to be sold at a good profit. After 1849 the Old Spanish Trail also became a route for prospectors and their families to California's gold fields in northern California. The North Branch of the Old Spanish Trail ran north from Taos or Abiqui along both sides of the San Luis Valley, then joined together near today's Saguache and went over Cochetopa Pass, and eventually met the main Old Spanish Trail near today's town of Moab on the Colorado River in Utah.

The first town in the San Luis Valley, located just south of the present-day Colorado-New Mexico line and east of the Rio Grande River, was probably Costilla. It was built on the Costilla River in 1851, but a few settlers had been living there before 1850. Further settlements in the future Colorado portion of the valley were soon established on the east side of the Rio Grande River and were the towns of San Luis (June 21, 1851), San Pedro (1852), and San Acacio (1853). Only the town of San Luis has survived, so it is considered the first permanently populated town in

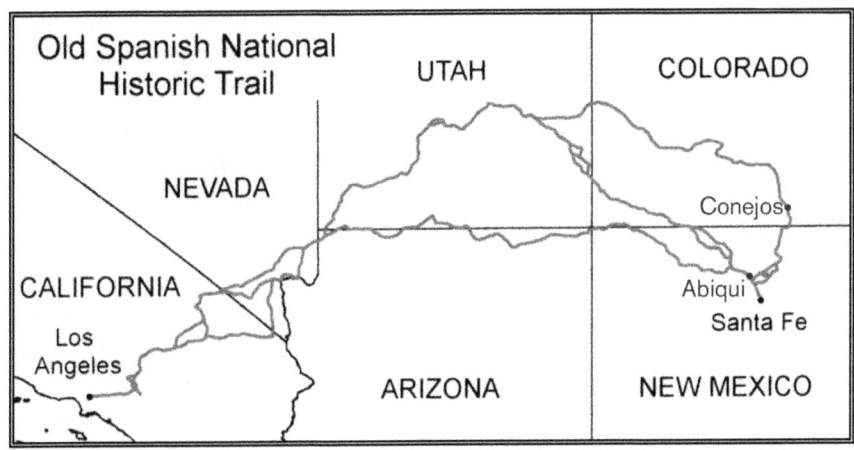

The Old Spanish Trail had several routes. The North Branch started at Abiqui and went up both sides of the San Luis Valley, then over Cochetopa Pass, down the Gunnison and over to the future Utah. The Main Trail ran from Abiqui to Green River (where it joined the northern branch). Later on there was a more southern route at about today's Utah-Arizona border.

Courtesy of Wikipedia.

CHAPTER 5

what would become the San Luis Valley. Fort Pueblo was built earlier in Colorado, but was abandoned for several years.

Even in 1850, two years after the Mexican-American War ended, the American concept of land ownership was foreign to the vast majority of Mexican-Americans. In Europe, and later New Spain and Mexico, feudal law still prevailed to a great extent. As mentioned, Spain and then Mexico authorized their provincial governors to provide land to their expanding populations by making land grants for agriculture, grazing, and other commercial ventures to individuals or groups who would settle on the land and establish communities. Title in fee simple (total private ownership) was sometimes given to wealthy or important private grantees who fulfilled the terms of their grants; but with community grants, individual fee simple title to the land was usually only given to small plots of residential and farming land, if at all. Settlers were allowed to use the land but did not own it, except perhaps for a small plot in the grant's town. This whole system fell into chaos as it became obvious to the Mexicans that the United States was interested in gaining their northern Mexican lands.

Worried Mexican officials made about half a dozen or so private land grants during the 1830s and 1840s that were huge. Among others, the 2.5 million acre Conejos Land Grant was created on the western side of the Rio Grande River. This grant covered the southwest San Luis Valley on both sides of the Conejos River, but it also extended west over the Continental Divide and into the San Juan Mountains almost to the future Creede and Pagosa Springs.

In 1833, José Seledon, José Maria Martinez, Antonio Martinez, Julian Gallegos, Stanley Valdez, and others had petitioned the Spanish government for a grant of land in the San Luis Valley along the west side of the Rio Grande and centered on the Conejos River for the purpose of creating a community settlement. One of the two aforementioned Martinezes may have been Martina Martinez Head's father and it is possible his grandson by a slave (José) was given to Martina to raise. The petition for land was granted on February 8, 1833, but there were conditions. Foremost, the land had to be settled on, farming done, and houses built. This never happened on the first Conejos Grant, as the Utes quickly ran the settlers out of the area. Then a few months later, after the settlers had returned, planted their crops, and even dug parts of a few irrigation ditches (but before their crops could be harvested or homes built) the Navajo drove a large herd of horses across the planted land and sent the settlers again fleeing to the south.

An application for the same land was made by forty-three families (including some of the first grant's petitioners) on February 23, 1842. The

A Home in the San Luis Valley and the Ute War of 1855

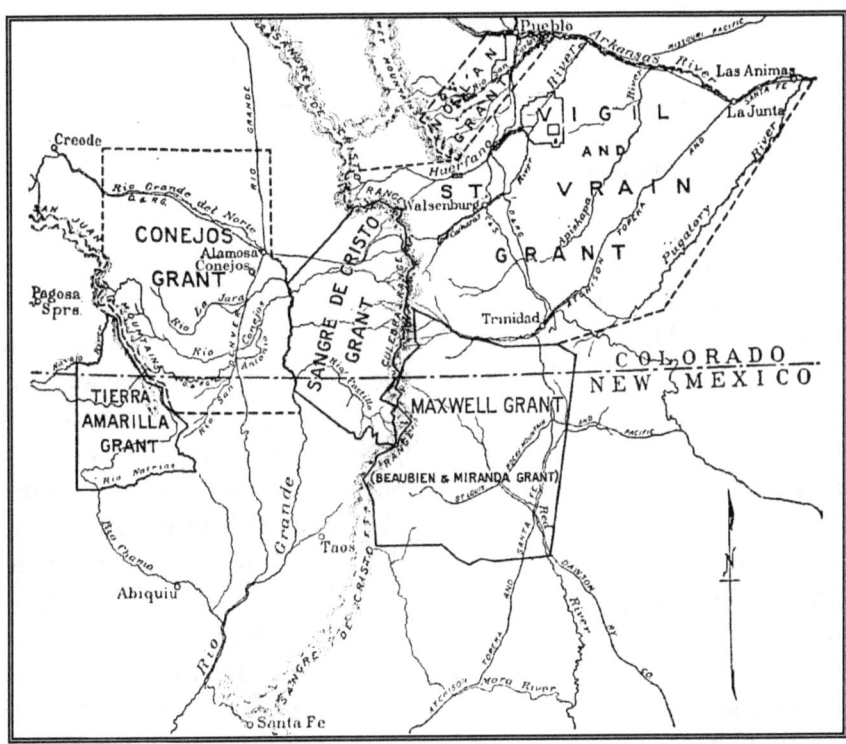

Very large land Grants were made in the Province of New Mexico as shown here on a current-day map. The Conejos Grant was the only grant not at least partially approved.

From Taylor, *Colorado, South of the Border.*

original grant application and charter were resubmitted, but the Mexican government decided a new grant should be made, as it was noted that the conditions of the first grant had not been complied with and that it was considered null and void. In the second grant, it was noted that this time the land covered by the grant had to be cultivated and a fort built within twelve years; and, if not, "the land shall be given to another person." The settlement to be built there was to be called "San Francisco."

On October 12, 1842, the Taos Alcalde (similar to an American Justice of the Peace) went to the land and explained the provisions of the grant to the heads of families or their attorneys that were present. All together there were now eighty-four families. The grant was for 3,600 square miles or 2.5 million acres. The Alcalde stated:

> *I took them by the hand and declared in a loud and intelligible voice that, in the name of the sovereign constituent Congress of*

CHAPTER 5

> the Union, and without prejudice to the national interest or to those of any third party, I led them over the tract and granted them the land; and they picked up grass, cast stones, and exclaimed in voices of gladness, saying "long live the sovereignty of our Mexican nation!"[42]

The grant's settlers started moving into the area near the junction of the San Antonio and Conejos Rivers in 1843. In making the second Conejos Land Grant, all the formalities of an original grant had been followed, and it was again noted that the previous grant had been abandoned and was void because the settlers had not built their well-fortified town or harvested their crops before they were run off by Native Americans. It was further noted that the possession under the second grant would be by feudal tenure and not in fee simple and that it would be called the "Conejos Grant." The settlers under such an agreement had the right to build houses, a right to grow and sell their crops and animals, and other uses of the land; but they did not own the land in all respects. The title to the land remained with the Country of Mexico. This was an important point, as much later the U.S. courts stated the land at the time was being reserved for the use of all the people of the Mexican nation and not just the original (actually the second) group of settlers.

Once again, the Native Americans soon drove the second group of land grant settlers out. This group tried to settle again on the Conejos River in 1846 at a small camp evidently called "San Margarita," but they were again driven away. Then the Mexican-American War started and all efforts to settle on the Conejos Grant land ceased for eight more years. However, shortly after the U.S. took possession of New Mexico, on October 5, 1846, Julius Gallegos and some of the second Conejos Grant settlers did ask then U.S. Governor of New Mexico, Charles Bent, to affirm their property rights under the Conejos Grant; but Bent stated, correctly, that he did not have the power to do so. The original Conejos Land Grant petitioners did nothing more, including talking to other U.S. officials, until petitioning in the U.S. Land Grant Court fifteen years later; although they evidently talked with Lafayette Head, José Maria Jacques, Crescenio Valdez, and others who they wanted to settle on the land and perhaps comply with the conditions of the grant for the second group of settlers. The original Treaty of Guadalupe Hidalgo of February 2, 1848, provided that the U.S. would verify the Spanish and Mexican land grants and preserve the property rights of Mexican citizens regardless of whether those Mexicans retained Mexican citizenship or chose to be American citizens, but the land grant provision (Article X) was struck from the treaty by the U.S. Senate before it was ratified.

One problem in determining what Lafe was trying to do at Conejos is that the names of Martina's parents have not been ascertained, except that it was probably Martinez (as common a name as Smith or Jones to Anglos). José Maria Martinez, Antonio Martinez and Santiago Martinez were definitely three of the petitioners for the first or second Conejos Grants, but it has not been determined if any one of them was Martina's father, grandfather, or father-in-law. It is clear that Martina's father urged Lafe to settle on the Grant, and the early Colorado historian Frank Hall even refers to it as the "Martinez Grant."

In 1847, a small group of settlers from El Rito, New Mexico, followed Anatansio Trujillo to the area that was later called Los Cerritos, about five miles downstream from the confluence of the San Antonio and the Conejos Rivers. Trujillo was a trader with the Utes and supposedly paid them for permission to settle there, but it was a deal with the Native Americans (who in fact were the ones who probably "owned" the land, although they had no concept of that at the time). Trujillo had no dealings with the Mexican or American governments, and no one is exactly sure what happened to those settlers.[43]

No attention was paid to any of the Spanish or Mexican land grants by the United States until six years after the Treaty of Guadalupe-Hidalgo, when the Office of the Surveyor-General was established in 1854 in an effort to straighten out Spanish-American titles to New Mexico land. Meanwhile, many Spanish and Mexican legal papers had been lost or even fabricated in several fraudulent attempts to get title to the land. Eventually the controversy and litigation concerning these lands would reach the level of a national scandal.

As of 1847, Aloncio Trujillo and his son Luis Raphael Trujillo had sheep camps on the Conejos; and, in 1849, Aloncio came back with two of his brothers, but again they only established a temporary summer camp, which was not sufficient to own the land under Mexican or U.S. law. During the very late 1840s and very early 1850s, a few other small groups, mostly sheepherders who were not included in either of the original grants or represented any of the petitioners, spent the summers in the area of the Conejos River and may have even raised a few crops; but they built no homes, and once again their actions did not qualify them under the U.S. Preemption Act or the Mexican Land Grants. In the mid-1850s, other settlers started moving into the eastern San Luis Valley on the Sangre de Cristo Grant, presumably claiming their land under the U.S. Preemption Act (passed in

CHAPTER 5

1841). These settlers almost always immediately built a plaza (similar to a home fort) with the houses of several families inside or part of the fort. Most Americans of the time considered the start of a plaza the start of a town; so in the 1850s, the southern San Luis Valley was soon covered with what the Americans and some Mexican-Americans described as dozens of "little towns."

The issue with the Conejos Grant (sometimes referred to as the Guadalupe Grant) later became one over whether the Mexican settlers had complied or not with the conditions of their grant; and, if they did not, was it because of conditions beyond their control. An unstated point, but one that was evidently a major factor in the U.S. Conejos Land Grant case, was that neither the original owners nor the second group or their representatives tried to keep other settlers off the land; and evidently Lafe's efforts were not clearly enough taken for the grant owners, or perhaps his efforts were never brought up in the court.

A claim was officially submitted for the Conejos Land Grant to the U.S. Land Court on June 3, 1861 (shortly after Colorado became a territory). However no official action was taken on this claim by the Court at that time, probably because the Civil War was raging and considered more pressing. Titles to virtually all the land in the Conejos Land Grant were still clouded.

In the meanwhile, after the Mexican-American War had ended, and with the U.S. Army establishing its presence in the San Luis Valley in 1852, settlers had felt much safer and started to move into the Ute occupied 100 to 125 mile long and 30 to 50 mile wide (depending on just where you measure) San Luis Valley. The fact that some of the land titles in The Valley were clouded by the Conejos Land Grant on the west side and the Sangre de Cristo Grant on the eastern side did not seem to bother the new arrivals. However, settlers in the San Luis Valley in the mid-1850s now had more to worry about than their land titles. In 1854, New Mexico Territorial Governor David Merriweather, who was also Superintendent of Indian Affairs, wrote in his annual report of that year about the current situation with the Utes, and it was not good:

> *The Utes of New Mexico are a part of the tribe of the same name inhabiting the Territory of Utah (at the time Utah Territory spread east to the Continental Divide where it borders New Mexico Territory).... From the best information which I have been able to obtain, that portion of this tribe properly under the charge of this superintendent numbers* **five to six thousand souls** *(emphasis added); and they inhabit and*

> claim all the region of the country embracing the sources of the northwest tributaries of the Arkansas river, above Bent's Fort, up to the southern boundary of Utah Territory, and all the northern tributaries of the Rio Grande which lie within New Mexico and north of the 37th parallel of latitude... but they often extend their wandering beyond these limits.
>
> ... This is a highly warlike tribe of Indians, well-armed with firearms, and have committed many depredations upon the unoffending inhabitants of New Mexico. They do not cultivate the soil, but depend on the chase and robbery for subsistence. A continued feud has existed between the Utahs on the one side, and the Arapahoes (sic) and Cheyenne of the Arkansas on the other, for many years past; and lately, the latter Indians have been supplied with arms and ammunition by our Indian agents and traders, and have proved more than a match for the former, and consequently the Utahs dare not visit the buffalo regions in search of food. This, together with the fact that game is becoming comparatively scarce in their country, has induced if not constrained the Utes to keep up their ancient customs of theft and robbery.... The Utahs are probably the most difficult Indians to manage within the Territory.[44]

Few could blame the Utes for their actions up to this point. Although they had their troubles, the Utes and Spanish had lived next to each other in relative peace for over 200 years. However, starting in the 1800s, many of the Mexican Land Grants adversely affected the Ute people, as the grants encouraged large groups of Mexicans to encroach upon what had been Ute land for over 500 years. The invaders were killing the game, building houses without permission, and plowing up Mother Earth! The rising anger of the Utes caused them to raid and drive off the settlers found on their land.

The Americans knew the Utes were nomadic, and they also recognized that the Utes wanted to try to live in peace. Most of the American authorities realized that the Ute transgressions were because they were hungry or even starving at the time since their game was being killed off by the Americans. The Utes were not savages and were being described by the Americans who actually knew them as very smart, perhaps the most intelligent and "civilized" of all the Native American tribes. This acknowledgement was probably due to the Utes' close ties to Spanish and European culture for over 200 years before the Americans arrived in New Mexico.

CHAPTER 5

Most Native American tribes being conquered by the Americans did not have this advantage.

From 1850 to 1852, the real trouble had started—it had all the makings of a true tragedy, with the villain being the U.S. government. The Americans had opened an Agency for the Utes in Taos, but there was no food supplied as per the treaty that had been made. The Utes complained that they were due these supplies under the 1849 treaty, but still no food was forthcoming. When the Utes started to kill settlers' livestock to replace their game, the American settlers were justifiably upset; but the Utes had to eat or die. More food supplies were promised by the U.S. government, but did not come. Then the Taos Agency closed. When the Agency reopened under Kit Carson, it supplied a small amount of food, which was meant to be only for the Mouache and Capote Utes. Then not just Mexican plazas, but Fort Massachusetts was built in the middle of the Utes' favorite hunting grounds, and soldiers arrived. Once again, when the Utes were starving and did not get their food supplies from the U.S., they killed American livestock or stole American crops. However, now the soldiers from Fort Massachusetts, who the Utes thought were there to protect them from their Native American Plains enemies, came to punish or even kill the Utes who had done the raiding. It was not hard to see why the Utes considered the American actions as a war being waged against them, and they were determined to not give up their land.

Now to the American side of the problem. The Spanish for centuries had traveled through, but never permanently settled, in "El Valle," and the first Americans to visit the San Luis Valley came as trappers and mountain men, not true settlers, just after 1800. The San Luis Valley was first revealed to most Americans back East after 1809, when Zebulon Pike wrote of building his stockade on the Conejos River; and it was near Pike's Fort that Lafe and other very early pioneer farmers and ranchers would arrive in 1854. The spot that they chose on the Conejos Grant to build their settlement was a favorite Ute campsite, but the Americans knew the Utes were nomadic and only visited the San Luis Valley for a portion of the year. They also knew that this was prime agricultural land and that the Utes did not want to be farmers. So why shouldn't the Americans settlers use it?

Meanwhile, the spot where Fort Massachusetts was built in the San Luis Valley was not working out. In the summer of 1853, Brevet Colonel Joseph H. F. Mansfield became the first of many high ranking officers to criticize publically the location of the fort as being indefensible. He also felt the fort's troops needed better training and equipment. He noted some of the fort's men did not even have shoes to wear (they were probably wearing moccasins), although this was the fault of their supply depot. The main problem at this time was there were only fifty-four men stationed at Fort Massachusetts.

Later that summer, both Captain John W. Gunnison and his second in command Lieutenant E. G. Beckwith suggested that the Ute land to the west of the San Luis Valley (the San Juan Mountains) was of no use for settlement and might make a good reservation. Captain Gunnison further reported, while making his survey for a transcontinental railroad, that the high mesas that ran away from the Rio Grande into the San Juan Mountains or Sangre de Cristo Mountains were covered for some distance away from the creeks by:

> ... a thick carpet of curled "grama"—the most nutritious grass that grows—affording abundant and unfailing pasturage, during every season of the year, to unlimited herds of cattle and flocks of sheep.... Forty seven thousand and three hundred sheep were driven off by these Indians (from New Mexico) within eighteen months prior to the first of September, 1850. Doubtless the Indians took many flocks from the shepherds in the mountains that were not officially reported....[45]

Gunnison therefore saw hope for living in peace with the Utes:

> I believe we are beginning better to understand the "red brethren" and soon will accord them some of the rights due to true "native Americans...." Savage warfare will then cease, and the resources of New Mexico—agriculture, pastoral, and mineral—will be developed, and if they choose, the people may build cities and aqueducts in the deserts, as did the Spanish....[46]

This belief was very ironic as Gunnison was killed just a few months later in a surprise attack by Utes in Utah.

Why were the Mexicans and then the Americans so determined to settle in the San Luis Valley in the middle of the Utes' best hunting grounds? Some of the reasons given by the Americans were the need for more good irrigated and range land than was left for settlement at the time in the Territory of New Mexico, the need for a closer and better market to trade with the Utes and Apache, and some settlers even mentioned the move as an escape from religious persecution, which will be discussed in more detail in Chapter Eleven. This view was expressed by a group called the "Penitentes," and a large number of the new settlers in the San Luis Valley were already or soon became Penitentes. However, the main reason the settlers came were the very good agricultural and ranching possibilities in The Valley, which was exactly why there was so much game in this area before the settlers arrived.

CHAPTER 5

Josiah Gregg, in his book *Commerce on the Prairies*, has left us a very good and fair description of the San Luis Valley and northern New Mexico at the time the first American settlers were moving there in 1851.

Gregg points out the agricultural prospects of New Mexico:

> *Wheat especially has been produced of a superlative quality, and in such abundance, that, as is asserted, the crops have often yielded over one hundred fold.... Agriculture, like almost everything else in New Mexico, is in a very primitive and unimproved state. A great portion of the peasantry cultivate with the hoe alone.... The* labores *and* milpas *(cultivated fields) are often indeed most usually without any enclosure. The owners of cattle are obliged to keep herdsmen constantly with them, else graze them at a considerable distance from the farms.... Only a chance farm is seen fenced.... The necessity of irrigation has confined, and no doubt will continue to confine agriculture principally to the valleys of the constant-flowing streams.... Where water is abundant, however, art has so far superseded the offices of nature in watering the farms.... On the one hand the husbandman need not have his grounds overflowed if he administers the water himself, much less need he permit them to suffer from drought. He is therefore more sure of his crop than if he was subject to the caprice of the weather.... One acequia madre (mother ditch) suffices generally to convey water for the irrigation of an entire valley, or at least all the fields of one town or settlement.... It is conveyed over the highest part of the valley, which on these mountain streams, is, for the most part, next to the hills. From this, each proprietor of a farm runs a minor ditch.... Each farmer has his day, or portion of a day allotted to him for irrigation; and at no other time is he permitted to extract water from the* acequia madre. *Then the cultivator, after letting the water into his minor ditch, dams this, first at one point and then another, so as to overflow a section at a time, and with his hoe, depressing eminences and filling sinks, he causes the water to spread regularly over the surface.*[47]

But Gregg ends his chapter on foods and dining with the following statement:

> *But by far the most important indigenous product of the soil of New Mexico is its pasturage. Most of the high table-plains*

afford the finest grazing in the world...are (they) mostly clotted with a highly nutritious grass called grama, which is of a very short and curly quality. The highlands upon which alone this sort of grass is produced, being seldom verdant till after the rainy season sets in, the grama is only in perfection from August to October... (but) it cures upon the ground and remains excellent hay—equal if not superior to that which is cut and stacked from our western prairies.[48]

There were also Mexicans in the Trinidad area as early as 1833, and the town was founded in 1842 by Mexican traders who were taking advantage of the Santa Fe Trail running through the area. However, this little settlement was far to the east of the San Luis Valley. So at least initially, the land that Lafe and his group were moving onto was good farm land and a rancher's paradise, neither of which the Utes cared about. They did, however, care about their best hunting ground being destroyed and settlers occupying Ute land, and this was causing great trouble.

Whether they knew the details or not, many of the early settlers in the San Luis Valley claimed their land under the U.S. Preemption Act of 1841, but they needed to comply with its provisions. The Act entitled a head of family, widow, or single man of the age of twenty-one or older to a homestead of 160 acres if he or she filed the paperwork correctly and took the steps needed to be considered living on and developing their land. The grantee under the Preemption Act needed to be a U.S. citizen, or have filed an intention to become a U.S. citizen, and could not already own 320 acres or more in the same state or territory. The settlers' rights under the Preemption Act were specifically subject to any Spanish or Mexican Land Grants, if the grant was found to be valid.

However, because grazing land in The Valley was so arid except along the rivers and creeks, 160 acres or even 320 acres was not really sufficient land for grazing even a medium size herd of cattle or sheep except in places of expensive irrigation. As a result, later ranchers in The Valley (and actually over the entire arid West) often had employees, relatives, or friends claim a preemption homestead and then transfer the title after a patent (the first legal title) for the land had been issued by the U.S. government. In this way, some of the cattlemen in Colorado and New Mexico accumulated huge ranches for very little cost. Another way to get enough land to raise cattle was to buy acreage out of one of the big land grants or even buy the entire grant.

It was generally sensed by 1854 that there might be a land rush to the San Luis Valley despite the fact that it was still Ute land, and that they were

CHAPTER 5

The first time that San Luis Valley soil was plowed it would usually be necessary to use two or three teams of oxen to break the soil.

Harper's Weekly, May 9, 1868.

still fighting to retain control of it. Small settlements were beginning to spread along the rivers and creeks of the southern half of the valley and a few merchants were opening little stores. All of the new arrivals relied heavily on stock (especially sheep) herds or agriculture, and they lived in plazas at night for protection from the Native Americans and tended their fields and flocks during the day. Besides sheep, they brought pigs, oxen, goats, cows, and horses to the valley, and their herds grew rapidly. Typical crops were corn, wheat, oats, barley, beans, peas, lentils, pumpkins, and various other vegetables, and their yields were large.

In May of 1854, while Lafe was still living in the small settlement of Servilleta near Ojo Caliente, he had been named a special Agent for the Jicarilla Apache; and Lafe reported to Kit Carson that "General José Maria Chavez is leaving with 200 militiamen and a month's worth of supplies to fight the Apaches."[49] Lafe also wrote that the Ute Indians who came to his Agency would not join the Jicarilla Apache in their war against the Americans. In this case, the mere appearance of the U.S. military seemed to subdue the Jicarilla Apache; and the newly elected New Mexico Territorial Governor David Merriweather, in his annual report to the Indian Bureau in Washington, praised the actions of Kit Carson and Lafayette Head: "The judicious management of Agent Carson and Special Agent Head prevented a war with the Utes and Jicarilla."⁵⁰ However, it would remain a time of great unrest among the Utes and Apaches.

The title to virtually all the land in the San Luis Valley (ignoring the Ute question, as Americans did at that time) would be uncertain until the Spanish and Mexican land grants could be settled in the American courts; but it seems Lafe may have formulated a plan to take care of this contingency. Although we have no written confirmation that he was trying to meet the terms of the Conejos Land Grant, he obviously was involved and followed the grant's terms to the letter. He must have discussed the grant's requirements in detail when he met with the heirs of the Conejos Land Grant, and as mentioned this may have included members of Martina's family. Several people have started tracing the genealogy of Martina's family to compare it with the applicants for the second grant; but as far as this author knows no firm connection has yet been made, although it seems very possible. Lafe's goal was to fulfill the requirements of the Conejos Land Grant and at the same time he and his friends were settling the area under the U.S. Preemption Act. The only question was why didn't he keep other settlers who were not part of the grant off the land?

There is much confusion involving the first settlers along the Conejos River in the summer of 1854. José Maria Jacques and a few others from the small town of El Llanito visited the area on the north bank of the Conejos River across and upstream from the future town of Conejos and found excellent pasturage for ranching and water for farming. An extra benefit of the Conejos River area was that the river had a hot springs and did not freeze, even in the middle of winter. Jacques' group came back with settlers and established a small camp on the north side of the river, which they called "El Cedro Redondo" or "Round Cedar."

In August of 1854, a larger group led by Lafe settled four or five miles downstream from El Cedro Redondo. Lafe and his group built or occupied an existing temporary fort at that spot on the north side of the Conejos River and called the log stockade "Servilleta." Lafe came from the little town of Servilleta, which was about ten miles south of Tres Piedras and where his office as Marshal and Sheriff was located for a while. Lafe named the fort for the town he came from, which was a very common practice of the time. Lafe had met the requirements of the Conejos Grant that a temporary fort be built within twelve years, but just barely. In October, the group from El Cedro Redondo, which had now been joined by other settlers from El Rito, Abiqui, and Ojo Caliente, decided to move to very near the Servilleta fort to have better protection from the Utes. They called their new location "Guadalupe."

CHAPTER 5

Both Lafe and Jacques could claim a permanent fort or settlement, thus fulfilling one of the twelve year requirements of the Conejos Grant. The second Conejos Grant also stipulated that while waiting for the town to be finished, the settlers would move upon the land "and build their shanties for the protection of their families." The stockade built or occupied by Lafayette's group and available to Jacques probably fulfilled this requirement as it had "barracks" for the settlers. Lafe was the only Anglo in any of the groups that settled on the Conejos that year, but it is very possible that he and Jacques were jointly trying to comply with the terms of the Conejos Grant.

Servilleta was evidently the first American built structure on the Conejos River after Pike built his stockade in 1809, but it was evidently, like Pike's structure, meant to be only a place of protection, as it had no place to sleep other than "barracks;" and, as no homes were built in the fort, it was not meant to be a plaza.

The "barracks" in the log stockade at Servilleta on the north side of the Conejos River allowed the settlers and their important animals to stay there for extended periods in case of Indian attack. In October, 1854, yet another group of settlers came from the Chama River Valley. This one was definitely led only by Lafe and included a fair number of horses, oxen, cows, sheep, and goats. There are, however, other versions of the time frame of the original settlements along the Conejos River. Respected Colorado historian, Frederick Athearn, in *Land of Contrasts*, writes José Maria Jacques founded El Cedro Redondo, then Lafe founded Plaza de Guadalupe, then Lafe built Servilleta, and then Mogota was founded—all in 1854. Athearn believed Head was the most influential settler at the time in the whole Conejos area. Athearn also wrote that Head definitely was representing the claimants under the 1842 Conejos Land Grant when he first arrived.

On the other hand, Frances Leon Swadesh, Mexican-American rights activist, wrote in 1974 that Guadalupe was established in the valley area in 1847 or 1849 under an informal agreement with the Tabeguache band of Utes stating they would not attack the Mexican-American settlement. This was probably the same group led by Antanasio Trujillo, mentioned earlier, that tried to buy land and ended up renting from the Utes. Swadesh also writes that San Pedro and San Acadio, on the east side of the Rio Grande River, were deserted soon after being built, leaving only the towns of San Luis and Guadalupe/Conejos—one on each side of the Rio Grande in the southern San Luis Valley. Swadish, in *Los Primeros Pobladores*, takes the position that the Mexican-American Jacques was the leader of the first settlers, but even some of the descendants of Jacques admit Lafe was the sole leader of both groups that made the large migration from the Chama River Valley. Most historians write that Lafe, not Jacques, led the first large group in August of 1854 and that the second group was led by Lafe a month or two later.

When D. W. Workman was writing *The History of Colorado Agriculture* in 1925, he corresponded with Evangeline Hill, great granddaughter of Lafayette Head. In a letter dated February 7, 1925, Attorney J. H. Thomas of Antonito, Colorado, wrote Workman that he felt Head had visited the future site of Guadalupe as early as 1852, but he could not remember his source. Thomas personally knew Head and wrote that as a boy he often sat and listened to his many stories. He said that Lafe said that in 1852 he did not build anything; rather his group was only surveying the land and looking it over. Thomas also wrote there were several people still living in the Conejos area in 1925 who had close relatives that had come to the area with Head to settle in 1854, and that Head was considered the leader of everyone there—"the people looked to him for counsel and advice…from the earliest records we have he was the temporal leader, in politics, finance, and every conceivable subject where leadership might appear."[51]

The original site of Guadalupe near the Servilleta Fort was washed away in the spring floods of 1855, causing many of the settlers, including Lafe, to re-establish on the south side of the Conejos River near the mouth of the San Antonio River. Those settlers remaining on the north side of the river re-established their settlement of Guadalupe, but opposite Conejos on higher ground. A small (16 by 30 foot) jackal chapel was started at Guadalupe, and the settlers at Guadalupe and Conejos began building permanent homes. By 1858, a bridge had been built between the two settlements, but it was soon badly damaged in several floods and eventually was not rebuilt. Lafe would spend the rest of his life in the town of Conejos.

The small jackal chapel that was started in Guadalupe also served the Conejos settlers for a few years. Because this chapel was named "Our Lady of Guadalupe" and was located at Guadalupe, there is some confusion between it and the first true church building using the same name; however, the first actual church in the area was started in Conejos in 1856. The process that Lafe and Jacques were following in building their communities of Conejos and Guadalupe was predictable. Spanish and Mexican settlers usually built a *placita* (small plaza) almost immediately upon arrival in a new area, then built a *morada* (a small non-consecrated place to worship and honor their patron saint), and then a *capilla* (a chapel meant for divine protection and intervention during the settlement of their land). Only then would they build their main plaza.

A small Ute group raided Guadalupe and Servilleta and took a few horses and cattle from there in the summer or fall of 1854. It must have

CHAPTER 5

made the settlers realize just how vulnerable they were at the time, and perhaps Lafe (the only known settler with military experience) made plans with the settlers for the future protection of the town. When a bigger attack came in a few months, they were better prepared and ready to defend themselves at the fort at Servilleta. In later years, settlers coming to the Conejos River area used the fort at Servilleta for protection from the elements and the Native Americans while they were building their more permanent structures. The fort was said to never have more facilities than just "barracks" (sleeping rooms for temporary occupants), a jail, and a lookout tower on the northwest corner. After the Utes were removed from the San Luis Valley, the lookout corner became the town hall; and around 1900, one corner was made into a house.

Lafayette Head had lived his entire life up to this point on the frontier in Indian country, so he showed little concern in being in the midst of the San Luis Valley among Native Americans who were often on the warpath, and he was known to help some of his neighbors when they were attacked by Indians. Head was already an up and coming figure when he moved to Conejos and was soon called "Uncle Lafe" or "Don Raphael" by the locals. Martina was called "Doña Head" or "Doña Cabeza." Most of the settlers were poor *genizaros*, and their new homes at Conejos were their only hope for a better way of life. Martina Head's family had money and, if tradition was followed, they had provided a dowry for the couple that set them up in Conejos and perhaps even earlier with the store in Abiqui. Lafe and most of his Anglo friends were among the few Anglo-Americans that were greatly respected by the early Mexican-Americans settlers, and Lafe quickly became their friend and leader. The quick respect Lafe received may have been given in part because of Martina's family having some wealth and a good position in New Mexico society; or it may have been that Lafe became Catholic in order to marry Martina and totally embraced and became a leader of that faith. However, it is likely that the main reason for that respect was that Lafe was a good, brave, intelligent, and experienced pioneer, who treated the Mexican-Americans fairly and as equals and returned their respect.

Shortly after establishing Guadalupe/Conejos, Lafe's and Jacques' groups planted crops—thereby meeting another requirement of the Conejos Land Grant. Most Mexican-American farmers of the time still used wooden plow heads that were handmade from oak, if it could be found; otherwise, pinyon (Lafe and a few others probably had metal plow heads). Hand rakes or hoes (usually totally wooden) were used to cut grass and grain crops. When they gathered their first year's grain crops to be milled, the Conejos locals had no local mill to make their grain into flour, so those who could afford it loaded their crops into two-wheel carts (called "carretas") and hauled the grain south to a mill. The round-trip to the nearest mill took them almost a week. Most settlers were too poor to take their crops to a mill, so they cut their corn with a crude wooden hoe, and used a scythe to cut wheat, then threshed the wheat by laying it on hard ground and used long clumsy poles to beat the wheat kernels loose. Animals were sometimes driven over the area. Americans, including Otto Mears as late as 1865, tried to introduce threshing machines and metal plows into the community of Conejos, but they were not very successful. Most Mexican-Americans thought the threshing machines cheated them by keeping much of the wheat.

The new settlement of Conejos was soon well-fortified, with an adobe fortress built around a large plaza, but there were not yet any living quarters, as it was then only a place where horses, oxen, and mules could be driven if Conejos was attacked. Built into the fort would be Lafe's first home at Conejos, which would not be finished until 1856, when it was said to become the center for social life in the southern valley. His house at that time had only two rooms and was part of a duplex; the home attached to Lafe and Martina's may have been occupied by Don Jesus Velasquez, who was definitely living there by 1859. Lafe's influence quickly spread from just the Conejos area to throughout the entire San Luis Valley.

Coming from Abiqui in 1855, the west side of the Rio Grande was basically uninhabited except along the Conejos River. All of the families in Lafe's group received 200 *veras* (about 400 feet) of tillable river frontage—some on the San Antonio and some on the Conejos River itself. They

Horses could not pull very heavy loads, so Mexicans usually used wooden carts pulled behind oxen.

Monaghan, *The Book of the American West.*

CHAPTER 5

also received water rights from the *acquacia madre* (the main irrigation ditch), could cut trees on the grant for building construction or firewood, and could run their livestock on land owned in common by the settlers. However this may have made them talk about the fact that the second Conejos Land Grant made only small tracts available to individuals and most of the huge grant was given in common. If they filed under U.S. law, Lafe and the other settlers would own the land in fee simple (total outright ownership for the individual).

Besides their farming and ranching efforts that consumed the vast majority of their time, the men of Conejos made adobe bricks with which they built their houses; and they raised and butchered the livestock, which were mainly sheep but a good number were cattle. Many of the cattle at this time were oxen meant to pull carts, plows, and wagons and not cows meant for meat or milk. Following Spanish custom, the men usually did the weaving, using a hand loom. The women made the meals, manufactured candles, dried meat, and washed the wool sheared by the men. The women also plastered the interior of the house with adobe mud and whitewashed it nearly every year, spread muslin on the ceiling to catch falling dirt, and regularly sprinkled the dirt floor with water and packed it until it was firm.

The increasing number of settlers, livestock, and farmers that came to the San Luis Valley between 1851 and 1855 meant the supply of wild game in the valley greatly diminished. The early settlers found wonderful grass in many places, although the center of the valley was basically barren, and with irrigation some huge ranches were eventually established. Although ranching was the first choice of many early settlers, eventually the grass was overgrazed and not only the original wild game but, in time, the great herds of the valley's cattle and sheep ranching days disappeared. Meanwhile, the Utes were substituting cattle and sheep on their food menu, in part because the disappearing wild game now took much more time and effort to hunt than killing domesticated animals.

Fort Massachusetts' soldiers did not get their provisions in time for their first winter in the San Luis Valley, so most of the troops left and only a few guards were present at the fort from October 1853 to April 1854. The Utes took advantage of this six month absence during the winter of 1853-54. Unfortunately, the settlers did not understand the livestock thefts, and the first chase of Utes in the San Luis Valley by U.S. soldiers occurred shortly after the soldiers returned in May of 1854 with Kit Carson as their guide.

> *On May 23, 1854, Carson left his Agency to accompany Major James H. Carleton in his pursuit of the Indians. They*

> *traveled north into the San Luis Valley, crossed the Sangre de Cristo Mountain Range through Huerfano Pass and found the Apaches in the vicinity of Fisher's Peak in the Raton Mountains (near Trinidad, Colorado). There Carleton's troops surprised the Indians and a number were killed.*[52]

The Utes did not want war; they simply wanted the food that had been promised them, and now they were being killed because they were trying to keep from starving. In September of 1854, a party of Utes visited Carson at his Agency, after which he reported:

> *The Indians seem to manifest the most peaceful intentions towards the United States. They complain that they are poor and that the game is scarce—and that while all of the Indians of the North are receiving (goods) they are receiving none. I would respectively request that as the inclement season is now very near, that you, at the earliest day as possible call them together and (provide them) blankets and shirts… I deem this to be a matter of utmost importance.*[53]

In October of 1854, Merriweather and Carson met with the Mouache chiefs and gave each a woolen blanket, but soon thereafter the recipients began to die of small pox. Kit Carson rounded up the Utes and reported:

> *On their way to their hunting grounds, the smallpox broke out among them. The leading men of the band of Mouache Utahs died. They came to the conclusion that the Superintendent (Merriweather) was the cause of the disease being among them, that he had collected them for the purpose of injuring (them), that to the head men he gave each a blanket coat, and that everyone that received a coat died. That the coats were the cause of the deaths the Indians firmly believed and the murderer of the Indians being allowed to escape unpunished and they having but poor faith in anything the Superintendent promised them, they commenced preparations for war. They joined the Mouaches and drove off nearly all the stock and murdered citizens as they be found.*[54]

The Mouache Ute tribe in particular was decimated by smallpox. Colorado Indians had no contact with contagious diseases before the white man arrived, so smallpox was especially deadly for them and now tensions were reaching a boiling point. The Jicarilla Apache and some of the Utes

CHAPTER 5

thought the Americans were trying to kill them off without having to get into a war! Settlers were replacing the roving Mexican sheepherders who had grazed their flocks on San Luis Valley grass in the past few years. Now farmers were plowing up the land. Payback was in the air!

Fort Pueblo (also called El Pueblo) had been established on the Arkansas River by mountain men in 1842 and had grown to a population of about 150 at one time. However, it got the reputation as being inhabited by bad men of all types, and the population had shrunk to only about fifteen or twenty people by 1854. It had been visited by many famous mountain men; but many traders left in 1849 when the U.S. cracked down on the illegal trade of whiskey to the local Native Americans. Mexican custom was to celebrate Christmas Eve on December 23, and a Ute attack happened when many of the men at El Pueblo were sleeping off their hangovers on the morning of December 24, 1854.

The fort was located on the north side of the Arkansas River across from the mouth of Fountain Creek and about a mile from Marcelino Baca's home on the Baca Land Grant. The fort was occupied at the time of the attack by sixteen Mexican-Americans, three Mexican-American women (one of whom had two children), and a Canadian mountain man. Some of the men living at the fort worked for Baca on his grant. Tierra Blanca (Spanish for "White Earth") was chief of the Mouache Utes; but in the attack on Fort Pueblo, he also had members of other Ute bands and Jicarilla Apaches with him. As mentioned, conflicts had occurred throughout 1854, but this attack was major and horrific. Everyone at the fort had feared trouble, as just ten days earlier, a Mexican trader had been killed by Mouache Utes and/or Jicarilla Apaches at nearby Greenhorn. Then just two days

This drawing is not Fort Pueblo but is a very similar structure, including lookout towers.

Fossett, *Colorado*.

before the Fort Pueblo attack, mountain man Dick Wootton had stopped by the fort to warn that he had seen tracks of a large Indian party and that there would probably be trouble.

When Baca heard Indians were in the area, he sent a boy at daybreak on December 24 to warn the settlers downstream on the Arkansas River and to get help; but the boy soon returned to report he could not go for help as all of their livestock, including their horses, had been stolen. Then Tierra Blanca showed up at Baca's home fort riding Baca's best white horse. Although he asked to trade, he was not let in. About 8 a.m., the men and women at Baca's home heard a lot of shooting coming from the direction of Fort Pueblo. When they carefully investigated several hours after the shooting had stopped, they found a dead body near the river. Then a man came staggering towards them with a terrible gash in his stomach. He died before being able to tell them what had happened.

Near the fort, Baca's group found the dead bodies of three Indians. Another injured white man was at the gate and was conscious; but he could not tell them what had happened, because he had been shot in the mouth and his tongue had been cut in two by the bullet. Most later reports of the slaughter exaggerated this into his tongue being cut out by the Utes. By using Indian sign language and writing notes, the man communicated that Chief Blanca had ridden up to the gate, said he was hungry, and asked for some corn. When he asked to come in, he was at first refused entry. Ultimately he was let in by Bonito Sandoval, leader of the fort. Sandoval knew Chief Blanca and had traded vegetables and milk with the Mouache Utes and Jicarilla Apache over the years. The two men had a couple of drinks despite the early hour; and after a debate over who was the best shot, they ended up having a shooting match outside the fort. Sandoval then invited Tierra Blanca and some of his men to come inside the fort to eat.

Evidently Sandoval thought the Utes were friendly, but Tierra Blanca was quickly followed by about fifty armed Native Americans (out of about 150 to 200 reportedly with Chief Blanca). They rushed into the fort and killed most of the occupants with their own guns, as the Utes for the most part had only bows and arrows, spears, and tomahawks for weapons. In all, sixteen of the fort's men were killed and one of the women and her two children were taken captive. Several Utes had also been killed within the fort. Two Mexican-American women had been able to escape the massacre by hiding in the willows along the river.

It was late January when the scalp of the captured woman was found tied to a tree. Her death made seventeen people from the fort that had been killed. Her children had been sold as slaves by the Utes, but were eventually delivered to and purchased by the Americans. The woman had been shot through the chest with an arrow, probably just a matter of days after the attack, but had actually been killed as she lay on the ground by Ute squaws stoning her to death. Later a Ute said she was killed because she had cried too much.

Immediately after the massacre, the Jicarilla Apache and Utes continued to attack settlers along the Front Range near today's Colorado Springs and Pueblo, and after a while they moved into the San Luis Valley. When he learned of the fighting, Kit Carson notified the New Mexico Territorial Governor that the regular troops in the valley were not numerous enough to fight an estimated combined Ute-Jicarilla Apache force of about 1,000 men and that they would need a small army. The fact that El Pueblo was located nearly 150 miles northeast of Guadalupe and Conejos did not sooth the settlers' fears. The United States decided this was a time to inflict major damage on the Utes. Governor Merriweather of New Mexico was absent from the territory, but acting Governor William Messervy called for the death of the entire Jicarilla Apache tribe saying, "… The best interest of this territory and the highest dictates of humanity demand their extinction."[55] A call went out for four or five companies of volunteers to enlist in the New Mexico Territorial Army (Colorado Territory had not yet been formed out of New Mexico Territory) for a six month enlistment to fight the Utes and Jicarilla. Lafe was one of the first to sign up. The Americans spent January and February of 1855 gathering the large military force needed to attack the Utes, and the officers planned their campaign against the Jicarilla and Mouache.

Two of Lafe's Lodge brothers, Colonel Ceran St. Vrain and next in command Lieutenant Albert Pfeiffer, were assigned to Fort Massachusetts and were in command of the volunteers. Another Lodge brother, Kit Carson, agreed to be chief scout for the small army. Four hundred men volunteered altogether. The New Mexican volunteers each bought similar colored hats and woolen shirts, but with different colors for each regiment.

St. Vrain was a famous mountain man born in today's St. Louis, Missouri, and was one of the partners in the establishment of Bent's Fort. His father was a French aristocrat and had money, but Ceran chose instead the excitement of frontier life. He was partners in the largest of the Mexican Land grants, the four million acre Vigil-St. Vrain Land Grant from Mexico (also called the Las Animas Land Grant). Their grant was eventually reduced by a U.S. law that limited all later approved Mexican Land Grants to a maximum of 96,000 acres. St. Vrain had organized the 1846 volunteer force that accompanied the U.S. Army to put down the Taos Revolt, and he had served as a Mexican and Native American translator in the trials of

A Home in the San Luis Valley and the Ute War of 1855

some of the rebels. In 1855, St. Vrain started a grist mill and several saw mills near Mora, New Mexico, and supplied flour and became the sutler (a licensed private merchant) to the garrison at Fort Union. He also became the publisher of Santa Fe's first English-language newspaper, *The Santa Fe Gazette*. St. Vrain died at the age of sixty-eight on October 10, 1870.[56]

After Ceran St. Vrain was appointed commander of the Mexican-American volunteers, he raised, armed, and obtained supplies for his soldiers, and headed to Fort Massachusetts in February 1855. The four companies of volunteers under St. Vrain joined with one battery of U.S. artillery, two regular companies of U.S. Dragoons, and one group of "spies" (probably either scouts or friendly Indians) under the command of Lucien Stewart, a mountain man. The whole group at Fort Massachusetts was under the command of Colonel T. T. Fauntleroy. That same month the army took to the field with Kit Carson as head scout. The entire force went west across the San Luis Valley to the Big Bend of the Rio Grande River. Then from about the future site of Alamosa, they headed north to the Saguache River Valley. There were only minor skirmishes until they got to the Saguache River, where the Utes were found in force and a battle ensued on March 19, 1855. Chief Tierra Blanca of the Utes was very obvious in his presence as he always wore a red woolen shirt. Somehow he escaped injury, but two chiefs and six of his warriors were killed in the fight and many more were wounded. About 150 Utes and Jicarilla were soon in full retreat when they realized how badly they were outnumbered and outarmed. The Americans were able to capture the entire Ute herd of extra horses. Only two Americans were wounded in the battle and the numerous skirmishes that followed with the Utes as they retreated up Cochetopa Pass, where the Utes split up into many small groups and disappeared. During the skirmishes the Americans had a problem in keeping up with the Utes because the soldiers' horses were being fed grain at the fort and did not have the stamina needed when forced to graze on grass.

Ceran St. Vrain was a good friend of Lafe's. This portrait was painted from an image from 1845, several years before he met Lafe.

Courtesy of Wikipedia.

CHAPTER 5

Cochetopa Pass was the main route in central Colorado from the eastern to the western Slope for 10,000 years. This drawing was made by the Fremont Expedition.

R. H Renn, Artist.

Another small battle occurred on March 23 near Poncha Pass, with a few Utes killed and some wounded. The rest of the group was chased into the Wet Mountain Valley, where again they split into many small groups and disappeared. The whole American force returned to Fort Massachusetts, as the weather had been very cold and the men and their horses needed rest, more supplies, and additional ammunition. When Fauntleroy was in the Saguache Valley, he had noted and reported the corpses of many Indians who had died of smallpox.

Even Fort Massachusetts had felt threatened by Tierra Blanco's group at this time, with so many of its soldiers gone to fight in the valley. Trees and branches were cut from around the fort to allow a better view of the enemy and to allow better shots by the soldiers. Breastworks were added outside vulnerable parts of the fort, and sentries were posted day and night. The fights with the Utes and Jicarilla Apache came to be called part of the "The 1855 Ute War."

Chief Kaniache's Mouache Utes continued raiding in the San Luis Valley in the spring of 1855. They killed several men and drove off the Costilla livestock. Then the Jicarilla Apache attacked Costilla. During this time, the Mouache Utes and Jicarilla Apache were also beginning to attack many small ranches on the Front Range and in the San Luis Valley from Fort Garland to Taos.

One story arose from a conflict with the Utes at the time, but parts of it may be only legend. Ute War Chief Kaniache had repeatedly told the settlers to get out of the San Luis Valley "... or face the alternative, which was death." Kaniache was protected in his battles by a thick umbrella-shaped shield of hides that the bullets of the day could not penetrate. One morning while Lafe was home on leave from the 1855 Ute War, he awoke with his home fort being attacked by Kaniache and a large group of his Utes, who started a furious fight. Perhaps it is only a legend, but Lafe supposedly raised his hat on a stick and took careful aim at the spot where Kaniache's head would be if he lowered his umbrella shield. Kaniache moved forward firing at Lafe's hat and eventually lowered his shield to see better. Lafe then fired and wounded Kaniache so severely that the Utes retreated, carrying their dead and wounded, including Kaniache, with them. Several of the town people were wounded, but no one was killed. The worst damage for the Americans was that the Utes carried off much of the Conejos settlers' livestock. Lafayette was evidently only slightly wounded in the battle.

The wounding of Kaniache ties in to another possible legend about Chief Ouray's first act as a chief that occurred in 1855. Ouray was asked by an Indian runner to send help to Kaniache, who was in a fight with the Mexican-Americans in the San Luis Valley (probably the fight at Conejos). Ouray not only refused to do so, but sent a runner to Kit Carson, who was in the Raton Mountains at the time, to tell him to send reinforcements to the settlers. Ouray then supposedly rode to Conejos/Guadalupe, picking up a few of his warriors along the way, and the little group of Ouray's Utes helped defend the settlement, during which time Ouray was said to have wounded Kaniache, and the Mouache then fled with about a dozen of their men killed. In this story, Ouray was said to have captured Kaniache after he was wounded, taken care of him until his health was regained, and then released him. It is factual that Lafe and his settlers were attacked by Kaniache and a major battle of six to eight hours ensued. Kit Carson reported the battle to his superiors:

> *An estimated 800 to 1,000 Indians drove off 1,000 head of sheep, 25 head of horses, mules and burros, and 40 head of cattle from the little settlement (of Conejos).... (Kit) Carson understood that the 60 to 70 families held the stock in common and he reported to his superiors that probably every family suffered losses.*[57]

CHAPTER 5

However, exactly what happened with Lafe and Kaniache is unknown. The Native Americans were followed by Fort Garland troops to near Trinidad with more Utes being killed until finally the whole group was "routed in every direction."

Kaniache is an interesting Ute who has almost as many unanswered questions concerning his life as does Lafayette Head. "Kaniache" means "One Who Was Taken." The name was given him in later life when he first appeared on the historic scene back in 1849. He was thirty-one years old at this time and one of several head chiefs of the Mouache Utes band. As mentioned, the Utes and the new American conquerors of New Mexico were not getting along well, and U.S. Cavalry units were stationed at Abiqui. Kaniache was considered relatively peaceful at the time and was asked to bring in the other Utes for the 1849 Ute Treaty, but was only given twenty days to do so. He and some other chiefs were a few days past the deadline but were supposedly coming to Abiqui when they heard soldiers had already left to come after them. When they met up, Captain Chapman ordered Kaniache's arrest, and he was thrown into the guardhouse with, of all people, Mexican-Americans who were charged with killing Old Bill Williams and Dr. Benjamin Kern when they had gone back into the San Juan Mountains to retrieve equipment left behind in the disastrous Fremont expedition. The Mexicans had been incarcerated when they were found with some of the Fremont expedition's equipment and extra clothing, although there was general agreement that Kern and Williams had been attacked by Utes.

There was no evidence of Kaniache being involved with the stealing of the clothing and equipment, but he evidently overheard talk by the guards that all the prisoners would be hung the next morning for this deed. Kaniache escaped wearing nothing except his moccasins, and he was slightly wounded twice during the escape. Kaniache then supposedly came back with other chiefs, but he was not recognized and signed the 1849 treaty with someone using a different variation in the spelling of his name before he signed his "X". At this time the Utes could no longer go onto the plains to hunt because the Comanche and Arapahoe had moved into that area, and the Plains Indians were well-armed and had plenty of horses. Kaniache and his Utes were therefore forced to move out of their traditional area on the plains between Colorado Springs to south of the Raton Mountains and into the San Luis Valley.

Apparently, Kaniache very logically thought that because the treaty of 1849 stated that Fort Massachusetts was to be built to protect the Utes as well as white settlers from their enemies that the soldiers would defend the

Utes from their Plains Indian enemies. There was a statement to that effect in the 1849 treaty, but the Americans ignored it. Article VI of the treaty stated:

> *In order to preserve tranquility and afford protection to all the people and interests of the contracting parties, the Government of the United States will establish such military posts and agencies, and authorize such trading-houses, at such times and in such places as the said Government may designate.*[58]

However, when Kaniache came to the Indian Agency in Taos in March of 1852 to complain that the Mouache were not being protected from the Plains Indians, Agent Greiner told him that such protection was not going to happen. When the Utes were again attacked by their Plains enemies, Kaniache decided to take it out on white settlers and changed from being basically peaceful to being very warlike. After this time he also became very unpredictable in his relationship with the Whites. One moment he was helping them as their friend and the next he might be killing them. The Jicarilla Apache had always been less friendly toward the Whites than the Utes and in the future they often joined with Kaniache's Mouache Utes to cause trouble.

Back at Fort Massachusetts, after a few weeks rest, in April the Americans involved in the Ute War of 1855 were split into several groups, as there was not enough grass in the valley to graze the entire group's horses at one spot. Some, including Lafe, were ordered back out with Ceran St. Vrain and pursued the Jicarilla Apache into the Raton Mountains. On April 25, sixty Native Americans were surprised by St. Vrain's group, with thirteen killed or captured. The rest took flight. Other soldiers were left to guard Fort Massachusetts; and at the same time Colonel Thomas T. Fauntleroy had several companies of regular U.S. soldiers with him, and they made a thirty-six hour forced march north through the San Luis Valley, so as to not give any warning to the Utes. He caught the Utes dancing at night (presumably a war dance) in the Arkansas Valley near the north end of Poncha Pass. Because the Americans came so quickly, they surrounded and totally surprised the Utes. Many of the Utes were killed with many more wounded. Then Fauntleroy and his men went to Cochetopa Pass and fought eighty Utes in a skirmish before going back to Fort Massachusetts. After these major American victories, the threat of war from Native Americans decreased substantially for the next few years.

As mentioned, Lafe already knew Carson, St. Vrain, and Pfeiffer, his leaders in the 1855 Ute War, but he must have gotten to know them much

CHAPTER 5

better during this time. The muster rolls of the company of the New Mexico Mounted Volunteers in which Lafe was enrolled, listed ninety-two men. When the Second Lieutenant of Lafe's company resigned in May 1855, the company, probably at the suggestion of his officer friends, elected Lafe to take his place. He only served at his new rank for about a month before going home, but it was an honor he appreciated.

By July 1855, the Indians involved in the uprising were asking for peace and the next month a treaty was made with the Tabeguache and other Utes who had not participated in the war. In early September the hostile Mouache Utes and Jicarilla Apache asked for peace. The treaties were made near Abiqui with David Merriweather, New Mexico's Territorial Governor, and Kit Carson representing the United States. The parties met September 10, 1855, and the Mouache agreed the next day to accept a reservation of 1,000 square miles west of Rio Grande to the San Juan River. The Jicarilla Apache made a similar deal for a 160,000 acre reservation. Although neither of the treaties was ever ratified by the U.S. Congress, relationships did improve.

Lafe had plenty of work to do when he returned to his ranch and house. Conejos and Guadalupe settlers replaced their stolen stock with animals that included the first flock of chickens in the San Luis Valley. Lafe understood that under U.S. law he could file an "Indian depredation" claim with the United States government. If accepted, the claim would be paid out of the annuities due the tribe responsible. He probably encouraged his fellow settlers to do the same. He valued his particular stolen animals and his part of the common herd at $735, but it took decades to receive payment on his claim. Since he had volunteered to battle Indians for six months, Lafe was especially bothered by the inaction, and it was an issue that chafed him for the rest of his life. Some sources state Head reported he had personally lost three cows at $35 each, an American bull valued at $200, and a bay horse valued at $45 for a personal total of $350.

At the end of the 1855 Ute War, many of the Conejos group of settlers decided it was too dangerous to share the San Luis Valley with the Utes nearby and they left. The number of settlers at Conejos shrunk to only about twelve families in 1856. However Lafe probably felt right at home, as his family had constantly fought Native Americans in Missouri. On the positive side for Lafe, it would have given him a chance to buy out the property rights of some of the settlers who were leaving for a very low price or perhaps no money at all, thereby increasing his land holdings around Conejos.

However, Indian troubles aside, the movement of American settlers into The Valley would again be limited when the amount of land available for homesteading was markedly decreased in 1860 after the U.S. Congress approved the 1.7 million acre Maxwell Grant on the east side of the Sangre de Cristo Mountains. This would mean that homesteading was not a viable choice for settlers on the east side of the Rio Grande River, and most settlers had no money to purchase land. Future settlers, however, still had plenty of land to homestead on the west side of the San Luis Valley, along both sides of the upper Rio Grande River, and further north up the San Luis Valley; but, what did that mean for the Utes?

CHAPTER SIX

Conejos, Fort Garland, Indians and the '59ers
(1855-1859)

Lafayette Head is "a most efficient and competent officer... friend of the Administration... and greatly respected by the Mexican population, whose language he speaks with fluency."

William Gilpin, first Governor of Colorado Territory

The Valley of the Rio Grande Del Norte, which lies between 7,000 and 8,000 feet in elevation, was well-known to be fertile, but it suffered from lack of snow and rainfall. However, the many rivers and creeks running through the parks along its lower elevations, as well as the Rio Grande River itself, meant many parts of it could easily be well-irrigated. Planting crops was a priority for Lafe in the early summer of 1855, since the Utes had destroyed the fields his settlers had planted in the summer and fall of 1854. The settlers knew they needed to dig irrigation ditches (called *"acequias"* in Spanish). During the Spanish and Mexican period, the location and construction of the *"acequia madre"* was one of the first actions taken after building a defensive fort when founding a new town.

Water is more bountiful on the west side of the San Luis Valley, with its numerous creeks and rivers filled by the melting of plentiful San Juan Mountain snows. Besides the Rio Grande River, there are, among others, Rock Creek, San Antonio, Saguache, Alamosa, La Jara, and the Conejos on the west (most with tributaries) and the Trinchera, Cuelbra, San Luis, Costilla, and their tributaries on the east. From 1855 until the Utes were removed from the area in 1868, there were small settlements up and down most of the creeks and rivers in the southern half of the San Luis Valley, usually built in close proximity to each other for protection. Early on, the area around the Conejos River was proclaimed "a most fertile region" of the San Luis Valley.

Evidently a few irrigation ditches had at least been partially constructed by the first and/or second Conejos Land Grant settlers, but the citizens of the new town of Conejos were expected to volunteer their labor for the construction of the Conejos Main Ditch and for maintenance of the main canal. These citizens would be under the watchful eye of an elected official who would make sure everyone contributed their fair share of work. The family plots of land ran in long, narrow strips of land away from the river or the main ditch, so that at least a good part of it could be irrigated. The smaller canals were the responsibility of the individual families.

The settlers also had the use of the common pasture and timberland of the grant. Those who could afford it had sheep to graze, although the original sheep were later said to be of poor quality and, if their wool was not used by the owner, it was often simply thrown away after it was sheared, as there was no market for it. The sheep were used for meat, and for a while the wild game (mainly deer and rabbits) supplemented that meat.

The "Law of the Indies" was used by the Spanish crown to set guidelines for laying out and building a new town in a plaza shape. It also gave instructions on the town's location (basically "high and dry") and the town's main public buildings were to be built on the central plaza. While U.S.

Irrigation was necessary for New Mexico and was used early in the settlement of the San Luis Valley. In the early days it was a source of drinking water and a place to do the laundry besides water for the crops.

Wood, *Over the Range to the Golden Gate.*

CHAPTER 6

towns used the central plaza mainly as an economic spot, the Spanish and Mexican towns used it for social interaction and a market place for small farmers.

One of the first things Lafe did after coming home from chasing Indians during the Ute War of 1855 was to file for water rights with the New Mexico Territorial government in Santa Fe. Approval of the application came on June 1, 1855. Since many of his initial settlers had left Conejos, he hired men from some of the other small settlement on the Conejos River to help him dig his main ditch on the south side of the Conejos River, and the twelve-foot wide *acequla madre* ran for about two miles to where he was building his house. He filed on the water for domestic use, for a mill, and for irrigation of his group's fields. The rights were later transferred to Colorado when that territory was formed and then later to the State of Colorado. Lafe claimed as much water as needed to fill his ditch to two feet deep and keep a grade of three inches to every 100 feet of ditch. Under the system used by New Mexico and later Colorado, Head's Ditch received a #2 Priority, which was only exceeded on the west side of the Rio Grande by Jacques' ditch. The #1 Priority of the San Luis town site had been issued on April 10, 1852, on the other side of the San Luis Valley and it was the first priority in all of Colorado. State engineers figured that Lafe's water claim amounted to 117 cubic feet of water per second (as much as a good size creek). By the end of 1855, the paperwork for forty smaller irrigation ditches had already been filed in the San Luis Valley.

The winter of 1855-56 was again very cold and there was scurvy at Fort Massachusetts. Kit Carson went to meet with the Indians at Abiqui to give them "presents" (basically their annuity goods) and food. After the presents were given, Kit reported:

> …*They appeared to be content, then there was a disturbance. The next day a Tabeguachi (sic) Utah tore up the blanket given him. It was old, had been worn and he was dissatisfied. He wished to kill the Superintendent but was hindered by the other Indians. I cannot see how the Superintendent can expect Indians to depart satisfied (when) he has called (them) to see him from a distance of 2 or 3 hundred miles, (and) compelled (them) to go several days without anything to eat, unless they have carried it with them.*
>
> *They are given a meal by the Superintendent then the presents are given. Some get a blanket; those that get none are given a knife or hatchet or some vermillion, a piece of red or blue*

cloth, some sugar, perhaps a few more trinkets. They could more than earn the quantity they receive in one day's hunt, if left in their country. They could procure skins and furs and traders could furnish the same items to them and they would be saved the necessity of coming such a distance, thereby not causing their animals to be fatigued and themselves have to travel without food.

If presents are given they should be taken to their country. They should not be allowed to come into the settlements, for every visit an Indian makes to a town, it is more or less injury to him.[59]

In the late summer and fall of 1856, Lafe finished building his two-room house inside the northwest corner of his large plaza in the new Town of Conejos. Head's house faced the town plaza and a church was eventually built across the way. Two foot thick cottonwood tree trunks had been placed upright in the ground to form Lafe's plaza walls. Adobe mud was then used to fill in the cracks between the logs. More logs were used for the flat roof of the house, with small aspen or cedar tree trunks and branches used to cover the logs. Then a mixture of adobe was placed over the top, which pretty well sealed the roof. Head's house was only two rooms, but his and the other part of the duplex were the largest in the 200 by 200 foot house fort, with all windows and doors located inside the compound and a sturdy wooden gate made for the entrance. The windows to his house, if any, were probably small and made of mica or sheepskin parchment and had wooden shutters that could be barred if necessary. The whole house was plastered with adobe-like mud. It was a true fortress that was designed to withstand the worst of attacks from the Native Americans, and it would be badly needed. When Lafe moved from the north side to his new house on the south side of the Conejos River in 1856, "the center of community life moved with him."[60]

Martina whitewashed the walls on the inside of their two-room house. The smaller room was used for storage and preparing food. The larger room was used for living and as a bedroom. She covered the lower parts of the walls in the large room with fabric to keep the whitewash from rubbing off. Above the fabric she would have hung paintings, religious objects, and mirrors, as well as strings of chilies, dried fruits, and herbs that were hung higher. Lengths of bleached muslin were stretched beneath the cottonwood ceiling beams to catch bits of earth that might filter down from the roof.

CHAPTER 6

Homespun wool carpets, called *jergas*, covered the earthen floors. Thick, wool-filled mattresses were rolled up against the walls and served as seats during the day. Rolled out on the floor at night, the mattresses became beds. Piñon wood burned in the corner fireplace. It gave off strong heat and a pungent odor.

Martina would have fried tortillas on a stone griddle, used iron kettles for cooking, and roasted meat on an open grill. Lafe had learned to enjoy the food of the Southwest—primarily beans, chilies, and tortillas. He hunted deer and rabbits; and, sometimes, he butchered a lamb. Meat not eaten immediately was cut into thin strips and salted, then dried and stored in wooden boxes for winter. In the spring, Martina gathered the wild spinach, onions, and asparagus that grew along the streams and irrigation ditches to supplement the vegetables from their garden.

The next few years for Lafe and Martina were full of construction, politics, and religion. In 1856, the first mass was held at the Conejos church, of which Lafe was one of the leaders. That same year, Guadalupe leader José Maria Jacques supposedly built a mill two and one half miles northeast (downstream) from Guadalupe on the northeast side of the Conejos River; and probably the year after (1857), Lafe built a mill near his house at Conejos on the south side of the Conejos River. Several sources report that Lafe built a flour mill at Conejos as early as 1854 and that it was one of the earliest in all of Colorado, but the 1854 date is improbable. Lafe was

Grinding corn into a paste was the first step in making tortillas, usually done with a mano and metate in the early days. There was no kitchen, just a room in which the meals were prepared.

Author's collection.

too busy building the jackal fort at Servilleta in late 1854, then he was away from home fighting Indians for the first five or six months of 1855, and then he was building his adobe home fort and digging irrigation ditches in the summer and fall of 1855. He did evidently have plans for a mill in 1856, but he probably did not finish it until early 1857. The mills of Head and Jacques could handle all the crops from the surrounding area. Lafe and Jacques used native lava for grindstones, and small pieces often broke off, making the flour gritty. Flour was not separated from the bran at the early Mexican flour mills, which made the flour red. The course ground "Mexican" flour made from red wheat also often contained dead bugs and was not very appetizing, and this may be the reason for so many discrepancies of the dates for the building of the earliest San Luis Valley flour mills, ranging from the mid-1850s to the mid-1860s, when "American flour" mills were being built.

One reason for having a mill was that the ground products (flour, cornmeal, etc.) were a favorite barter item—used almost as much as cash, and it was common for farmers to give payment of part of their crop to the miller to pay for the milling process. When you had flour to sell, it was also easy in those days to sell other purchased or bartered items, and before you knew it, you had a store. This happened later to Otto Mears in Saguache, and probably happened about this time for Lafe.

In addition to his other projects, in 1856 Lafe (noted on the records as La Fayette Head) went back into politics and was chosen to fill a vacancy in the Sixth Session of the New Mexico Territorial Council representing Taos County, where Conejos was located, a position left by the resignation of Juan Baptiste Valdez. Lafe would be reelected to another year in 1857, and served as President of the Council (Senate) in 1858.

In June of 1856, orders had been issued to move Fort Massachusetts to a new location six miles south of its first location. The original fort continued to have a garrison of fifty-four men until the new fort was finished. The new fort was called "Fort Garland" in honor of Mexican-American War veteran Brigadier General John Garland, who was a hero at the 1846 Battle of Monterrey, Mexico, and was then commander of U.S. troops in the Territory of New Mexico. Fort Garland was located on a twenty-five year lease of land from the Trinchera Estates of the Sangre de Cristo Grant, and a ditch was run from Ute Creek to the fort. The post's grounds were six miles square with its buildings, which formed a very large stockade, in the center.

The building of the fort proper promptly started. The fort was built by 150 men of Company E of the U.S. Mounted Riflemen, but many local civilians who were experienced in doing adobe work were also hired. The adobe walls were three feet thick and the roofs were also adobe. Charles Autobees directed the construction work, except for a period of time when he was injured after being stabbed by a worker. Mountain man Tom Tobin came to the fort to fill in while Autobees recovered. Tobin liked the area so much that he homesteaded a 160 acre tract at a spot about a mile and a half to the south west of the new fort.

Fort Garland was finished in 1858, and the old Fort Massachusetts was closed on June 24, 1858. The new post (much the same today as when it was built, except a few outlying buildings are missing) consisted of a large parade ground completely surrounded by adobe buildings. It had room for 100 men in each of the two barracks, and each barrack included a large kitchen, its own mess hall, storerooms, the company office, and squad rooms. The infantry quarters were on the west side of the fort, and the cavalry barracks were on the east side near the stables (now gone). The officers' quarters were on the north side facing south,

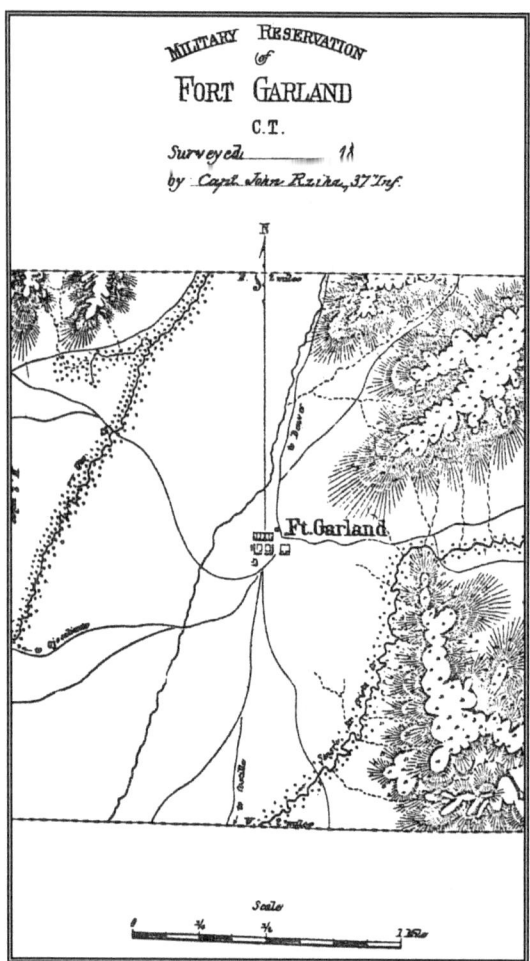

The original location map for Fort Garland, showing only a few buildings but all the roads led from it. Note the trees along the creeks.

From U. S. National Archives.

so they could "get the morning sun." The commander had his own kitchen, office with fireplace, dining room, and rooms for a wife and children. He could use his own furnishings if desired. Each of the six other officers had

Conejos, Fort Garland, Indians and the '59ers

only one room for living quarters. Non-commissioned officers and the rest of the soldiers lived in the barracks, two men to a bunk and clothes racks used for their uniforms. Gun racks were made around each barrack's ceiling posts, and a fireplace was at one end. The one fireplace did not supply enough heat, and it was often very cold in the barracks in the winter. The fort also had a jail described as a box with a small hole cut in the roof. On the south side were a chapel, billiards room, and a room for visiting performers who entertained the troops or other guests. Over the years Fort Garland had a band room, family quarters for all officers, rooms for civilian employees, and a room for the laundress.

Food for the soldiers was usually purchased from farmers and ranchers in the San Luis Valley. Before the railroad arrived in the valley, food was sometimes a problem, as the fort was so isolated, especially in the winter. After the railroad came near in 1877, the situation reversed itself, and the fort was used as a place for the U.S. Army to procure beef, grains, and potatoes from The Valley for use at other military forts. Nearly all the food coming in by train went to the Anglos. When using "Mexican flour," Major Hugh Fleming, one of the commanders at Fort Garland wrote, "Some calculate that our flour is composed of one-third flour, one-third earth, and one-third manure."[61] Some of the mills in The Valley, including Lafe's mill, soon made improvements so they could produce "American flour." Among the permanent units to stay at the fort over the

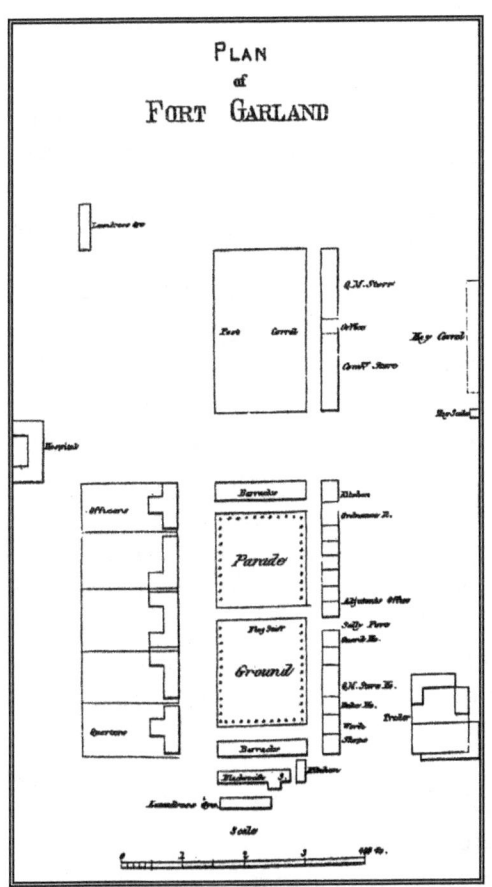

Original Plan for Fort Garland, showing main gate on right, corral at top, and parade grounds in middle of bottom.

From U. S. National Archives.

CHAPTER 6

years was the largely Hispanic First New Mexico Mounted Volunteers. They were garrisoned there in 1862-63 and 1866-67, and the renowned Buffalo soldiers were stationed at Fort Garland in 1876-79.

The winter of 1857-58 was another bitterly cold one in Conejos and many of the settlers' spring lambs died. When the heavy snows in the San Juans melted, flooding was widespread. However, despite the difficult spring of 1858, there was also some good news for Conejos—the new French Catholic Bishop of Santa Fe (installed in 1857), Bishop John-Baptiste Lamy, made his first trip into the dangerous San Luis Valley in the northern part of New Mexico Territory.

In 1857, U.S. officials recommended (but their recommendations were not accepted) that the Capote Utes and Jicarilla Apache be removed to the San Juan River Basin and be made to farm and ranch to a point where they became self-sufficient.

In that same year, Diego Archuleta had been appointed Agent of the Jicarilla Apache and Capote Utes at Abiqui. However, the following year officials decided the Tabeguache Utes would also be attached to that Agency. Kit Carson had been Agent for the Mouache and Capote Utes as well as for the Jicarilla Apache at Taos after August 31, 1858. Carson was having trouble controlling the Indians in his charge at Taos and, during this time, hostilities were also breaking out between the Navajo and the Utes. The Utes also remained at war with the Plains Indians who came into Ute Territory, and the U.S. still continued to refuse to help them in their battles. A fight between the Kiowa and the Utes occurred just east of Conejos in 1857, and the Utes killed about sixty Kiowa in a decisive victory. Mouache chief Kaniache and a small party of his Utes also attacked a party of Arapaho on the Plains who were escorting Charles Autobee's wagon that was carrying grain for the Arapaho's annuity. The Capote and Jicarilla Apache were also fighting the Navajos at this time; and in 1858 the Capote and Jicarilla captured twenty-one Navajo girls and several dozen horses. It was one of the greatest losses of their children that the Navajo ever sustained and is preserved in pictographs in their rock history.

When Archuleta refused to move to Abiqui, James L. Collins, the Superintendent of Indians Affairs, appointed Albert Pfeiffer as its Sub-Agent. One of Pfeiffer's first orders was to get an accurate count of the Native Americans at his agency. Pfeiffer's interpreter, John Maostin, wrote: "The Tabeguache have been attached to this Agency (Abiqui).... It is impossible to give exact numbers.... They live in parties of ten to twenty lodges and have no permanent residences...." This was a constant problem among Ute Agents. As late as 1875, the Agent at Los Piños, H. F. Bond, wrote in

Conejos, Fort Garland, Indians and the '59ers

his reply to a request for a Tabeguache Ute census that "a count is quite impossible. You might as well try to count a swarm of bees on the wing." Collins, in a letter to Pfieffer at this time, pointed out that the Jicarilla lived on the east side of the Sangre de Cristos and were not picking up their food, and if they could not be made to do so, it might be necessary to move the Agency from Abiqui to Kit Carson's Taos Agency so as to be closer to their homeland. Superintendent Collins went to Abiqui and personally presented the annuities on September 15, 1858, to 1200 to 1500 Mouache and Tabeguache Utes.

Although the military would not help the Utes, Indian Agents were responsible for protecting the Indians and investigating the complaints of Whites against those Native Americans within their care. There were provisions for trying the Indians for transgressions in American courts; but they naturally felt they would never be given a fair trial, so this remedy was seldom used. Carson decided that perhaps withholding the Native Americans' annuities would "make them feel the consequences of their acting in bad faith."[62] Unfortunately this only increased their shortage of food and made matters worse. One problem faced by some Agents at this time was that Utes would often go to more than one Agency to try to collect their annuities. Another problem was that many of the Native Americans

View of Fort Garland from Sierra Blanca. Stables are to the left and trees line Ute Creek to the west (background).

From *Croffutt's Gripsack Guide to Colorado.*

119

CHAPTER 6

would often take the goods, flour, or livestock they wanted without letting the Agent know they were doing it. Different members of a band would also appear at different times or perhaps not come at all, making it difficult for an Agent to know if he should hold back rations for some Ute group they knew had not come yet.

A visitor arriving in the San Luis Valley in the spring of 1858 was A. P. Wilbar, Deputy Surveyor General of New Mexico Territory, who came with a six-man crew to do a survey of the western lands in the San Luis Valley. His was the first official U.S. Survey in the mountains of today's Colorado. This meant the settlers land in the San Luis Valley would soon be eligible to be owned under the U.S. Preemption Act. Wilbar noted that the San Antonio River was a quarter of a mile wide at this time due to spring snowmelt. The Conejos River would have been much wider; sometimes its floodplain was said to be almost two miles across.

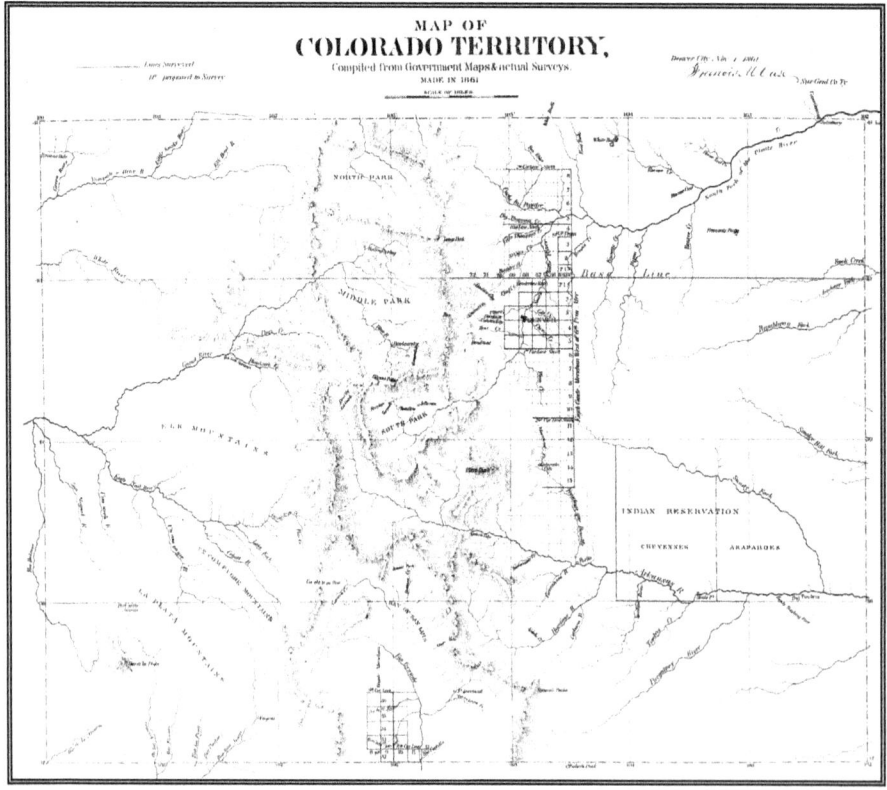

The government survey that Lafe helped make is shown in the bottom middle of this map.

1861 U. S. Government Survey of Colorado Territory.

Wilbar also mentioned that Lafe's stockade (Fort Servilleta) was still standing with peaceful Indians camped around it at the time the survey was taken. For several miles going downstream on the Conejos, he noted small "little Mexican" settlements including Guadalupe, Conejos, Servilleta, Brazoso, San Francisco, Canon, Mazetta, and San Raphael , "all on the Conejos River." Wilbar jotted in his notebook "cultivated land… soil rich… bottom land…abundant cottonwood timber, very good grass." He also noted that there were many Indian camps all along the rivers in the area, and that there was a bridge over the river between Conejos and Guadalupe.[63]

On the morning of June 16, 1858, three men quit Wilbar's crew, likely from fear of the numerous Native Americans in the area. Wilbur found replacements two miles away in Conejos, and Lafe was one of the men hired. His job was placing corner stones for survey markers. The work was finished within a few weeks and the crew left the San Luis Valley. Wilbar filed his survey report in Santa Fe on July 20, 1858.

The years 1858 and 1859 were the time of the "Rush to the Rockies." White men came to the Rockies like "endless swarms of grasshoppers." In July, 1858, gold was discovered at the mouth of Dry Creek (a short tributary of Clear Creek) by brothers William, Oliver, and Levi Russell, along with ten other men. Word back East was there was gold in the "Pike's Peak Region," although it was called such only because most gold seekers followed the Arkansas River to the west and Pike's Peak could be seen from far out on the Plains. The Clear Creek diggings were sixty or seventy miles north of Pikes Peak. It is worthy to note that some of the first miners in the Clear Creek area included Mexican-Americans placer mining on what was called "Mexican Bar." By the spring of 1859, an estimated 50,000 to 100,000 people had set out for the gold fields of today's Colorado, but about half never made it or went back East after a very short time. Almost everyone ended up in the Denver/Golden area; but it is known that a few prospectors were at Fort Garland, looking for gold in the nearby Sangre de Cristo Mountains in 1859, a year in which most Colorado students are taught that the first "pioneers" arrived in today's Colorado. Lafe and his family had been living and/or working in what would become Colorado or New Mexico Territory for fourteen years.

A story in the *Rocky Mountain News* on July 9, 1859, featured this headline: "Trouble with the Indians—Our miners shot and scalped by the Ute savages without provocation." There were many other such reports of difficulties between the Whites and the Utes, but most were exaggerated tales of murders and scalpings reported by an unscrupulous press.

In the summer of 1859, Agent Pfeiffer took some time off and acted as a guide for Captain J. M. Macomb's expedition of topographical engineers from Santa Fe along the Old Spanish Trail to the junction of the Green and Colorado Rivers in Utah. One of their major discoveries was the hot springs called Pagosa that Lafe had known about for years. Macomb also noted the many small rivers running south out of the San Juans, including the Los Piños, which would play an important part in later Ute history. He also noted that the name already given the La Plata Mountains by the Spanish must indicate that silver was found there.

A *Rocky Mountain News* correspondent in November 1859 wrote:

> While in Taos, New Mexico... I was requested by Kit Carson, government Agent for the Ute Indians, to say to the Miners here, that he hoped to visit this region early next spring, with several leading 'braves' of the tribe, to conclude a permanent peace between them and the Whites. He deems this very desirable, as the Utes are the most dangerous of the mountain Indians, excellent shots with the rifle, and if hostile, will be likely to destroy many small prospecting parties and solitary travelers next spring.

More than 1,000 Tabeguache and Capote Utes were in the San Luis Valley during the winter of 1858-1859. Kit Carson wrote a letter to the *Rocky Mountain News* notifying residents there that he had in his possession mules that he believed the Tabeguache had stolen near Denver and

Almost 100,000 men headed for Pike's Peak in 1859-1860, but only about 50,000 made it or stayed any length of time.

Harper's Weekly, August 13, 1859.

proceeded to explain how the owner could pick them up if he could identify them. He also said "this year's presents will not be given them on account of their deeds of murder."[64] He further wrote that he had reason to believe the same band that had stolen the mules had killed a Mr. Kennedy, but they were refusing to give the killer up. He ended his letter: "Government will force them to comply."[65]

Because of administrative changes, in 1860 and 1861, quite a bit of shuffling was done with the Ute Agencies in Colorado and other Indian Agencies as well. This reorganization was apparently due to the U.S. War Department being in control of pre-1861 Colorado Indian Agencies; then after Colorado became a territory in 1861, the Indian Agencies were under the control of the Territorial Governor.

The Tabeguache Agency at Abiqui, under Pfeiffer and then Head, was closed in late 1859 and moved to Denver, which was not a good spot. Kit Carson had tried to get it moved to Taos; but Carson failed, and he then requested that the Tabeguache Agency be moved to Conejos with Lafe proposed as Agent. The Indian Bureau agreed, and on June 27, 1860, the United States Senate approved the appointment of Lafayette Head as Indian Agent of the Tabeguache at Conejos. In 1861, when management of the Native Americans was placed under the first Colorado Territorial Governor, William Gilpin, he continued with Lafe as the Agent for the Tabeguache Utes at Conejos. Lafe served as Agent for the Tabeguache Utes for the next eight years (until 1868).

Both Lafe and Kit Carson had thought for several years that Conejos would be a better place for the Tabeguache Ute Agency, as the Tabeguache were often in the western edge of the San Luis Valley. About 2,000 Tabeguache Utes soon showed up, supposedly trying to stay away from the Plains Indians.

In simple terms an Indian Agent's job was to protect the Indians and investigate white complaints, but there were many more details. Back in 1857, Superintendent of Indian Affairs James Collins had written a detailed letter to the new Agent at Abiqui, Albert Pfeiffer, that explained his duties as Agent, duties which would have applied equally to Lafe in his duties as Special Agent and soon to be Agent of the Tabeguache Utes.

> In the discharge of your duties you are expected to make yourself acquainted with the condition of the Indians under your charge embracing, of course, the several tribes that are now and have been under the control of Agent Archuleta and Carson. You are aware that the government has made provisions by the

CHAPTER 6

> *appropriation of money, to feed and subsist the Indians over which you will have charge, and of course it is intended that they shall receive the greatest possible benefit from these appropriations. To this end the whole tribe should be the recipient of the issues that may from time to time be made to them. To accomplish this object it is deemed most advisable to make the issue monthly and always at the Agency, which is for the present established at Abiqui. In carrying out this policy it will be necessary to give the Indians notice of the days on which the issues are to be made and to endeavor as far as may be possible to collect the whole tribe. If however you find they are not all present you should retain a portion of the provisions that are intended to be issued, for those who are not present, and to give the absentees notice that the provisions are on hand for them.*[66]

Collins continued:

> *… Your traveling expenses while in the discharge of your duties will be paid by the Govt., but it is expected and required that you on all occasions use a proper economy in your expenses. You are expected for the present to furnish your own horse, but will be allowed to feed him at the cost of the Govt., provided the cost is not more than forty cents a day.*
>
> *You are required by regulations to make monthly reports of the condition of the Indians, their conduct during the month; whether robberies have been committed by them, and to what extent; and every other matter of importance connected with the business at the Agency.*
>
> *Corn is believed to be the best article to issue to the Indians, but as it is becoming scarce in the vicinity of your Agency, it may be necessary to use wheat. Beef or Mutton in small quantities can be occasionally issued, but care should always be had to see that the tribe is equally supplied. This can only be done by making yourself thoroughly acquainted with them. The Indians most needy are often the least likely to present themselves to the Agency and unless care is taken they may go unsupplied and be forced to steal to obtain food. The Govt. is liberal in the allocation of money for the subsistence of the Indians, and if the Agents act in good faith, and with proper industry in the discharge of their duties, it is believed that no Indian will give*

> us but little trouble, especially those that will come under your charge.
>
> ... I desire you to be present on all occasions when issues are made to the Indians at the Abiqui Agency, and as often as convenient when they are made by Agent Carson....[67]

Lafe estimated that there were about 5,000 Utes at his Agency during the year 1861. There were similar over-estimates among other Indian Agents across the country. One historian wrote "the most common practice was for an Agent to inflate the number of Indians under his charge and order food and supplies accordingly. The surplus items would be sold or traded off the reservation or used as payment to an Indian for a favor..."[68] Lafe was referred to specifically by the author of this quote, but there is no proof of that. The Utes were very hard to count and control, as they were constantly shifting from one place to another. It is more likely that Lafe wanted to be sure to have enough food as his Indians were very spread out and hard to get word to; he seemed to have more and more Indians coming to his Agency each time he distributed supplies, and he knew from past history that his request would probably be cut severely. Kit Carson advised his Ute friend, Ouray, that the Utes needed a treaty with the United States and that he was going to try to get a treaty in Denver in 1860.

By the end of 1859, Colorado mining men and prospectors had already deduced that there was a rich "Mineral Belt" in the future Colorado that ran from Boulder southwest to the new discoveries in California Gulch, and that it evidently continued southwest into the San Juan Mountains. A few successful Colorado mining men in the future Leadville area put together a small party to explore the region under the leadership of Charles Baker. If anything was found, Baker was to file claims (although the San Juans were in Ute country and the claims would not be legal), establish a toll road into the "diggings" (they too were looking for placer gold, panning the streams for nuggets), locate a town site in the best place possible near the diggings, and sell lots in the new town. All of these activities were illegal and the minerals were in the heart of the rugged San Juan Mountains with no easy access and in the heart of Tabeguache Ute territory

During "The Rush to the Rockies," the future area of Colorado would also go through some political turmoil. In 1859 today's Colorado was part of Kansas Territory, unorganized Utah and New Mexico Territories, and the Republic of Texas. On October 24, 1859, the locals decided to become Jefferson Territory with boundaries similar to present-day Colorado. Jefferson Territory supporters originally wanted it to be a state, but this idea was dismissed when it was discovered it would be cheaper to be a territory. The supporters of Jefferson Territory also tried to merge into Kansas Territory, but Kansas did not agree.

At the end of the 1859 session of the New Mexico Territorial legislature, Lafe did not run for reelection. He probably realized that he may not have been eligible or perhaps was waiting for Colorado to become a state or territory. The area that Lafe lived in was covered for sixteen months by Jefferson Territory, but was also considered as part of both the potential Colorado Territory and the existing New Mexico Territory.

Perhaps because he did plan to get back into politics, Lafe continued to join fraternal and business organizations. The Fifty-Niners Pioneer Association held its first meeting in 1859 in Denver, but did not hold a second meeting until June of 1866, and Lafe attended both. To be a member, one had to have arrived in the territory by 1859. Lafe beat that by five years. Besides Lafe, there were thirty-three other members, including Indian Agent D. C. Oakes, newspaper publisher William N. Byers, future Territorial Governor A. C. Hunt, and future silver king H.A.W. Tabor. The members selected uniforms—red flannel with white collars to be worn with black pants. They initiated a July 4th celebration in Denver that included a band, parade, prayers, reading of the Declaration of Independence, and a speech. Lafe and other pioneers also later formed the Society of Colorado Pioneers. He was elected one of sixteen Vice-Presidents, probably one from each Colorado County. The organization also hosted a Fourth of July Pioneers Reunion with a banquet at Denver's Broadwell House. They only had one other activity, another reunion seven years later.

As mentioned, most of the Colorado prospectors' initial activities were north of Ute lands, in the area around today's Golden and Denver in what was then Kansas Territory; and the new prospectors were in the area controlled mainly by the Plains Indians, some of whom were peaceful and some of whom were very warlike. By 1860, most of the good claims in the Denver/Golden/Boulder area seemed to have been taken and prospectors headed south and found new discoveries in the future Leadville-Fairplay (California Gulch) area. Now the prospectors were in northern Ute territory, and skirmishes became common between the Utes and the Americans in South Park and the upper Valley of the Arkansas River. It was obvious that the prospectors would soon be in the San Luis Valley.

The main purchasers for San Luis Valley foods and manufactured items were now in the Denver, California Gulch, and Golden areas; and those goods were cheaper than from back East, as the San Luis Valley was much closer to the prospectors. In fact, the San Luis Valley became "the bread basket" of Colorado until the railroad arrived at Golden and Denver in 1870. Horses, mules, and burros became a very important commodity from the San Luis Valley. Burros were especially useful to the new prospectors, as they could carry a larger load than a horse, they ate almost any vegetation, and they were very sure-footed in the mountains. They also cost much less than a horse or a mule and were more social, like a dog. Cattle and sheep would become sought after as American "meat eaters" came to Colorado. Lafe was far-sighted enough to see the trend and made a trip to the East in the spring of 1859 to buy more cattle and visit his family. However, from his mother's home in Howard County, Missouri, he wrote a letter (uncorrected) to his friend and the Fort Garland Sutler, Mr. Francisco on April 16, 1859.

> *Dear Sir upon my arrival here I find that Cattle are very high. They average from 85$ to 100$ per yoke and scarce at that. Mules are worth 300$ to 225$. Such prices does (sic) not suit Me consequently I will leave here for Kansas City about the last of this month, hoping that you and the Col. Are well and buying goods at reasonable prices. I remain Yours very Truly, Lafayette Head.*[69]

Unfortunately the same food being grown for newly arrived Americans was also a prime target for the very hungry Utes, although they preferred corn to flour.

Probably as a result of the white men rushing into the foothills of the Front Range, the Kiowa and Cheyenne raided Conejos in 1858; then, in 1859, the Kiowa again attacked the Utes near Conejos. However, except for the marked increase in raids by Native Americans, the start of the Colorado Gold Rush of 1858-1859 resulted in the San Luis Valley entering a time of prosperity. Because of spoilage, the newly arrived prospectors could not get items like fresh meat, vegetables, or milk and butter from back East at all. There were stores established in the late 1850s in the settlements of Costilla, Conejos, and San Luis to provide manufactured goods, food, and animals to the settlers (store owners usually bartered with the settlers—merchandise for crops) and to the prospectors, who usually paid in cash or gold.

The Native Americans were not just fighting the Whites, they were still fighting each other. In 1859 the Navajo raided American settlers and prospectors and stole thirty oxen and eight horses from one man. The Americans decided to retaliate and the Utes asked their Agent Pfeiffer if they should keep the peace treaty made between themselves, the government, and the Navajos; or if the United States wanted them to help fight the

CHAPTER 6

Navajo, who were the Utes' traditional enemy. Pfeiffer wrote New Mexico Superintendent of Indian Affairs James L. Collins to ask what to tell the Utes, and he also asked:

> Will you give me permission to raise a Company here like they have in Connejos (sic) only for to get arms for the people, then I believe in the whole river (area) there are not ten rifles to be found. It would be a good thing and I believe I would soon have opportunity to chastise the Navajo for their robberies.[70]

Evidently Pfeiffer was told to use the Utes; and on June 1, 1859, he was made Captain of Company A of the New Mexico Mounted Volunteers at Abiqui. Pfeiffer, who by now was good friends with the Utes, raised a force of 500 to 600 Ute warriors, as well as a few Mexican-Americans, to confront the Navajos.

Lafe's good friend and fellow Indian Agent Albert Pfeiffer was another Colorado mountain man who is famous for two fights he participated in with Native Americans. He came to New Mexico in 1844 and he joined

The first known drawing of the Pagosa Springs drawn from a sketch by Dr. J. S. Newberry.

Courtesy of the National Archives.

the U.S. Army in Santa Fe when the Mexican-American War broke out. Pfeiffer married a Mexican woman after he came to New Mexico, and he moved to Abiqui, where his in-laws had a trading post. In 1862, during the Civil War, he led Fort Garland troops against the Confederates at Embargo Creek. He had a deep hatred of the Apache Indians after his wife's death at the hands of the Mescalero Apaches.

The date of Pfeiffer's first famous fight varies, but it probably occurred as early as the 1850s and was at the springs called Pagosa (there was no town of Pagosa Springs yet). There was a controversy as to whether the Ute or the Navajo tribe would control the sacred hot springs. The Utes believed their gods had sent them to Pagosa hot springs to help them stop an illness that was killing many of their people. The sick Utes received a vision that they should build a huge fire and dance at a particular location. They did so all night and when they woke up there were hot springs at the spot where they had danced. They bathed in the springs and were cured. The site had been shared with the Navajo for many years, but then fights started to break out over who owned the springs. Eventually the Navajo started a battle with the Utes over possession of the springs.

The Utes eventually sent for Pfeiffer, who came and convinced each tribe to have a representative fight the other for ownership. The Navajo appointed a huge powerful warrior, a giant of a man, as their representative. Then Pfeiffer, who was only five-foot five inches tall, but very muscular, told the Utes he would fight this man, but the two must be naked and only have knives for weapons. Pfeiffer chose the Bowie knife, and then threw or perhaps stuck his knife into the giant, killing him; and the Utes had ownership of the springs. The Navajo thought the Bowie knife to be too big to be thrown accurately. This tale may only be a myth, as the American newspapers that still exist from this time make no reference of this fight; but local Whites claimed there were at one time papers that confirmed the event. The Pagosa Springs fight

Albert Henrich ("Henry") Pfeiffer was a good friend of Lafe, especially in later life. Pfieffer was an officer in the military, an Indian Agent, and he was a prospector.

Courtesy Rio Grande Museum.

was covered in an article by the *Colorado Historical Society Magazine*,[71] which states that there was at that time (1932) still considerable evidence that the story was true and the Albert Pfeiffer probably had the original claim to the springs. Author Ann Oldham states in her book *Albert H. Pfeiffer: Indian Agent, Soldier, and Mountain Man*[72] that Pfeiffer chose to fight because he had also just been "adopted" by the Utes. After this fight Pfeiffer had a strong dislike of the Navajo.

The other historic fight in which Pfeiffer was a participant, resulted in his hatred of the Apaches and took place in June of 1863 near the future Truth or Consequences, New Mexico, at hot springs that were located to the south of Socorro and three miles east of the Rio Grande River. He, his wife, and a half dozen others from nearby Fort McRae were enjoying a soak in the hot springs on June 20, 1863, while being guarded by six soldiers. Two of the soldiers escorting the group were killed and two were wounded when Mescalero Apaches attacked and took Pfeiffer's wife, Antonia, and the two other women present. Pfeiffer, who was wounded twice, realized the women would probably not be killed if the Apache were not threatened (as they could be sold later for a large bounty). He ran naked with an arrow in his side for six miles (another had passed all the way through his body), carrying only a knife, to get troops from the fort to go after his wife and the other women. He was beaten to the fort by two soldiers who were not injured. Pfeiffer later called them cowards who had run away from the Apaches. He was rescued a short way from the fort by a group of soldiers who had been sent out to look for his group, and he was taken to the fort's hospital.

Unfortunately Pfeiffer did not have an opportunity to tell the rescue party that they should carefully trail the Apache without their knowing they were being followed, and the Mescalero shot the three women when they learned they were being followed by the soldiers as the women were slowing them down. All three women were found alive, but barely. Pfeiffer's wife and one other woman died within minutes, and the other lady eventually died from the mental stress and physical wounds she incurred. Pfeiffer was left with four motherless children to take care of while still having to earn a living and serve in the military, and he now understandably hated the Apache. It is said that Pfeiffer killed every Mescalero Apache he saw after his wife's death. He supposedly said, "I fight them night and day—everywhere, in all seasons!" He found someone to watch his children and served as an officer with Kit Carson in the attack on the Navajo at Canyon de Chelly and the Long Walk in 1864; yet he remained friends for life with the Utes, instead of hating all Indians.

Although the story is certainly true, Pfeiffer and Carson greatly embellished the attack when spending a night in 1866 at Lucian Maxwell's Ranch with a reporter present. Both of the men loved to "shoot the bull" and did so to an author who believed that version of their story about the "Fort McRae Massacre." The story was printed in the *New York Evening Post* on November 1, 1866. That version was supposedly read many years later by historians who questioned its validity, and which led to some uncertainty about whether the event ever happened. However it is a certainty that it **did** happen. There were many references to the Truth or Consequences Fight in reports Pfeiffer made to the Army, requesting leave after the death of his wife by Apaches.

CHAPTER SEVEN

Colorado Territory, San Juan Excitement, the Utes, and the Civil War in Colorado
(1860-1862)

> *He (Lafayette Head) was a major player in territorial politics in both New Mexico and Colorado for over a quarter of a century.*
> Creating the American West, Derek R. Everrett

Major events and changes would be made in what is now southwest Colorado in the new decade of the 1860s—many of the prospectors disappeared during the Civil War; the Homestead Laws were passed and homesteaders began to outnumber prospectors; Colorado Territory was formed, but only after a lot of confusion; and a shift was made in what had been Lafe's home in extreme northern New Mexico to the new Colorado Territory. Colorado's first Territorial Governor William Gilpin, a friend of Lafe, heavily promoted the new territory and predicted gold in the San Juan Mountains, as well as a good economy in the San Luis Valley. He even wrote a guidebook for the area and gave lectures about southwest Colorado back East, in great part to bring settlers to the area so he could try to sell them land.

All of the confusion over land titles also brought many attorneys and land investors to the San Luis Valley early in its occupation; and wealthy Americans, such as Territorial Governor William Gilpin had begun to buy whatever rights they could from whoever had settled on various parcels of land. In some cases, the investors were receiving the land by merely paying the back taxes owed. Gilpin was a man who felt the possibilities for the future Colorado-New Mexico area was great, and he believed very strongly in Manifest Destiny.

However the biggest event was to occur in the eastern San Juan Mountain foothills, which are considered part of the western San Luis

Valley. Ever since Coronado's time, the Spanish had known there was gold and silver in the San Juan Mountains; but there was little placer gold, and no one knew an economical way to extract the precious metals from the rich veins found in the barren rock of the San Juans. Among others, Lafe's good friends Albert Pfeiffer, William Gilpin, and Kit Carson had all reported gold and silver in the San Juans in the 1840s and 1850s, but no one had paid much attention. A prospecting party of thirty-six men headed by Miles Johnson had gone down the Gunnison River and up the Uncompahgre in 1859, and "encouraging results" were found near today's town of Ouray. They then went into the heart of the San Juans the next summer and reported in Conejos, where they had gone to get supplies (perhaps at Lafe's store), that they had prospected the Rio Grande River's tributaries with some luck. La Loma de San José was established along the upper Rio Grande (after it turns west) in the spring of 1859 by fourteen families from Santa Fe, Ojo Caliente, and Conejos; and it became another early San Juan supply town along with Conejos.

William Gilpin, the first Territorial Governor of Colorado, issued $375,000 in worthless drafts just before the beginning of the Civil War.

Hall's *History of Colorado, Vol. 1.*

Charles Baker and six men first came into the San Juans in July of 1860 by going over Poncha Pass, then over Cochetopa Pass, then down Tomichi Creek and a short way on the Gunnison River, up the Lake Fork of the Gunnison River to Cinnamon Pass, and finally down from the headwaters of the Animas River to what was named Baker's Park. They found signs of gold and silver along the Lake Fork and the Animas Rivers, but nothing spectacular. However, when Baker returned to Denver in the fall of 1860, he reported that a major discovery had been made in what came to be called "Baker's Park," and that the men had recovered twenty-five cents **per pan** in gold, which would be about ten dollars a day when wages were about a third of that amount. He also wrote to the *Santa Fe Gazette* predicting that "there will be no less than 25,000 Americans engaged in mining and agricultural pursuits (in the San Juans)…within a year, perhaps double that number." The *Rocky Mountain News* also printed Baker's letter, in which he stated he

CHAPTER 7

was unhappy to learn that some people were going to come into the area from the north. Baker himself then went to Denver, had an interview with William N. Byers of the *Rocky Mountain News* in which he gave the proposed new route, and set off from Denver with a much larger party, which varied in size as people gave up, joined the group, stopped because of problems, or rode ahead of the main group trying to get to the "diggings" first.

Instead of going up the Lake Fork River as Baker did the first time, or even the Rio Grande River as some other prospectors did in 1859 and 1860, the second Baker Party (1860-1861) made a very circuitous route. The party went down the Front Range and over Sangre de Cristo Pass in the middle of the winter and almost had a disaster:

> On the 14th of December 1860 they left Denver… their party ranging at different times on the journey all the way from one hundred to three hundred persons.… They traveled south by way of Colorado City and Pueblo, crossing the Sangre de Cristo Mountains through Sangre de Cristo Pass. Here they suffered greatly from the inclement weather and the difficulties of travel. Roads had to be built and there was no feed for their stock except that obtained by cutting down trees for them to browse upon. They were fourteen days crossing the mountains. After getting down into San Luis Park, they were overtaken by a terrific storm of wind and snow that scattered their stock and caused intense suffering to many of the people. Wagon boxes and other property were burned for fuel. **On the 4th of March they passed Conejos** (emphasis added) and traveled thence via Abiqui, Chama River and Pagosa Springs. April 1 they reached Cascade Creek.[73]

Although we do not know all the details, we do know that much of the party stopped at Conejos—those in better shape for only a day or so rest; those in worse shape for several weeks while they tried to regain their strength, buy more animals, or repair their wagons. During this time some of the leaders of the group talked to Lafayette Head. Lafe probably knew at least the first half of the route that they needed to follow (the portion to the future Durango) because of his time in Abiqui, interaction with traders who came down the Old Spanish Trail, and his stint as Arriba County Sheriff and U.S. Deputy Marshal. Not only did Baker want to know the route, but he also talked Lafe and some of the other Conejos locals into signing his paperwork as founders of a toll road to Baker's Park, which ultimately became the route into the central San Juans from the south.

It is unknown if Lafe traded food or animals for a stake in the road, paid for partial ownership of the road, or was made a part owner for giving advice and directions. Or it might be that the New Mexico men signed the toll road petition because New Mexico's laws required a certain number of New Mexico signers and many of the incorporators were not citizens of New Mexico Territory. Throughout his life, Lafe never seemed to be interested in prospecting, but he and other residents of Conejos may have had hopes to "mine the miner" by selling them food, lumber, and supplies. Lafe also knew more roads and bridges were badly needed in the San Luis Valley at this time and now had a chance to get part of the future tolls from those traveling the route. Baker left the toll company the next year. However, Lafayette and several other signers of the original petition claimed to still have ownership as late as 1869 and perhaps later.

Lafe, as an Indian Agent, probably kept a pretty close eye on Baker and his parties, as they were traveling into the heart of Ute land. Perhaps that is the reason he did not go with them, but he apparently did not try to stop them, and he must have warned them about the danger. The men who later traveled the Baker Toll Road into the San Juans from the south were in dangerous territory. In one day, one party traveling over the route

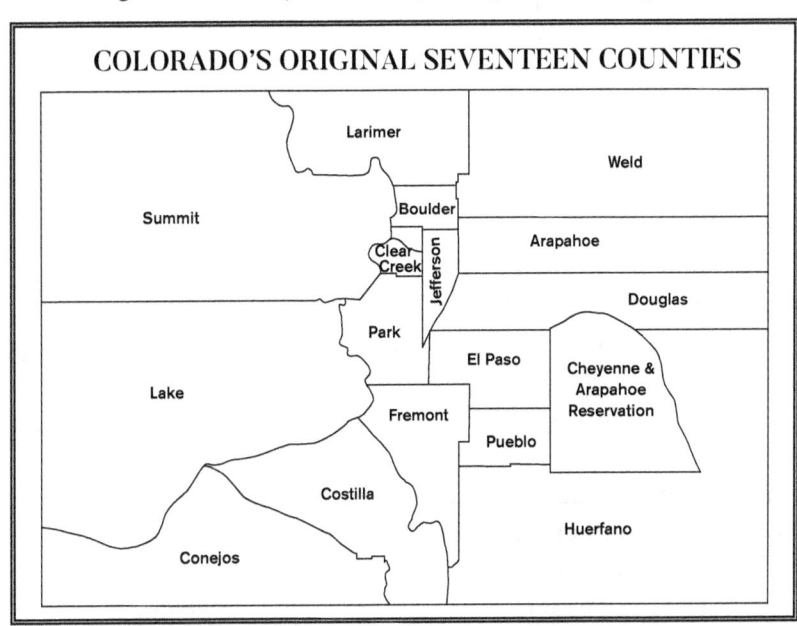

Colorado originally had seventeen counties, and Conejos County was huge— running all the way to the Utah border. The dividing line between Costilla and Conejos was the Rio Grande River.

Western Reflections Publishing Co. Map.

CHAPTER 7

found sixteen bodies of men killed by Indians. Lafe reported that the killings were done by the Navajo, who altogether had killed forty Americans and fifteen Mexicans along the road by 1862. Another of the travelers on the toll road was a merchant carrying his first load of goods to Baker's Park, and he was forced to trade his goods on the road for four Navajo children. Then the fledgling settlement of Animas City was set on fire by the Native Americans, probably the Navajo.

"The San Juan Excitement" was short-lived at this time, as the 1861 prospectors only averaged about twenty-five cents a day instead of the per pan that they had been told they could expect. By the time Baker got back to Fort Garland that winter, all was quiet again in the San Juan Mountains and would remain so for about a decade. On his way back to civilization, Baker and a few companions reported they were well received at the fort. Fort Garland's hospitality was also recognized by C. H. Adens a few years after Baker was there:

> *Then to the accompaniment of music by four native performers (Mexican-Americans) all gave themselves up to the enjoyments of the dance. The señoritas in their best array, the soldiers in their well-brushed uniforms made as fine an assemblage as could be seen anywhere, and notwithstanding the frequent visits which custom sanctioned to the adjoining room where the drinkables of all kinds were afforded, the most perfect good order and decorum prevailed.... Again and again did the unwearied dancers respond to the flowing music of the slow waltz... and unconscious of the lapse of time, the night sped on until the drums of reveille (day break) awoke them from their trance. After a hearty breakfast the visitors began to return home....*[74]

The San Luis Valley flour mills were now getting unexpected orders from Whites in the Denver and Boulder area as the *Rocky Mountain News* had announced that after October 1860 flour would be available in the San Luis Valley.

Meanwhile, Colorado, with the discovery of more rich metals, was on its way to becoming a territory. In 1860, the U.S. Congress began discussion of the possibility of forming what it hoped would be two new states—Colorado and Nebraska. However, in the 1860 census, only 35,000 people were shown as living in future Colorado, not counting Native Americans, who ironically were not considered citizens (Native Americans were not made citizens until 1926 unless they were paying income tax). Because of the impending Civil War, many Colorado men were leaving at the time to go back East to their "home state" to fight, but Colorado was an especially desirable area for annexation because of its newly discovered gold, which could help finance the war for either side in the Civil War. As mentioned, most of the gold and silver veins in the Denver/Boulder area had been staked, and many prospectors were also leaving because of their disappointment. For these and other reasons, Colorado's population was dropping drastically; and, there was even some doubt as to Colorado's eligibility as a Territory, which required 25,000 citizens to be living in the area. Furthermore, the Indian question was far from settled in Colorado. The Utes were co-existing with the Americans and were fighting the Plains Indians near Denver, especially the Arapaho. Since the Denver area was a favorite Ute and Arapaho campsite, both tribes often passed through the area. Sometimes during 1859 to 1862, one tribe or the other would bring fresh scalps they had taken from other tribes into Denver.

The name of the proposed new territory or state that would become Colorado was changed several times. At first it was called "Jefferson," then on January 30, 1861, it was proposed that the name "Jefferson" be changed to "Idaho." The name "Lafayette" was even suggested, but it is not known if this is a reference to Lafayette Head. On February 4, 1861, the name was changed to Colorado. Then on February 6, Illinois Senator Stephen Douglas argued that Congress should reconsider having the southern boundary of the proposed Colorado at the 38th Parallel. He argued that as it stood the boundary was not consistent with the Treaty of Guadalupe Hidalgo. There was a great debate about whether any part, all, or none of the San Luis Valley would be included in the new Territory or State of Colorado. With the vast majority of the valley area being Spanish-speaking residents, there was a valid position that it should remain in New Mexico Territory. Don Miguel Otero, the non-voting delegate to Congress from New Mexico Territory, argued vehemently that the residents of "the northern bit of the New Mexico Territory were 'homogenous' with and should stay a part of New Mexico Territory."[75]

The San Luis Valley had long been considered Spanish, then Mexican territory; however, the other side of the argument was that the San Luis Valley had received nearly all of its non-Native American residents in just the five or six years before Colorado Territory was being considered. Before that time, all of the future Colorado was totally controlled by Native Americans. Some U.S. legislators admitted they were simply trying to get as much territory as possible into a slave-free state. New Mexico had slaves, but many U.S. legislators did not realize they were left over from the Spanish system and were mainly Native Americans with very few blacks in New Mexico.

CHAPTER 7

Some Congressmen actually said they simply preferred straight lines for state boundaries, because they felt "it looked better on a map."

The reference to "straight lines" was that the north boundary of New Mexico which ran along the 38th Parallel, but only to the Continental Divide where it then went south to the 37th Parallel. The resulting bump was called "The New Mexico Notch." The notch had been formed when New Mexico Territory had been created, and the area north of it was to be designated "Unorganized Territory." The Territory of Utah was on the western side of the Continental Divide and the notch, was cut out of what would become Utah Territory because it was an area that was much more like New Mexico than Utah. The notch also included the Sangre de Cristo Mountains on the east, including the towns of Walsenburg and Trinidad and north all the way to the headwaters of the Rio Grande in the San Juans. The same argument was now made that the notch, which included the settled part of the San Luis Valley, should be left as part of New Mexico.

New Mexico's Congressional delegate, Otero, fought hard to keep the notch with New Mexico, claiming that the culture of The Valley required it be so, as well as The Treaty of Guadalupe-Hidalgo having that intent. On February 6, Senator Stephen Douglas made an impassioned speech that giving the notch back to New Mexico avoided "raising the slavery question,"

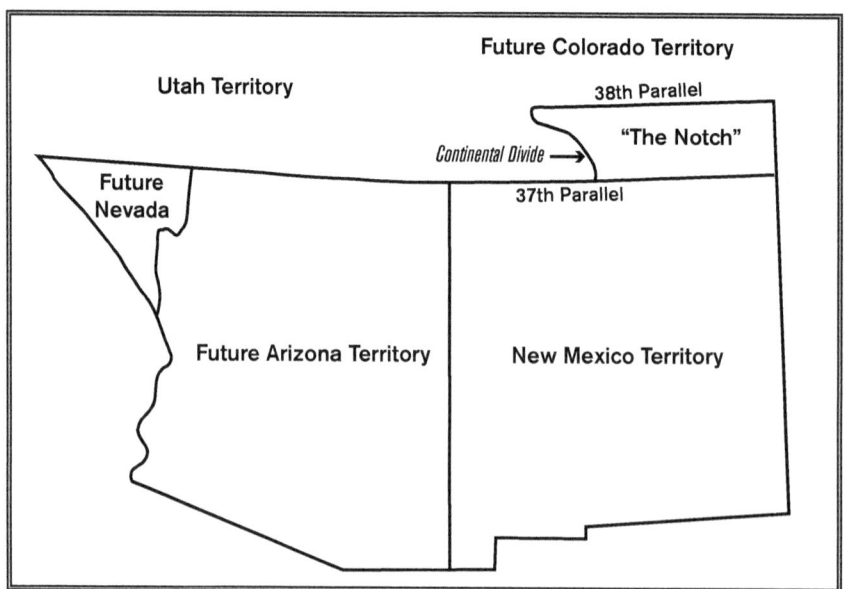

New Mexico was eventually divided into two states and a portion given to Nevada.

Map modified from Thompson, "Don Miguel Antonio Otero and the New Mexico Notch."

and the notch went back to New Mexico. Then the bill went to the House of Representatives, and Colorado supporters rallied others to their side on the final vote. The 37th Parallel instead of the 38th (the more northerly) parallel would be Colorado's southern boundary, and it would also encompass much of the former Utah Territory. On February 4, 1861, The New Mexico Notch was officially given to Colorado Territory.

Colorado Territory was created from western Kansas Territory, eastern Utah Territory, and small bits of Nebraska and New Mexico Territory. Using the 37th parallel as the boundary made most of the San Luis Valley a part of Colorado. However, a surprising twist was coming. The residents of what was to be the State of Colorado voted not to become a state, but instead chose to be a territory. Becoming a territory meant the federal government would pay the costs of territorial administration; when, as a state, Colorado residents would be taxed to pay those expenses.

On September 9, 1861, the first Territorial Congress convened with Lafe having been elected a new legislator and with Hiram P. Bennett the new representative to Congress (territories were only allowed one non-voting representative). Most of the estimated 7,000 private citizens and all the government officials of the San Luis Valley and northern New Mexico had wanted to remain in New Mexico Territory. Their language, culture, and heritage were all closely tied to New Mexico. The issue of Colorado Territory's southern boundary was therefore seriously debated in Congress for several more years; and even today, it is obvious that the middle of the extreme southern part of Colorado is much more similar to the State of New Mexico than to the rest of Colorado.

Hiram P. Bennett was the first Colorado Territorial Congressman. Territories only were allowed one delegate to Congress who did not have the right to vote but who could make a speech and sit in with elected officials.

Hall, *History of Colorado*, Vol. 1.

When Colorado Territory was formed, there were three huge counties (Conejos, Lake, and Summit) that included most of the San Luis Valley land west of the Rio Grande and the southern part of the Western Slope of

CHAPTER 7

Colorado, running all the way to today's Utah border. Costilla County was on the east side of the Rio Grande, but also took in the all of the San Luis Valley north of the Big Bend. Conejos County was on the west, and ran all the way to the present-day Utah state line

The southern half of the San Juans east of the Continental Divide was in Taos County, New Mexico, until Colorado became a territory. The settlement of Taos was the county seat until that time. After Colorado became a territory on February 28, 1861, the northern San Juans from about present-day Silverton on the north was partially in Costilla County and partially in Lake County in the new Colorado Territory. After December 29, 1866, part of the northern San Juans was also in Saguache County, which had been carved out of Lake County. Over the next thirty-two years, a total of thirteen counties would be carved out of the San Juan Mountains. Because of the rugged San Juan Mountain terrain, it was very difficult in the middle or northern San Juan Mountains to know which county you were in.

The Territory of Colorado was officially created November 1, 1861, by the United States Congress at the same period of time as the southern

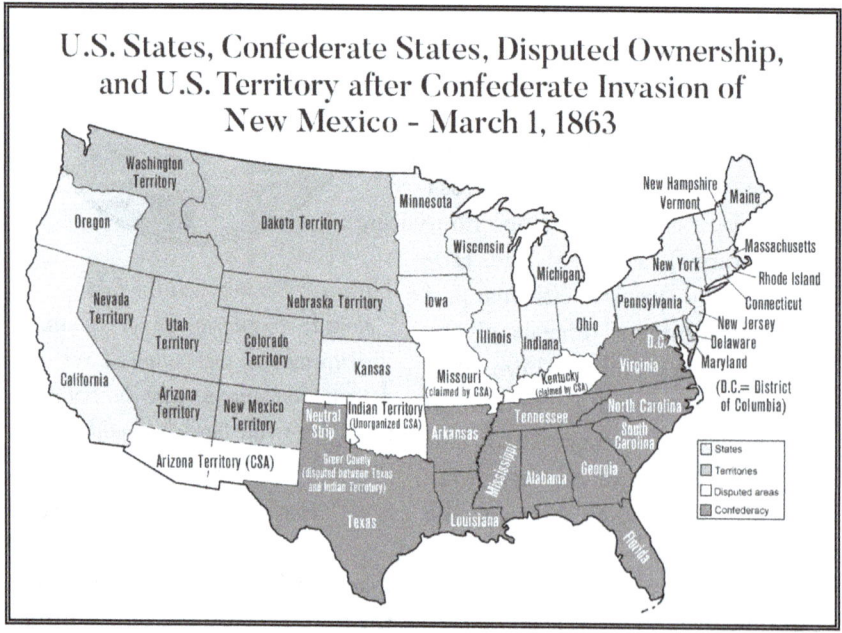

The United States after Confederates invaded New Mexico in March 1863. Colorado, Kansas, Washington, and Nebraska Territories and the State of Oregon have been formed and the Gadson Purchase in southern New Mexico had been made.

Courtesy of *Colorado Encyclopedia*.

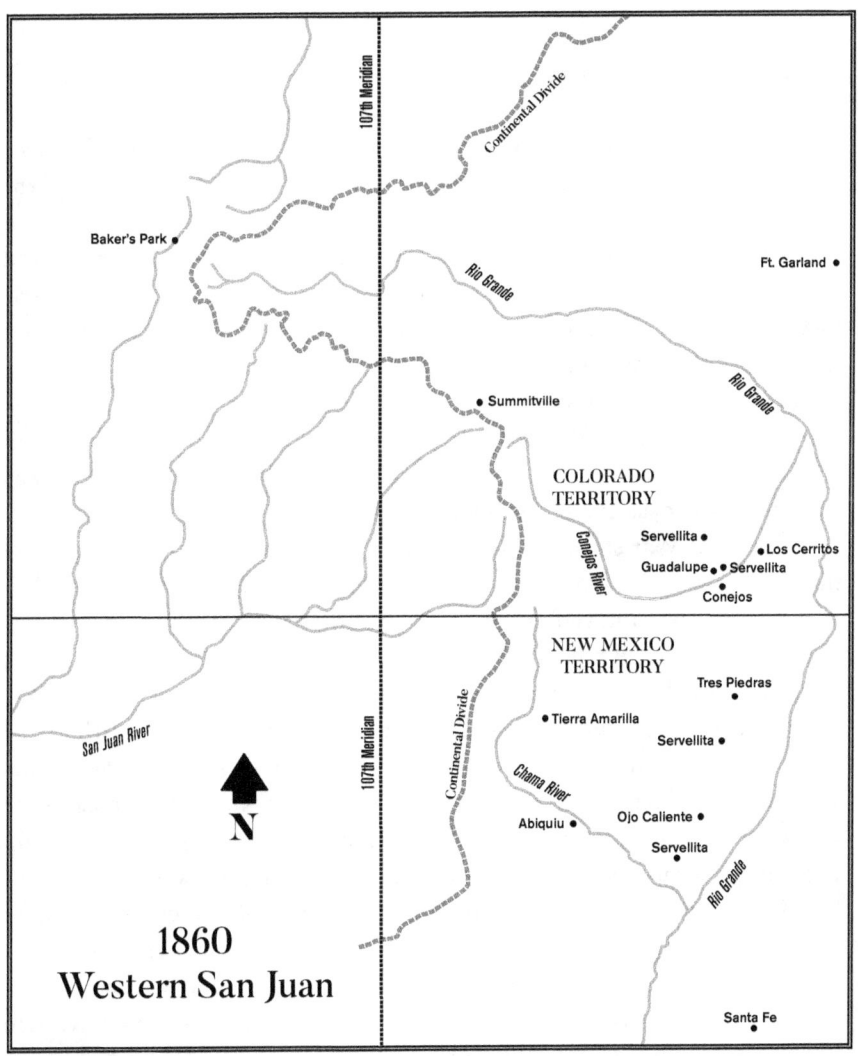

Map showing the early settlements named Servellita in the San Luis Valley on the west side of the Rio Grande in 1860.

Western Reflections Publishing Co. Map.

states were seceding from the Union. New Mexico had been a U.S. Territory since September 9, 1850. "Guadalupe County" was created on November 1, 1861, as part of the new Colorado territory; but, although the settlement of Conejos was smaller, the name was changed within a week (on November 7, 1861) from Guadalupe to "Conejos County." The reason for the change in the county's name and the county seat was probably that Lafayette Head requested it in the Colorado Territorial legislature.

CHAPTER 7

The prospectors in the San Juan Mountains would have known little of the national news; but if they had, they would have known that the Civil War was fast approaching. Abraham Lincoln, who favored the abolishment of slavery, was elected in November of 1860 and took office as President of the United States in January 1861. In February of that year, Jefferson Davis became the President of the Confederate States of America, and on February 28, 1861, the U.S. accepted Colorado as a prospective territory and outlined the procedure to be followed to make it official. Jefferson Territory was terminated, but with many of its actions later ratified or made into law by the new Colorado Territorial Legislature. In April of 1861, the first shots of the Civil War were fired. The main reason Lincoln appointed William Gilpin as the first territorial governor of Colorado was that he was strongly against slavery and was a Unionist.

The Civil War started in the East, so the western territories had a little time to prepare before the war spread to the West. Colorado and New Mexico Territories stayed in the Union, but there were many Confederates in both territories. At the outbreak of the war, Kit Carson enlisted and was made a Colonel in the New Mexico Volunteers of the Union Army. Albert Pfeiffer also joined and became Carson's right hand man during the Civil War. Lafe filled in for his two friends, while Indian Agent replacements were sought, which was not an easy task. Lafe was asked not to enlist in the army, since his experience as an Indian Agent was greatly needed to help keep the Colorado Native Americans peaceful during the war.

The isolation of the West from that portion of the country east of the Mississippi River made it hard to defend the area. Most people felt that the winner of the Civil War would take the entire West. There were even worries that Mexico might try to take Colorado and New Mexico back during America's "War between the States." With the beginning of the war, most of Fort Garland's regular federal troops were sent to the East and were replaced by Colorado volunteers. In 1861 and 1862, Fort Garland was a Union volunteer enlistment center and a rendezvous point for the Union soldiers in the area. During the Civil War, the War Department neglected Colorado's forts as they were nowhere near the war zone; and the Colorado forts basically became social centers for activities and entertainment for Union soldiers and local settlers. After Colorado became a territory, Lafe stopped by Fort Garland often on his way to, or coming back from the new territorial capitals of Colorado City and then, after 1862, Golden. Most Union troops in Colorado were either at Fort Lyon or Fort Garland; and Colorado and New Mexico were basically in charge of their own defense.

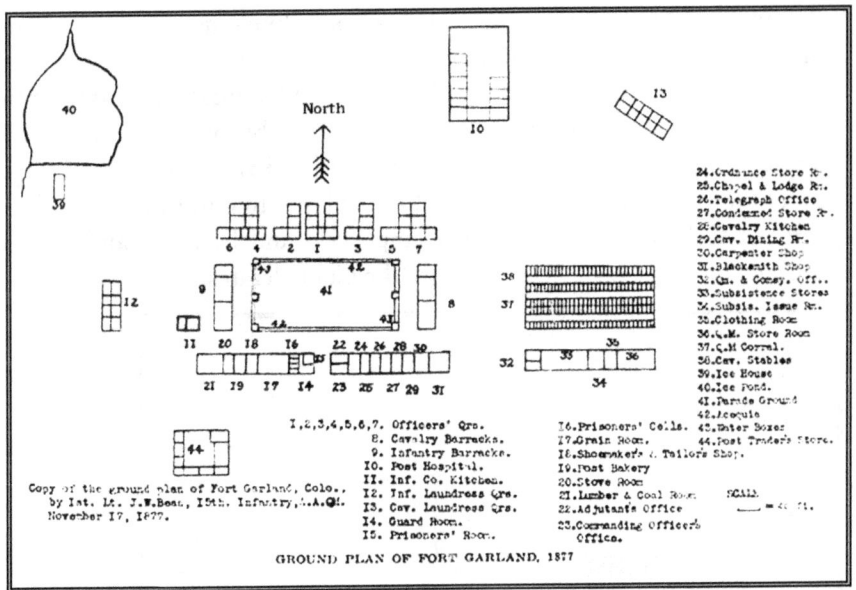

A sketch of Ft. Garland in 1877 showing use of space and new additions.

Courtesy of Ft. Garland Museum.

The First Regiment of Colorado Volunteers was formed at Camp Weld near Denver; and the 2nd and 3rd Colorado Volunteers were formed in Cañon City, and were soon marched to Fort Garland. John Chivington became the commander of the Colorado Volunteers in Colorado on November 1, 1862, and Kit Carson helped organize the 1st Regiment of New Mexico Volunteers and became the first commander of that regiment. Those Colorado Territory residents who did not join the military during the Civil War were generally pro-Union, and most Colorado Confederates hid their affiliation or left the territory.

Governor William Gilpin had a major problem. His territory was brand new and, although the need was not seen to be as great as back East, it had few funds of its own to defend itself from the Confederacy. Nearby Texas had joined the Confederacy and many believed that New Mexico would do the same or would soon be conquered by Texas. This was one of the main reasons Charles Baker had made his loop to travel into the San Juans from the south. He wanted New Mexico to be a Confederate state, including the mineral riches of the San Juans. He had hoped to encourage migration into the San Juans from New Mexico and not from the Union-leaning Denver/Boulder area.

CHAPTER 7

Immediately upon taking office, Governor Gilpin requested funds from Washington to outfit the Colorado volunteers, but the money did not come. In desperation, he issued drafts on banks with U.S. funds in Washington without having the authorization to do so. Most businesses in Colorado accepted Gilpin's drafts, which eventually totaled $375,000. It was a huge sum of money in those days, and it allowed Gilpin to outfit the three companies of Colorado Volunteers at Camp Weld and Fort Garland, which were soon sent to New Mexico to fight the Confederates.

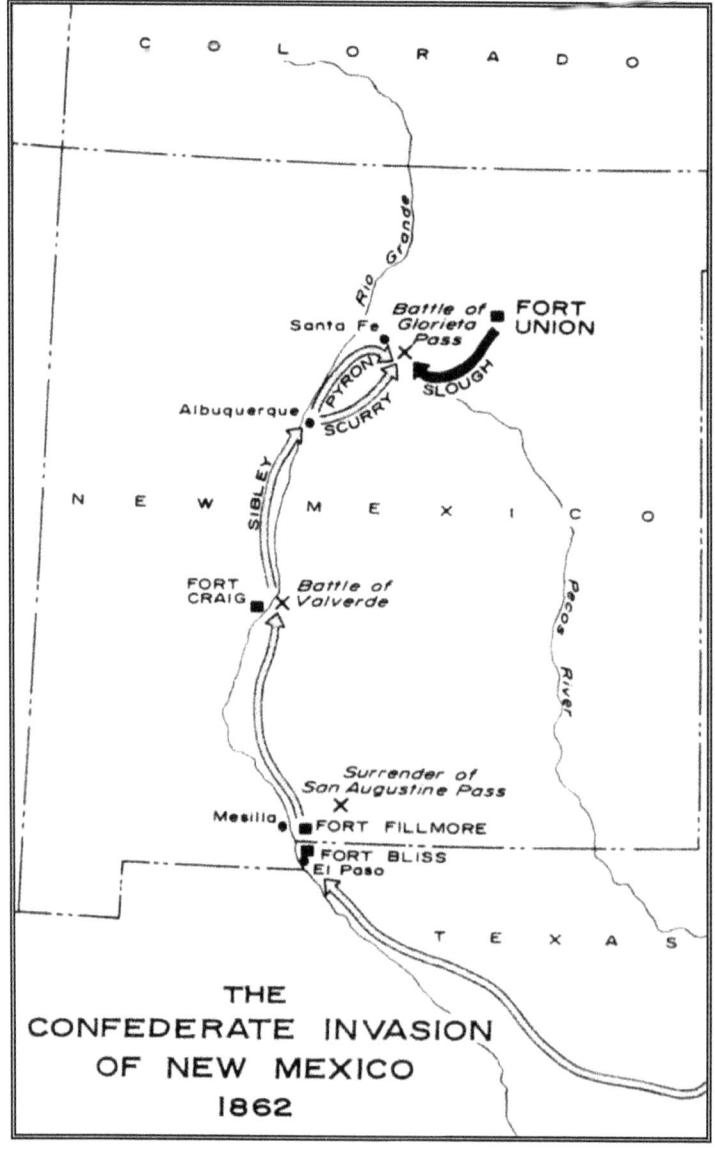

Map showing Confederate battles in New Mexico in 1862.

Courtesy National Park Service.

When the Gilpin drafts were not honored by the federal treasury, the local Colorado merchants, farmers, and ranchers who had received them as payment were outraged and turned against Gilpin. It would be part of the reason he would soon be relieved of his position as Territorial Governor, but Gilpin was also relieved of office because of his scandalous land and business dealings.

Colonel Edward R. S. Canaby, the commander at Fort Craig in New Mexico, began to assemble all the troops that he could muster. He had quickly asked Colorado to send reinforcements, and on December 14, 1861, eighty-four men were sent from Fort Garland to New Mexico. Two more companies soon followed. Canaby then moved his troops to Fort Union. The Civil War reached southern New Mexico in July 1862, when Confederate forces left El Paso and came north up the Rio Grande River. On February 20 and 21, 1863, the Confederates defeated New Mexico Union volunteers and the few U.S. Army regulars who had stayed in New Mexico at the Battle of Valverde. At that point, southern New Mexico was declared to be a Confederate state. Colorado and the San Luis Valley were now definitely in danger of being attacked. On March 23, 1863, the Confederates occupied Santa Fe. Union soldiers from Fort Union and the volunteer units from Colorado met the Texans at Glorieta Pass on March 26 to 28. Some of the Union soldiers made a loop around the Texans and captured their large supply train. They then burned seventy-three wagons filled with supplies and killed 600 horses and mules, leaving the Confederates with no option but to retreat. After another battle at Perleta on April 14 and 15, the Texans left New Mexico. The Colorado forces then returned to Colorado, and under the leadership of Kit Carson turned their attention to the Navajo.

Back in the San Luis Valley in 1861, Lafe, who had become a very important link between the Mexican-Americans and Anglo-Americans in New Mexico Territory, now had become even more important as an elected representative to the new Colorado Territorial legislature. However Lafe's reputation among the Utes was hurting after establishing their Agency at Conejos on August 25, 1860. The Tabeguache Agency had been closed at Abiqui in late 1859. Lafe had been appointed Conejos agent on June 27, 1860, and the Agency was moved to Conejos. Lafe had only been allocated $1,000 in expenses and food besides his and his interpreter's salaries ($750 and $175 respectively) for the rest of that year for the almost 2,000 Utes who had come to the Conejos Agency as soon as it opened. The government had only allocated $2,600 to $4,600 for the next fiscal year, but Lafe could not explain "a fiscal year" to the Utes, little less why the money needed had not been allocated.

CHAPTER 7

In 1861 the Utes were still short on food and complaining that Head had not distributed rations fairly. The Utes said they did not like Head because he had no money to buy them "presents." They felt he must be robbing them, as they were not getting what was promised from the federal government. The Utes thought the U.S. government would never lie or cheat them. They did not realize that the failure to get their rations was the U.S. government's fault, not that of Lafayette Head. A delegation of Utes even went to Fort Garland to complain, and a young sub-chief named Ouray told the commander that they thought Lafe was selling their supplies and pocketing the money. The Utes said their sugar had dirt in it, and that the rice supplied them had worms. Further, many hardware items were defective. They also complained that the Ute interpreter at Conejos could not speak Ute. On the other hand, new Territorial Governor William Gilpin was describing Head in 1861 as "a most efficient and competent officer, a sincere Republican, and friend of the administration and greatly respected by the Mexicans whose language he speaks fluently."[76] Unfortunately Head could only speak a little Ute at the time.

The Utes had not understood that Lafe had to get the money for their food and supplies from Washington, and that when the "Great White Father" did not keep his promises to send food or money, Head had even used his own credit to try to keep them fed. The Utes had been especially upset when Head suggested they be moved to western Colorado, but it was an honest opinion shared by Kit Carson that eventually became necessary. Both men backed off this position, but only for a while.

By 1861, Carson was actually feeling bad about withholding Ute annuities and knew it was not the solution to their misbehavior. The Utes and Jicarilla Apache were starving. Carson wrote:

> *Scarcely a day passes but I have from five to twenty-five to feed and take care of, their only resource is upon the Government and as they come in I must provide for them and send them away, only to be visited again when their supplies are exhausted.*[77]

Head now estimated that he had 8,000 Utes under his care, but that figure was definitely high. Governor Merriweather and Head had originally estimated the number of Tabeguache at 5,000, but the actual number was closer to 4,000. Due to disease brought by Americans, the fact that the Tabeguache were starving, and wars with the Plains Indians, there was no doubt that the actual number of Utes was shrinking fairly fast.

It did not help that some deplorable incidents were occurring frequently at Taos, where the Kit Carson Agency was located. For example in 1861:

> *An Indian of the Utah tribe was in Taos recently where certain parties are said to have gotten him drunk, then to have saturated his clothing with turpentine and set fire to the clothing.... From the effect of the burning the Indian is said to have died. The Utah tribe to which he belonged is ... very incensed at this unhuman outrage and threatened to be avenged.*[78]

Events like this happened so often in Taos that after Kit Carson's resignation as Agent so as to enter the Union Army in 1861, the Agency for the Mouache and Jicarilla was moved to Maxwell's Ranch. The Capote stayed in Abiqui and the Tabeguache with Lafe in Conejos. The new Mouache Agency site was on the Cimarron east across the Sangre de Cristo Mountains, so that they would be further away from the "Taos Lightning" being made there. However, the move did not help much, as there were soon people making and delivering whiskey near Maxwell's Ranch, as well as that area being described as a den of inequity with prostitutes and gambling. One author said it had a reputation for debauchery with gambling, women, and cheap whiskey in abundance.

The town of Conejos remained a Mexican-American community, and its farm products and livestock were still badly needed in the Denver/Boulder area. Besides becoming a spokesman for southern Colorado's Mexican-American farmers and ranchers, as a Tabeguache Ute Indian Agent Lafe was about to become an important link with the Utes, the federal government, and the government of the new Territory of Colorado. The San Luis Valley flour mills were getting unexpected orders from the Anglos in Denver, California Gulch, and Boulder.

Lafe used his home and then a building nearby as the Ute Agency headquarters, and he often had hundreds of Utes camped around his plaza. During the time he was Agent, he ran a school, a general store, and a stable, that were associated with the Agency. However, in addition, he farmed, ranched, milled, and operated his own store and stables for the Americans in the area. Lafe spoke Spanish fluently, but not much Ute, so he badly needed a good interpreter.

At the suggestion of Kit Carson, twenty-six year old Ouray would soon be appointed to fill that position. It was a very smart move on Carson's part. At this time Ouray was just an unknown but bright young sub-chief, but he was of great benefit to Lafe in his efforts to explain that he was trying to help the Utes. Even though Ouray had been critical of Lafe's Agency

CHAPTER 7

Ouray and his brother Quinche were two of the Utes that went to Washington City in 1863. This is thought to be the earliest photograph of them transferred into a drawing to be published in a French book, Le Tour Du Monde *in 1868.*

Author's Collection.

work in the past, Lafe hired him to fill the position of interpreter. He gave Lafe wonderful insight into Ute life and the way the Utes were thinking. Ouray was just at the beginning of his rise to influence, and because he had been indentured to a Mexican family during his younger years, Ouray could speak fluent Spanish. Ouray did not know many of his people's ways or much English, but he learned quickly. He did, however, have perhaps the best understanding of European life of any other Ute. Ouray often traveled to Conejos just to listen to other Ute chiefs discuss tribal matters. He also soon gained a reputation as an adept and ferocious hunter and warrior, and he could ride, shoot, and use a knife better than most of the other Utes. No one wanted to cross Ouray. He loved to fight, and he killed several men for Chief Nevava just to enforce discipline within the Ute tribe.

Kit Carson often talked to Ouray about Ute-American relations, and when Carson had brought up the idea that the Utes needed a treaty so they would own their land under U.S. law, Ouray passed the idea on to Chief Nevava. At first Nevava just laughed and said that there was no need for that, as everyone knew the Utes owned the southern Rockies. They had lived there "forever," and they would only be demeaning themselves to ask the white man for something they already owned. However, Ouray pressed the matter, and Nevava finally sent him to California Gulch (the future Leadville) to see what the white men were up to. Ouray came back to report many thousands of white men were swarming around the mountains in just that area, and that many were shooting at the Utes on sight. Even at this early date Ouray felt that it was just a matter of time before the white man would take all of the Ute territory.

New roads, bridges, and ferries in the San Luis Valley were making traveling easier. Lafe was able to help the transportation problem by building several new bridges or ferries at strategic points across the Rio Grande River; and until the bridges were finished, he and his partners had the authority to operate ferries for up to five years at the approximate bridge sites. In 1861, Lafe and José Maria Jacques helped establish a ferry over the Rio Grande River just south of where the present bridge goes to the town of San Luis from the area of Conejos. Before this time there had been a ford at the spot, but it was very dangerous and impossible during the spring run-off. The ferries and bridges allowed the settlers to easily get back and forth across the Rio Grande River, and it did much to tie the two sides of the San Luis Valley together.

Concord stages were now beginning to run on the main roads in The Valley. These stages carried up to thirteen passengers and were pulled by two to six horses. Horses were switched every eight to ten miles. The emphasis was speed of travel and not necessarily comfort, and a change of horses only took four minutes. In July of 1861, the first Barlow and Sanderson Concord stage arrived in the San Luis Valley, and in 1862, there was a free road from Cisco to "Head's Ferry" and another free road from Head's home to the south boundary of Colorado Territory.

Besides Baker's toll road, Lafe had joined Baker's "Rio Arriba Bridge Company" in 1860. Their largest project proposal was to build a bridge across the Rio Grande River near the point where the Chama River meets the Rio Grande. The New Mexico Territorial Legislature approved the project on January 22, 1861. Twenty men were owners in the company,

CHAPTER 7

including Lafe, Albert Pfeiffer, and Charles Baker; so it is very likely that this bridge was a connection with the previously mentioned toll road to Baker's Park.

In October 1861, Lafe met with John M. Francisco, the sutler (civilian merchant) at Fort Garland from November 4, 1856 until 1862. Francisco was involved with Fort Garland even before it was built, as he was the supply contractor for the adobe bricks that were used to build the fort. He had a large cattle ranch in partnership with Henry Daigre and supplied meat to Fort Garland as well to Fort Union and two other forts. He was now a Territorial Senator from the San Luis Valley. Francisco and Lafe applied to the new Colorado Territorial Legislature for permission to establish a ferry and bridge on the Rio Grande River at the small Mexican-American settlement of La Loma, which was established in 1859. At the time it was the northernmost settlement in the San Luis Valley and the only settlement located on the north side of the Rio Grande after it turned west near Alamosa. The two men obviously recognized

Colonel J. M. Francisco was an early settler in the San Luis Valley but moved to the Cucharas Valley after the Civil War started. At one time he supplied four Colorado forts as their sutler and ran a large cattle ranch.

Hall, History of Colorado, Vol. 1.

the importance of that spot for getting into the San Juan Mountains and also realized that it would probably be used by U.S. government troops stationed at Fort Garland who might be fighting Utes or Confederate rebels. Francisco was a Confederate supporter, which was why he left his job at Fort Garland in 1862. At that time he built Francisco Plaza north of the Spanish Peaks near the Cucharas River. This was his headquarters for a trading post, farm, and his cattle operation.

Although, La Loma would eventually be totally outdone by nearby Del Norte (Del Norte was a new town organized by mainly Americans directly across the Rio Grande), on November 7, 1861, a bill was passed authorizing the ferry across the Rio Grande at La Loma until the year 1900. Then it would become the property of the State or Territory of Colorado. During that time, no one else could have a bridge or ferry within 2 ½ miles up or downstream.

Rates were set by the legislature at $2 for a wagon with two horses, mules or oxen, and $1 for a single horse, mule and buggy. A single rider on a horse or mule was fifty cents, loose horses, mules, cows or burros were ten cents each, and sheep or swine cost five cents each. Head was to have a business and personal relationship with John Francisco for the rest of their lives.

With the better roads and bridges, on February 25, 1862, Thomas J. Barnum carried the first official U.S. mail from Pueblo to the towns in the San Luis Valley.[79] The first Colorado mails had arrived in Denver on August 10, 1860. Previously the stage from Denver charged twenty-five cents to carry each letter back East to be mailed. Barnum had just recently been hired for the job of postman and his pockets bulged with letters, as his mail bags had not yet arrived (it would be two more months before they did). To reach the San Luis Valley, Barnum followed trails over the Sangre de Cristo Mountains. There were still no completed bridges over the Rio Grande River, but some of the Rio Grande ferries were evidently operational. However, there were no bridges or ferries over the Culebra, Trinchera, or Costilla Rivers, and their waters ran deep and fast from snow melt in the spring and early summer. Only one horse was used by Barnum for the entire trip.

Delivering the mail was never tougher than in the winter from Pueblo or Denver to the San Luis Valley.

Crofutt, *Crofutt's Grip Sack Guide.*

CHAPTER 7

The mail route Barnum followed was used three times a week, depending on weather, floods, and hostile Indians. There was very little civilization along the route, and Barnum kept a constant watch out for unfriendly Native Americans and wild animals. Barnum recounted that the few ranches along the way were "scarcer than angel's visits." Lafe welcomed the stranger when he arrived in Conejos and offered him a meal. The first letter Lafe received in Conejos contained his commission as postmaster for the Town of Conejos.

There were now a string of small villages along the Conejos River from Los Cerrites to Las Mesitas. The Head household was the center of activities along the Conejos River. His home was a half mile north of the Conejos County courthouse, and his flour mill adjoined his plaza. There were many merchants in the town, which made it the principal trading area of the southern San Luis Valley. The opening of the new Tabeguache Ute Agency at Conejos in 1860 also helped spur on business in the town. Utes would come to trade furs for goods such as tobacco, cooking utensils, and powder and lead to use for their guns. The area farmers had a place to sell flour and vegetables to the Americans, and the Utes traded for food and goods that were not included in their annuities.

Because Head and his interpreter, Ouray, were together a lot, Ouray began to see that it was the U.S. government not Head that was causing most of the Utes' problems, and that Lafe was actually trying to help the Ute people by getting them to take title to their remaining land. On March 21, 1862, new Governor John Evans arrived in Denver and he took office on March 26, 1862. On June 6, 1862, the *Rocky Mountain News Daily* reported that Lafe, Carson, and Ouray were in Denver on business with the new Territorial Governor John Evans who had replaced Gilpin and was now also Superintendent of Indian Affairs. Gilpin's worthless drafts may have possibly saved Colorado, but they had cost him his job. Ouray told the government that all the Utes would

John Evans, second Territorial Governor of Colorado, served for three years but favored the attack on the Native Americans at Sand Creek and was asked to resign by President Andrew Johnson.

Hall, *History of Colorado, Vol. 1.*

be friendly and agree to a reservation of 5.8 million acres in the mid-section of Colorado, but he wanted the Tabeguache to get ownership of the heartland of Colorado Territory's mountains, plus the Utes wanted $10,000 in supplies per year, monthly rations of food for ten years, 150 cattle per year for five years, five "Virginia Stallions," and 1,000 sheep annually for two years, then 500 sheep a year for three years. Evans accepted the proposal on the spot, but unfortunately this would only be an agreement with the Territory of Colorado and not the United States, and nothing significant happened to fulfill the plan.[80]

Lafe attended the Golden City Convention while in Denver as a delegate of the southern portion of Colorado Territory. Delegates were from all over the Territory. The *News* noted that Lafe "desired to cultivate relations with this (the northern) portion of the Territory, which will be mutually beneficial." At this time the purpose was simply to get people from all over the state together, but Lafe would go on to be an important part of the entire state's ranching and agricultural community.

Over the years, Lafe continued to join many organizations, mostly in an attempt to unite the southern part with the central and northern portions of the Territory and later State of Colorado. On July 13, 1861, thirty-two prominent citizens issued a message via the *Weekly Colorado Republican* and *The Rocky Mountain Herald* newspapers. They called for a convention on July 31, the purpose of which would be to "organize a society to assist in the development of our Agriculture resources…." Among those thirty-two citizens were William Gilpin (first Governor of Colorado Territory), Thomas Gibson (founder of the *Rocky Mountain Herald* newspaper), Alexander Majors (founder of the Pony Express), William Larimer, Jr. (one of the founders of Denver), and Indian Agents Amos Steck, A.G. Boone, and Lafayette Head. The Colorado Agricultural Society later organized the first Colorado Territorial Fair in September 1866, as well as doing a good job promoting Colorado agriculture.

Another of the organizations that Lafe joined was the Society of Colorado Pioneers, which began in 1859 but soon disbanded. Then in June of 1866, it was reestablished, and Lafe was elected to represent Conejos County. They held a Fourth of July reunion with a banquet at the Broadwell House, but no further meetings are recorded.

Ex-Governor Gilpin was making good profits from his Colorado land—not from farming, but from selling land. As mentioned, Gilpin, who was removed from his office in April 1862, after only one year in office, made his best deal ever in 1863 in partnership with a syndicate of foreign investors that bought the Sangre de Cristo Grant in 1863 for $41,000 (about 4 cents an acre). Then Gilpin began to evict the settlers located on the property. He was mainly successful, but controversy and litigation over the land grant and its original settlers continues to this day. After the Sangre de Cristo Grant, Gilpin bought other grants and used the same tactics. He quickly made a large fortune off these transactions, but some of his actions were questionable and possibly even illegal.

The United States Preemption Act was replaced with the U.S. Homestead Act on May 20, 1862, after the secession from the Union of the Southern States. The Homestead Act meant more farmers and ranchers moving west, many to the San Luis Valley. This act virtually gave away public land in the West to settlers. The people responded, and almost ten percent of the public land in the Union portion of the United States was taken by private settlers at the time. After farming and living on the land for five years, the settler owned the land; so some of the San Luis Valley settlers were able to get U.S. title to their land at this time. The purpose of the Homestead Act was to encourage farming, but the Union also felt that by creating numerous small farms they could help eliminate the need for slaves on big plantations. It was further seen as a way to "tame" the West and protect it from the Native Americans and Confederacy. However, wealthy land owners and land speculators like Gilpin saw it as a way to get land cheap or even for free, and sometimes they even paid the homesteaders to settle on the land, make a claim, and then transfer the land for little or nothing to the speculators. Corrupt officials took bribes for the best land, as much of the land was too arid to farm or ranch. Under the act, Lafe could have had his "adopted children" file on land when they were twenty-one, then turn it over to him five years later, although it is not known if this actually happened.

Colorado was raided by small groups of Confederates during the Civil War, especially in South Park, the Arkansas River Valley, and the San Luis Valley. Most of the attackers were Colorado citizens who had stayed in Colorado to fight a guerilla war. They raided supply trains, disrupted communication lines, and had a few skirmishes with Union troops. Most Confederate actions were, however, considered more of a nuisance or criminal action rather than a threat. Confederate Captain George Madison captured some of the U.S. mail in 1862, and it was learned that he planned to attack Fort Garland. However federal troops captured forty-four of his men before that attack could happen. In 1864, Confederate guerila James Reynolds and his marauders operated out of South Park, trying to capture Union gold shipments, supposedly for the Confederacy, but probably for themselves. Reynolds' gang was quickly put down; although other

Confederates were later caught trying to smuggle gold out of Colorado for the Confederacy.

The biggest and very realistic fear was that the Confederates would start a general Native American uprising, and Lafe's job during the Civil War was to prevent that from happening. The Colorado Indians often made statements that they knew the Whites were fighting their own brothers. It was a very dangerous situation fueled by the fact that the Utes were literally being starved; and it was said that "in the San Luis Valley that priests were carrying guns."

Lafe's task was not easy. Even though the Civil War was raging and Colorado was losing part of its population to men going back East to fight, a few prospectors continued to arrive in Colorado Territory during the first half of the 1860s, and merchants were establishing stores to meet the prospectors' needs. Some of the new arrivals were settlers who came to raise cattle or sheep or to grow food the prospectors did not have the time or the desire to produce for themselves. The Utes tried without success to run the

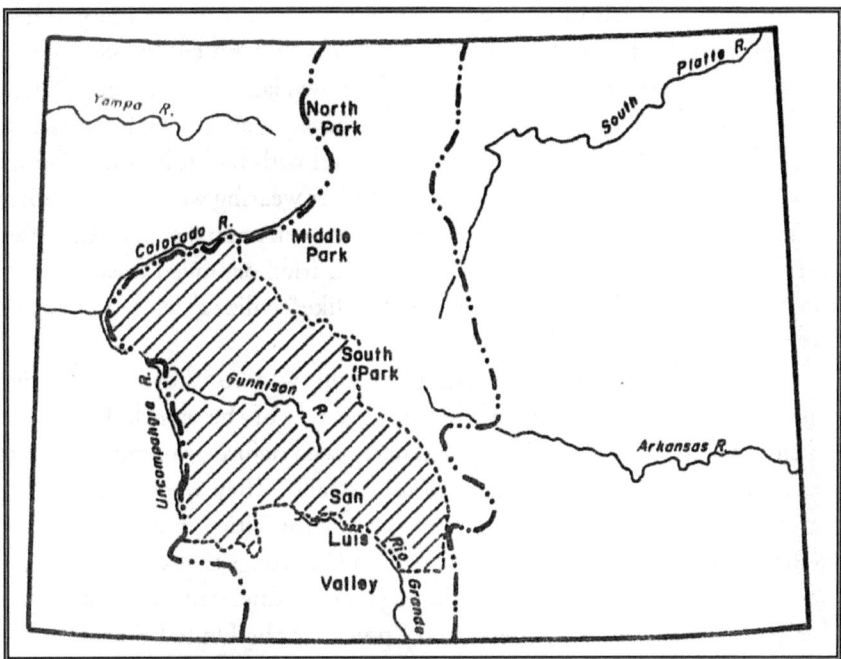

By the treaty of 1863 the Tabeguache received some very good land for a reservation, although it gave up the southern San Luis Valley, South Park, and Middle Park, which had been prime Ute hunting grounds.

From Smith, *Ouray, Chief of the Utes.*

invading Americans off Ute land. The prospectors and merchants in return complained to the federal government that the Utes were taking up much more land than they really needed and demanded that they be removed from Colorado. As a result, Hiram Bennett, the first Colorado Territory's representative to the U.S. Congress, suggested to William Dole, Secretary of the Interior at the time, that a delegation of Ute chiefs and their Agents be brought to Washington for a treaty council.

Governor John Evans anticipated more trouble with the Utes, since his "Denver Treaty" had not been accepted by the United States, and he requested preparations be started to council with the Utes. The problem was that the Utes had no overall chief; and, in fact, the seven bands of Utes had hundreds of chiefs—a chief for each of their small (ten to fifty people) nomadic groups, plus two to five chiefs (such as war chiefs and peace chiefs) for each of the seven bigger bands. Governor Evans nevertheless was developing a plan to take a delegation of Utes to Washington City (there was not yet a Washington, D.C.) to impress the Utes with the military might of his country and make them more willing to sign a treaty.

Inviting the chiefs of Native American tribes to the nation's capital had become a standard prelude of the United States government before holding actual treaty negotiations with them on their own land. The Americans had many hidden motives. One was to teach the "savages" about "civilized" living. After sleeping on a feather bed in a large hotel with bathtubs and running water, who would want to live in a teepee? After wearing well-fitting clothes made from fine fabrics, who would want to dress in animal skins? And after tasting fine food, who would want to live on fried or boiled meat? Surely the Native Americans would choose to live like "civilized" white people, or so the people back East thought.

Another reason for a Washington trip was to show the Native Americans how isolated they were from the rest of the world. They were taken to zoos to see animals they had never seen before or to factories that the Indians could not even begin to understand. They went to plays, listened to large bands playing strange music, and saw cities with many tens of thousands of people, brick-paved streets, and buildings that were many stories tall. But the main reason for bringing Native Americans to Washington was to impress them with the military power of the United States, to the point where the Native Americans knew they could not possibly win a war with the United States, even while the Americans were having a major war among themselves.

One somewhat unique reason that a new Colorado treaty was needed with the Utes was to get them to give up their mineral rights to Colorado's mountain land. Evidently, U.S. officials had simply ignored this important point before this time, but if the Utes owned the land they also owned the minerals. Yet another reason was that the U.S. was now fighting the Plains Indians in Colorado and could not afford to be engaged in a war with the Utes. Colorado needed the Utes to leave the San Luis Valley. One possible solution, already brought up years earlier by Kit Carson and Lafayette Head, was to move them west of the Continental Divide to a reservation. This solution was now being discussed frequently by both the Utes and the Americans.

By November 1862, there was much talk and many letters passing back and forth about the proposed new treaty with the Utes. A series of correspondence began between Colorado Governor Evans and Secretary of the Interior (which included the Department of Indian Affairs) William Dole. Kit Carson made the point to the Utes that the only valid treaty in existence was that of 1849, which simply stated the Utes agreed to stay on their "traditional territory" without any boundaries being set. Another possible solution would be the reservation proposed by Ouray, Lafe, and Kit Carson to Governor Evans located in the Elk Mountains and northern San Juan Mountains between the future Gunnison and Aspen.

On November 6, 1862, Bennett suggested to Secretary of the Interior Dole that the normal prelude to a treaty be followed—that a delegation of Colorado Indians should be brought to Washington City, since none of the Utes had ever been there. Secretary Dole soon authorized the visit. Dole sent instructions to Territorial Governor John Evans to "bring a delegation of Ute, Comanche, Kiowa, Cheyenne, and Apache … to this city from Colorado Territory." He allowed for six Utes plus one interpreter and noted they should travel "with as little expense as possible." Dole instructed that the five Colorado Native American groups should meet at St. Joseph, Missouri, and from there they would travel together to Washington City. Evans quickly shot back an answer that the Utes could not possibly go to Washington with the Plains Indians, as they were mortal enemies. Dole then agreed to a separate visit from the Utes, and the Plains Indians were to go to Washington first.

Lafe had indicated that the Tabeguache Utes wanted him to serve as one of the treaty commissioners. The method of picking the Utes who would go to Washington City appears to have been that Head and Ouray assembled the delegation, and they soon left for Denver. The Ute delegation had no more than left the Conejos Agency when accusations about the qualifications of the Utes in the group surfaced. In a February 7, 1863, letter, A. H. Gilbert notified Captain Ben Cutler at Army headquarters, New Mexico that:

> *Major Head* (n.b. note the title) *has just started out for Washington City with 6 Utes reporting them to be chiefs when they are not. Neither are they men of any influence in the tribe. They are quite young.*"[81]

Another letter dated February 8, 1863, from E. A. Eaton informed Captain Cutler:

> *The Head delegation is not legitimate. The delegation he is taking does not consist of any of the chiefs of the tribe* (n.b.— Ouray was a chief or subchief of the Utes at this time). *The tribe knows nothing of this visit to Washington.*[82]

On February 21, 1863, W. F. Arny, Acting Governor of New Mexico Territory, sent a message to Dole that began "Re: Head Delegation—Not Chiefs." Two more letters from American officials expressed concern that the Utes were not chiefs, but gave information that they were influential,

Shavano was a long-time Ute Chief, shown here in his younger years with his peace medal from the 1863 treaty, which was made null and void by the U. S. changing its terms before they signed it.

Le Tour de Monde–
Author's Collection.

especially among the young Utes. The complaints being made had some truth. The Ute men going to Washington were generally young, and chiefs were usually picked by Native Americans for age, experience, and leadership ability; but it was the young Utes who were most likely to go to war. All the Utes going to Washington were generally influential, and would likely someday be the "Head Chiefs" of the Utes. For example, one of the Utes going to Washington who was not yet a "chief," was Shavano, who was a man of great influence among his people and soon was to become a chief. Two others were brothers of men considered very influential (one of whom was Quinche who had no great influence himself, but was Ouray's younger brother). Two were Mouache Ute chiefs, and as the Mouache were a very small but warlike band, they were probably needed. However, the main reason for the choices of young men to go to Washington, which all the men writing these letters missed, was to show off the U.S. military power to Ute warriors and to create in the Native Americans a fear of such an enemy. The Utes would be taken on carefully planned tours of military bases, where they would see huge numbers of assembled troops and demonstrations of cannons and other powerful weapons. A treaty would not be made in Washington (although it was later suggested); but, hopefully a clear message would be sent through the younger Utes—the United States could easily win a war with any tribe of Native Americans, even if the United States was in the midst of a Civil War and fighting the Plains Indians at the same time.

Taking even a small group of Native Americans all the way across the country was not an easy task. Lafe had to spend several months preparing for the trip to Washington City for his small group. He first bought two cows for $30 each and 100 sheep at $2 each. These animals would feed the families of the Utes going to Washington while the Ute warriors were gone. On January 16, 1863, Lafe bought four complete suits of clothes from F. W. Posthof, the new sutler at Fort Garland. Each outfit included a flannel shirt, flannel coat, pants, vest, hat, shoes, socks, cap, gloves, underwear, suspenders, and a belt. He noted on the receipt: "Purchased for the Utah Delegation." The clothes were not for the Utes. Lafe was making sure that he and the three other white men who were traveling with the Utes would be well and warmly dressed.

William Godfrey (Godfroy was German and later changed his name to the more American sounding Godfrey), Clerk of the Conejos Agency, joined Lafe on the trip. They hired two Special Agents as freighters, brothers John and Clarence Clark, to travel with the group for $2 per day each. Ouray filled the position of interpreter. Besides Ouray, there were now six members of the Ute delegation: Pu-u-wich, Pa-bu-sat, Sho-was-she,

CHAPTER 7

Yu-pu-wa-at, Tu-pu-wa-at, and Quinche (Ouray's brother). The party of Utes had somehow grown from six to seven.

Lafe had supplies to buy in Denver for the seven Utes and four Anglos for the next leg of the trip. The nearest railroad station was at St. Joseph, Missouri. It was 750 miles east of Denver, and the group would go there by wagon in mid-winter. Therefore, while in Denver, Lafe went shopping for food and cooking equipment, which included a coffee mill and large coffee pot, a wash basin, two wooden buckets, three camp kettles, a frying pan, a dozen tin plates, cups, and spoons, and a large quantity of matches. He bought warm woolen clothing for the seven Utes, and he added a dozen buffalo robes for bedding. For his own use, he had purchased writing material, postage stamps, and a notebook. One seemingly unusual purchase that Lafe made was a variety of different colored paints meant for the Utes, as they enjoyed body decoration. He also added two bales of smoking tobacco and seven sets of combs, brushes, and mirrors. Food for the trip included 486 pounds of fresh beef still on the hoof, one eighteen-pound ham, thirty-one pounds of beans, thirty pounds of bread (flour?), five pounds of fried apples, ten pounds of dried peaches, 100 pounds of sugar, twenty-five pounds of coffee, a keg of syrup, and a sack of salt.

On February 19, 1863, the delegation left Fort Weld, two miles north of Denver, in two wagons. A team of four horses pulled each wagon, with extra horses bringing up the rear. They followed the Platte River eastward. It was a slow, cold trip, often through deep snow. Thirty-one days later they arrived in St. Joseph, Missouri. At "St. Joe," Lafe bought "city clothes" for the Utes. His expense report listed seven suits with shirts, neck ties, shoes, and hats. The group boarded an eastbound train the next day. Fare to Washington City from St. Joe was $29 per person on a through train with a dining car and a place to sleep. However, the Civil War was raging and rail travel was dangerous at the time. Lafe had therefore chosen a route to Chicago; then, after a day and a half layover, they took a train to Detroit. They waited there for two days before taking a train into Canada, and then went back into the U.S. at Buffalo, New York, and arrived in Washington City on March 28, 1863.

Two days earlier, on March 26, 1863, the *Washington Evening Star* had reported that the "Apache, Comanche, Kiowa, and Cheyenne met with the Secretary of the Interior. They stated they would make treaties with the United States, but never with the Utes and Pawnees." The Plains delegation left Washington just shortly before the Utes arrived.

The Americans in Washington listed the names of the Utes taken to Washington two different ways. The Bureau of Indian Affairs listed "Ule or Ulah" (Ouray), Quinche (Ouray's brother), Grouley and his brother (Mouache Utes from New México), Shawana (Shavano), and others unnamed. A *Washington Star* reporter lists Ouray as one of the seven chiefs; and the *Washington Times* lists Ure (Arrow), Pu-u-wich, Pa-bu-sat, Quinche, Sho-wa-she-it, Tu-pa-wa-at, and Tu-pue-pa. This was the same as Lafe's list. To make matters even more confusing, according to *The Ute System of Government* (a publication of the present-day Ute tribe), ten Utes participated: Ouray, Kaniache, Antkatosh, Pubiwich, José Maria, Nicaagot, Guero, Paant, Piah, and Pabusat.

The spelling of the written names of the Utes taken to Washington was not constant among the Americans recording their names. It must be remembered that the Utes have no written language and their oral language is very guttural and hard to decipher. Head lists the men as Ure (the Arrow), Pu-bu-wich, Pu-bu-sat, Quinche, Sho-wa-she-it, Tu-pu-wa-at, and Tue-pue-pa.

Ouray posed in this photo with the silver handled cane that President Lincoln had given him to designate him as the first chief of all the Utes.

Author's Collection.

CHAPTER 7

While in Washington, the Utes met with President Lincoln, who gave Ouray a silver-capped cane, which was traditionally given only to the head chief of an Indian delegation. It was a risky decision, but the Whites had decided to unilaterally appoint Ouray as head chief of all the Utes. The Utes had never had an over-all chief, and Ouray would be the one acting in this capacity for the first time. Ouray remained head chief over the later objection of some of the Utes and even some Americans, but he was a good choice; and Carl Schurz, a later Secretary of the Interior and Indian Superintendent, called him "the brightest Indian I ever met."

Lafe and Carson evidently felt Ouray had the ability to properly present the Ute's case and represent his people. The fact that Ouray, Lafe, and Kit Carson had met with Governor Evans shortly before going to Washington indicated that he was already influential and had standing with the Tabeguache band, if not with all the Utes.

The Monday issue of the *Washington Evening Star*, April 12, 1863, reported their arrival:

> *Seven of the chiefs of the Ute tribe of Indians from Colorado Territory west of "Snowy Ridge" (Continental Divide) arrived in this city Saturday. They are in the charge of Major Head and have come to make a treaty with the Commissioner of Indian Affairs.*

The Utes and Lafe met many times with different government officials. Finally a treaty was drafted. Ouray performed his duties admirably, and further wisely said he could not sign the treaty at that time. He said the U.S. officials must visit Colorado and meet with all the Ute chiefs. He also wanted to seek counsel from some of the other chiefs before signing an agreement.

It would, of course, be a great triumph for Ouray if he could make the Americans come to the Utes; but Ouray knew that he did not have the authority to bind all the Utes. If he did sign for them, the Utes would claim the treaty was not legally valid. However, the Americans were desperate for a treaty. When President Lincoln went to council with Ouray and the rest of the Ute delegation, he agreed to send a delegation to Colorado, but with his right hand man, John Nicolay, representing him. The Utes accepted the switch. After the meeting, the Utes were given a tour of the White House.

While the delegation was in Washington, Lafe received a letter from P. T. Barnum, who wanted to arrange a special appearance of the Utes at his American Museum in New York City. Lafe replied by letter to the invitation as follows:

> *I am in receipt of your letter related to the Ute Indians.... You suggest they should be allowed to see New York. I thoroughly concur... It happens, however, that while on the plains... I met Major Leland of the Metropolitan Hotel... who invited them and myself to stay at his hotel... free of expense.... The Utes are the best looking and most intelligent of any Indian tribe. They are the finest shots with a rifle. I scarcely know how they would get along with the Indians you now have at the Museum, for they are deadly enemies.... The (Utes) are much better looking than your Cheyenne and Kiowa and are far hardier men.... My party of Utes will reach your city on Thursday next, but I shall be unable to allow them to remain beyond a very few days as I am bound to send them back to their homes as quickly as possible.*[83]

Lafe and the delegates did visit New York City, but as guests of Major Leland. On April 30, 1863, *The New York Times* reported that "the Utes frequently expressed themselves highly gratified with their brief visit to this city."

Secretary Dole in his 1863 report stated that his plan for a reservation along the San Juan River was brought up at the conference in Washington, but it was found that the it would not work. The Capote and Weeminuche, who claimed that land, were not willing to give it up; and it was doubtful there was enough room there for all the Ute bands. The Utes also made it clear while in Washington City that they would not agree to a treaty that would force them into agriculture. When asked again to try farming, the Utes were adamant that they wished to keep their nomadic ways and rely heavily on hunting and gathering. They even said "We are not that low yet." It was further noted that the agricultural possibilities of Colorado were very limited and that much of that land, especially the land that needed to be irrigated, was already taken by Americans. It was recommended as an alternative that the Native Americans might raise livestock of all kinds and that much of the land not already taken had been found suitable for ranching. However that choice was ignored.

Many of the Ute bands other than the Tabeguache stated later that most of their leaders were in Utah at a meeting for another treaty and that the Tabeguache who went to Washington gave up land that was the territory of other Ute groups that were not included in the meetings. Even the Tabeguache complained that important terms of the proposed treaty had later been changed without their knowledge, and that they never got the supplies promised them under the agreement.

CHAPTER EIGHT

Family Man, the Utes, and an Exciting Trip Back From Washington City
(1863-1864)

> "... Fine fields of wheat, barley, oats, and corn at Conejos and immense herds of sheep.... Major Head owns a sawmill, grist mill, and a large store."
> The Denver Mirror, November 30, 1863

The Ute delegation left New York City on April 30, 1863. On this part of the trip, the Clark brothers, the men Lafe had hired as Special Agents before leaving Colorado Territory, took charge of the Utes. The group traveled to St. Joe, Missouri, over the same confusing route they had taken to Washington City a month earlier. Lafe and Godfrey had purchased tickets for a quick trip to Jacksonville, Illinois. While waiting for Lafe and Mr. Godfrey in St. Joe, the Clark brothers restocked their wagons with supplies for the return trip. One of the Clark brothers also signed the delegation up with a large wagon train leaving in mid-May.

It had been twenty-two years since Lafe ran away from home, and he had only seen his sister, Eliza Downing, once during that time, although they had kept in touch. Lafe and Godfrey arrived to find Eliza in great distress. A coffin lay in her parlor, and in it was her eldest son, John. He had died on April 10, 1863, from wounds received in a Civil War battle, and his remains had arrived the same morning as Lafe. The family was just opening the coffin as Lafe arrived. Eliza was totally overcome with grief, but her family could immediately see that Lafe was "a warm-hearted, real man." It was a God-send that Lafe arrived at that very time, and he totally took charge of the funeral and the burial. Then he convinced Eliza that it would be good for her to come with him to Conejos for a visit. She and her two younger children, Finis and Lucy, packed quickly, as all knew that the Ute delegation was waiting for them and the Utes had not been under Lafe's supervision for nearly two weeks.

Family Man, the Utes, and an Exciting Trip Back From Washington City

On May 14, 1863, Lafe, Eliza, Finis, and Lucy boarded a Wabash Railroad train bound for St. Joe. Godfrey had gone to take care of some business of his own and had said he would meet them in St. Joe. Finis was a tall boy of sixteen. He was so thin that people called him "spindling." He reminded Lafe of himself at that age and, in St. Joe, Lafe outfitted the boy for the West. Finis wrote that "Uncle Lafayette Head read my disposition fairly well and humored my every whim...."[84] Finis was thrilled when Lafe bought him cavalry-style boots that came up over his knees, a U.S. cavalry belt complete with cartridge box, a new broad-brimmed hat, a jewel-handled Bowie knife, and two six-shooters. Eliza was not pleased that her son had the weapons; but if she had known the very real dangers that lay ahead in the West, she likely would not have agreed to make the trip.

St. Joe was a steamboat port on the Missouri River, as well as a telegraph center. At this time, it was also the western terminus of the Hannibal & St. Joe Railroad and a major staging point for wagon trains going west. It was a city caught between sides in the Civil War with its citizens' loyalties split between the Union and the Confederacy. In 1861, the Confederate Army had captured the city, but Union troops had run them out and then tightly controlled St. Joe until the end of the war. Residents needed passes to enter or leave the city during this time. Lafe, his family, Mr. Godfrey, the two freighters, and the Ute delegation joined the large west-bound wagon train that was escorted by three companies of the First Colorado Cavalry with Major Downing (no relation to Eliza's husband) of New Mexico in command. The troops were there to guard the wagon train against rebel forces in Missouri and Native Americans while they were on the Plains, but especially to guard the Utes in the party, who were at war with practically all the prairie tribes. All together there were about 500 travelers of which Finis wrote there were not seven, nor ten, but thirteen Utes going back to Colorado.

The wagon train was composed of about 200 civilians, 275 military, and the Ute delegation. When the Ute delegation had been traveling eastward in the winter, it was relatively safe because most of the Native Americans were in their winter camps; but now the Native Americans had moved onto the Plains to do their spring hunting. Trouble was already brewing on the Plains between the Americans and the Native Americans. That trouble would culminate in the Sand Creek Massacre on November 29, 1864. The caravan would pass through Cheyenne, Arapaho, and Comanche territory.

While in St. Joe the newspaper reported:

> *These Utes are noble specimens of the Native Americans, with all the pride and obstinacy peculiar to the race. While in*

CHAPTER 8

> Washington they threw themselves upon their "reserved rights" refusing to make a treaty, and when an intimation was given to their spokesman that he had better conduct himself with propriety and not be so haughty he promptly told the Commissioner something like this: I and my party came here because we wished to come. You may give presents to other Indians, but we don't want any presents. You want our land because there is plenty of gold there, but all that you are willing to give us is copper. Do you think we are fools? You talk as if you could whip us. You are now fighting your own brothers and can't whip them. You will find it harder work to whip us. We wish to go home, and when we get there we may be willing to make a treaty.[85]

While traveling, Lafe taught Finis to drive a team of horses pulling a wagon. Lafe or one of the Utes always sat beside Finis as he was driving, and the cavalry rode in lines on both sides of the long wagon train. Finis was the "Color Bearer," carrying a U.S. flag mounted to his wagon. Finis really liked the Utes.

> These Ute Indian chiefs were wonderful fellows; quick to learn and understand and they were grateful and kind to those they reposed confidence in, but as sullen and hard as flint when they were suspicious or felt that someone was wronging them.[86]

Like many travelers, Lafe and Godfrey carried a lot of cash to pay travel expenses and for use at the Conejos Indian Agency. The money was "in greenbacks, in the original (uncut) sheet form, strapped around their backs."[87]

In early June, the wagons approached Julesburg in northeast Colorado Territory. A scout brought news that cattle herders had recently witnessed a Sioux war dance with fresh scalps displayed. It was also learned that a large group of Plains Indians was waiting in nearby Julesburg to try to capture the Ute "chiefs" in the party. Some weeks earlier a Ute band had attacked a Plains Indian camp and taken captives. These Plains warriors wanted to trade the Utes for the stolen captives. The wagons closed ranks as they approached Julesburg with the cavalry in a tight formation on either side of the civilians. Every soldier and civilian was armed except the Ute chiefs, who were stripped of any type of weapon so they could not start a fight. They were carefully hidden away in the beds of two of the wagons.

When the wagon train topped a hill, there was a huge number of Indians blocking the trail. Finis estimated their number at 10,000; but later he admitted that his sister Lucy told him that she thought he counted the number of Indians twice. Finis remained in the lead wagon. The soldiers and Lafe agreed they should keep moving. For the first 200 yards, the soldiers had to force their way through the "bold, jeering, and taunting Indians;" but the soldiers kept pushing forward and the Indians stepped back, opening a path for the wagon train to drive into their midst. They were forced to stop when a chief commanded them to halt and grabbed the bridle ring of a lead horse. Lafe quickly elbowed his way to where the chief stood. The lead soldier drew his sword just as Lafe jumped to the ground. Lafe spoke to the Plains chief in sign language, but a soldier who spoke the Plains Indian's language soon joined him. The three men conversed until the chief finally let go of the bridle. The soldier interpreter quickly jumped into the bed of the wagon that Finis was driving. The wagon surged forward, and the whole caravan raced twelve miles to a horseshoe bend in the South Platte River, where the wagons circled. Every man and woman held a gun. The pursuing Indians stopped within sight of the wagons, but slightly out of effective gun range.

Later Finis said he did not know what had spooked his horses. There was a rumor that someone tossed a freshly killed animal hide under the horses' bellies; or it might have been a well-placed slap by the interpreter soldier who had jumped into Finis' wagon. When darkness fell, a military scout slipped away and rode to Fort Weld near Denver for help. The soldiers and civilians waited through a long night with guns drawn; but just before dawn, a company of 150 soldiers from Fort Weld arrived. As the sun rose on a quiet morning, the weary travelers saw no sign of Native Americans. A few of the soldiers scouted the area for some distance from the wagon train, but still found no sign of Indians. Only then did the travelers relax. Lafe and his group went to Fort Weld, where they stopped for ten days. Lafe had been gone from Colorado for almost four months.

During this time, Lafe and Ouray reported the details of the successful Washington City meeting to Governor Evans, who was much more in favor of sending the Native Americans to a reservation than Gilpin had been; and the three began to discuss the follow-up treaty council to be held in October in Conejos. Governor Evans also asked Lafe to prepare a budget for the 1865 fiscal year, as the budget was due to the Commissioner of Indian Affairs by the end of September 1863. They came up with the following:

50 head of beef cattle at $30 each	*$1,500*
300 head of sheep at $3 each	*900*
200 fanegas of wheat at $3 each	*600*

Pay of Agent	1,500
Pay of Interpreter (Ouray)	500
Keeping and feeding four public animals	500
Office Rent	200
15 cords of wood at $5 each	75
2 boxes of candles at $15 each	30
Shoeing four public horses	25
Stationery	50
Total	$5,880

Lafe also included an "Estimate of Merchandise Required" for the "presents" to be given the Utes at the treaty conference." The list included blankets, fabrics, thread, wool shawls, wool hats and shirts, coats and pants, combs and mirrors, needles, assorted beads, knives, wire, fishing line and hooks, axes and spades, bridles, pans, kettles, spoons, coffee, sugar, rice, tobacco, pipes, and pipe stems. The total cost of these goods and presents, plus many more items was $15,507.25, which brought Lafe's total cost for these goods and other services at the Agency to $21,387.25. However, after reviewing Lafe's request, Governor Evans increased the amount to $30,000 (Governors often got part of the pie and Evans was part of the "Denver Ring" of lawyers, politicians, and wealthy but crooked men). Then Governor Evans added a note to the request: "The estimate for Major Head's Agency will need to be changed if the treaty just concluded with the Indians is ratified, so that we may at once commence to carry out its stipulations." The Governor further requested $40,400 for the Uintah and Grand River Utes and $27,000 for the Office of the Superintendent of the Native Americans for Colorado (an Agency which the Governor managed). He explained that the growing costs were caused by white settlers moving on to the traditional hunting grounds and killing a large share of Ute game, but the vast majority of the items requested were not food.

Herman J. Viola in *Diplomats in Buckskin* points out that many Indian Agents of the time sold some of the goods meant for the Native American to local settlers. Some items ordered by the Agents (such as petticoats) would simply not have been used by the Native Americans. There were perhaps times when the Agents paid their friends more money than the Native American's items were worth, and/or perhaps received kickbacks. Whether Lafe did this or not is uncertain; but in his defense, if he did, there were also times when he personally gave large amounts of his personal food to the Utes when they were hungry. Why would he do such a thing if he was selling their food to others? Territorial Governor McCook was later fired for grossly misappropriating goods and cattle meant for the Utes and sometimes reimbursing himself for as much as five times what he actually paid for cattle and other goods. He was also paying salaries to relatives who did no or little work to earn the money.

As a result of the cheating going on by many Indian Agents, the Superintendent of Indian Affairs started having their Auditors check the purchases of Indian supplies carefully for anything that looked suspicious, and on-site audits were even occasionally being made. Many times the Agents might claim an item that supposedly had already been distributed was of the very best quality, and therefore was worth the high price. There were also major problems involving expenditures when a Native American group was taken to the East. There were tickets bought for shows the Native Americans would obviously have not been interested in (such as opera). There were fancy silk handkerchiefs or gold plated collar buttons that the Native Americans would not use. (One exception was Ouray, who had his photo taken in Washington wearing them, but it is doubtful if he ever used these items back in Colorado). The Utes were taken to fancy restaurants and hotels that their white companions obviously enjoyed more than the Utes. Colorado Governor Charles Adams was charged with such misconduct while on this trip to Washington, but somehow talked himself out of any repercussions at the time. No charges were made against Lafe verbally or otherwise.

Well-rested and with his business finished with the Governor in Denver, Lafe's group went on to Manitou, where there were only the springs at the time—but no buildings—and to Colorado City, where they spent a few more days. Then the party continued to Pueblo, which Finis reported having only a few shacks; and they had to ford the Arkansas River, as there was only a foot bridge at the spot. After crossing Sangre de Cristo Pass, they were in Ute territory and no longer needed the soldiers. The Utes were even allowed to go hunting. The families of the Ute chiefs and Martina Head were waiting at Fort Garland, and Lafe and the rest of the Anglos in the group traveled with their families to Conejos. They arrived in late June.

Besides the Native Americans, a few Mexicans took the start of the Civil War as an opportunity to rebel against what many of them called "the American occupiers of their country and their sympathizers." The worst of these were the Espinosa brothers, Felipe and Vivian. In the winter and spring of 1863, Vivian and Felipe Espinosa started killing Americans or their sympathizers and stealing horses. Their motives were not mainly political; although they always took any opportunity to state they were trying to

CHAPTER 8

get rid of the racism of the Americans in the San Luis Valley. The Espinosas lived in San Raphael, just a few miles from the Town of Conejos. Before their killing rampage, they were known to be horse thieves; and when they robbed a man on a wagon, they were recognized. Fort Garland sent troops to arrest the Espinosas at their family home. A fight ensued, and one of the soldiers was killed. After the brothers escaped, the other soldiers then looted the Espinosa family home in retaliation. Felipe and Vivian vowed revenge for their parents' loss and started their killing spree, quickly murdering eight men including the brother of one of the officers at Fort Garland.

A posse was sent out from Leadville, as several of the men killed were from the Arkansas River Valley. Troops were also sent out from Fort Garland again, and Vivian Espinosa was killed in a shootout with the posse near the future Cripple Creek. A written agreement between the two brothers was found on Vivian's body, and it showed that the two had made a pact that they would kill at least 600 Whites. Felipe went back to San Raphael, killing two more men along the way, as well as a man fishing in the Conejos River. It was almost time for Governor John Evans to come to Conejos for the treaty with the Utes, and Felipe sent a letter to the Governor that he was going to kill him. This resulted in a reward of $2,500 being offered for Felipe—dead or alive. Felipe was not successful in even finding the Governor, but he did kill two more men.

After the treaty negotiations were over in mid-October, Colonel Samuel Tappan, commander at Fort Garland, sent Tom Tobin, the famous Colorado mountain man who now lived close to the fort, after Felipe. Tobin was an uncanny tracker. Some said he "could follow a grasshopper's trail through sagebrush." Tobin was told he would get a reward (although the $2,500 figure

Tom Tobin was a real mountain man, who was a scout for the U. S. Army for many years. He became one of the best trackers in the country and had no trouble finding the Espinosa brothers.

Courtesy of Colorado College.

was not mentioned) if he "brought in Felipe's head." Felipe had, meanwhile, recruited his nephew, José Espinosa, to join him, and the men continued the rampage, killing two more men and raping a Mexican-American woman who was simply riding with a white man in a buggy. Felipe called the woman a "whore," proven by the fact that she was with a white man. Tappan sent eighteen soldiers with Tobin, who said he did not need them, but Tappan insisted. In one day Tobin had picked up the trail. On the third day out, Tobin found the Espinosas by going to a spot where birds were circling because the Espinosas were dressing out a cow they had stolen.

When Tobin stepped on a twig he alerted Felipe, who Tobin immediately shot, and who fell screaming into the campfire. Some of the soldiers fired at José as he was running away, but it was Tobin who killed the fleeing man with a very long shot. He brought the two men's heads back (he had cut Felipe's head off while he was still alive) in a sack along with the agreement the two brothers had made and a diary that showed they had killed over thirty people. The governor never fully paid Tobin the reward he was due even though in 1900, when Tobin was an old man, bedridden, and destitute, he pleaded for the money. Tobin died on May 15, 1904, but had received only $500 of the $2,500 reward due him.

Lafe was doing well enough financially that he had built a much larger adobe house for his family. Finis described the second house Lafe had recently built in Conejos:

> (Conejos is) ... a town of 'dobe houses. Uncle's was the largest and best, built like a fort around a square plat of 200 feet, with solid walls outside, windows and doors all inside the square. A look-out was two stories up.[88]

> It had adobe walls two feet thick, was one story, and had "a frontage of 210 feet and a sixty foot depth ... almost entirely surrounded by a wide porch. (It faced) the oldest church in the state on one side, the old town on another, the second oldest mill on another.... (This) place stands preeminently as a historic spot."[89]

It was nicely furnished at this point; but when his granddaughter Piedad later moved in it was "extravagantly furnished" by her.

After Head's new home had been finished in Conejos, some called it the finest in the San Luis Valley. Still, the town of Guadalupe was said to be bigger than Conejos, and Guadalupe was incorporated in 1869. Conejos has never been incorporated (it is the only County Seat in Colorado that

CHAPTER 8

is not incorporated). Lafe had built his mill nearby to supply the Utes and Fort Garland, but he also did a little business with the locals, although most were very poor and had little money. Lafe's sister Eliza and her daughter were the only non-Mexican-American women in the village, but the town was filled to overflowing at the time because the 1863 Ute Treaty conference with the Utes was soon to be held there. Finis said:

> *During all the time we were in Conejos there were never less than 500 soldiers to preserve the peace. There were about three hundred Mexicans, 500 soldiers and some Jew merchant traders....* [90]

As mentioned earlier, President Lincoln had agreed to a treaty conference in Conejos with all the Utes that would come to receive presents. The date was now set for October 1, 1863, as that was the time of year when the Southern and Tabeguache Utes received their government annuities, which would hopefully assure a good attendance. The meeting would be held near Conejos. In September, Finis and Godfrey had made a trip to Denver to pick up the shipment of government goods that would be distributed to the Utes at the treaty conference. Finis later wrote that Godfrey hired wagons and drivers in Denver and "ten large wagons with three yoke of oxen each were required to haul the goods back to Conejos." [91]

The trip back to Conejos was filled with bad omens. On the way out of Denver, one of the ox teams clipped the corner of a new drugstore that was a frame building set on a flimsy rock or block foundation, and the entire building collapsed "with such a crash of bottles and glasses you never heard." Finis said it took a promise from government officials that the U.S. would pay for the damage to quiet the angry store owner. Dark storm clouds were gathering as they started into the mountains. Thunder, lightning, and a driving rainstorm soon slowed their travel. On a high mountain pass, the back wheel of one of the wagons slid off the slippery trail. The side of the wagon gave way, and the heavy load tumbled into a steep ravine. Barrels filled with sugar burst open and frosted the rocks below. They spent that night in a mountain snowstorm—Finis wrapped in a blanket and a buffalo robe. He fell asleep beside the campfire and the next morning found the buffalo robe badly singed by the fire. Finis was lucky, as the falling snow had doused the flames.

Some Colorado citizens believed that it would not be necessary to sign a treaty with the Utes because, as *The Denver Weekly Commonwealth* declared, "the prospect for a fight was good." *The Commonwealth* declared that not only were the Utes upset, but so were the Mexican-Americans. The article was referring to the Espinosas in particular, but in general the paper wrote "....The (Mexican) people are notoriously bad and lawless." *The Rocky Mountain News* wrote that "the bitterness and acrimony between the few Americans and Mexicans residing in that section, if allowed to fester, will result in bloodshed." These accusations were simply not the case among the vast majority of the valley's citizens.

John Nicolay brought treaty instructions to Governor Evans from Indian Commissioner William P. Dole. Dole asked to be sent a survey of the lands the Indians might be moved to, but no such survey had ever been made of those lands. Dole also mentioned that he thought the Indians' destiny was to submit, go to reservations, and take up agriculture. The northern Utes announced they were at a "treaty conference" in Utah and would not be able to come to the Conejos gathering. As previously mentioned, Nicolay reported back to President Lincoln that the agricultural prospects were very limited for the Utes and noted that almost all land that could be irrigated had already been taken. He also wrote that "The lessons of civilization must of necessity be taught them gradually," and "it would be wiser to promote stockraising among them." [92]

This photograph of (Left to right) John Nicolay, President Abraham Lincoln, John Hay was taken November 8, 1963.

Courtesy U.S. Library of Congress photo collection.

CHAPTER 8

Because of the good possibility of a Ute or even a Mexican-American uprising, Head was worried about not having enough troops at Fort Garland during the treaty negotiations. He knew the Utes were hungry and needed cattle and other food supplies from the Americans if they were going to make it through the winter. Head also pleaded for more troops to help in the war going on with the Navajo at the time, who he said had killed forty Americans and fifteen Mexican-Americans in just the last few months. (He was probably referring to the Navajo attacks along the Baker Toll Road.) The worried Governor told Head to try to get more food and supplies for the Utes from the Indian Superintendent in New Mexico, and the garrison at Fort Garland was beefed up with Colorado volunteers.

Trouble with the Native Americans in the area had been building. The Navajo had caused a lot of trouble for the United States at the beginning of the Civil War, and Kit Carson was ordered by Brigadier General James Carleton to quiet them down. He was given the authority to employ 100 Utes in the effort, "as they had done well when recruited by Colonel Fauntleroy in 1860." Carleton said the "Utes are very brave, and fine shots, fine trailers, and uncommonly energetic in the field." He believed that they "would be of more service than twice as many troops."[93] The Mouache were fully equipped with provisions, clothing, and equipment and were also given permission to take Navajo livestock as pay for their service. The U.S. eventually decided that the Navajo had to either be exterminated or isolated totally at a remote location from the rest of the inhabitants of Arizona and New Mexico. Kit Carson was assigned to round up and move the tribe. Carson started the round-up in 1863 and launched a full scale assault on the Navajo in January of 1864. This he did by instituting a "scorched earth policy," and by spring of 1864 Carson started taking starving bands of Navajo to Bosque Redondo in New Mexico. By the end of the summer of 1864, the Utes had so many Navajo sheep that they had to designate part of their group to take them home, while the rest of the Utes stayed with Carson and helped to move the Navajo who had been captured for the "Long Walk" to Bosque Redondo.

The Long Walk (actually involving fifty-three different groups of Navajo) was a major event that was hoped would keep the Native Americans in New Mexico, Arizona, and Colorado peaceful. Prior to the Long Walk there had been a series of treaties signed between the Navajo and Americans in 1849, 1858, and 1861; however, there were many fights between the two nations inbetween these treaties. The Navajo (who had traditionally been warlike) were having the same situation as the Ute—the Americans were killing their game and not giving them promised food. The Navajo had yet another major problem—they had large flocks of sheep that they raised mainly for their wool, and American livestock was eating the little grass available in their area.

During the later "Long Walk," the Navajo were moved 300 miles east to Bosque Redondo in the Pecos River Valley. The Navajo men had to walk, although the women and children could sometimes ride in the wagons. At least 200 Navajo died during the nineteen day trips, and between 8,000 and 9,000 Navajo were eventually relocated. The Utes with Carson saw how badly the Navajo were being treated during this time and perhaps realized that the same could happen to them.

Back in late September 1863, the Utes had begun to arrive at Lafe's ranch near Conejos. Their teepees soon dotted his land. The Tabeguache Utes turned out in great numbers, but only a few of the Capote and Weeminuche were present. The Mouache and Jicarilla Apache did not want to participate at all, as they were being asked to give up their traditional territory in the San Luis Valley and both sides of the Sangre de Cristo Mountains north of Taos. The Grand River, White River, and Uintah Utes could not be located, but they were evidently visiting Ute Chief Black Hawk in Utah.

On the last day of September, the Americans who would negotiate with the Utes met ahead of time at Lafe's house. Besides the Utes and negotiators, there was a regiment of cavalry, 500 soldiers of all kinds, and many of the local citizens from Conejos. John Nicolay arrived with Territorial Governor John Evans; Dr. Michael Steck, Superintendent of Indian Affairs for New Mexico Territory, came from the south; and Indian Agent Simeon Whitley was also present, supposedly representing the Jicarilla Apache. They discussed the challenges of the treaty they hoped would be agreed to by the Utes.

On October 1, 1863, Lafe took Nicolay and the other men to meet the Utes. A unit of Colorado cavalry accompanied them. The first order of business was the distribution of the promised supplies. Finis later wrote:

> The sight of the throng of Indians reminded me of the Julesburg affair, for there were, as I remember, over 5,000 of them. They sat or stood in rows around the annuity goods, and each received his allotment… Then they got down to the business of the treaty.[94]

Finis again overestimated the number of Indians he was seeing, in this case the number was probably closer to about 1,500. An article in *The Denver Commercial Record* stated:

CHAPTER 8

> The Governor, Col. Chivington, Lieutenant Col. Tappan, and other prominent officers of the Colorado troops are here. It is the current belief of those who ought to know that the Utes will make no acceptable treaty, unless force be used to compel them to; and it is equally the general opinion that force will be used .... We are expecting six companies and a battery of artillery here from Fort Union, which added to the troops already here, will make a force capable of whipping two Ute nations.[95]

The President's Secretary later reported to the Secretary of the Interior that only one Capote chief was present and only three of the Mouache. The Weeminuche were reported to have had some chiefs who had started to come, but then went back before reaching Conejos; and the Northern bands did not come, because they said "their horses could not make that long a journey." Actually many of the Ute bands were in Utah, and they were meeting with Ute Chief Black Hawk about a possible war in Utah. Of course they could not report the truth. Black Hawk was actively recruiting Utes from other Ute bands to join in his war, which started in 1865.

Since nearly all the Tabeguache had come, it was decided that a treaty would be made only with the Tabeguache; and because of this some call this "The Treaty with the Ute Tabeguache." Even the Tabeguache had not agreed in Washington City to move immediately onto a permanent small reservation, as they would not abandon their nomadic life and they felt such a move would make them easy targets for their Native American enemies. Nicolay again reported that stock ranching seemed to be the way to get the Indians to be self-sufficient, and that it conformed much better to their present way of life. He also mentioned that the Tabeguache themselves had mentioned sharing their land with the Mouache. The hope of the commissioners was that as the other Ute bands saw the success of the Tabeguache Utes at raising livestock they would want to take up cattle or sheep ranching to support themselves. Again these suggestions were ignored.

The concept of land ownership or a reservation were both completely foreign to the Utes. They were a nomadic people that roamed most of the mountainous part of Colorado and extreme northern New Mexico, as well as the nearby valleys and foothills, searching for their seasonal food. Farming the land seemed crazy to the Utes, who had for 600 years simply picked natural food and killed game, both of which also gave them materials for other uses. Prospectors and settlers were starting to intrude on their land, and the Utes wanted them to leave. However, after their visit to Washington, some Utes, like Ouray, realized that they were greatly outnumbered by the much

Family Man, the Utes, and an Exciting Trip Back From Washington City

better armed Americans. Most Americans wanted the Utes to entirely leave the Territory of Colorado, their abundant homeland for centuries.

The annuity distribution and treaty talks lasted for six days, and on October 7, 1863, the parties reached an agreement. John Nicolay, Michael Steck, Simeon Whitley, Lafayette Head, and John Evans signed for the United States. The Utes signing the document included Un-Cow-Rat-Gut (Red Color), Sha-Wa-She-Yet (Blue Flower), Colorado, U-Ray (Arrow), No-Va-Vetu-Quar-Et (One Who Slides Under Snow), Sa-Wa-Wat-Se-Wich (Blue River), A-Ca-Mu-Che-Ne (Red Wind), Mu-Chu-Chop (Lock of Hair), Sa-Patchi (Blue Warm) and Cinche (Left Hand). The Tabeguache agreed to stay on the western side of the Snowy Range (the Continental Divide) until they moved to their reservation land, and they would allow roads, mail stations, Indian Agencies, and military posts to be built on their land. In return, the government would provide them with legal title to their reservation and $10,000 per year in household goods and food for ten years. They would also receive 750 head of cattle and 3,500 sheep, and it was stipulated that their new Agency would have a blacksmith's shop and a farrier for the Utes' use. The U.S. government again agreed to protect the Utes as long as they complied with the terms of the treaty. Quinche, Ouray, and Sho-Wa-She-Yet were the only members of the Ute delegation to Washington who signed the treaty itself, but most of the actual Tabeguache chiefs signed. The men all smoked the peace pipe to seal the agreement. Then Nicolay awarded silver peace medals to seven Ute chiefs, including Ouray.

Ouray was considered overall leader of the Utes from that point on by the Americans, although it was recognized that it was a precarious leadership. The U.S. proclamation of Ouray as the Utes' single leader was perhaps the only positive thing to come from the treaty. Many historians feel it remarkable that Evans got any agreement whatsoever, but the agreement was only with the Tabeguache. Ouray learned from this experience that he would have to give up

This photo of Ouray may have been taken in 1863 in Washington as it was one of the few times he dressed like a White man when there, wearing a vest, shirt and watch fob. Chamberlain Photo.

Author's collection.

≈ 177 ≈

some Ute land to get guarantees of the Utes' right to the remaining land. In order to convince the other Ute bands to sign the treaty he had brazenly signed, Ouray began to formulate the idea that the Utes could protect themselves, not by fighting, but by bargaining with the Whites. He was evidently trying for a middle course between the two cultures. Ouray hoped the Utes would reduce their hunting grounds and start raising at least some cattle, sheep, crops; using buckskins and other items to trade with the Whites for extra income. However, his control over any of the Ute bands other than the Tabeguache was questionable, especially during the time right after the signing of the 1863 treaty. Many members of the other bands felt Ouray was selling them out to the Americans. It was a very tough problem, and Chief Ouray stated that the negotiations from the Ute point of view—they were like the agreement made by the buffalo after it has been pierced by many arrows. "All he can do is lie down and cease every attempt to escape or resist."[96]

Nevava was the main northern Ute leader of those Utes whose bands were not nearly as close to the Americans as the Utes in the San Luis Valley; and only after Nevava's death did Ouray gain much power among the northern bands. What was surprising was that Ouray did, for the most part on his own, continue to function as the overall chief until he died.

> *Ouray's hold upon his people was always precarious except for the members of his own band (the Tabeguache), who were usually loyal to him. He accomplished his objectives primarily through patience, diplomacy, and the strength of his personality, rather than by any power that he might have had as head chief of the tribe.*[97]

U.S. Secretary of the Interior Carl Schurtz wrote of Ouray:

> *I have become acquainted with several chiefs of so-called "wild" tribes, who had won a reputation as men of ability, such as Spotted Tail, Red Cloud, Chief Joseph, and others, and while I found them to possess considerable shrewdness in the management of their own affairs according to their Indian notions, their grasp of things outside of that circle was extremely uncertain. I may except only Ouray, the late chief of the Ute nation, a man of a comprehensive mind, of large views, appreciating with great clearness not only the present situation of his race, but also its future destiny and the measures necessary to save the Indians from destruction and to assimilate them with the white people with whom they have to live.*[98]

Although the Tabeguache had again refused to be moved to a reservation, they did agree to the stipulation that they would take the territory that was supposed to become their reservation (possibly with the Mouache) after the Plains Indians were moved to their reservations. They wanted Ute enemy tribes to be put on reservations first, hopefully outside Colorado, so that their enemies would not know exactly where the Utes were located and attack them. It was actually a very reasonable point, especially since the U.S. was not protecting them as it had agreed in two different treaties.

Most importantly, in the Treaty of 1863 (as later amended unilaterally by the U.S.), the Tabeguache gave up the part of the San Luis Valley that was populated by Americans and the U.S. recognized the future reservation as being Ute land under American law. The Tabeguache admitted the supremacy of the U.S. and its right to establish roads, railroads, mail lines, Indian Agencies, and military posts on their land. It was specifically agreed that miners and prospectors could come on Ute land to prospect and mine. It was further agreed that if a white man committed a crime on Ute land, he would be tried in American courts and be sentenced as if the crime had been committed on White soil. If a Ute committed a crime, he would be turned over to American authorities for like punishment. The 10,000 to 15,000 pounds of "presents" was given out in Conejos when the treaty was signed by the Tabeguache. However, the entire treaty was eventually found to be null and void, as the United States unilaterally changed important parts of the treaty without the Tabeguache's knowledge and kept it a secret from them for some time after ratification. It was also becoming obvious that the Ute bands not present at the treaty talks would not agree to be bound by an agreement that was basically made only by and with the Tabeguache.

The fraud on the part of the U.S. government in changing the terms of the agreement added more confusion to the already confusing situation. The U.S. Senate had changed three pages of the seven page treaty without the knowledge of the Utes and did not honor its other commitments made under the treaty. Alexander Cummings wrote that the three pages of changes were so "difficult, if not impossible for even an intelligent (White) reader… to understand what changes were accomplished" that there was no way the Utes could understand it, "even if someone had translated and read it to them."[99]

Although the U.S. later tried, not even the Tabeguache Utes would agree to ratify the amendments that the U.S. had made to the treaty. The important changes made by the Senate were very basic to the agreement and reduced the size of the boundary of the reservation that the Utes were agreeing to eventually be confined to and reduced the amount of food they were to receive. The reservation that the Utes had agreed to (but would not immediately move to) was described in the original treaty as from the headwaters of the Uncompahgre (the Mineral Point area) down the Uncompahgre and the Gunnison Rivers to the future Grand Junction, then up the Colorado River to future Glenwood Springs, then up the Roaring Fork to Independence Pass, south down the crest of the Collegiate and Sawatch Ranges to where it meets the Sangre de Cristo (Marshal Pass), then over to the Great Sand Dunes, across the San Luis Valley to the Rio Grande River, up the Rio Grande to its headwaters and over to the Mineral Point area at the point of beginning. This was the first time that any definite boundaries had been given to proposed Ute land.

In the treaty's later unapproved form, it was stated the Utes would give up the entire San Luis Valley, while the original treaty description had them giving up only the southern portion of the San Luis Valley below a line from the "Great Bend" in the Rio Grande River to the Great Sand Dunes. The Utes had actually made the point very clear in Washington that they would not give up **any** part of the San Luis Valley, so even giving up the southern portion was a major concession probably agreed to at the treaty conference because so many Americans lived there as well as the soldiers of Fort Garland. The number of stock cattle that the Utes were to receive was also reduced. Agent Head agreed that the original treaty had been severely altered without Ute knowledge and was null and void.

Life in Conejos returned to normal after the Utes left. Lafe's sister Eliza regained her health quickly during her time in Colorado. Eliza was probably scared to death by being surrounded by thousands of Native Americans and having Mexican-Americans who were said to be dangerous living nearby. Her son Finis loved being in Conejos, but there was now a major problem. Finis described Martina as:

> ...*a full-blooded Spanish woman, large and portly and used to having her own way. She was kind to me but as to mother, I sensed trouble from the start. I knew mother would not obey orders from anyone....*[100]

Martina owned a young Navajo slave girl and often hired her out to other Mexican-Americans, who were said to beat her on occasions. Martina kept the girl locked up at night because she was afraid she would run away. Eliza hated the idea of slavery, and she was very upset by the way the young girl was being treated. One night, Eliza took the key to the girl's room, brought a horse from the stable to the house, and released the Navajo girl. By morning the girl was well on her way back to her people. It should be noted that the only offense that Lafe and Martina were said to have personally committed at this time was locking the girl up at night.

When the loss was discovered, Martina was furious, and Eliza announced that she and her two children were going home. Finis argued for them staying, as he liked Western life, and Lafe had offered to send him to a fine school in Santa Fe. However Eliza was determined that she and her children were going back to a more civilized area. The Espinosa episode and the number of Utes surrounding the Head house at the treaty negotiations had helped firm up this opinion. Finis said he could not let his mother and sister travel alone, so their family left on November 12, 1863. However there is evidence Finis may have either soon come back or never left.

The United States never did provide the provisions promised to the Utes in the 1863 Treaty; and the winter of 1863-64 brought early, heavy snows that prevented the Utes from hunting buffalo on the plains or in the foothills in the fall, so they had little meat prepared for the winter. Soon the Utes were literally begging for food in Colorado City, and in desperation they decided to again get their meat from the livestock of the American settlers.

CHAPTER NINE

Otto Mears, New Mexico Slavery, and Starving Utes
(1864-1866)

> "... There were few military or civil officials who did not own captive slaves and they were found even in the service of the Indian agents."
> Hubert Howe Bancroft, Historian

It soon became apparent that the large number of Utes who had come to Conejos for the 1863 treaty had scared some of Lafe's neighbors as well as his sister Eliza. A group of Conejos residents soon signed a petition requesting Lafe's removal as Indian Agent. It was sent to the U.S. Attorney for Colorado. The petition read (without corrections):

> *We consider Lafayette Head to be the Indian Agent as having been the cause of all the trouble and difficulties which the people of this county has been subject to for these last two years and that we do also consider him totally unfit for the office he occupies and undeserving of the confidence of the Government for the following reasons.*
>
> *1st... charges having been made against him... of having bought Indian children with government property, contrary to the laws of the United States can be fully substantiated.*
>
> *2nd Because his loyalty to the Government is very doubtful to us, as he has on a certain occasion expressed himself in the most disrespectful terms of whom our President... and is a regular subscriber to the Ohio Crisis (a Democratic newspaper which pushed for the ouster of Lincoln and the Republicans from power).*
>
> *3rd Because by false and malicious representations he has induced Gov. Evans to establish a military post in our midst,*

for which there has never been an occasion and three of our citizens have had premature and violent death at the hands of the soldiers.

4th Because all those persons who have known him for years pronounce him to be a bad and dangerous man of a mean and revengeful disposition and public opinion points him to be the cause of the deaths that have been recently committed.

Therefore we earnestly believe that his removal from the office he occupies as Indian Agent would not only serve the best interest of the Government but would restore quietness and harmony of feelings in this community....[101]

The petition was dated at Conejos on January 18, 1864, and signed by forty-three residents (out of about 300 living in the town at the time), but it included three county commissioners, the county treasurer and coroner, the probate judge, and two constables. One interesting question is why his neighbors felt Head was vengeful? Nowhere else during the research into his life by this author has that accusation been found, but it is very possible that these people were perhaps being vengeful themselves for some perceived

The Utes, especially women and children, were often forced to beg for food in the mid-1860s as much of their game had been killed by whites.

Harper's Weekly, March 16, 1876.

CHAPTER 9

wrong. The signers of the petition were mostly government officials who had no money at stake with the loss of the Conejos Ute Agency, and who would have the same salaries with less trouble if the Utes were gone. On the other hand, Conejos businessmen were said to be furious about the petition. Lafe may have had a conference with the Governor or the U.S. Attorney regarding this petition; but no apparent action was ever taken, and Lafe remained Indian Agent. Most, if not all, of the allegations were false, and the probable motive was that these Conejos citizens did not like the large number of Utes constantly camping near their town. The problem would solve itself when the Utes were removed from the San Luis Valley in 1868.

It was at this time that Otto Mears became an important new player in Lafe's life and in the lives of many San Luis Valley settlers in the second half of the 1860s. Mears had been discharged from the Union Army on August 31, 1864, at Las Cruces, New Mexico, near the Mexican border. Michael Kaplan, one of Mears' biographers, writes that Mears worked his way north while walking along the Rio Grande River from Las Cruces, New Mexico, to Santa Fe, doing odd jobs along the way. In Santa Fe, Mears was an efficient manager of the clothing shop of Elsberg and Amberg, and he came to the attention of their chief competitor, Z. Staab Brothers, who approached Mears with a proposal. They would back him, if he opened a general mercantile store using his own name, so his present employer would not know who was financing him. This was a huge opportunity for Mears that he quickly accepted, and he operated his store as "Mears and Company." Then, in early 1865, he took his considerable stock by wagon to Conejos.

Mears was only twenty-four or twenty-five when he came to Conejos, where he originally opened a store in his name on the north side of the Conejos River at Guadalupe. However, Mears usually referred to his store as being located in Conejos. He went into partnership with Head to build another grist mill and a saw mill in Conejos, as lumber and flour were in great demand in the area. Otto Mears was supposedly the one who noted that Fort Garland was paying $20 per 100 pounds for flour and $80 per 1,000 board feet for lumber—very high prices at the time. Prices were so high at the fort because freight costs for the 150 to 200 miles from Denver or Pueblo over Sangre de Cristo Pass doubled or tripled the cost of many of the goods. Iron materials were very costly at the time, and nails cost from fifty cents to a dollar each, as they were still handmade by a blacksmith; so the pieces for the two mills' equipment were fastened together with rawhide, except for the saw blade in the lumber mill.

Some historians feel Mears totally owned the flour and saw mills, others state he and Lafe were partners, and yet others have written Mears simply worked for Head. The most likely scenario is that they were partners, but with Mears basically running the show because of Lafe's mild mannered ways. Lafe already had a flour mill and a saw mill, but apparently helped build these larger and better equipped mills to increase production and produce "American flour" instead of red course ground "Mexican flour."

The lives of Lafayette Head and Otto Mears were a contrast in personalities. In their day, Mears was the most admired of the two, but today it might well be Head's character that would win out. Mears got his start by trickery, working secretly for a competitor of the men who employed him. Head was a farmer and stockman, who lived off the earth. Head was a man enjoying a somewhat simple life. Mears was a driven man who was out to gain power and money. Mears liked being with the rich and powerful. Lafe was equally friendly with the rich and the poor. In his day, Head was often seen as a "simple" man, but he was greatly admired for his honesty, trustworthiness, and courage—all traits that Mears lacked. Mears used his supposed friendship with the Utes for his own gain, and they eventually tried to kill him. Head was a good, close friend of the Utes, who were cautious, but felt him trustworthy and knew that he was trying to help them. Although the Utes said at one time that Carson and Pfeiffer were their two favorite Indian Agents, it is a good bet that Head was number three. Head fed the Utes when they were hungry. Mears would not have done that and even cheated them out of some of their food. For example, at one time he recycled just the hides of fifty cows, which he claimed had been killed and the meat given to the Utes. Mears was totally engrossed in the "San Juan Mining Excitement;" and he was a gambler who especially loved poker and was good at it. Head was tempted, but never got involved in mining and did not seem to be the type of man who would gamble. His favorite game was chess. For forty years, Mears migrated to wherever he thought he might make more money. For over forty years Head liked to sit on his front porch at Conejos with his wife and many friends.

Otto Mears.
Hall, *History of Colorado, Vol. 4.*

CHAPTER 9

As the Civil War neared its end (which occurred on April 9, 1865), Coloradoans did not give up in their quest to become a state. In 1864, Territorial Governor Evans persuaded the U.S. Congress to adopt an enabling act to make Colorado a state, but a majority of Colorado citizens (6,192) voted against it. Then in 1865 Colorado voted to approve statehood and adopt a constitution; but the Democrats claimed fraud in the election. In May of 1866, President Andrew Johnson vetoed a successful bill intending to kill statehood, but the Democrats overrode the veto. It would be almost ten more years before Colorado would obtain statehood, during which time Colorado's population rose from 35,000 in 1866 to 150,000 in 1875.

Shortly after he became Colorado Governor John Evans made a treaty in Denver with Lafe, Ouray, Kit Carson and a few other Utes, but Congress did not approve his action at the time.

Author's Collection.

Meanwhile, in the early winter of 1864 and 1865, the Utes had become very rebellious. They were hungry and realized they could not trust the Americans or the U.S. Government; and they had just learned that changes had secretly been made to the 1863 treaty by the U.S. Senate.

Kit Carson was now often at Fort Garland and soon would be its commander. He described Fort Garland's garrison as "a very motley crew," as it was made up of mostly volunteer soldiers who had not yet been released from the Union Army after the Civil War—probably because they had nowhere else to go. And, given the unrest, Lafe's calm manner and negotiation skills would soon be badly needed.

Colorado's territorial military had turned its attention at this time to the Native Americans on the Colorado Plains, who the Confederates were enticing to join them in their war against the Union men in Colorado. It was not long before chasing hostile Indians was a full time job for the Union soldiers, culminating in the Massacre at Sand Creek. On November 29, 1864, 700 men of the Colorado Territorial Mounted Volunteers under the command of General John Chivington, attacked a village of peaceful Cheyenne and Arapaho led by Chief Black Kettle. The Native Americans were camped along Sand Creek on the Colorado Plains near Fort Lyon military post. Most of the men of the Indian village were out hunting, so the vast majority of the 160 Native Americans killed at Sand Creek were women, elderly men, or children. Black Kettle was flying an American flag from his tepee, and as soon as the fighting started he ran out with a white flag of truce. When Chivington saw a soldier trying to protect a young Indian boy, he told the soldier to kill him as –"nits become lice." Sand Creek was one of the worst massacres by U.S. troops in American history. Chivington had been a hero at Glorieta Pass and in civilian life was a minister; yet, after Sand Creek, he married his deceased son's wife, participated in several business scams, was accused of forgery, and fled to Canada to escape prosecution.

The residents of Colorado Territory feared Indian attacks in retaliation for the Sand Creek Massacre. Lafe spent a great deal of time assuring San Luis Valley residents that they need not fear the Utes because the Native Americans who were killed by Chivington's troops were mortal enemies of the Utes. He also talked to the Utes and told them to avoid the Whites for a while, as they might be trigger happy because of the situation. Colorado Territorial Governor Evans foolishly backed Chivington's actions as being necessary.

News of the Sand Creek Massacre ignited a full-scale Plains Indian war. Attacks against American travelers increased dramatically and Denver lost contact with points back East for a month. Even after the massacre,

The Sand Creek Massacre on November 29, 1864, was the worst massacre in U. S. military history, as U. S. troops killed 160 women, children, and old men in a surprise attack while they flew an American and a white flag of truce. It ignited a full scale Plains War against the Americans that lasted several years.

Dunn, *Massacres of the Mountains*.

CHAPTER 9

the U.S. government did not send food to the Utes, and as a result of Sand Creek, the Native Americans on the Plains of Colorado went on a massive revolt, even burning the Town of Julesburg to the ground in January 1865. In the San Luis Valley, the Utes were sure the same type of massacre would happen to them as at Sand Creek. Kit Carson's and Lafe's efforts to keep peace were hampered by small periodic Ute and Jicarilla Apache attacks on the settlers, mainly efforts to steal food.

Besides the Plains Indians being on the warpath, early in the spring of 1865, groups of hungry, begging Utes appeared at Colorado City and Pueblo, as well as continuing to do so in the San Luis Valley. Frightened residents notified Lafe, and he rushed to intervene. To reassure the citizens, he sent the following letter to *The Rocky Mountain News*, where it appeared on April 19, 1865.

> *Pueblo C.T., April 7, 1865*
>
> *EDITORS NEWS: I met the Tabeguache Ute Indians, under my charge, on the 5th instant, at Colorado City, and had no trouble whatsoever, on prevailing upon them to leave said place for their own reservation, as I found them in a truly destitute condition. I was obliged to issue to them a reasonable amount of flour for the support of their families, while on their journey homeward. The current report of their aggression toward the Whites in the vicinity of Colorado Springs, was without foundation and to a person familiar with these Indians, no trouble need be apprehended from that quarter. Owing to the difficulties on the plains, these Indians did not receive their presents from the Government last season, and are therefore poor and needy; they will now return to their Agency and wait the notion of their Superintendent, who is doubtless doing all he can to hurry their goods onward across the plains.*
>
> *LAFAYETTE HEAD*

Until this time, there had been little in the way of an attempt to restrict the Utes to a reservation, except for the disastrous "Treaty of 1863." However, in 1865, there was a movement to at least get the Utes off the Front Range. In addition to the hungry Southern and Tabeguache Utes, the Northern Utes were coming to Denver and Boulder on the Front Range to meet with Territorial officials or trade for supplies. The Mouache and Jicarilla Apache also came to Denver from the south. Governor Evans reciprocated with the northern Utes and went to their territory in July of 1865 in an effort to see if they would stay in the part of Colorado west of the Continental Divide. However little was accomplished.

In the summer of 1865, the Utes were killing or stealing the stock of the Whites on the upper Arkansas River, and the Plains Indians were still on the warpath on the plains because of the Sand Creek Massacre. By this time, Chiefs Shavano and Colorow had become leaders of an angry faction of the entire Ute tribe, including the Tabeguache. This group did not want to give up the San Luis Valley and were causing considerable trouble. Since Lafe did not know which Ute belonged to what group, he asked and was allowed to move the place for dispensing of annuities to a point away from Conejos.

Fortunately for Lafe, his half-brother, Jesse Arnold, had moved his family to Conejos in 1865, and was able to help out at the mill and on the ranch as Lafe's Indian Agent duties increased and became more demanding. Jesse and his wife had a son, David Lafayette Arnold; and a daughter, Mary, was born in Conejos the following year. Jesse set up shop as a merchant, and for several years Lafe enjoyed having some of his own family living nearby. However, in the early 1870s, Jesse and his family moved to California.

By the time this photo was taken of Shavano he had become more hostile towards the Whites. Shavano was an early friend of Ouray, but became a war chief and made attempts to take Ouray's position. In this photo he wears a peace medal and carries a gun.

Author's Collection.

CHAPTER 9

In addition to his usual Agency duties and the increasing unrest among the Utes, Lafe received another major time-consuming project. On June 28, 1865, President Andrew Johnson had directed every Indian Agent in the Southwest to conduct a survey to determine persons holding Native American captives as slaves, although they were not at this time asked to free Indian slaves. When Lafe submitted his list of Indian captives to Colorado Governor John Evans on July 17, 1865, he recorded over 160 names in Costilla and Conejos Counties. His full transmittal letter reads as follows:

> *In the company of E. R. Harris, U.S. Marshal, I called upon all those persons that hold Indian captives in Costilla and Conejos Counties and interrogated the Indians themselves, and their replies to my inquiries, you will please find in the accompanying lists which embrace within my knowledge every Indian Captive in these two counties, and to the credit of the citizens here I would add, that they all manifested a prompt willingness on their part to give up said Captives, whenever called upon to do so, and in view of the facts, I would most respectfully recommend, that all the Navajo Captives here be returned to their Reservation in New Mexico. Also the few Ute Indians residing in private families here, it is generally understood that they are there with the consent of their parents or friends, and enjoy the full privilege of returning to their people whenever they have the inclination or disposition to do so. Very many of these Ute children are orphans, and therefore homeless and perhaps under these circumstances, their condition would not be so much benefited by your order. Yet if your order is imperative, and you are instructing me to have them all removed, I will promptly do so.*
>
> *I have notified all the people here, that in the future, no more Captives are to be purchased or sold as I shall immediately arrest both parties caught in the transaction. This step, I think, will at once put an end to this most barbaric and inhuman practice, which has been in existence with the Mexicans for generations.*
>
> *There are captives here who know not their own parents; nor can they speak their mother tongue, and who reconise (sic) no one but those who rescued them from the Merciless (sic) Cap-*

> tors. What are we to do with these? I would here add that I have not incorporated in the accompanying lists the large number of Captives that have legally married in the two Counties.
>
> I shall wait for further orders from you in regard to their removal. Please also instruct me what course I shall pursue in the premisis (sic) in regard to those who are not willing to return to their people.[102]

A number of well-known men in the San Luis Valley were on Lafe's list of slave owners, and Kit Carson was said to have three such captives. There were the names of six Anglo owners on the list turned in by Lafe. Lafe was accused, many years later, of getting rich taking ransoms offered by the parents for captive children that he as Agent, Marshal, or Sheriff had taken from the slave owners for little or no money. However, it was found that there was no proof of that charge.

Governor Evans promptly forwarded Lafe's July 17 list of captives to the Commissioner of Indian Affairs in Washington with the good suggestion (probably influenced by Lafe's transmittal letter) that those "slaves" who did not want to return home not be forced to leave their adopted families, and he considered the project closed. Governor Evans, however, was not aware of one major problem with Lafe's list—that it did not include any of the Indian children living in Lafe's home or living with other families in the Town of Conejos. Lafe would later submit a second list that would include himself and other Conejos residents that were slaveholders.

Obviously Lafe was not following exact orders when he chose not to submit the names of those residents of the Town of Conejos who had Native American "slaves" living with them. In Lafe's defense, however, he was probably sure that the American officials back East would not understand the Mexican-American practice of slavery and was trying to protect his friends and the children who had been adopted by them as young orphans and who had become an integral part of their families. Those who defended holding slaves usually did it by pointing out that even military officers and government Indian Agents owned slaves. Lafe, as many others, countered this argument with the fact that if their parents were unknown they were almost always better off with a White family that loved them than with a non-related Native American family, where they might also be made true slaves, especially if captured from another tribe. It should be noted that Lafe did not steal the children taken in by his family. They had been lost or taken by others, and Lafe did not know who or where their families were. Without taking any moral blame off Lafe, if there was any, it is notable that

CHAPTER 9

Lafe did not take in any type of slave until after he met and was living with Martina, and we know that it was her great desire, as an act of charity, to take the children in on several later occasions.

Slaves were held among many Native American tribes long before the Spanish occupied New Mexico Province; but it was not until the Utes gained horses that Indian slavery became common. Horses were so valuable that only a slave or the more valuable possession of a European (like a gun) could be traded for one. The Utes tended to get slaves from tribes in the Great Basin or deep in Mexico. These Native American tribes were usually desperately poor and were often glad to trade a child for a gun or a horse, so as to make it easier to hunt for food for the rest of the family. These tribes sometimes knew the child they traded might well be saved from certain starvation, which would happen if the child stayed with them.

As far back as 1700, records of the New Mexico parishes show that many Native Americans, especially Apache, were baptized into the Catholic faith. The captives (*criados*) were given Spanish names and at first were listed as "servants" or "of the house of…." Children under eighteen were very desirable to the Spanish because they could be easily trained in Spanish ways, while adults usually resisted and almost always did not need to be taken in as an act of charity. There were hardly any black slaves in New Mexico, or for that matter, almost anywhere in the West before the Civil War; but there were many Native Americans slaves in the Spanish or Mexican based systems. This was true even after 1829 when slavery was declared illegal in the Province of New Mexico. The Treaty of Guadalupe-Hidalgo even contained this provision in Article XI:

> It shall not be lawful, under any pretext whatsoever, for any inhabitant of the United States to purchase or acquire any Mexican, or any foreigner residing in Mexico, who may have been captured by Indians inhabiting the territory of either of the two Republics (Mexico or United States) nor to purchase or acquire horses, mules, cattle, or property of any kind stolen within Mexican territory by such Indians.[103]

On April 9, 1866, the Republican Congress enacted the Civil Rights Act over the veto of Southern Unionist President Andrew Johnson. They felt the Act was important to support the Thirteenth Amendment (passed January 31, 1865). The Act defined "citizenship" as any person born in the United States and affirmed that all of its citizens were equally protected under the law, except that Indians who were not being taxed would not get citizenship (not until 1924) at this time, and that this protection applied regardless of race, color, or creed. This made the holding of slaves of any kind a violation of U.S. law, but there were no penalties attached to the legislation and it was not applied to Native Americans living on reservations. There were many Native American slaves in New Mexico Territory and also in the San Luis Valley, as the Mexican-Americans who had moved north into the San Luis Valley had brought their Indian slaves with them as servants, workers, or just a member of the family.

It was expected by the Spanish that the "masters" of any Indian slaves would act as a good parent or owner and have them all baptized or they could be taken away from them by the authorities. Lafe and Martina did as expected, and the Conejos Church records the couple as the parents of many baptized Indian children. They were also sponsors for the baptisms of many such children taken in by other families. Unfortunately, after the Civil War ended, there were many kinds of "Indian slaves" who were being lumped together in one category by the U.S. Congress and the Bureau of Indian Affairs.

There were also various explanations as to how young Indians came to be part of a Spanish, Mexican, or even later, an American household. First, there were those taken in because they were young and there was no one who was taking care of them at the time they were found. If they were not taken, they almost certainly died. An attempt might or might not be made to locate their parents or the ones responsible for them, and if anyone was found they were returned home. But often no one was found, so the children were kept and "adopted." However, they were free to leave any time if their parents found them or after they could take care of themselves.

Second, were those children left voluntarily by their Native American parents who had given them up for a good reason. Valid reasons included the parents could not support them, they had a medical condition that the Indians could not treat, they were to learn a trade, or their parents wanted them to learn fluent Spanish or English. The parents knew they could come get their children at any time. Chief Ouray and his brother Quinche were two of the most notable examples of this group.

Third, were those stolen from their families or whose parents were killed in a raid by another tribe. This group could include Mexican, Native American, and American children. Chipeta, Ouray's wife, was such a child. She was found by the Utes in a deserted Kiowa Apache village that had been attacked by another unknown tribe and was taken in by the Utes at the age of two or three. The Utes liked her and made her part of their tribe. If the Utes had not wanted to keep her, she would have been sold or traded. When the Spanish purchased a captive, he or she was expected to at least work off the price paid for them. If parents or relatives found a child who had been purchased, it was expected that whoever had bought the child would be reimbursed the price paid. One of Kit Carson's Navajo "slaves" met these criteria. She was with him for six years to work off the $300 he paid for her, but in the meantime she became part of the family and chose to stay with the Carsons when her time was up.

Fourth, as non-Indians began to question slavery, they were more likely to refuse to buy captives and the Indians would often then consider child slaves useless and kill them unless they were purchased. Kit Carson's wife, for example, traded the Utes a horse for a boy called "Juan," who was going to be killed. Everyone agreed Juan was treated the same as her own children. Juan lived with the Carson family until he was grown and found a wife.

The fifth category would be the true slaves, often being mistreated or abused. These were the only people (usually Navajo) who actually needed the new law's help, and they were a small percentage of the total number taken away from their Mexican-American or American adopted families by the new American law. As mentioned, Lafe suggested that all of the Navajo slaves be released immediately.

Navajo slaves were often treated badly by the Spanish, Mexican, and even some American owners. The Navajos were:

> ...the scourges of New Mexico, perpetrators of innumerable raids in which thousands of head of horses, cattle, and sheep were carried off and hundreds of ordinary, unoffending people, herders, and inhabitants of small villages and ranchos were killed or made captives. To them it (slavery) seemed reasonable and justifiable, a custom sanctioned by long practice, to exact some degree of retribution by taking Navajos captive in town.[104]

As mentioned, Martina evidently kept her Navajo slave(s) locked up at night, although she did not mistreat them. They were eventually allowed to go home; but, not until after the Civil War ended and the Thirteenth Amendment was adopted.

Another aspect of the Indian slave issue had arisen in 1866 that involved Lafe and Martina—this time Lafe was accused of stealing the children in the first place. In January 1866 (before the 1866 Civil Rights Bill was enacted), Sam F. Tappan, Commander at Fort Garland, wrote to the Commissioner of Indian Affairs and reported he had received information in the fall of 1863 that Lafayette Head was engaged in the "kidnapping and enslaving of Navajo women and children." Why Tappan did not bring this to the attention of his superiors or act on it sooner is unknown; but he only suggested to the Indian Bureau that perhaps Lafe "should be removed to some other Agency." A government investigation followed and, according to Tappan, Lafe "succeeded (sic) in proving that all the Navajo women and children in his family were purchased by his wife as an act of charity." This was at the same time (autumn of 1863) Kit Carson was chasing Navajos. It was very likely these Navajo were abandoned or captive Navajo brought to Lafe by Carson's soldiers.

The records of Our Lady of Guadalupe show the baptism of most of these "slaves," and indicate that the children were adopted "according to the custom of this country," and that after the Civil Rights Act of 1866 that the captives who chose to leave their "captors" were very few. Back on September 11, 1860, Lafe and Martina brought two little girls to church to be baptized by Padre Rolly. Rita Cabeza was ten years old and Estefana Cabeza was eight. The parents were listed in the baptismal book as Raphael Cabeza and Juana Martinez. These were "adopted" children, taken in from unnamed sources, treated well, and taught to do house and garden work. The Heads raised two Ute girls in his household, sisters or cousins, one of whom retained the Head surname all her life. Both returned to live as married adults on the Southern Ute Reservation. They were devout Catholics "of a distinctive Hispanic cultural orientation," as were other Utes raised in Hispanic households.[105]

Lafayette probably approved of the slave system involving Indian captives, or at least realized that individual circumstances needed to be considered; yet, it was evident that in 1865 he was also trying as an Indian Agent to follow orders that had come from Washington pertaining to Indian slavery. Head pointed out to his superiors that the heads of households having a child captive were encouraged to have them seek a mate at fourteen to sixteen years of age for girls and eighteen to twenty for boys, and once married, the captive was automatically free. The United States census records from 1860 to 1885 record a total of nine "adopted" Native American and Mexican children who passed through the Head household. Lafe and Martina had no children of their own; although, as mentioned previously, Martina had at least one and perhaps two children by her first husband, both of whom were now getting close to, if not already considered, adults.

The 1860 census identified seven children in the Head home ranging from eight to eighteen. Felipe, Juan, and Antonia were recorded as "Indian, birthplace unknown." These three, plus a girl named Rita, all had the surname "Head." Eight year old Estefana had the surname "Cabeza." Vicente Dominguez and Gertrudia Medina were listed as "Mexican children." From Lafe's point of view, all were probably adopted. The 1870 census showed three new Indian children and that only one of the earlier three reported in 1860 lived there. The 1880 census showed two of the 1870 Indian children still there, as well as one new Indian child, Miguel Head, who was "treated as a son for all purposes." As an adult Miguel Head in his own right owned a significant amount of ranch land adjoining Lafe's property. He was also listed as "son" in the 1885 census with his race changed to "White." The 1885 census list no "slave" children at the Head household, although it does list young children that were evidently "the children or grand-children" of "slaves" that had chosen to stay with Lafe and Martina. On February 28, 1866, Gov. Cummings reported he had interviewed Lafayette Head, noting the children in his home were "mostly orphans" and that Head and his wife had taken them "all in as infants as an act of charity." The children were now old enough to make their own decisions and were free to go if they wanted, so the Governor saw "nothing to be gained by disturbing the parent-child relationship." Cummings was the second Colorado Territorial Governor that verified that Lafe was doing nothing wrong.

It is also important to note that in 1868 the New Mexico Territorial District Court tried 171 residents of Rio Arriba, Santa Fe, and Taos Counties in New Mexico Territory holding Indian captives. Since he now lived in Colorado, Lafe was not one of them and the judge ruled that "because the social and economic exchange of captives played such an important part in both Hispanic and Indian societies, the Court (hereby) dismisses most of the cases."[106] The few cases not dismissed were captive children truly held as slaves and not allowed to go home.

While Lafe was compiling his first and then second list of San Luis Valley Indian "slave owners," unrest and hostilities among the Utes continued. In April of 1866, Kit Carson was transferred from Fort Union to become the commander at Fort Garland, a position he only held from May 19, 1866 until October 28, 1867, when illness forced him to resign. Carson had been promoted to Brevet General by the end of the Civil War; but when he was transferred to Fort Garland, he had been reduced in rank to a Lieutenant Colonel, as he had a much bigger command at his previous post at Fort Union. Major General John Pope Cummings of Fort Union said of Carson:

> Carson is the best man in the country to control these Indians and to prevent war, if it can be done. He is personally

known and liked by every Indian of the bands likely to make trouble.[107]

Since the Utes had been making constant trouble and their raids were becoming more frequent, it was hoped that Carson would not only prevent a full-scale war, but keep their raids to a minimum. Carson obviously thought firm actions were necessary, but could be accomplished only with a much stronger military presence in the San Luis Valley.

The principal duty of the men at Fort Garland at this time was to keep watch on the Utes and Jicarilla Apache, and Kit Carson was a good choice for the commander's job. Carson noted in one of his very first reports that the fort was "in very bad condition, attributed in my opinion to culpable neglect of the commanding officers."[108] He also mentioned that there were only seventy-three soldiers and ten officers at the fort, which he described as "a collection of log and adobe houses around a parade ground."[109] Carson saw that the fort needed more soldiers, and that the number would grow as Indian raids were growing more frequent at the time. War Chief Shavano's Tabeguache band and war Chief Kaniache's Mouache were raiding ranches and had killed several ranchers. Carson estimated that within fifty miles of the fort there were three bands of Ute Indians (Mouache, Capote, and Tabeguache) that had 800 warriors, and another 250 Jicarilla Apache

Kit Carson's house in Taos also doubled as the Ute and Jicarilla Agency.

Author's Collection.

warriors were also nearby. He knew the Utes were desperate for food and close to war, and he requested that he immediately be sent two companies of cavalry—one of infantry, and a battery of light artillery.

In June, Head came to Carson and told him that Shavano's band had again been raiding, this time east of the Sangre de Cristos. He had taken cattle, sheep, and other food items and beat a sheep herder severely. Then Head had received reports that three men had been killed in the same area. Carson said he could only afford to give Lafe ten soldiers and six friendly Indians to help put down the rebellion. Head was told he could kill or capture Shavano. Head left immediately, and three days afterwards Carson got some of his reinforcements. It is unknown if Lafe talked with Shavano, but by the end of June it looked like matters had quieted down, but Head still had no funds or supplies for the Utes and Jicarilla Apache. Carson had been giving what food he could from Fort Garland to the Utes.

In June, Albert Pfeiffer returned to Army Headquarters in Santa Fe, where he accepted a commission as Captain of a battalion of New Mexico Volunteers and was sent to Fort Garland, where he would work under his friend Kit Carson. Carson knew Pfeiffer had a drinking problem and required him to report to him every morning, every evening, and every roll call "for orders." During this time Pfeiffer was offered the position of Sub-Agent for the Ute Bands at Abiqui and Tierra Amarilla, but he wisely did not accept the offer. By August, 1866, Carson had four companies of volunteers as well as his regular army soldiers at Fort Garland.

Carson was the perfect choice not only to deal with the Native Americans, but also the local settlers:

> At (Fort) Garland, Carson kept an open house, exercising the most unbounded hospitality to all visitors and passersby.... (including) the Ute Indians of whom he had such a powerful influence that no trouble ever took place when an appeal could be made to him.... It was a study to see him sitting surrounded by them rolling cigaritos and passing the tobacco around, all the while laughing, joking, talking Spanish, or Ute tongue, with such abundant gesticulations and hand movements, that it seemed to me he talked more with his hands and shoulders that with his tongue.[110]

It was a difficult situation for the Utes, as they no longer trusted the Americans to keep their word, yet the Utes also knew the Americans could defeat them in war. However, it helped that the Utes now had the two Indian Agents that they liked and trusted the most as the Commander and

Second in Command at Fort Garland. Carson, in response, is quoted as saying that the Utes were the bravest and best "Red Skins" he had ever met in all his wild wanderings.

Carson and Lafe as Indian Agents had always wanted the Utes to be moved far away from the Whites to a permanent location; this time Carson suggested that they be moved near the Four Corners area. After it was obvious that the Utes would not move to the reservation provided for in the 1863 treaty, in his June, 1866 report Carson noted:

> *The time is fast approaching when the Government must take active definite measures for the Subjection and removal of these Indians to Reservations—A war will necessarily first ensue ere these wild men of the Mountains will Consent to leave their native haunt.... I am fearful that we are even now on the Verge of war with them.*[111]

Carson, however, was soon convinced that it was actually the Jicarilla Apache that were trying to talk the Utes into going to war with the Americans, and that the military needed to focus on that tribe and keep them away from the Utes.

It was July before the Utes were issued extra meat and flour that had just been received by Head. The justifiable but continuous begging of the Utes renewed an interest in getting them away from the Front Range, out of the San Luis Valley, and removed from at least the vast majority of Whites; and it was reported that it was obvious they were destitute and starving. Unbelievably, there were some legislators and military men who did not want Carson or Head to give the Utes their food annuities on time, as they felt that starving the Utes might help them decide to become farmers. The Jicarilla Apache were still busy trying to convince the Utes they needed to go to war against the Americans, and Kit Carson told the Jicarilla to return the property they had stolen or there would be no gifts that year.

On August 6, 1866, Kaniache's band was camped near Fort Garland, begging for food, when a Ute boy went missing and several days later his dead body was found. Carson and the fort's doctor felt the Ute boy had been hit in the head with a blunt object, but the doctor also stated he thought the boy might possibly have been poisoned. A Ute named Casador told Carson he thought the Ute medicine man might be responsible, since he and the dead boy both had love interests towards the same Ute girl. Some of those at the fort thought Mexican laborers might be responsible, but the laborers fled to the south and could not be found. Kit Carson sent for Head, who came to Fort Garland and met with Kaniache and his band. Several councils were held at the fort with Lafe and sometimes Carson attending, but there were no clues as to who had done the killing. The Utes were adamant it was a White who had committed the murder, but the Americans knew that it could well have been a Native American. After many meetings, Lafe established peace with Kaniache and his Utes. Kaniache had agreed with Lafayette to take 100 sheep in retribution for the murder, but he said there would still be revenge. Carson got upset at Lafe because he felt that giving the sheep made the U.S. look guilty when there was no evidence of that. It is unknown if Lafe talked again with Kaniache, but by the end of June it looked like matters had quieted down. As it turned out, the Americans discovered later that the death of the young man was due to a soldier putting something bad tasting in the liquor the young Ute was begging for, hoping to get him to stop the consistent begging, but not meaning to kill him.

Then there had been trouble at the Cimarron Agency when one of Kaniache's sons was shot and killed by a nervous sheepherder. There were also major food issues at that Agency at the same time. Albert Pfeiffer reported to Carson that there was a sense among the Cimarron Utes that no justice would be obtained by Kaniache, and that they needed to go on the warpath. This possibility, coupled with lack of food and the Americans not fulfilling their promises, had raised tensions at Cimarron to the boiling point. Then on August 19, Pfeiffer brought news Kaniache himself was now announcing there would be no justice given in this case or any other dealings with the Utes. Then the killer's case was dismissed in court. Carson was positive that this would be the action that started another major Ute war. Extra troops were sent to all the nearby forts and Fort Stevens had been ordered built on the eastern side of the Sangre de Cristo Pass from Fort Garland on a plateau at the foot of the Spanish Peaks. Captain A. J. Alexander was commander of a small garrison of about sixty men. Kaniache had come to Fort Garland while his son's death was being investigated.

There were several versions of what happened between the sheepherder and Kaniache's son,[112] but Taylor writes that the son was having no luck hunting and asked the sheepherder if he could have a sheep. A small band of Utes had evidently made the same request a little earlier and the sheepherder had given them one sheep, but then the Utes shot two more and left the two dead sheep behind. The sheepherder told Kaniache's son to take one of the dead sheep, but the son said he preferred to kill his own sheep and prepared to kill one that was alive by putting an arrow in his bow. The sheepherder then shot the boy and fled to Fort Union. Kaniache supposedly said the sheepherder's actions were not totally unreasonable, but "his other sons could scarcely be constrained." With some quick action, the Agents got Kaniache to realize that his son might have been at least partially at fault, he accepted $400 for the killing of his son, and matters became peaceful again.

Even with this close call, when General William Sherman (second in Command of the Army of the West at the time) was at Fort Garland on September 20, 1866, Kit Carson was not able to convince him that the Ute were a powder keg getting ready to explode, and no additional troops or food were authorized by Sherman. General Sherman was checking out the Indian problems for himself at this time, but he was arrogant and decided the problem was only the exaggerated claims of the local settlers with no proof. After reviewing several other forts, General Sherman soon came back to Fort Garland. Sherman said he was impressed with the way Carson dealt with the Utes, and he noted that Ouray was very influential among his people. Although he still did not authorize additional troops, Sherman did agree to keep four companies of soldiers at Fort Garland.

General Sherman then suggested another attempt be made to negotiate a Ute treaty, the terms of which would have forced the Utes to the reservation the U.S. had proposed under the 1863 agreement. This council was soon held near present-day Alamosa on the Big Bend of the Rio Grande. Kit Carson acted as interpreter, Lafe was present at the council, and Territorial Governor Cummings urged the Utes to accept the reservation and settle down "like White people." The Utes were adamantly against going to a reservation, as they again said if they stayed in one place their enemies could find and kill them.

Leroy Hafen, former Colorado State Historian, quotes Ouray as saying at this meeting:

> *Long time ago, Utes always had plenty. On the prairie, antelope and buffalo, so many Ooray can't count. In the mountains deer and bear, everywhere. In the streams, trout, duck, beaver, everything. Good Manitou gave all to red man; Utes happy all the year. White man came, and now the Utes go hungry a heap. Game much go every year—hard period to shoot now. Old man often weak from want of food. Squaw and papoose cry. Only strong brave live. White man grow a heap; Red man no grow—soon die all. Utes stop not in one place, and Comanches no find. But Utes settle down; then Comanches come and*

CHAPTER 9

kill. Tell great white Father, Cheyennes and Comanches go on reservation first; then Utes will. But Comanches first.[113]

The 1866 treaty council was a failure. General Sherman is reported to have said in disgust after the meeting, "They will have to freeze and starve a little more, I reckon, before they will listen to common sense."[114]

War Chiefs Kaniache and Shavano were getting extremely frustrated with the Utes not getting their rations. In late September and early October of 1866, Shavano and his band were in the Trinidad area and complaints were being made by the local settlers that they were stealing their sheep, horses, cows, coffee, sugar, flour, powder and lead, and corn. The settlers' concerns escalated greatly when Kaniache and his group appeared at the scene. The Utes then drove their horse herd over some of the settlers' crops. One of these settlers panicked and called for troops from Fort Stevens.

Kaniache caused trouble with the Whites after he was mistakenly captured and jailed before the 1849 Treaty. He loved to wear the red hat seen here into battle.

Author's Collection.

Captain Alexander first tried talking with Kaniache, who made the statement that Alexander was on Ute land, and if the Ute children were hungry, he would take whatever food they needed. Justice of the Peace, W. R. Walker, Uncle Dick Wootton's son, went to try to retrieve some of the stolen animals and calm matters down. Walker returned without any of the stolen items, although the amounts stolen were relatively small (twenty sheep, one horse, two cows, and a few of the few of the poor settler's meager supplies).

Alexander decided to let the matter rest for the night. Exactly what happened after this point is unclear, but evidently Alexander decided that he and his sixty soldiers would make the first move and fight the more than 200 Utes. Alexander chose to head up the Purgatory River with trumpets blowing and sabers drawn. When Alexander thought he saw the Utes raiding a settler's house, he and his men charged them. In fact the Utes were retrieving a Ute woman who had been shot by a settler named Gutierrez's trigger-happy son. The battle only stopped when the soldiers realized they were running out of ammunition. One Ute was killed in this fight, as well as one soldier. The Utes immediately went into retreat, but several more Utes were killed as they withdrew from the area. Alexander gave an exaggerated report that thirteen Utes were killed and Kaniache and other Utes were wounded. Another version of the fight was that Kaniache challenged Alexander to a fight, but Alexander refused, saying he was there to keep peace and not to cause a war. Then Kaniache started a battle and very soon saw he was losing the fight and decided to make a run for it.

This fight could have been yet another spark that started a massive Ute war; but on October 6, Ouray arrived at Fort Garland and said that his people would not fight like Kaniache or Shavano, and he would try to calm Kaniache down. In the meanwhile, Alexander was still chasing Kaniache, who killed several settlers on the Huerfano River and took a woman and four children captive. At Carson's request, Ouray brought his people to Fort Garland for protection from anxious white settlers, and then went after Kaniache with some of his warriors. Kaniache was told to quit fighting and come to the fort to make a treaty, which he did. He met with Kit Carson and agreed to stop fighting and return the stolen animals and supplies not already eaten. Carson had already asked Lafe to come help with a treaty council. On October 11, 1866, Head felt compelled to write *The Daily Mining Register* in Central City the following letter from Fort Garland, asking for the Mouache Utes to receive their allotment early:

CHAPTER 9

> *The Mouache band of Utahs have all come in and surrendered to General Carson. I leave this morning on official business for Fort Union. General Carson will, by letter, explain to Superintendent Cummings my temporary absence. Send over immediately to General Carson the beef cattle that were reserved for general distribution on the 25th instant. I will return in ten days.*

When the Utes got their food, they returned the stolen livestock, and Kaniache went back to New Mexico. The captured woman and her four children had already been released, and matters settled down again.

After the skirmishes, Territorial Governor Alexander Cummings explained the rising amount of trouble with the Utes to the Commissioner of Indian Affairs in October, 1866:

> *They (The Utes) are quite intelligent and point with great earnestness to the condition of all the places where the Whites have obtained a foothold. And they say with great force that if roads and settlements are allowed to be made in their present hunting grounds, which is all that is left to them, the game will vanish and they will soon be left to starvation.*[115]

In the winter of 1866-1867 an estimated 1,000 Tabeguache camped on Fountain Creek near Colorado City and survived by demanding and being given flour and other food by the people of that town. In May, Kaniache was again raiding and Ouray came to Fort Garland and sent Shavano to bring Kaniache to Fort Garland.

The Medicine Lodge Treaty was made in October 1867, with the Plains Indians agreeing to go to a reservation in western Indian Territory (Oklahoma), and they would also be allowed to go north up to the Arkansas River to hunt buffalo in the fall. Many of them went to Oklahoma, but other Native Americans stayed in Colorado and continued to fight. The Plains Indians who stayed became disorganized, they could not get enough food for winter, and they lost most of their battles with the U.S. soldiers. Soon they were on the run. There was no time for them to make war against the U.S. or their traditional enemies the Utes; although it was 1875 before they were totally gone from the Plains. By 1868, the Utes were basically the only Native Americans left to freely roam in Colorado. Their argument was now gone that they could not go to a reservation unless their enemies went first. Virginia Simmons wrote of another trend in the Northern part of Colorado:

Meanwhile, a slow migration of Utes was going to the Unitah Basin (in Utah). Regardless of whether they had been historically members of the Uintah band, they and others who followed were later called "Uintah" Indians and were assigned to the Uintah Valley Agency. [116]

CHAPTER TEN

The Kit Carson Treaty of 1868 and Saguache
(1866 - 1870)

> *Perhaps the most influential settler of the time was Lafayette Head.*
> Frederick Athearn, Land of Contrast: A History of Southeast Colorado

Despite the troubles with the Utes, in the fall of 1866, the San Luis Valley agricultural and ranching possibilities were still described in glowing terms by a reporter from the *Pueblo Daily News* of September 28, 1866, who was going to a treaty conference:

> ... (It is) covered, far as the eye can see, with salmon-colored grass, soft and silky as velvet, short, but of luxuriant richness, and waving in the fragrant air as if nature was swinging her censers, whose smoking ashes were of roses.... We rested upon the banks of the Rio Grande, broad and swiftly flowing, whose waters breaking in the shining foam-flocked waves, rushes grandly melodious to the gulf.... In the distance, beyond the river, under the cottonwoods, whose giant shadows loom grandly against the sky, and in whom's (sic) lofty branches the sighing wind is singing itself to sleep, are the lodges of the (Ute) tribe with whom we treat.

Head was truly trying to help his Ute Indian charges; but at the same time (the mid-1860s), he was greatly expanding his sheep and wheat operations.

The first large flock (about 1,000 head) of sheep was brought into the San Luis Valley by Lafayette Head in the mid-1860s. They were driven from the Taos area to Conejos and were not of a very good grade. However, within twenty years, Lafe had doubled the amount of wool they produced.

The Kit Carson Treaty of 1868 and Saguache

After evidently doing well financially in Conejos, Otto Mears moved on from that town and bought 1,240 acres of government land in the Saguache area for $3,000, and put eighty acres into cultivation—forty in wheat and forty in potatoes. It appears Lafe was not a partner in any of the Saguache ventures, probably because he did not want to move from Conejos, even though many of his friends saw Saguache as being a wetter spot than Conejos and therefore a better spot to farm and raise cattle. Mears and others from

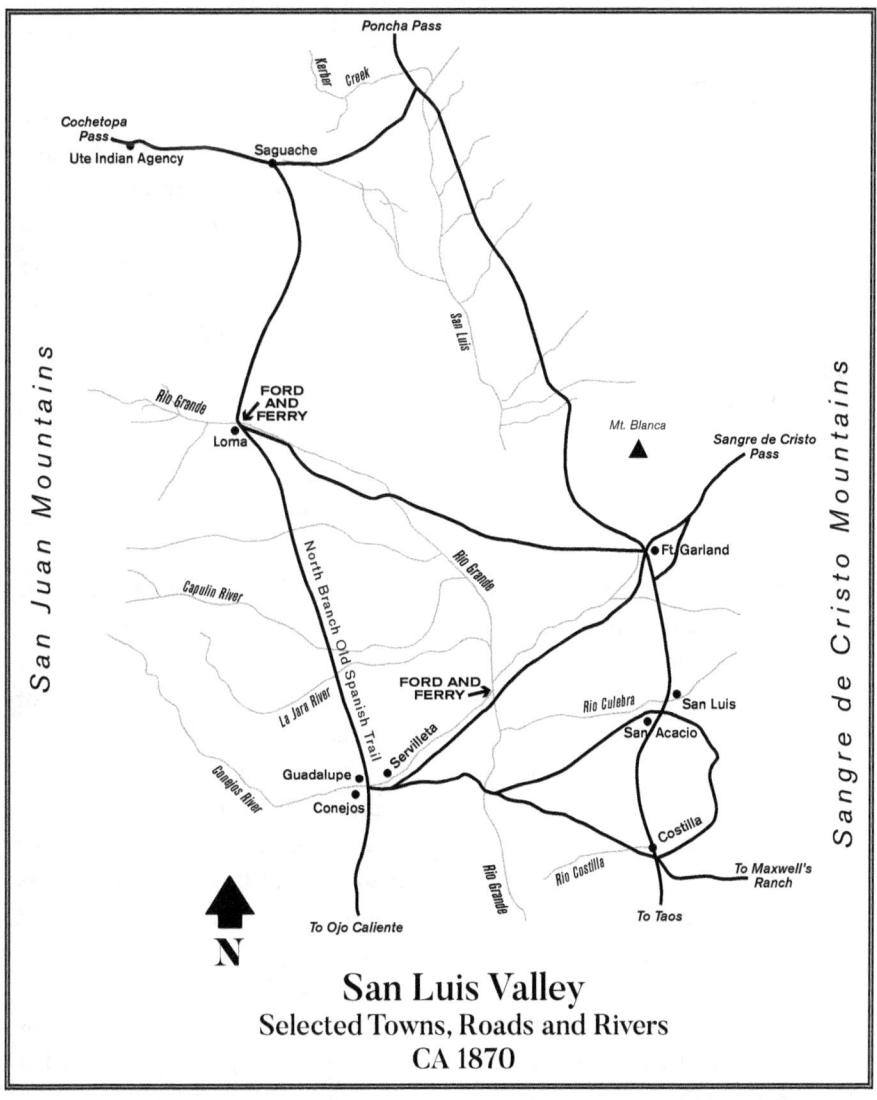

Map of Selected Roads, Rivers and Towns in the San Luis Valley about 1870.
Western Reflections Publishing Co. Map.

CHAPTER 10

Conejos, like John Lawrence, soon formed the Saguache Town Company so they could sell lots in the new settlement. Lawrence was even able to get a new County of Saguache approved by the Colorado Territorial legislature, even though the County's population was extremely small. Mears became the first treasurer of Saguache County.

When Mears had come to Conejos, Lafe was already considering giving up his Agency job so Lafe started teaching Mears about the job, which he hoped Mears would eventually take over. Conejos' businessmen were doing very well serving the American settlers, Native Americans, and soldiers. Mears never became an Indian Agent, but Lafe was able to help Mears become the official trader for the Conejos Ute Agency, a position in which Mears knew he could (with a little manipulation) make considerably more money, with much less danger or trouble, than being an Agent. Mears met and became friends with Chief Ouray at Conejos. The time that Mears was in Conejos was a hard one for the Utes, and they were often at the Agency begging for food. Mears got to see what it was like to work with the Utes in a crisis. Later in 1873, after Lafe had retired as an Indian Agent, Mears did take over or help for a few years with the duties of Agent at the later Los Piños Agency on Cochetopa Pass, but he never officially became an Indian Agent.

A few scattered Mexican-American families were the first settlers in the far northern part of the San Luis Valley. The first cabins may have been built by ex-Civil War veterans filing on free land given them for their service, but who had turned prospectors in 1865-1866 when gold and silver were discovered on nearby Kerber Creek, west of today's town of Villa Grove. A few Mexican-Americans had settled in the Saguache River Valley about the same time. During 1866, the area around the future Town of Saguache was homesteaded by Nathan Russell, representing Fred Walsen (who later founded the town of Walsenburg) and Christian Stollsteimer. Natural arroyos were used for irrigation ditches, and wheat was grown to make flour; but there was not enough to meet even the small needs of the Saguache Valley. Then a third group headed by John Lawrence (known as "The Father of Saguache County") and other men from Conejos settled near the present site of the Town of Saguache.

John Lawrence's parents, like Mears', had died while he was very young, and he was raised in an orphanage in St. Louis. He received a very poor education, but was said to read a lot and had a very good memory. He left the orphanage at age fifteen and went to Iowa, where he worked for various farmers, and when he was twenty-four, he moved to Colorado. Lawrence came to Conejos in 1861, and already had friends in the Saguache River

Valley when he moved there on February 28, 1867. John Lawrence made his move to the future Saguache with two ox teams, one horse, a wagon loaded with wheat and oat seeds, enough personal provisions to last a few months, three Hispanics, and a Navajo boy. Lawrence wrote in his diary:

> *In accordance with a command of God, which says, "In the sweat of thy brow shalt though eat bread all the days of thy life," I, John Lawrence, having passed thirty-one years of my life, eating bread, and rather poor bread, in this way was anxious to change it for better, and as to make such change it was necessary to change from my old to a new home. I therefore changed from Conejos to Saguache.*[117]

Other settlers were with Lawrence, as well as loose cattle (for their carts, or perhaps to start a herd). By 1870, cattle ranching and grain production were the predominant industries of the Saguache area, with most of the stock and grain coming from small ranches along the various rivers and streams. In the meanwhile, there was a constant back and forth shuffle of men, wagons, and carts over the eighty to 100 miles (depending on the route taken) from Conejos to the Saguache River. As an example, on March 17, 1867, men with three yoke of oxen (for plowing) arrived from Conejos with more supplies, and the next day a man was sent on an errand to Conejos. Just a little later that month, Lawrence got some seed potatoes from Mears, but it was unclear if Mears was now living in the northern part of the valley or was still back in Conejos. Somewhere around the end of March 1867, Lafe's clerk at the Indian Agency, William Godfrey, decided to settle in Saguache, supposedly to "keep track of Head's wards." He did in fact become one of the substitute Agents for two years while waiting for the appointed Agent to arrive. By April 1, one of the men along the Saguache River was taking two yoke of oxen back to Conejos, so evidently most, if not all, of the needed plowing had been done. The Saguache men's time was taken up with planting in April and May.

Lawrence went on to found the first public school in Saguache and became good friends with Lafe, the Utes, and Chief Ouray. He served two terms in the Colorado Territorial legislature. Like Lafe, Lawrence eventually became mainly a sheep rancher and did very well in that business. Later, he moved to the Town of Saguache, where he was a partner in a mercantile business, named "Lawrence and Williams." Lawrence died February 13, 1908. His obituary describes him as "a kind-hearted man and had many good traits of character, which made him friends of all who knew him. He was a great friend of the poor and will be greatly missed."[118]

CHAPTER 10

The *Rocky Mountain News* further mentioned:

> He had a bright sunny disposition, the kindest of hearts, and a helping hand always extended to those in need. He was beloved by all that knew him and the whole valley will mourn his loss.[119]

Otto Mears first became interested in the future Saguache area in the winter of 1866-67, when he realized that he and Lafe needed more land to grow wheat for their mill. Mears could tell the land near the Saguache River was more fertile and water more abundant than in Conejos; but, as in Conejos, the local Mexican-American farmers refused to use mowers, reapers, and threshing machines, thereby severely limiting the amount of grains that could be harvested.

In early June of 1867, the Saguache men could not get to Conejos as the Rio Grande River was too high and fast from snow melt to cross (evidently dangerous even on the ferry); but, by June 20, Lafe got two head of cattle to Saguache, probably crossing the Rio Grande after the water had gone down a bit on one of the ferries he helped establish. The next day a load of straw showed up in Saguache from Conejos, so that the new settlers could start making adobe bricks for their homes. Then, the following day, twenty-two head of cattle were brought back to Saguache to keep until the Rio Grande went down enough to allow them to ford the river and get back to Conejos.

By late July 1867, there was a major disaster threatening Saguache, as a hoard of locusts arrived. Lawrence wrote in his diary that "the crops were black with them." The locust continued to increase until mid-August, with the farmers doing everything they could think of to fight them, including dripping kerosene into irrigation ditches to kill their larva and dragging trees behind horses in the fields to try to knock the locust off the plants and kill them on the ground. The locusts were a problem over much of Colorado, including Conejos, and would return periodically in years to come.

The first of September, 1867, Lafe stopped in Saguache after going to Cañon City to look at a locomotive, as the Southern Railroad had an interest in moving into the San Luis Valley and was looking for investors. Governor Hunt also soon showed up on vacation to rough it in the Saguache area, and in one day he is said to have caught sixty pounds of trout out of the little streams nearby. Conservation had certainly not come yet to The Valley. From November 21, 1867 to April of 1868, Lawrence was in Denver at the Territorial legislature.

In 1867, when Mears had definitely moved to Saguache, only a handful of Americans resided in the upper San Luis Valley; however, they felt

A locust plague leaves little hope for farmers.

From Clamp, *Echoes From the Rocky Mountains.*

they should have a county seat and other government offices closer to them. Lawrence (who was acting as an interpreter for the legislature) was successful in establishing Saguache as a county and gaining himself a seat for the county on the territorial legislature in an election that had only eight voters (evidently the Mexican-Americans were not used to voting). Otto Mears was elected the first treasurer of Saguache County. It was the only political office Mears held besides a single two-year term in the initial State of Colorado legislature in 1876.

Mears and John Lawrence were friends one day and enemies the next. Mears was a Republican and Lawrence a Democrat and their arguments occurred over and over. Mears expanded his operations into roads and freighting. Lawrence was a rancher. Mears gained power all over Colorado, but Lawrence stayed close to Saguache. Mears was a promotor, always looking for business opportunities. Theirs was basically the same type of relationship that Head had with Mears in Conejos. Mears, Lawrence, and others incorporated the town of Saguache in 1867. Mears could have been a very powerful politician, but he realized he could get more of what he was after, with less time and trouble, by sponsoring and controlling others who ran for office. He saw electioneering and serving the people as a waste of time.

CHAPTER 10

Instead, he was a skilled manipulator, using people he knew he could control so as to get what he wanted, even if it meant giving bribes or coercion.

Back in the summer of 1866, Alfred Pfeiffer had come to Fort Garland as second in command to Kit Carson. Since Pfeiffer's wife had recently been killed by the Apache, and he was now drinking heavily, there was some concern about how well Pfeiffer would react to the many Utes present. However, Pfeiffer got along well with the Utes, and he ended up purchasing a ranch near Del Norte at this time and often went there to camp when getting away from the fort.

By this time Carson was sick with the ailment that would soon kill him. Carson had to officially resign as Agent for the Weeminuche, Capote, and Mouache in November 1867; but he was appointed Superintendent of Colorado Indian Affairs in January 1868, and would still help make a peace treaty with the Utes that would last until 1879 and the Meeker Massacre.

Tragedy struck the Head family that summer. On June 26, 1867, *The Rocky Mountain News* reported the death of Martina's son José:

> It becomes my painful duty to announce to you the sudden and melancholy death of José Crecincio Cisneros, an adopted and only son (Note: This could indicate that Martina also had a

An early flour mill at Saguache showing some of the abundant produce that also came from the local garden.

Author's Collection

daughter) of Major L. Head, who was drowned on the morning of the 12th inst., while attempting to cross the Rio Grande River. This unexpected circumstance has cast a gloom over the entire community here, as he was a young man in the bloom of life, and cherished and esteemed by all who knew him.

José left a young daughter (this also indicates Piedad was born before 1867)—Piedad (pronounced pee-uh-dad, which means "Piety" in Spanish) Cisneros. José's birth father and sister (if any) were not mentioned in the obituary and were presumably dead, but Lafe and Martina (Piedad's grandmother) took the little girl and raised her as their own daughter. She eventually inherited the Head estate. No mention has been found of José's wife—perhaps she died in childbirth—nor is any mention made of his possible sister by Martina's previous marriage.

Over 500 Utes went to Denver in June of 1867 to complain about the inconsistency of getting their food and the fact that when they did get it, the food was dirty, rotten, or otherwise inferior. They also complained that when they did get their food it was always late and never enough to feed all of them. Their appearance in such large numbers made enough of an impression that the U.S. agreed to another treaty conference.

In the summer of 1867, Lafe still had the same serious Ute Indian problem in the San Luis Valley, and a large number of Utes were camped at the Conejos Agency. Another group had also gathered at the Agency managed by D. C. Oakes for the Yampa and White River Ute in northern Colorado (the Uintah had moved to their Utah reservation on October 3, 1861). The Native Americans were again desperate for food. On July 10, 1867, Lafe and Agent Oakes sent a joint telegram to the Commissioner of Indian Affairs that read "No money received at our agencies since January last." They warned of "open hostilities" if they did not receive funds to buy food for the Utes. The two Agents were quite angry and sent the telegram "collect." Lafe once again provided sacks of flour from his flour mill to feed the hungry Utes at his Agency.

In 1867, after receiving numerous complaints, the U.S. was finally ready to try and make another treaty with the Utes. There were three major problems before the negotiations even began. The first and largest problem was the United States kept breaking its promises—usually because the U.S. Senate would not ratify the treaties made in the field or the U.S. Department of Indian Affairs was not sending good food or money to buy it in a timely manner. Secondly, the United States never seemed to realize how deeply engrained the hunter-gatherer life was in the Ute culture. They

CHAPTER 10

could not change their more than 500-year Ute lifestyle overnight. The Utes could not be farmers—it simply was not in their DNA. Many Americans pointed out to the federal government that the Utes might become ranchers, but the government did not seriously push that occupation for the Utes.

While in Washington there were many photos taken of different men involved in the 1868 treaty negotiations. The four principal men that escorted the Utes are seen in this photo. Left to right they are Hiram Bennett, first Colorado delegate to Congress, Kit Carson, Colorado Commissioner for Indian Affairs, Lafayette Head and D. C. Oakes, Indian Agents. This is one of the last photos of Kit Carson, who died just months later.

Author's Collection

Thirdly, the United States kept trying to have treaties with the Utes as one entity, when in fact they had seven different bands and each band was composed of numerous family groups of fifteen to forty people, and each family group had its own chief.

Now in 1867, the government was trying to get the Utes to move further west to the Pacific side of the Continental Divide. So in the winter of 1867-1868, another attempt was made by the United States to get a treaty with all the Ute tribes left in Colorado. This time, the reservation suggested was basically all the land in Colorado west of the Continental Divide and would include the Uintah as part of the reservation. As mentioned, most of the Plains Indians were or soon would be forced out of Colorado, so the argument that their enemies would find them if they were on a reservation was now gone.

In and after 1868, Bosque Redondo was being closed, and the Navajos returned to New Mexico. They were a beaten people and did not cause any more trouble in New Mexico or Colorado. The Utes had helped capture and take the Navajo on the Long Walk, and even though the Navajo had been their hated enemies, they must have had the thought that this same tragedy could also happen to them if they kept fighting the United States. It was probably one of the main reasons that the Utes had changed their hardline in 1867 that they would never give up their land.

In January 1868, Lafe took another Ute delegation to Washington City. The reasons for the Americans desiring the Treaty of 1868 with the Utes was described by some as a mixture of getting the Utes away from the Whites, especially in the San Luis Valley, and trying to Christianize and civilize them. Lafe and William Godfrey left Denver with Ouray, Waro, José Maria, Pah-bu-sat, An-ka-tosh, Piah, Su-ru-ipe, Nic-a-a-gut, Kan-i-a-che, and Pa-ant. Since their previous trip, a railroad line had been built to Cheyenne, Wyoming, which reduced their total round-trip travel time by nearly a month. They went to Cheyenne by stage and then proceeded by train. On January 22, 1868, Head, Godfrey, and the ten Utes met up with Kit Carson, Territorial Governor Alexander Hunt, and others in the delegation in St. Louis.

Otto Mears was part of the group, supposedly as interpreter, but probably to make sure he got the new contract as Agency trader to provide annuities to the Utes as he was doing in Conejos, even though the Utes were bitterly complaining about the poor quality of the food. Lawrence, for example, had described 400 head of cattle delivered to the Utes as "the poorest, scrubbiest, and most ordinary Texas cattle that ever passed through the territory," even though Mears' contract specifically stated there should be no

CHAPTER 10

Texas cattle (longhorns) delivered to the Utes.[120] The cattle were in such bad shape that the Utes refused to accept them.

By February 5, the entire delegation was in Washington and met with President Andrew Johnson. The expense report shows that there were ten Utes in Washington, accompanied by Governor Alexander C. Hunt, Kit Carson, Agents Head and Oakes, Colonel A. C. Boone. Also in the group, but not meeting with President Johnson, were U. M. Curtis, Interpreter; Edward M. Kellogg (Hunt's brother-in-law); George M. Vhilcoot, Colorado Representative to Congress; Hiram P. Bennett, first territorial delegate to Congress; and Otto Mears. By this time some historians feel that Governor Hunt, Ouray, and Mears had formed a mutually beneficial alliance that would last until Ouray's death in 1880.

On February 10, 1868, Governor Hunt signed for $625.50 worth of clothing purchased for the ten Utes at S. L. Hable & Company in Washington, D.C. The clothes bought on this trip were ten suits, twenty shirts, socks, drawers, gloves, collars, neckties, six satchels, ten suspenders, nine pairs of boots, and one pair of shoes.

On March 2, 1868, the Utes supposedly signed a treaty at a Washington hotel with Head acting as a witness. Signing as the Treaty Commissioners were Kit Carson and Colorado Territorial Governor Hunt. The seven bands of the Utes were all represented. Before leaving Washington City, the delegates met as expected with President Johnson at the White House, and the President took them on a tour. Ouray supposedly later confirmed that a treaty

had been signed in Washington by all the Ute chiefs that had come. There was severe dissention among the Ute tribes about being a part of the treaty. However, Ouray soon said no treaty had been signed,[121] evidently realizing that there were many Ute chiefs who would not recognize his authority.[122]

Specifically, Ouray said there was not a treaty, as Kaniache and Ankatosh's signature "Xs" were forged.

Whether signed or not, by the terms of the 1868 treaty, a single reservation was formed for all the Utes on the west side of the Continental Divide, which was roughly the west one-third of Colorado less a strip all along the north above today's Meeker. It was the first valid treaty that set definite and exclusive boundaries for the Ute land. The treaty recognized 15,120,000 acres as Ute land that they were promised they could "keep forever." According to the treaty, no unauthorized white men would "...ever be permitted to pass over, settle, or reside in Ute territory." This was a major point because one purpose of the treaty was to keep the Whites and the Native Americans totally apart. However it seemed later that the Utes did not understand that they were not to leave their reservation; and prospectors did not care to honor the agreement.

On the way home, the delegation stopped in New York City. *The Rocky Mountain News* of February 7, 1868, reported that New York was struck with "the worst storm in years, a northeast gale with snow that halted street cars." Nevertheless the Utes attended a circus in the city—probably at P. T. Barnum's museum.

The official delegation to the 1868 Treaty is shown here and on pg. 216. Left to Right: Ankatosh, Piah (Chipeta's brother), Su-ru-ipe, U. M. Curtis Northern Ute Agent, George Chicott (Delegate to Congress), Sa-wa-ich, Col. Albert E. Boone (Grandson of Daniel Boone), Colorado Governor A. C. Hunt, Captain Jack, Hiram Bennett (First Colorado Delegate to Congress, Lafayette Head, Waro, Daniel C. Oakes (Indian Agent), Chief Ouray, Capote, and William Godfrey (Lafe's Secretary and perhaps acting Agent).

Author's Collection.

CHAPTER 10

Later Albert Pfeiffer reported to friends that Carson had been very sick during his entire time in Washington, and that Carson saw a doctor there and was given little hope to live very long. Carson had taken the train to Cheyenne and then a stage to Denver where he rested several days before continuing his journey home, helped by his long-time friend, Thomas Boggs.

When he got back to Denver, Lafe wrote to Pfeiffer, then serving at Fort Garland, on April 1, 1868:

> *My Dear Old friend: We all arrived here day before yesterday, but cannot go on any farther on account of the snow on the divide between here and Colorado City. The General (Carson) is quite unwell but I hope he will still be able to get Home. He will go by way of Pueblo and then down the Arkansas he will be accompanied by a friend who will take every possible care of him. He is very anxious to see you all and especially his family.*
>
> *With kindest regards to Mrs. Carson and family I am ever Fraternally yours,* (A reference to their Masonic membership)
>
> *Lafayette Head.*[123]

When Carson had bought land from Thomas Boggs, his brother-in-law, and moved his family before he left for Washington. Boggsville was near Fort Lyon, which had a hospital. Bennett evidently did not know that Carson had moved from Taos and incorrectly reported, "Upon our return to Denver, (Carson) started south with Major Oakes for his home in Taos, New Mexico. But he became worse and died at Fort Lyon." It was April 11, 1868, before Carson got to Boggsville, a town that used to exist on the Santa Fe Trail, where his third wife, Maria Joséfa Jaramillo Carson, was living with the Boggs family while Carson was in Washington. Joséfa was pregnant and about to give birth to their seventh child, Josephina. Carson got there just two days before Joséfa had their child; but his wife died on April 23. Carson was moved from Boggsville to the hospital at Fort Lyon because the Arkansas River was beginning its spring flood stage and his friends were worried that they might not get him across the river in an emergency. Carson followed Joséfa in death on May 23, when an aneurism in his stomach area burst. Pfeiffer sent a letter to Lafe at Conejos to notify him about Carson's death, but Lafe did not get it for a while, as he had gone to Saguache.

The death of Kit Carson, the man who had been his longtime friend and mentor, was a great loss to Lafe. Unlike his first few years in the West,

Kit had also been a good friend to the Native Americans during his last ten years, and at the time of his death most Utes called him "Father Carson." The bodies of Kit and Joséfa were returned to Taos for reburial about a year after their deaths.

The U.S. wanted all the chiefs of each band of Utes to sign the 1868 treaty for it to be valid. The Utes literally had dozens, if not hundreds of chiefs, and finding them during their nomadic season would be challenging. However, between August 15 and September 21, 1868, Lafe and fellow Agent D. C. Oakes collected the "Xs" of forty-seven chiefs who were ratifying the treaty, including possibly Ouray, who signed the treaty as U-re on August 15, 1868, and later for a second time as Ou-ray, a Mouache chief, not a Tabeguache.[124] It was late September before the Government said enough Ute chiefs had been contacted. However, who was to say what number a majority would be? By signing the 1868 treaty, the Utes were ratifying most of the provisions of the 1863 Treaty. President Johnson signed the treaty on November 6, 1868. The December 9 issue of *The Rocky Mountain News* presented the full treaty text and listed all the Ute chiefs who had ratified the treaty, along with the government men who witnessed each signing.

The huge chunk of land set aside for all seven bands of the Utes amounted to almost 5,000 acres per adult male Ute; however, in the rough mountain terrain a large amount of land was needed for the nomadic hunter/gatherer tribe. The Utah border was the western boundary; the present-day New Mexico northern boundary was the reservation's southern boundary, and the northern boundary was about fifteen miles north of today's Meeker. The Utes were basically giving up their ancient territories of Middle and South Parks, the Yampa Valley, and the San Luis Valley, but were keeping a large amount of good land. The reservation's eastern boundary under the Ute treaty was not the Continental Divide, but rather at the 107th Meridian. There was nothing the Utes could actually see or relate to on the ground. The 107th Meridian was roughly all of the Territory of Colorado west of a line through or near the present-day towns of Pagosa Springs, Gunnison, Crested Butte, and Basalt to about twelve miles south of Steamboat Springs; however, most Whites and Utes considered the east line of the reservation to be the Continental Divide. Albert Pfeiffer later pointed out that the 1868 treaty's description was one that the Utes certainly could not have used for reference; and if the Continental Divide had been the boundary, both Whites and Utes would have had fewer questions about the location. The majority of Utes were unhappy about the treaty, and they often ignored their reservation boundaries. The Americans basically did the same, and Ute incidents were still occurring in the San Luis Valley, even though the Utes were not supposed to be there.

The United States had been trying since 1849 to get the Utes to become farmers and, in an effort to do so, there were provisions in the 1868 treaty that a Ute family could claim 160 acres of farmland within the reservation as their own land. They would receive seed, farming implements, and instructions from the Agency farmer on how to farm. Any Ute over the age of eighteen who was not the head of a household could receive eighty acres, and the younger Ute children between the ages of seven and eighteen were to attend school. The Utes were promised $30,000 a year for clothes, blankets, and other supplies, and an additional $30,000 for food. The head of each "lodge" was to receive "one gentle American cow, as distinguished from the ordinary or 'Texas breed,' and five head of sheep."

The money payments under the treaty were to continue until the Utes could support themselves. In an effort to help change his people by example, Ouray later started his own farm and ranch near today's Montrose, Colorado, and was very successful in terms of American values. The treaty provided that the United States "solemnly" agreed that no person, other than certain government officers (such as the Agent and Agency employees), would be permitted to pass over, settle, or reside on the reservation. However there was an important exception: "roads, highways, and railroads as authorized by law" would be allowed. It was probably one of the best treaties ever offered an American Indian tribe. In part this was due to a change in the attitude of many of the American people, who now were beginning to realize how badly the Native Americans, and especially the Utes, had been treated over the past decades.

There were now individuals and groups who wanted to help the Native Americans—groups like The Indian Peace Commission and The Women's National Peace Commission. The 1868 treaty had all the elements of the often discussed strategy of Carson, Ouray, and Lafe — if the provisions had only been followed; but they were not. The prospectors and settlers just kept on coming.

Although the treaty was signed in Washington on March 2, 1868, the U.S. Senate did not ratify it until July 25, 1868, and there was one amendment at that time; then, after it was realized that there would need to be a new treaty, it was not signed by President Johnson until November 6, 1868. The deleted paragraph would have given the Utes "one bull for every twenty five cows." That same paragraph also struck out a bonus payment to the Utes of up to $45,000 per year for four years; the payment was to be split among all the Ute families that had increased their cattle herds during the four years. Taking out these provisions was very short-sighted. Its deletion meant the Utes were not being encouraged to become ranchers, and that the government would have to keep supplying them cattle or sheep for the foreseeable future.

Under the original 1868 Treaty, there were to be two Agencies set up for the Utes—one for northern Utes—the Yampa, Uintahs and White River bands on the White River, and one for the Tabeguache and Southern Utes—the Weeminuche, Mouache, and Capote bands—on the Los Piños Creek on the reservation near the future Durango and Pagosa Springs in Southwest Colorado. At each Agency, the United States was to build a warehouse, a schoolhouse, and houses for the Agency. Each Agency was also supplied with a farmer, a carpenter, a blacksmith, and a miller. A water-powered sawmill was also to be built at each Agency. The Agents were to be required to live at the Agency. Although the food that Mears supplied to the Utes at Cochetopa was no better than what they received in Conejos, the Utes found the game and wild food to be much more plentiful on the Western Slope. It was good enough that they stopped complaining that they were starving.

It was not until over five months later, on April 10, 1869, that the U.S. Congress gave the power to President Grant to resettle the Utes on their new reservation. The treaty specified:

> ... Agents for said Indians, in the future, shall make their homes at the Agency building; that they shall reside among the Indians, and keep an office open at all times for the purpose of prompt and diligent inquiry into such matters of complaint by and against the Indians, as may be presented.....[125]

As mentioned, Mears, Evans, and possibly Ouray were working very closely in secret with the Utes and various Colorado political figures to make sure the new Agency, which the treaty specifically stated was supposed to be on the reservation, would be as close as possible to Saguache and the San Luis Valley, even if it was not west of the 107th meridian. Mears also was working with Saguache citizens to get a road built to the top of Cochetopa Pass, where he wanted the Agency to be built if not in the town of Saguache itself. The good news was that there was now one unified reservation for all the Colorado Ute bands. Although we do not know the details, Mears was successful on both his efforts. As Virginia Simmons wrote:

> Never one to miss an opportunity, Mears quickly acquired the contract for delivering rations to the new Agency, which

CHAPTER 10

> *opened for business in 1869. To fulfill his contract, Mears purchased large quantities of provisions from farmers not only in the immediate neighborhood of Saguache, but also around the Rio Grande.... Complaints about the quantity and quality of the rations had been frequent at Conejos previously, and one can assume they continued at Los Piños. Agencies often received... old and spoiled (goods) with better products being sold to the military or to markets in towns.*[126]

When a chance of getting the Ute Indian Agency at Saguache came along in 1868, Virginia Simmons wrote in the same article: "it was a lot like acquiring a correctional facility today." It gave the town(s) close to the Agencies a very big economic boost; yet, it also meant the presence of hostile

Otto Mears, acting interpreter, and Chief Ouray (who did not need a interpreter) in Washington at the 1868 treaty. It was very unusual for a single White and Ute to pose together; thereby lending some credence to the rumor they had formed a "partnership."

Author's Collection.

Indians nearby. Mears had learned well about dealing with the government, the Mexican-Americans, and the Ute Indians through his business dealings in Conejos, his talks and lessons with Lafe, and his business with Fort Garland. He was determined Saguache would get the new Agency, even though it took some foul play before it happened.

During this time of confusion Godfrey evidently went to Saguache and was filling some of the functions of an Agent.[127] It was at this time in Saguache when Ouray first announced there was no treaty signed in Washington. A number of Utes were now coming to Saguache to buy corn and flour. The Agency was evidently unofficially moved to Saguache in the spring of 1868. According to Lawrence's diary quite a few Colorado political figures were in Saguache at that time, and an Indian war was even expected in June of 1868, and soldiers had been sent to Saguache to help protect the town. Godfrey, Lawrence, and Ouray had a long talk about a potential new treaty. Besides these three, Governor Hunt, Lafayette Head, Major Oakes, Mears, John Evans, and many other lesser political figures were in Saguache in July. Then Lawrence's diary is silent in August and September when the treaties were made, except on September 27, 1868, when Hunt "made a bargain with us to let the Utes have some wheat and beef."

When it came time to move the Agency for the Southern Utes and the Tabeguache, the Tabeguache refused to leave Saguache, but the Southern Utes went to the Los Piños River in southern Colorado near today's Durango, which was the spot that most people involved with the treaty had in mind for the new joint Agency. Exactly why the Tabeguache refused to go to the Los Piños Agency in southern Colorado will probably never be known. The spot where the Tabeguache Agency was eventually moved was not within the boundaries of the reservation (it was ten miles east), but the Tabeguache would not move further west and would not go south. To partially comply with the treaty, the government ended up naming a nearby creek on Cochetopa Pass "Los Piños," and the Tabeguache Agency was built there. Sidney Jocknick, in his book *Early Days on the Western Slope of Colorado* contends that Governor Alexander Hunt (McCook's predecessor) was the one who planned for the Tabeguache Agency to be built on Cochetopa Pass, but he was removed from office on June 14, 1869, before he could actually build the Agency. Jocknick insisted that this was Hunt's plan all along, that the Tabeguache were told to assemble there at an unnamed stream that Hunt planned to rename Los Piños, and that the Utes did not just coincidentally refuse to leave Saguache for southern Colorado. General Edward McCook replaced Hunt on the same day Hunt was removed. McCook was probably even more into political graft than Hunt.

There were actually several Los Piños Rivers or Creeks. One was near the central San Luis Valley and was a tributary of the Rio Grande, but it was much further east of the Continental Divide than on Cochetopa Pass. Although most authorities were surprised when the location on Cochetopa was announced; the Tabeguache did traditionally range further north than the Southern Utes and therefore evidently wanted their Agency in that location. The Cochetopa site was a very long way from the Southern Utes' normal territory and was at such a high elevation that there could be no real agricultural pursuits there.

The other Ute bands and many Tabeguache were not pleased with what eventually came to be called the "Los Piños" Agency. Its first name, before the Tabeguache split off from the Southern Utes, was "The Southern Ute Agency." Since the Cochetopa Agency was not on the reservation, the Utes had to leave the reservation to get their annuities, and it must have been tempting to do a little hunting while there. Lafayette Head objected strenuously to the site as the former Agent and wrote a letter to Governor McCook protesting specifically that there was no Los Piños Creek in the area of Cochetopa Pass when the location was put into the treaty. The *Santa Fe New Mexican* complained in January 1870, that the "Colorado Clique" in Washington had stolen the Tabeguache Agency's business from New Mexico. All of these very valid objections were ignored. One of the local Indian Agents wrote Washington that the new Ute Agency was near the Grand Cañon of the Colorado River (perhaps referring to Black Canyon, but it does not contain the Colorado River), "not less than 150 miles from any traveled road, and usually impassable by October 20." Only the last of those statements was correct. The Denver Ring had prevailed again.

New Territorial Governor McCook had become close friends with Ulysses S. Grant (who took office on March 4, 1869, and was later well-known for his administration's graft) during the Civil War. Grant removed Governor Alexander Hunt, who was actually well-liked in Colorado, to appoint McCook. The popular Samuel Elbert was later appointed for a year after McCook was removed by a petition of Colorado citizens; but he was also removed from office by Grant and McCook was appointed again. Then another petition from Colorado citizens in 1874 asked for McCook's removal due to his fraudulent dealings with the Utes and the way they had been mistreated and cheated. McCook was generally known to be crooked during both of his administrations, even though he was not found guilty of a specific crime. When McCook was again removed by petition of the people, it was after serving only nine months.

The Kit Carson Treaty of 1868 and Saguache

After McCook's first inauguration on June 14, 1869, he immediately signed the contracts for the new Tabeguache Agency buildings. When the Tabeguache had first stopped at the Town of Saguache and said they would go no further, they perhaps believed the Agency would be at the bottom of the pass. Mears had asked at the time to go to Denver and get Governor McCook's help. McCook came to Saguache with ten soldiers and they eventually got the Utes to move to the top of the pass. Fifteen thousand dollars was appropriated for constructing the buildings at the Agency for the Tabeguache, which was much more than needed to build the few needed buildings. McCook evidently made a sweet deal with the contractors.

After the Tabeguache Utes finally moved to the spot where their Agency was built, (they):

The new Territorial Governor Edward M. McCook also was the Colorado Superintendent of Indian Affairs, and he appointed his brother-in-law James B. Thompson Agent at the new Denver Ute Agency. Money seems to be the only reason for creating an Agency in Denver.

Author's Collection.

> …staged a frightening reception for (temporary agent Lt. Calvin) Speer and his party and the materials he was bringing to build the Agency buildings and its sawmill. Mrs. Godfroy who was part Indian, had gone along as interpreter. Eight hundred Utes in war paint, blocked the party's way, then galloped forward and so frightened Mrs. Godfroy that she fainted. The warriors then claimed that the party was a joke, but Speer reported that the Utes did not want him to enter the reservation until Ouray and others were assured that Speer was bringing them their annuities.[128]

The Tabeguache Agency ended up being built just over the top of Cochetopa Pass at an elevation of 10,000 feet. The spot was often totally impassable for months in the winter because of deep snow, so most of the Utes left the area in the fall and wintered for five or six months in the Uncompahgre Valley near today's town of Delta. The Agent and his employees were supposed to stay at the Agency, which they usually did, and

CHAPTER 10

The Los Piños Agency was at a high and rough elevation but it was not as bad as this artist made it look. There was actually a lot of fairly level land but crops could not be grown at the 10,000-foot elevation.

Author's Collection.

sometimes they were there with absolutely no Utes present. All of this was very upsetting to the Governor of New Mexico, Lewis Wallace, who was planning for New Mexico to get the Tabeguache Agency business when they were moved to the southern Los Piños River, with the closest supplies being located in his territory. The spot on the originally proposed southern Los Piños River was at a much lower elevation than Cochetopa Pass, had a much better climate, and had good agricultural possibilities with several large rivers being in the area. The Southern Utes were now in a good place, and the Tabeguache began to ignore their Agency in favor of staying at lower elevations in the Uncompahgre River Valley where the towns of Montrose and Delta are today. As an example, in 1869 there had been 120 lodges near the Agency on Cochetopa Pass, but in 1870 there were only thirty lodges. Then Ouray's home at the Agency burned from suspected arson, but was rebuilt on Cochetopa Pass.

When the 1868 treaty had been formatted in Washington, D.C. Lafe probably knew that his days as an Indian Agent were numbered, as even the eventual Southern Ute Agency was far from Conejos, and he would not move his home. His only hope would have been if the Agency was built on Los Piños Creek near his home, but that was unlikely. However, Lafe's exact reason was never stated. Perhaps he knew of the Ouray-Mears-Governor partnership and did not want to be part of it. Maybe after nine years as an

Agent, as well as several earlier years spent as a special Agent, he was simply tired of the job. But more than likely he just did not want to change his home from Conejos. The Tabeguache Ute Agency at the top of Cochetopa Pass was almost 150 miles north of Lafe's ranch; much too far from Conejos for him to remain their Agent. The Southern Ute Agency was almost as far and meant crossing the Continental Divide—almost impossible in the four to six month winter. Lafe submitted his resignation as Agent for the following term, but remained on the Bureau of Indian Affairs' official list of Ute translators.

On July 14, 1868, Secretary of Interior Orville H. Browning had sent the following letter to President Andrew Johnson:

> *Lafayette Head, who has been nominated as an Indian Agent for New Mexico, does not wish to continue in the service. Information to this effect reached me only this morning. I have therefore to request that you draw (sic) his nomination.*[129]

In the same message, Browning nominated James Shelly, Agent for Montana's Flat Head Indians, to fill Lafe's unexpired term. Most of the men who followed Lafe served only a year or two before they were either too scared to serve further or too disgusted with the United States government to stay. Browning's suggestion for the new Agent at Tabeguache Agency at Cochetopa Pass was ignored because under new regulations Agents were now assigned from different church groups, and the Utes were to get a Unitarian. The first official Agent at the new Los Piños Agency on Cochetopa was Second Lieutenant Calvin Speer, who arrived July 31, 1869. He was supposed to be a very temporary Agent until the new Agent arrived, but the permanent Agent did not arrive until almost two years later on April 23, 1871.

Lafe must have been thankful to not have been part of the Cochetopa Pass Agency mess, and now had the time to be more actively involved in his religious, business, and political ventures. In 1869, he represented Conejos County on the new Board of Trade of Southern Colorado. The organization was based in Pueblo, with directors from each of the Colorado counties. One of the board's early actions was to publish a pamphlet promoting the business advantages of Southern Colorado. Business was booming, as was the town of Conejos, which now had several stores, Head's flour mill, a blacksmith, and numerous adobe houses.

After the Treaty of 1868 and the end of the Conejos Agency, Head spent the next six years seemingly content to stay on his ranch, run his local businesses, and have a home life with a good dose of business marketing

CHAPTER 10

thrown in. Head, Godfrey, Mears, and Lawrence continued to visit and sometimes depend on each other. Head noted that crops in the Saguache area looked better than those back in Conejos, but he still had no intention of moving. Lawrence mentioned in his diary that Mears now had a store in Saguache, although Mears had really just stacked some of his extra supplies in a corner of his home at the time. However, the "store" would soon become much bigger.

Once again the Utes initially failed to follow many of the new treaty's provisions, especially the agreement to stay on their reservation. Many of the Utes still traveled to the Denver area and the San Luis Valley for their fall hunting trips and to sell or trade their furs and hides and buy supplies. The Indian Agents were issued orders to do what was necessary to keep the Utes on their reservation, but it was like trying to catch bees coming out of an angry beehive. The Mouache Utes continued to stay in New Mexico Territory for a while, although they were supposed to have moved to Colorado's Western Slope. The U.S. even stopped issuing annuities at Cimarron to the Mouache, but they still failed to move. Even Ute Chief

The area around Denver was a traditional Ute hunting ground, but in the 1830s their mortal enemies (Arapaho) also moved into the area, and the two tribes were bitter enemies. Even in the late 1860s and early 1870s, the tribes were hunting in the area and brought a trophy scalp into Denver like these Utes.

Author's Collection.

Ouray took several hundred Tabeguache to hunt around the Trinidad area, but the buffalo were basically gone from that area. When Maxwell's Ranch was sold to Denver and then British investors in 1870, the Mouache insisted that this was their land and could not be sold. They did, however, move back onto the Plains around Trinidad, as the Plains Indians were now gone.

The new Agent Jabez Nelson Trask was now at the Los Piños Agency and the Utes there were very unhappy. Lawrence reported:

> *Lots of Indians here (in Saguache which was fifty or sixty miles off the reservation). They have nearly all left the Agency as they do not like the Agent and one of them told the Agent yesterday that he was of no account and that none of the Indians liked him.*[130]

The Utes continued to come to Saguache to get away from Trask, and Trask kept going to Saguache to get away from the Utes and visit Lawrence.

CHAPTER ELEVEN

Friend of the Fathers
(1857-1897)

"Don Raphael Cabeza (I lead) has given us a half a steer."
Diaries of the Jesuit Residence
Lady of Guadalupe Parish
Conejos, Colorado
Sunday, June 15, 1873

In the 1850s and 1860s, Catholicism was, by far, the dominant religion in the San Luis Valley. It was brought from New Mexico by the very earliest settlers; and, at first, the San Luis Valley Catholic churches were governed from Santa Fe, New Mexico. After 1860, the Colorado Catholic churches became a part of the "Colorado Mission" administered in Denver by Bishop Machebeuf and they were operated as a part of the Denver Diocese in connection with Utah. A plaque on the side of the present-day church in Conejos gives a quick history:

> This tract was selected by Bishop Machebeuf for the first permanent church in Colorado. Here was built a jackal (picket) church later replaced by a larger church. The first parish of Colorado was erected 101 years ago in 1858 with Our Lady of Guadalupe as patron by John (Juan) B. Lamy, Bishop of Santa Fe. Father F. S. Montaño was the first pastor. The finished church, dedicated by Bishop Lamy December 12, 1863, was under the Jesuit Fathers 1871-1920. Since 1920, it has been under the Theatrine Fathers (A male religious order of the Catholic Church). Fire destroyed the church on Ash Wednesday, 1926. John Henry Tihen, third Bishop of Denver, dedicated a new church Dec. 12, 1927. In 1948 the church was enlarged and embellished with its towers by the Rev. Michael Pascual, C.R., pastor. The Most Rev. Joseph C. Willging, first bishop of Pueblo, dedicated an addition to the church on August 7, 1948.

Friend of the Fathers

However, there is much more history to tell. Our Lady of Guadalupe was at first a small jackal shrine constructed in Guadalupe on the north side of the Conejos River sometime in 1854 or 1855 to pay tribute to the patron saint of the community. By 1856, the shrine was expanded to a chapel by building a fence around the area, covering part of the structure with a flat roof, and plastering some jackal areas with adobe. Bishop Lamy later wrote that it was the first active chapel in today's Colorado. The building itself was only 16 by 30 feet. There was no actual "church," but there were worship services held. The first mass was held in Guadalupe in 1856 and is believed to be the first mass celebrated in what is now Colorado. The Reverend P. Gabriel Ussel celebrated the mass, but he was the priest in Taos and just visiting Conejos, which was considered a mission of his church.

In 1857, priests from Abiqui and Arroyo Hondo were coming somewhat regularly to Conejos, and Bishop Lamy made his first visit to the Conejos church on June 10, 1858, with Father Vincent Montaño accompanying him. Father Montaño was installed that day as the first resident priest at Conejos. Unfortunately, Montaño did not keep good records. Lafayette Head soon became the church secretary, but he did not do much better than the priest. Although a bad record keeper, Lafayette's appointment certainly showed that he was one of the most active and trusted members from the church's humble beginnings; and this heavy participation continued until the time of his death in 1897. In early 1859, the people of Conejos or Guadalupe still had no real church other than the small one-story chapel building surrounded by a low jackal fence in Guadalupe. Bishop Juan Lamy wrote in the church's early Baptismal Book:

Bishop Jean-Baptiste Lamy was from France and came to Santa Fe in July 1850. He baptized Lafe soon after he arrived, but did not make it to Conejos until June 1858.

Photo courtesy of Wikipedia.

> *Father Montaño was the first parish priest of this new parish that he established three years ago. He kept no records whatsoever, be it of baptism or marriages, or burials.*

CHAPTER 11

At Conejos in late 1859, Lamy dedicated the "chapel built of jackal." Lamy's visit was brief, but the Catholics of Conejos (virtually the entire town) were delighted. They rarely saw a bishop, and usually the people had to travel great distances to receive confirmation. Lamy also performed baptisms at Conejos. Lamy had been sent by Pope Pius IX to New Mexico and had arrived with fellow priest Joseph Machebeuf in Santa Fe on August 9, 1851. Lamy was made famous in Willa Cather's book *Death Comes to the Archbishop*. Bishop Lamy was from France and had answered the call for missionary work and moved to Ohio and then Kentucky before he was notified in 1850 by Pope Pius IX that he would be the Vicar Apostolic of New Mexico. It took him months to reach Santa Fe, arriving in the summer of 1851.

Bishop Joseph Machebeuf later wrote that, in December of 1859, he and Father Ussel traveled to Santa Fe and along the way visited the little town of Guadalupe. Joseph Machebeuf was also born in France and came to New Mexico from Ohio in 1851. He was the priest in Albuquerque from 1853 to 1858, then at Santa Fe from 1858 to 1860. By 1868, he had opened eighteen churches in the future Colorado as well as a school for boys in Denver, several convents, St. Joseph's hospital, and the College of the Sacred Heart. Machebeuf was made Vicar Apostolic of Colorado and Utah on March 3, 1868 and was consecrated the following August 16 as Bishop.

Immediately after Lafe returned from his cattle buying trip back East in 1859, he welcomed Fathers Ussel and Machebeuf. They met in Conejos with Head and Don Jesus Velasques, "the principal men of this miniature commonwealth." In his account of the trip, Father Machebeuf noted that Head was converted to Catholicism, had been baptized by Bishop Lamy in Santa Fe, and had married a Mexican lady from a very good family. He described the duplex in which Lafayette Head, Jesus Velasquez, and their families lived as having only two rooms for each family (a kitchen and a large "hall"), so apparently Lafe's bigger second home had not

Bishop of Denver Joseph Machebuef came to Santa Fe to be with his friend Bishop Lamy in 1851. He was made Bishop of Colorado and Utah in 1868.

Photo Courtesy of Wikipedia.

yet been built. Head's home served as a temporary church for two days, while Fathers Machebeuf and Ussel heard hundreds of confessions and offered communion for adults and baptisms for babies. The two visiting priests noted the local residents had selected a better site for a true church than the original chapel in Guadalupe, as the former was subject to flooding. The new spot was between the Conejos and San Antonio Rivers and was called "Conejos." During the visit, Father Machebeuf selected the site on the Conejos plaza for the new and much bigger church building. Each family in the church pledged five bushels of wheat or the equivalent to support the priest.

Until 1860, priests had stayed at Head's home when in Conejos; but on January 1, 1860, Father Ussel completed the purchase of a house near the new church site to be used as the rectory. For $350 he bought from Maria Trinidad Medina and her two sons "a house of seven rooms bordering on the plaza, bounded on the north by the arroyo that goes behind the said plaza; on the south by the site for Our Lady of Guadalupe Church; on the east by the gardens of Tia Gadaladon and José Lopez; and on the west by the house and land of Chipeta Tafoya."[131]

In 1860, Reverend José Miguel Vigil became the priest at Taos, but also had a supervisory function at Conejos and over the Franciscan priests in the area. He got the locals to start building the new church. Bishop Lamy visited Conejos in the summer of 1860 to bless the start of the new church, and its walls were already about twelve feet tall. In the church's Book of Baptismal Records he wrote:

> *On this 8th Sunday after Pentecost I visited the jurisdiction of Nuestra Señora de Guadalupe in Los Conejos, the priest being Father José Miguel Vigil, and I administered Confirmation. In this Parish there is yet no chapel. The church is started, and is four yards high, and the construction is very large, but for reason of the small number of people, and being so dispersed, and also because the people are fairly new here and poor, it has not been possible to finish the church. Since January (1860) when Father Vigil arrived, the church has been built up from three yards. Also, the rectory has been bought, in which the parish priest lives, along with 200 yards of land. All the felicitated people of this new parish are very happy with the good attitude and devotion of the present parish priest.*
>
> *Nuestra Señora de Guadalupe in Los Conejos, July 22 of 1860*
>
> *Juan B. Lamy*
> *Bishop of Santa Fe*[132]

CHAPTER 11

Father Montaño was Franciscan, but Father Vigil was Jesuit. These two brotherhoods had very different theologies, but both operated together in New Mexico at this time. Exactly the role Vigil played at Conejos is not known, but evidently Bishop Lamy was gradually blending in Jesuit priests and theology as the Franciscans retired, died, or moved away, and Vigil oversaw the Franciscan priests at Conejos and/or Taos, and perhaps an even larger area. The Franciscans basically had control of the Catholic Church in New Spain from 1598 to 1797. The Jesuits had been expelled in 1767, so there was no brotherhood controlling the church for about eighty years. After the Mexican-American War, the Jesuits started to return to the newly acquired U.S. Territory. The Franciscan priests held their ground for several more decades in the San Luis Valley at Taos under Father Antonio José Martinez, and Lafe must have known Father Martinez of Taos well.

Father Martinez was born in Abiqui, went to seminary in Mexico, and eventually became the parish priest in Taos. His family was well to do and owned considerable land. Martinez was trained as a priest in Durango, Mexico, and was there during the Mexican Revolution against Spain. His hero became Don José Miguel Hidalgo, the early leader of the revolution. Martinez returned to Taos in 1822 after Mexico became a country. He vehemently objected when there was a turnover in local leadership of the Catholic Church a few years after the Mexican-American War, when French-born Lamy and other European Jesuit priests were sent to New Mexico by the Vatican. Father Martinez felt that native New Mexicans should have been trained as local priests instead of importing European Jesuit priests; and as a Franciscan priest, he did not agree with many of the Jesuit practices, one of the greatest problems being that his bishop Lamy was anti-Penitente. Martinez was said to have been part of the Taos rebellion and was rumored to be a womanizer—a renegade priest in the eyes of the Jesuits. However, to the citizens of Taos, he was a beloved hero—a highly educated man from a rich family who fought for the rights of the poor. He had married before he became a priest, but his wife died prior to his acceptance into the priesthood.

Martinez and the Bents were bitter enemies, but Martinez still helped hide the Bent and Carson women and children during the Pueblo Revolt. Martinez never charged people who could not afford to pay for his services as a priest. He had learned fluent English and felt the Mexican-Americans needed to learn English to operate in their new American society, which he also admired. He started a primary school and opened a seminary in New Mexico, as well as buying a small press to publish books for local children and adults. He was able to stop the practice of forced tithing (the withholding of communion if a parishioner did not tithe) for the very poor. Martinez was elected to the New Mexico Territorial Legislature for six years. He was President of the first Territorial Legislative Convention and served on the Council (Senate) in 1852. He was against land grants for the rich, believing the land should be split among the poor. He pushed for this view, even though his family owned part of the two million acre Tierra Amarilla Land Grant.

Both Lamy and Machebeuf bumped heads with Martinez. They believed that New Mexico's Franciscan priests were all old, lazy, careless, and horrible lechers, who dreaded reform because of their sexual morals. Lamy reintroduced the forced tithe and withheld the sacraments from those who he knew did not tithe. Martinez saw Lamy as an inexperienced young man who blindly followed orders from Rome and extorted money from poor people. In 1857, Martinez was excommunicated by Lamy; but, Martinez said Lamy could not do so, as he had not followed due process as required by American law. Martinez continued as a priest at his own church in Taos.

The Franciscan friars who Lafe associated with in the 1850s to the early 1870s actually admired the Penitentes because their brotherhood shared the view that "humble men given to the conviction of holiness and humility are promoted through mortification of the flesh." A new member of the Penitente had to pledge to follow their rules and policies and was on probation for five years. They also had to memorize those rules and regulations, as they were never put into writing. Lafe was surely drawn into the Jesuit-Franciscan controversy, but we do not know which side he was on; however, a good guess would be that he backed Martinez until Martinez died in 1867.

Juan Vasquez and Lafayette Head had led the drive for labor, supplies, and money for the new church at Conejos, and they were part of a committee with John Francisco, Pedro Lobato, and Celedonio Valdez to cast the new bell for the church, because when the construction of the church was finished, there had been no money left to buy a bell for the tower. The people of the parish contributed jewelry and silverware (some items were said to be family heirlooms) to be melted down to cast the bell. Lafe was one of five men in charge of the casting. The bell was ready for use when Bishop Lamy dedicated the new church on December 12, 1863 (the date of the Feast of Our Lady of Guadalupe). Our Lady of Guadalupe quickly became the premier church in the San Luis Valley, and as more and more mission churches were set up in the valley, they were administered from and their records often kept in Conejos.

Father Montaño was the priest at the Conejos church for six years before leaving in 1863; and another Franciscan, Reverend Miguel Rolly, took over

CHAPTER 11

at that time and served until 1871. Father Rolly and Lafe enjoyed playing chess together, and when Lafe's old friend Alfred Pfeiffer, the Abiqui Indian Agent, visited Conejos, he always was eager to challenge Father Rolly to a chess match. When he retired from the Conejos Church on December 9, 1871, Padre Miguel Rolly became the last Spanish Franciscan priest assigned to Conejos. He then became the priest at the Jemez Pueblo church and then was later assigned to the Cathedral in Santa Fe.

At the December 12, 1871, Feast of Our Lady of Guadalupe, just three days after Father Salvadore Personé (Rolly's replacement) arrived, it was probably a little sadder than normal because Father Rolly was leaving. Personé recognized the poor state of the church with the reflection that "no other home in town is in such miserable and wretched shape." This was not recorded in the *Diary of the Jesuits* until months later, as the Jesuit priests and brothers were much too busy when they first arrived but tried to fill in the several months they missed later.[133]

Despite the harsh start, Personé was described as "… always cheerful, ready to joke, and glad always to share another's sorrow or trouble…a fine looking man with white hair."[134] At this time, the territory for the Colorado parish was extended to Saguache, greatly increasing the priests' work load. New Bishop Joseph Machebeuf, who was now a close friend of Bishop Lamy, visited Conejos in 1870 and offered mass as well as confirming 120 children.

Father Personé also caused an uproar when he announced an end to burials in the church's dirt floor. From the very earliest days in New Mexico, the local people had buried their dead inside the churches, even though burials inside churches had been banned by the Catholic Church as early as 1798 for health reasons. In the beginning, in Conejos, it was a way to protect graves from being disturbed by animals or Indians. Then it simply became a tradition. Graves were not marked, but the names of the deceased and the location of their burial in the church floor were recorded in a Burial Book kept by the church. Bodies were not embalmed, so they decomposed quickly, and later burials inside the church were often mixed with decayed bones. Burial locations had a social status. Location determined the price. A grave near the altar marked a person of importance. In 1872, for example, a burial near the altar cost $25 and the priest's fee was $100, a small fortune in those days. The price for burial in the "Fourth Section," the farthest from the altar, was $4 plus $25 to the priest. Burial in the churchyard cost $12, including a mass and benediction; but this practice was not very popular. Father Personé was firm in his decision, but promised a proper cemetery would soon be built outside the church.

Friend of the Fathers

One of the first repair jobs was to place wood over the dirt floor in the church. After the initial $600 was gone, Personé was able to raise the money for a second round of construction and repairs, and the church was still able to buy an organ. Things were going well enough at the church that on February 1, 1872, several Jesuit brothers and Father Alexander Leone arrived to help the priests. One of their first jobs was to round up and burn any of Father Martinez's books that were found anywhere in Conejos. "Brothers" were a member of a brotherhood like the Jesuits or Franciscans, but might or might not be ordained as a priest. One brother served as a cook and the other as a gardener. Father Personé implemented recordkeeping for the brothers' residence. *The Diaries (Diarios) of the Jesuit Residence of Our Lady of Guadalupe Parish, Conejos, Colorado*, were started on December 9, 1871 (the day Personé arrived) and continued until 1920, when the Jesuits were no longer at the church.

New settlers continued to arrive in the San Luis Valley in the early 1870s, and Fathers Personé and Leone covered a territory that included over 3,000 parishioners in 1872. They were spread among twenty-five little villages and towns on both sides of the Rio Grande River, and Father Personé requested more assistance. The new missions included Alamosa,

Lieutenant George Wheeler had his photographer take this photo on December 31, 1873. The gate opens to the cemetery where men are working. The tripod structure on the flat roof is actually the "temporary" bell tower and the ladders were used for access to ring the bell. Wheeler Survey Photo,

Courtesy of Wikipedia.

237

CHAPTER 11

Capilin, La Garita, Los Mesitas, Los Cerritos, Los Piños, Saguache, San Antonio, San Luis, Servilleta, and Tres Piedras. Three more priests were soon sent, as well as four more Jesuit brothers to handle the cooking, gardening, management of the household duties, and livestock at the Church of Our Lady of Guadalupe at Conejos.

Lafe also made sure that the Bishops always felt welcome in Conejos when they visited. Bishop Machebeuf paid another official visit in July, 1872. Father Personé and Lafe met him several miles from the church with wagons and 100 men on horseback and escorted him into Conejos. Bishop Machebeuf was very pleased with the reception and the church affairs.

The people of Conejos maintained many old Spanish religious traditions. Among others, at Christmas time, La Posada welcomed Joseph and Mary, who were looking for a place to spend the night in Bethlehem with bonfires in front of many of the homes. After the Christmas night mass, Martina served the traditional late supper of *posole*: a stew made with hominy, pork or chicken, chili peppers, and other seasonings. Semana Santos (Holy Week) was observed at Easter with many church services and Penitente ceremonies; and the celebration of *Dios de los Muertes* (Day of the Dead), observed October 31 through November 2, honored deceased family and friends.

On January 16, 1873, Father Lorenzo Fede arrived in Conejos. Since Lafe's second Conejos home had by this time been built just across the plaza from the church, Lafe had frequent contact with the priests and brothers. He also, as mentioned before, was a generous supporter. On November 16, 1872, for example, the diary records thirty-five *fanegas* of wheat (about fifty bushels) that were from the missions in the Valley were ground for the priests at no charge by Head's Mill. Lafe would also regularly give the priests a half a cow and other food. Lafe usually provided needed transportation for the priests—often a buggy or a cart and horse(s). The diary entry for May 29, 1873, for example, reports, "Brothers Tateo and Panfilo have gone to El Pueblo with Don Raphael's little cart and mules." The diaries always referred to Lafe and Martina as "Don Raphael Cabeza" and his wife "Doña Martina Cabeza." Outside of Conejos the Heads were usually called "Major Lafayette Head and Mrs. Martina Head." On January 30, 1873, it was reported that Lafe gave a field to the church, probably for growing vegetables or a pasture for horses that the priests and brothers were beginning to collect.

Father Personé described the San Luis Valley in a March 1874, letter to his old Parish back in Italy. He diligently copied the letter into the *The Diary of the Jesuit Residence of Our Lady of Guadalupe Parish*.

The climate here is very cold. The rivers freeze over for months on end, so much so that they can be passed over safely with wagons carrying heavy loads. The snow falls here most abundantly; at the moment that I am writing to you, the snow is piled more than two meters high in certain parts of our garden. In the surrounding mountains, especially this year, the snow has grown so deep that it has not been possible for people to go look for wood as has been the custom, and many cattle and sheep that were in the snow-covered mountains have died of hunger and cold, being unable to find a blade of grass uncovered to eat. The frosts commence in September and finish towards the end of June. Therefore there are few things that can grow to maturity here, and so there is no fruit here of any kind, no figs, no grapes, no apples, no pears—in sum, nothing. The whole produce of earth reduces itself to wheat, corn, peas, potatoes, a few beans, grass for the animals—and that is all.[135]

He went on to describe the residence of the priests near the church to be "one of the best in New Mexico and Colorado," but he also complained that the extensive travel needed to reach so many missions spread over such a great distance was very tiring for the priests and wearing them down. He noted that most travel was also long and hard, especially when the rivers were flowing high in the spring.

It is also interesting that several *Diaros* entries indicate that Martina's mother was evidently living with her and Lafe, at least part time. One entry indicates she was with Martina when they went together to an Easter Sunday confession. An entry of February 11, 1874, indicates "Doña Barbara," who a footnote[136] indicates may have been Lafe's mother-in-law, was sick and in bed at Martina's house in Conejos and that communion was taken to her there.

On February 20, 1874, when Lafe returned from his trip to Washington, D. C. as interpreter for the 1873 Treaty with the Utes, he was warmly welcomed back. Father Salazar visited him the next morning. Then Father Fede visited him the next afternoon. They thanked God for his safe return and wanted to know the details of his trip. The number of people in the area continued to grow rapidly. Rich mineral discoveries were already being made in the San Juans in several locations, including at Summitville, located on the eastern side of the Continental Divide between Conejos and Del Norte. Prospectors were combing the mountains for more riches, and merchants were arriving daily in the San Luis Valley with their wares, so they could, as said before, "mine the miner."

The December 12, 1873, Feast of Our Lady of Guadalupe began with a procession. One hundred sixty men on horseback circled the church. Children with flags followed. Eight young women carried the statue of Our Lady of Guadalupe. They were protected by a canopy carried by Don Raphael Cabeza, Don Manuel Sabino Salazar, Don Celedanio Valdez, and Don José Gabriel Martinez. The procession made one circle of the church before entering the building for the high mass and a sermon. An entry in the Jesuits diary of January 31, 1874, indicates four priests and four brothers were present at Conejos.

A January 19, 1874, entry discusses the building of the promised "proper cemetery" outside the church and recognized that on January 21, 1874, "Doña Martina's laborers came to work." On July 22, 1874, Martina's workers were back and building the cemetery's walls. Martina Head was also personally present and instructed her workers on how to prepare the new burial ground. There were thirty-eight workers building the cemetery's walls on one day or another in September of 1874. Few of the graves at the cemetery had headstones; and often there was just a rock with some initials scratched into the stone or perhaps a wooden cross, which eventually decayed, for identification. Also in September 1874, more rooms and stables for the priests were being added to their existing residence.

Some rather ordinary details are also included in the diaries. For example, on May 13, 1875, the diary simply records "Don Raphael, Mr. Meyer, and Mr. Fayfer dined with the priests." Mr. Meyer was a German man who

The front of Our Lady of Guadalupe was very attractive and included these twin bell towers. Also note a gable roof was added.

Hafen and Hafen, *The Colorado Story*.

operated a general merchandise store at Costilla; and "Fayfer" (the priest had trouble spelling his Scottish name) was none other than Lafe's longtime friend, fellow Indian Agent and skilled chess player, Colonel Albert H. Pfeiffer.

One April day in 1875, Father Personé and Don Raphael Cabeza left for Denver, and they did not return until two and a half weeks later. The diary gives no details or reason for the trip, but on May 9, 1875, records show preparations to add nine rooms to be used as a convent for the Sisters of Loretto, "who will open a school." Perhaps the trip to Denver was to gain permission for a school, arrange for the teachers, raise money for the convent or the school, or all or part of the above. In 1876, the people of Conejos were also building a large addition to the south side of the church, with plenty of rooms for a school to be run by the Sisters of Loretto.

When approached, the Bishop had stated that if the church would build the convent and the school, he would provide the nuns. About this time, Donald Gasparri, from the Jesuit Society of Jesus (a Jesuit scholarly and benevolent society of the Catholic Church) gave a retreat at the Conejos church and suggested to the participants that a good memorial for the retreat would be to build the convent. The Jesuit society did the project, and three sisters were sent to Conejos—Sisters Vinceta Gonzales (the mother superior), Mary Mahoney, and Ophelia Conell.

The Sisters of Lorreto established separate schools for boys and girls. The women of the church furnished them with all the necessities for a school, which was started in September of 1877 and called "Sacred Heart Academy." It was a private Catholic academy, but the Sisters also taught at times in the nearby public school. Unfortunately Sister Mary (Mahoney) came down with smallpox and died. The other sisters were devastated, but stayed and even expanded the school. The Sisters had a commodious independent academy near the church by 1895. Both the church and the academy had been made attractive by shade trees, lawns, and flowers. The school continued until 1918.

The people of Conejos also tried to get a hospital started. The Sisters of the Order of Mercy was founded in Ireland in 1831, and trained nurses. The Order spread rapidly throughout the world. In 1882, Bishop Machebeuf asked the Sisters of Mercy Order in St. Louis to send volunteers to care for the sick in Colorado. Four sisters were eventually sent to Conejos, where they started a hospital in an old store building, but they were still thinking and praying about where to permanently locate in Southwest Colorado. Unfortunately, they were only in Conejos for two months before they decided or were ordered to go to the new and bigger town of Durango. This

CHAPTER 11

decision may have been made because Fort Garland had a medical facility, but so did Fort Lewis, now near Durango but originally at Pagosa Springs.

Lafe perhaps had a secret that he kept from the Jesuit fathers—that he was a member of the Penitente Brotherhood. The Penitentes were lay brothers who "expiated their sins through self-flagellation." They were regarded by the national Catholic Church as extremists, but even Bishop Lamy of Santa Fe could not stop their practice in Colorado or New Mexico. The Brotherhood supposedly still survives in Colorado, but in small numbers in Conejos, Costilla, Alamosa, and Saguache Counties. Their practice is continued in secret, usually during Holy Week, and today they operate independent of the Catholic Church.

The Brotherhood of Penitentes was started in medieval times in Europe by the Franciscan priests and was brought to New Spain by them and Spanish conquistadors in the 1600s. The Franciscan Brotherhood helped supplement the shortage of priests in New Spain. After 1821, when Mexico received its independence from Spain, the Franciscans in Spain were evidently worried about their brothers in Mexico and pulled them back to Spain. Many of the Franciscan priests were replaced by independent priests who did not belong to any particular order. Father Martinez was one of these priests, and he pretty well ran the local Catholic churches in New Mexico until Bishop Lamy arrived. During this time (1800 to 1848) the Penitentes flourished. The early Conejos Jesuit priests tried to keep on good

This photo of Our Lady of Guadalupe in the 1880s evidently shows a procession forming outside the church with girls in white gowns for their first communion.

Denver Public Library Western History Department Photo (X-7530).

terms with the Penitentes and even blessed several of their *moradas* (their meeting places). "Most moradas were adobe structures. They were nearly windowless and very plain so that they would not attract attention."[137] Moradas still exist in the San Luis Valley, but those still standing were usually built in the late 1800s or early 1900s. All unusual religious practices were considered to be a problem by the Jesuit priests in the southern San Luis Valley after they arrived in the 1850s and 1860s, but the Brotherhood of Penitentes, in particular, caused major concern.

Although the author has no problem with Lafe being a Penitente, if he was, the "proof" that Lafe was a Penitente comes from an article that has perhaps been misunderstood.[138] This article was written during the time when Alexander Darley, a Presbyterian minister, was doing missionary work in the San Luis Valley and was viciously attacking the Penitentes in books and newspapers, as well as in his preaching. In one article he reported that Lafe was not only a member but that he was a "conchatario" (leader) for his district and that he had joined for political reasons.[139] The article discusses the Masons and the Penitentes and states that Lafe was a member of "the brotherhood." Both the Masons and the Penitentes called their fellow members "brother." William Gillette Rich, in his private journals, listed Lafe and another renowned early pioneer as members of the "Brotherhood" from 1850 to at least 1878 (the time of Rich's writing); and perhaps Lafe was a member until the time of his death in 1897. To this author it is impossible to determine if Rich is referring to the Penitentes or the Masons when he uses the word "Brotherhood."

Another source wrote:

> *Americans who are accused of joining them ("the Brotherhood") for power and politics:*
>
> *Theodore D. Wheaton—a lawyer and several times a member of the legislature. He lived in Santa Fe, Taos, and Mora, since the American occupation. He died in Mora County.*
>
> *Lafayette Head was a member of the Legislature from Taos County. In 1877-78 he was Lieutenant Governor of Colorado. His residence was at or near Conejos. He was a Republican in politics.*

Penitentes were the most active in northern New Mexico and southern Colorado from 1850 to 1890, almost the entire time Lafe was living in the San Luis Valley. He would have kept it from the priests and the bishops, as Lamy and his Jesuit priests not only attacked the Penitentes, but denied their members the sacraments if they knew for sure they were a Penitente. Bishop Lamy called the Penitentes "Faith Healers" and "Witches," and he said their medical issues usually were resolved with only folk remedies. By 1900, the Penitente sect was secretive, even among most lay people.

The Penitentes were primarily Hispanic and their songs, prayers, and ceremonies were in Spanish. As the Catholic Church began to move against the group, the Penitentes made efforts to protect themselves by "consolidating their forces behind political candidates sympathetic to them or at least not hostile."[140] Their secrecy allowed them to deliver an unexpected bloc vote during elections to candidates who could not have supported them publically, but would privately. Although not recognized by the Catholic Church, in 1861 they were recognized by the New Mexico Territorial legislature as a benevolent society.

Some Penitentes would parade with their counterparts while whipping themselves or carrying large crosses.

Richardson, *Beyond the Mississippi.*

Rueben Archuleta, author of *Land of the Penitentes, Land of Tradition*, writes that the Presbyterian evangelist Reverend Alexander Darley alleged that Lafe "was initiated into the Penitente brotherhood so he could secure the necessary votes to win election as Lieutenant Governor of the new State of Colorado in 1876."[141] Of course the election was twenty-six years after Lafe supposedly joined the Brotherhood.

There were very good reasons for the Penitentes' early presence in the San Luis Valley. There were long periods in the first half of the nineteenth century when remote communities in New Mexico rarely saw a priest. The Brotherhood helped keep the presence of the Catholic Church alive and helped Catholic people in need. The Penitentes did much good. In the absence of a priest, the Penitentes would hold non-sacramental services; and, even when a priest was assigned to their church, the Penitentes bought clothes for the poor, cut firewood for the sick and elderly, helped bury the dead, took care of orphans, and comforted the sorrowful. The date that the Penitente practice started in New Mexico is not known, but it was before 1776, as Escalante-Dominguez in their travels stopped at a Penitente service. The Penitentes were especially prevalent in the early 1800s, when there were only seventeen Catholic priests covering all of New Mexico, and many of them were old and decrepit. In 1832 Antonio Barreiro, an advocate for the Country of Mexico doing more for New Mexico's churches, wrote:

> *Nothing is more common than to see an infinite number of the sick die without confession or extreme unction. It is indeed unusual to see the Eucharist administered to the sick. Corpses remain unburied for many days and children are baptized at the cost of a thousand hardships. A great many unfortunate people spend most of the Sundays of the year without hearing mass. Churches are in a state of near ruin, and most of them are unworthy of being called the Temple of God.*[142]

The Penitentes also led prayers and administered blessings in the absence of a priest. During Holy Week, they did acts of penance, and this included whipping themselves and re-enacting the crucifixion by tying a chosen member to a cross. When Bishops Lamy and Machebeuf tried to abolish the Penitentes, their members simply became more secretive and moved most of their activities to confidential meeting places. It is not known if Lafe "expiated his sins by flagellation," but he was the type of man who would have belonged to the Penitentes for the good they did and not for political votes. His strong attachment to the Catholic Church before the Jesuits arrived in Conejos in 1870, and the shortage of priests in the San Luis Valley at the time, may have also led him to organize and lead non-sacramental Penitente services when no priest was available.

The Penitentes served one other function in New Mexico during the first half of the nineteenth century. Before about 1920, Penitentes sometimes established rules of conduct for daily life and administered justice in their communities. Local citizens paid fines for criminal acts or they were forced to leave town. From 1870 to 1920, every town in the San Luis Valley probably had a *morada* where justice was dispensed. "Moral righteousness and the capacity for responsibility were characteristics of the Penitentes."[143]

Rueben Archuleta writes:

> *Los Hermanos Penitentes may still exist in the San Luis Valley and/or Conejos in secret but in very small numbers.*

The sect has definitely declined in numbers over time. The decrease was due at first to an influx of European priests into Colorado and New Mexico, then the Penitentes being persecuted by Protestants because of the harm they do to their bodies, and then the arrival of the railroad which gave faster and easier transportation for priests from one parish to another. Their whips were made of yucca plants which have very sharp edges, but the primary purpose of the organization was to carry on religious practices and worship. They also aided the sick, fed the poor, buried the dead, and cared for widows and orphans. They modeled the behavior of the bible and sought justice for their communities.[144]

CHAPTER TWELVE

The San Juans and A Political Leader Once Again
(1870-1875)

He (Lafe) had a cordial welcome for friends and strangers alike, and the poor found in him always a considerate and substantial benefactor.
Rocky Mountain News, March 10, 1897

In the 1870s, the extremely valuable minerals of the San Juan Mountains came to light and eventually the area proved to be one of the richest and largest treasure troves of precious minerals in the United States. Within a few years, tens of thousands of people were living in the San Juans; and they brought "civilization" with them. For example, by 1875 Lake City, founded in 1874 on the Lake Fork of the Gunnison River, had a cigar store, a women's dress shop, and was receiving eastern newspapers regularly (although several weeks late). Conejos was no longer a part of the forgotten and unexplored Southwest Colorado. Governors and Lieutenant Governors came from this area, and millionaires were made in the San Juan Mountains or bought their ranches in the San Luis Valley.

As Conejos County grew in wealth, so did Lafe's personal estate. The 1860 census showed Head had $3,000 in real estate and $5,000 in personal property, probably invested in his livestock. In 1870 this had increased to $21,000 in real estate and $38,000 in personal property. The census also showed the county's population grew from 1,500 to 2,500 during the years 1860 to 1870. Up until the 1870s, the population of the San Luis Valley was composed mainly of Hispanic settlers who had come from the families along the lower Chama River with a few others from Taos or other areas. However, starting in the mid-1870s, an influx of Anglos began, mostly in the cattle or land business, and especially later in the 1870s, after it became obvious that the Denver & Rio Grande (D&RG) Railroad was coming to the valley. Many of the new San Luis Valley enterprises were funded by foreign or eastern capital. They made inroads into the Mexican-American community, but:

CHAPTER 12

... by paying nominal sums to key members or certain grantee families, by representing clients in land confirmation cases with payment in land, and by considerable trickery, speculators took whole grants from their rightful owners.[145]

The first gold or silver found in any amount was very near Conejos in early 1870 near the future site of Summitville; and, as in many cases, the

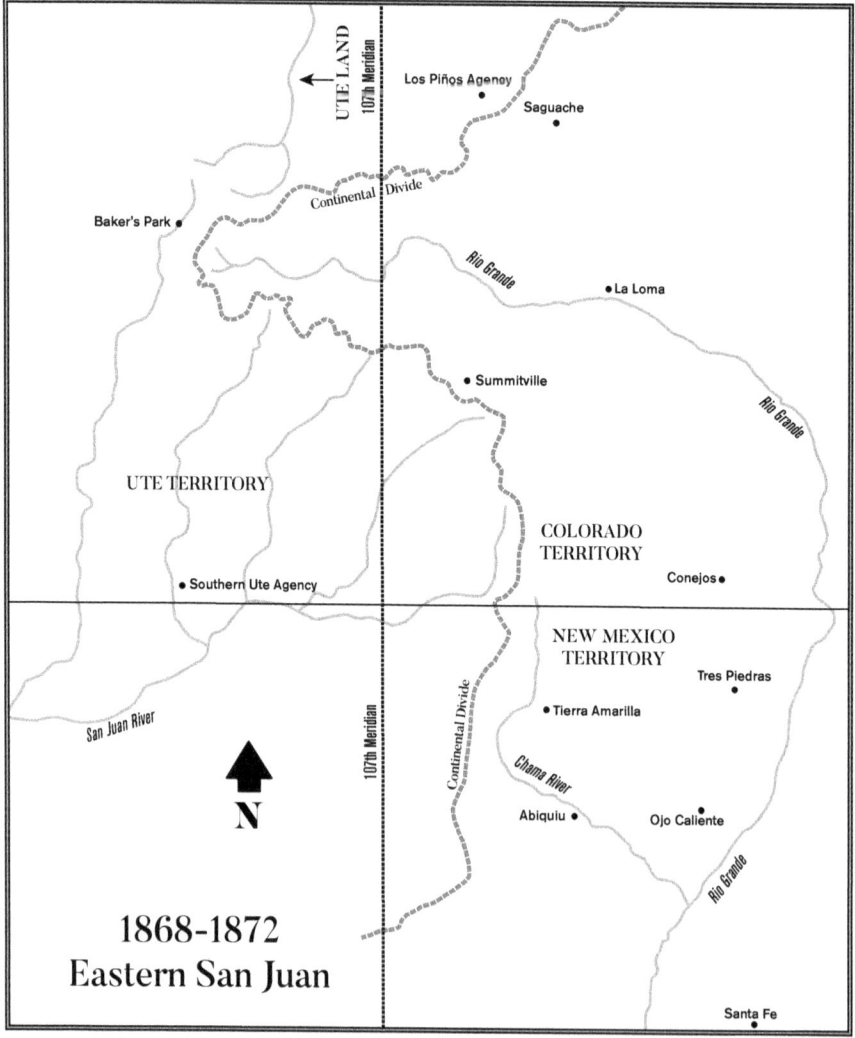

Map of the eastern San Juans and San Luis Valley about 1872. The 107th Meridian was the eastern boundary of Ute land, not allowing prospectors to go into Baker's Park legally, although Summitville was in White territory.

Western Reflections Publishing Co. Map.

precious minerals were found under unusual circumstances. John Esmond, who owned a ranch near Conejos, discovered a ledge of free gold while helping to look for a neighbor's daughter and another girl, both of whom had run away into the mountains. When Esmond stopped to check out a meadow, he found a promising-looking ledge. He later picked off fifty pounds of what proved to be very rich specimens. He filed four claims on the spot, but never did any assessment work during the next few years to meet the requirements under the Miners' Code or the General Mining Act of 1866. The Mining Act of 1872 was the first all-encompassing mining law in the United States.

In the last part of June 1870, gold was also discovered in a nearby stream in Wightman Gulch at the future Summitville by James Wightman and Dempsey Reese. The next year, about 150 prospectors were at Summit, soon to be called Summitville, which under the 1868 Treaty with the Utes was on U.S. soil, but barely on the east side of the Continental Divide (hence the name Summitville). Prospecting in 1871 was not as good as the year before, but a few locations were made and the prospectors visited Conejos, La Loma, Fort Garland, and Saguache to get supplies. It was obvious to the prospectors that the small gold nuggets and flakes they found in the streams came from mineralized veins; and the prospectors who found an outcropping of a vein filed lode claims.

In 1871, J. Carey French left the San Juans via the Rio Grande River to get lumber and needed supplies. He went first to La Loma, but he found neither available there and then went to Conejos to get the items. Several other groups at this time were reported to have gone to Conejos to replenish their food and other supplies and to get lumber. The 1871 prospectors were panning or sluicing for gold nuggets, as had been done in California ten years earlier; but by 1872, the prospectors shifted their attention from gold to silver, which was found in abundance in numerous San Juan veins of sulphurites, gray copper and brittle silver. However, the prospectors still had not realized that the even more abundant veins of galena ores carried silver as well as lead.

By 1872, Lafe's store must have done well, as he sold lumber, "American flour," and fresh meat from his own operations, as well as many other items at his store. Conejos was an early supply town for prospectors in the San Juan Mountains, although not the only such town.

Meanwhile, not all prospectors were staying east of the Continental Divide. By 1872, the San Juan Mountains were being explored all the way to their heart at Baker's Park, where Silverton now stands. Although claims could not legally be filed on the west side of the 107th Meridian in Ute

Territory, there were still prospectors staking claims there who traveled all the way to Conejos to try to file their claims, presumably in an effort to show they were the first to discover and work the claim. Summitville was the largest gold district at the time in all of Colorado Territory, but after the town of Del Norte was formed in 1871 and 1872, Conejos got little of Summitville's business. The major benefit to Conejos was that the prospectors in the southeastern San Juans after the Treaty of 1873 were required to come to the Town of Conejos for one very important reason—to file the legal notices for their mining claims.

It would only be a short while longer before the San Juans were recognized as a treasure trove, and Mears would move his base of operations to the Uncompahgre Valley, where he could still service the Indian Agency, but also reap much bigger profits from the prospectors and, after 1875, the people of the new town of Ouray. Mears also got the contract to move the Agency from Los Piños to the Uncompahgre Valley near today's Montrose. The move gave him the opportunity to build more toll roads, two railroads (the Silverton and the Rio Grande Southern), and even to invest in some of the local mines.

In the spring of 1873, when Esmond came back to the outcropping that he had discovered in 1870, "legal claim jumpers" were working his claim.

Lafe's second house dominated the Conejos plaza as well as his general store and mill (behind the store). The store may have been the original Indian Agency.
Courtesy Luther Bean Museum, Adams State University, Gift of Gwendolyn Hill, 1975.10.1i.

The site was one of the richest gold discoveries in the United States, and three of his claims—the Little Annie, the Del Norte, and the Margaretta Lodes—turned out to be the very richest in the future mining district. The claims were sold in 1874 for $410,000 (many millions in today's dollars).

As exciting, prosperous, and nearby as the San Juans were, "during the 1870s...the main characters (in the San Luis Valley) proved to be not (the miners) but the undramatic farmers and ranchers...."[146] Prospectors and miners had no desire to grow their own vegetables or raise cattle, hogs, or sheep for food, so the San Luis Valley became the breadbasket of Colorado (and especially the San Juans) and boomed. Agriculture progressed rapidly, not only because of increased demand, but also because of the new Homestead Act, the end of the Civil War, and extensive immigration from Europe. Flour, hay, vegetables, sheep, hogs, and cattle were especially desired among the prospectors. An added reason for a greater influx of settlers was that land patents were now being given by the U.S. government in the San Luis Valley near Conejos, even though some of the Mexican Land Grants were still in dispute.

Besides the prospectors, in 1873, homesteaders on Ute land in the lower Animas Valley around today's Durango were already filing paperwork at the Conejos courthouse. In 1874, Conejos' western and northern boundaries were shortened by the legislature, but Conejos County still contained all of today's Conejos and Archuleta Counties.

The first cattle in the San Luis Valley were brought by Mexican-American settlers in the 1850s to provide food and milk for their families or to pull plows to till the land for crops. Since it was the Spanish who first brought cattle to New Mexico, it was their tradition that prevailed in

CHAPTER 12

This mill was built when Lafe's Mill burned in 1874. The mill was expanded and renovated many times over the years.

Courtesy of the Luther Bean Museum, Adams State University, Gift of Gwendolyn Hill, #1975.10.1d.

the San Luis Valley, instead of the European cattle system that Lafe would have experienced back in Missouri. Cowboys were used to patrol the cattle that ran loose on "open range" instead of being fenced in. Brands had to be used to identify your cattle from those of your neighbors, calves had to be branded soon after birth at the "round-up," as well as your brand being registered with the authorities. The basic concepts of Spanish range law (and also water law) were adopted in the San Luis Valley and eventually the Colorado statutes as well. Range law also provided that the first to use a spot of public land for grazing got the first opportunity for that use each year thereafter as long as it was used, and that those who did not want livestock on their private land were required to fence in their land to keep the cattle out instead of vice versa.

The cattle industry did well after Texas cattle began to make an appearance in Colorado in the 1860s; but it was not until after the Civil War ended that the cattle industry boomed, as Texas ranchers were then allowed to drive or ship their cattle north. Colorado land was especially desirable, as its rich western mountain grass was adapted to Colorado's cold, dry climate, and cattle and sheep could often winter in the state without needing hay. Most of the early cattle from Texas were longhorns, and small farms and ranches were still the norm; but Hereford cattle and large ranches soon came to the San Luis Valley.

By the 1870s, the composition of the Indian Affairs Section of the Department of the Interior had changed to one made up of reformers.

One of the Board's first actions was to assign a Protestant denomination to each of the Indian Agencies, with the Agent appointed to that specific Agency being from the "assigned" denomination. After Head's resignation, Lieutenant Calvin Speers served for several years as the Los Piños Agent, but he was supposed to have been only temporary. The Unitarian Church finally realized there was no Unitarian at its assigned Los Piños Agency at Cochetopa Pass. They assigned Jabez Nelson Trask, but he had to delay his arrival for almost two years because of the illness and eventual death of his wife. Trask can only be described as "weird." His arrival did end the corruption at the Tabeguache Ute Agency involving Mears and the Territorial Governors in the early 1870s, but only for a year.

Trask was a graduate of Harvard College and Cambridge Divinity School; and he finally arrived at the Agency on May 3, 1871, dressed in an eccentric manner. Most of the Utes immediately made fun of him. He usually wore a navy blue, swallow-tailed coat with brass buttons and out of date trousers, which were skin tight except where they flared out at the ankles. He wore enormous green goggle glasses and an old-fashioned tall beaver hat. Upon his arrival, the Utes had immediately asked the governor for his dismissal as Agent. In time the Utes also complained that he did not associate with them, refused to give them their full rations, and treated them as inferiors. Virginia Simmons wrote:

Huge cattle herds ranged on "open range" (no fences) in the San Luis Valley in the 1870s and 1880s.

Author's Collection.

CHAPTER 12

> *The agent's quirky personality and especially his self-righteousness isolated him literally and figuratively both from the Utes and from Saguache's residents, as he shut himself up in his quarters at the Agency to avoid physical harm.*[147]

Trask was terribly stingy with the Tabeguache Utes' money, but he was not stealing the money. It was found that he had a savings account for the Utes of almost $25,000 when he left his position. That amounted to about half of all the money allotted to the Tabeguache Ute Agency for that year. He was described by Sidney Jocknick as "an eccentric, of sterling honesty, and guileless simplicity." Trask was totally inept, mentally and physically. Although he lasted a year, it was said he still was totally devoid of any knowledge of the Utes at the end of that time. The Tabeguache said they would like Albert Pfeiffer as their Agent, but Pfeiffer did not wish to serve. Shortly after the Civil War ended, Pfeiffer had purchased a small ranch about ten miles up the Rio Grande River from Del Norte where he planned to retire and raise cattle. However, retirement did not seem to fit Pfeiffer, and he spent little time there. Instead he seemed to roam aimlessly during the next ten years, no doubt because of his alcoholism and the loss of his wife. Pfeiffer died April 6, 1881, and is buried near his ranch.

The confusion at the Ute Agencies had been duly noted by the Department of the Interior's Office of Indian Affairs. The Denver Agency was started on January 17, 1871, with the Governor's son-in-law appointed as Agent in May of that year. Why the Governor would want the Utes to come to Denver is unknown. On November 15, 1871, a report was issued in which the Department recognized that there was "a confused and unsettled state of affairs (with the Utes) … particularly at the Los Piños Agency.…" A secret fact finder had been sent to determine the reasons and had found that, among other things, the frequent change of Agents, the inexperience of the present Agent in charge (Trask), and the many obstacles to getting supplies to the Utes at their present Agency were all factors. The report also mentioned the great number of prospectors on Ute land and suggested that a land survey needed to be done so prospectors would know where the boundary was. However, for practical purposes, both the Indians and the Whites knew it was very near the Continental Divide and that had not stopped most prospectors or Utes from crossing that boundary.

No one at the Agency, except for Trask, seemed surprised when he was replaced by another of Colorado Territorial Governor McCook's brother-in-law, General Charles Adams ("General" was a Territorial Army rank), in June of 1872. Adams was Catholic and not Unitarian, but McCook evidently wanted someone who would join his, Mears', and Ouray's ring. However, Adams actually turned out to be fairly capable as an Agent.

The Office of Indian Affairs sending a secret fact finder to the Cochetopa Agency was the start of a movement to move the Tabeguache Agency to the Uncompahgre Valley, but the actual move did not happen until 1875. One point not known by the Office of Indian Affairs about the confusion at the Agency was that without an official Agent, Mears, Governor Hunt, Governor McCook, and possibly Chief Ouray had for the most part been running the Agency for their own profit for almost two years. After Trask left, General Adams, the new agent, continued to control the Agency with the cooperation of Mears, McCook, and possibly Ouray.

> *Adams had a remarkable ability to get along with everyone, especially with Mears and Ouray, and this triumvirate held the reins at the Los Piños for a short period.*[148]

The Mouache were still at Maxwell's Ranch and continued to come back to the area of Trinidad. On January 1, 1872, they went to Colorado Springs to see the new Denver and Rio Grande train and then went to Denver. There was no trouble at that time, but the next year they came north again and were accused of a rape and of raiding. Ouray, Charles Adams, and troops from Fort Garland were sent to get Kaniache out of the area, but he refused to recognize Ouray's authority (even though Kaniache had signed the treaty of 1868); and, after refusing to go to the Los Piños Agency, Kaniache and his group went on "a drunken spree, killing cattle and running their ponies through planted fields." The Denver Agent, James E. Thompson, banned Kaniache and his band from the Denver Agency.

In 1872, the *Rocky Mountain News* published an account of annual government expenses incurred under Indian treaties for fiscal year 1871. In excess of $100,000 had been spent on the operations of the Ute agencies and for the annual annuities purchased for the Utes. About $89,000 was spent in clothing, blankets and supplies—goods that Otto Mears and former Governor A. C. Hunt were accused of making great profits on from inflated prices and charges for delivery. The $89,000 was eight times more money than the amount spent for food that year; and, although the Utes' food situation was better on the Western Slope of Colorado, they were complaining that they did not have enough food besides wild game. Otto Mears, who supplied their food, got along pretty well with the Utes during this time. Thanks to Lafayette Head, he spoke their language, honored their customs, and was not condescending toward them. However, he found his dealings with the U.S. government and the Utes to be very lucrative and did not hesitate to line his own pockets with money or goods that were meant for the Utes. By 1872, he was supplying the Cochetopa Tabeguache Los Piños Agency with a hundred head of cattle per month, together with oats, beans, potatoes, flour, and hay—even though there were very few Utes at that Agency most of the time.

In July 1872, Adams, Ouray, and ten other Utes went to Denver to meet with Territorial Governor McCook about selling the mining rights of the San Juans. Negotiations had been started in 1871, at which time the U.S. asked the Utes to sell only the right for Americans to own and mine the San Juan minerals. The Utes were willing to do so, if no houses were built by the Americans and the miners would come in the spring and leave in the fall. The Utes also only wanted one access point from outside the reservation and would absolutely sell no part of any of the valleys. The Utes were surprised when the government negotiators said the Ute proposal could not even be considered, so the Utes said they would absolutely not sign a new agreement and continued to ask the government to remove American trespassers under the 1868 agreement.

It was only a month later, on August 26, 1872, that Governor McCook, Governor Arny from New Mexico, Felix Brunot, Lafayette Head as interpreter, members of the Commission on Indian Affairs, and others met with 1,500 Utes at the Cochetopa Agency to again discuss giving up at least the

This sketch was drawn from a William Henry Jackson photo of the Utes waiting for the 1873 treaty negotiation. Some Utes were still nervous about being photographed and would not allow it to be taken.

Ingersoll, Crest of the Continent.

The San Juans and A Political Leader Once Again

Indian Agent Charles Adams, Agency employees, and Utes at the Los Piños Agency sat and stood for their photograph in front of the Agency during the 1872 unsuccessful treaty negotiations.

Author's Collection.

mines in the San Juans. (Brunot was a philanthropist as well as chairman of the Board of Indian Affairs in 1872. Both Agent Adams and Jerome Chaffe, Colorado delegates to Congress, had pushed to have Brunot made a new Commissioner for the treaty, which he was). Ouray stated emphatically that the Utes did not want to sell any of their land. The Utes wanted the government to keep the Whites off their reservation as promised; but the United States was now pushing for the Utes to sell their entire rights to the San Juan Mountains, since more precious minerals had been found there. Twice in 1872, troops were sent out from Fort Garland under orders from Washington to get the prospectors out of the San Juans. It was a hard task because it placed American against American, when they both thought they were in more danger from the local Utes.

The second attempt at negotiations with the Utes in 1872 also failed completely, but while Brunot was still at the Agency he learned from Otto Mears of Ouray's missing son. At an August meeting at Los Piños, Brunot brought up the subject and Ouray told him how he had lost his son.

> *The Utes had a fight with the Sioux on the Platte. We killed one Indian, and knew it was a Sioux by his shirt, which was of a peculiar kind worn only by the Sioux. After the fight, my boy, about five years old, was missing; and a Mexican who traded with the Sioux has since told me that Friday (an Arapaho chief) had my boy, and a Mexican woman who was married to a Sioux also told me a year ago that she had seen my boy, and that Friday still had him.* [149]

CHAPTER 12

The kidnapping gave an opening to the Americans to get the treaty signed. Ouray said he had been told by a Mexican trader that a chief of the Sioux named Friday had his boy. Soon Brunot found out the boy had been captured by or passed on to the Southern Arapaho.

Then Brunot was told by Mears that Ouray said he might make the Utes agree to a new treaty if the U.S. could find his son, which the U.S. commissioners eventually did; but the winter of 1872-1873 had already set in, and the Utes went to their winter quarters in the Uncompahgre Valley and the commissioners went back to Washington.

During his second term, which began in March of 1873, President Ulysses S. Grant tried to change the attitude in the Indian Affairs Office to one of more severity. In 1873, the official policy was a combination of "humanity and kindness" and "all needed severity to punish them for their outrages." He tried to again appoint military officers as Indian Agents, but Congress prohibited this action. Grant's official "Peace Policy" was still one of "reservation or extermination."[150]

The *Rocky Mountain News* of May 9, 1873 reported:

> *Ouray has given strict orders that none of his men shall go to the San Juan Country, as he does not wish to come into contact with the miners or soldiers at all and has runners out all over the reservation ordering the absent ones to come to the Agency at once; he also sent an order to Kaniache, who is now supposed to be somewhere on the plains… to come in immediately to this (Los Piños) Agency…. There need be no apprehension of trouble with the Utes, as they studiously try to avoid to come in contact with the settlers and miners.*

On May 28, 1873, Brunot had the secretary of the commission write to T. R. Cree to ask him to write the Arapaho and Cheyenne Agent to ask about Ouray's son. Cree did and wrote back that it was probable that Ouray's son was with the tribe, but that he seldom came to the Arapaho Agency. It was noted that everyone involved already understood that contacting him was going to be touchy. On June 25, 1873, Ouray and Agent Adams met at the train station in Cheyenne, Wyoming Territory. Brunot had planned to also be there, but he still had not found Ouray's son. However, at that time Ouray supposedly said "The Government is strong and can do what it wants; if the Government will do what it can for me and get my boy, I will do what I can for the Government in regard to our lands."[151]

Arapaho Agent Daniels did find an Arapaho Chief who remembered the boy being captured, and the details matched what Ouray had said at Cochetopa. On June 30, 1873, Agent John D. Miles wrote from the Cheyenne Agency and said another Chief had filled in other details and said they knew Ouray's boy was with a war party the Arapahoe had sent out against the Utes, but he would not come in.

The Utes had been told to assemble in mid-August of 1873, which they did with 1,800 Utes present; but prospectors were by then swarming into the San Juans and many of the Utes were anxious to fight them. Somehow Ouray managed to keep them peaceful while they waited.

Brunot was still trying to find Ouray's son, causing the commissioners to show up for the treaty council at Cochetopa two weeks late on September 5, 1873. The White River Utes had left the council because of the delay as they realized they would not be affected by the treaty. The Americans met with the other Utes on September 8, and Brunot admitted he still had not found Ouray's son, but also said he thought he was very close to finding the young man. Ouray asked that the government keep trying to find his boy. At this point it was suggested by General Adams to the Treaty Commissioners that they talk again with Otto Mears, who suggested a salary to Ouray of $1,000 a year for ten years "to allow him to build up retirement money for his old age." Ouray accepted the offer.

Ouray "was greatly disappointed," but Brunot told him the details of what was going on with the hunt and promised to keep working on it. The Utes left at Los Piños agreed to the treaty in September, mainly due to Ouray's influence and the government promise to keep up the search. Brunot actually did what he had promised and found the boy, who was brought to Washington with a delegation of Arapaho.

On September 12, the Utes at Los Piños signed the agreement. A copy was sent to Denver, White River, Cimarron, and Tierra Amarilla for the Ute chiefs there to sign. The 1868 treaty had included one safeguard that looked like it might save the Ute land. It provided that a majority of all the Ute men in the entire tribe had to confirm any further treaties made, and the U.S. confirmed that, although there would be no more treaties with Native Americans, that this provision would also cover "agreements."

To this day historians still disagree over whether Ouray sold out his people or realized that the Utes' time had simply run out. The Commissioners forced the Utes, the Arapaho, and the Cheyenne to meet together with the boy present and tried to make a truce, noting that all Indians should live at peace with each other. Brunot told everyone how Ouray's son had been taken and how Arapaho chiefs had verified the event, so they thought they had the boy. Brunot said, however, that whatever the boy decided to do, the three tribes should still make peace. One of the Utes went to the boy and

CHAPTER 12

said they had played together as children and they were cousins and that his Ute name was Cotoan.

The Commissioner then told Cotoan that Ouray did not want him to come back to him if he did not want to do so. Then Arapaho Chief Powder Face made a long speech about how the Utes and the Arapaho had killed each other for decades and they could not make peace. The boy had asked him to say he did not understand the Utes and did not want to go with them. Brunot asked the boy to tell about his capture, but he said he wanted the Utes to tell their story first. When Ouray started to tell the story, Powder Face broke in and said Ouray's son was captured thirty miles further north of where Ouray said. Ouray said the Utes never hunted the Cheyenne or Arapaho, but that they came to Ute territory to hunt his people. Powder Face admitted that was true. Brunot told him if they did it again the Americans would punish them. Powder Face agreed to be friends and the Arapaho agreed to stay on their own land. The record of the conference (which was only discovered in 1939) ends here; but Brunot's biography states everyone there knew they were father and son, but the boy would not believe he was Ute, as he had been taught to hate and fight them. "Convinced at last of his sonship (sic), the boy promised to go home... but he died on the journey, and his poor father (Ouray) twice lost his only son."[152] This, however, sounded like a good way for the boy to simply disappear. In September of 1873, Ouray, Chipeta, Wahnrodes, Antero, Tabby, and Kanosh visited Washington with the agreement signed by the Utes and which now needed to be ratified by the U. S.. The Utes later said they felt that:

When the Utes were in Washington, it also gave a chance for Ouray to meet his son who had been missing for over a decade. This picture shows the boy, but he refused to admit he could be Ouray's son as he was raised by their enemy the Arapaho.

Photo Courtesy Bureau of American Ethnology.

With military force, displays of technology, gifts, medals, trips to the east, and salaries (to Ouray and a few other Utes), government officials had created confusion among the Ute leaders." [153]

Mears, Charles Adams, and Herman Lueders (Adams' secretary), were on the three month trip to the East and Washington. Some historians called it a "victory party" for getting the Utes to give up the San Juans, but it was also a time for Ouray to see the man who had been found that the U.S. said was his son. The total cost of the trip was about $15,000; including a ball given at the White House and a trip to the circus. The Utes also went to a play, *The Black Crook*, which they did not particularly like. Mears also took them to Central Park, where the Utes were especially enamored by the camels kept there. Jocknick wrote that the tour was meant to:

...impress their minds with permanent convictions of their inferiority to the Whites in knowledge and power, and thus restrain them from entering into any warlike schemes.[154]

An official photo of the participants in the 1873 treaty (sometimes called the 1874 treaty as it was not ratified by the U.S. until then). Otto Mears is at the far right, center row.

Author's Collection.

CHAPTER 12

That plan certainly worked, and there was no war. The Utes were heard to say in one of their conversations among themselves that at some time in their past history they must have done something that offended their Gods and that the Gods therefore decided to be more favorable to the Whites than to the Native Americans.

Lafe went on this trip as an official interpreter. The Utes had agreed to sell the San Juans out of their territory, which left a strip, 100 by 15 miles along the border of southwestern Colorado that is now basically the Southern Ute Reservation, a 20 by 80 mile strip on the Utah-Colorado border, and another larger strip at the north. The Utes were to receive a sum of money that would give them $25,000 in interest each year forever, although it could after twenty-five years be paid in one capitalized amount. There would be a separate reservation for the Weeminuche, Mouache, and Capote along the southern border. The 1873 agreement basically split the Ute territory in two, except along the far western border of Colorado.

Lafe returned from Washington in February 1874. The treaty of 1873 opened up 3.7 million acres of mineral rich land that had formerly been part of the Ute reservation. Many historians see Otto Mears as the real power behind the movement of the Utes from their firm stance. Famous historian David Lavender quotes Mears as saying "in his harsh accent:"

> *I think I can get them to sign if you let me offer them a perpetual annuity of $25,000 a year. And for Ouray, $1,000 a year for the next 10 years.*[155]

Ouray is quoted as saying at the treaty council:

> *I realize the destiny of my people. We shall fall as the leaves of the trees when winter comes, and the land we have roamed for countless generations will be given up to the miner and the plowshare… and we shall be buried out of sight. My part is to protect my people and yours, as far as I can. From violence and bloodshed… and bring them into friendly relations.*[156]

Lafe turned in a salary report to the Indian Agency for first quarter of 1874 for his involvement as an interpreter with the 1873 negotiations.

In late 1873, the Mouache were back to receiving their food at Cimarron, but their Agent negotiated an agreement where they would go to the San Juan River, where a Consolidated Southern Ute Agency would be established for the Mouache, Capote, and Weeminuche. The Jicarilla received a reservation in New Mexico at the same time. Although there would be refinements, this did in effect get the Utes out of the area east of the Continental Divide and the western side of the San Juan Mountains.

Now it was time for the Americans to cause trouble in the San Luis Valley. The Travelers Insurance Company bought thousands of acres of dry land, put it under irrigation, and filed on or bought so much water that, between 1860 and 1896, 65,000 acres of the 125,000 acres in cultivation in the middle of the San Luis Valley had to be abandoned for lack of water. A wave of racial violence and terror during this time caused many Hispanics to move out of the San Luis Valley.

The basically Anglo cattle industry boomed in Colorado between 1860 and 1880, although it arrived a little later during this period in The Valley. Free public land spurred the industry in the northern part of the San Luis Valley; but most of the southern San Luis Valley was now private land, except in the mountains, and the sheep industry was predominate because it was a Mexican-American heritage. In the early part of this period, most of the valley was "free range," meaning there were no fences. Cattle and sheep ranching was much more profitable at this time, so many settlers around Conejos tried that industry. With free land and water, a $10 grass fed calf could be turned into a $40 hunk of beef in four years—a 400 percent profit. The same percentage applied to sheep.

A sketch of the Town of Conejos that appeared in Harper's Weekly *in May 1876 shows the town almost at its peak.*

CHAPTER 12

There were, unfortunately, land speculators who arrived along with the new cattlemen. With them came foreign capital, lawyers, and sometimes trickery. Even the "Santa Fe Ring," another group of crooked lawyers and bankers, got involved with the land speculation that centered on buying grants from family members who still had disputes pending in the Land Grant Court.

A few historians even claimed that Lafe was involved in this effort. Supposedly during this time Lafe attempted to form a partnership with Celedonio Valdez to gain control of the "Guadalupe" Grant, if there was such a grant or if it was misidentification of the Conejos Grant. Don Celedonio was the second richest man in Conejos, second only to Lafayette Head. He was also one of the original petitioners for the Conejos Grant in 1833 and in 1842. He settled along the Conejos just shortly after Head and Jacques, and by this time, like Head, owned a large amount of land. In November 1873, he was visited by wealthy English investor William Blackmore, who was at this time promoting the recently approved Sangre de Cristo Grant; and the two supposedly reached a tentative understanding about acquiring the Conejos Grant. However, nothing was ever formalized. There are some who feel that Lafayette Head may have been involved in this scheme, but there has been no proof of that seen by this author.

On April 28, 1873, about 1,100 Utes returned from their winter camp near Delta to the Los Piños Agency. They had been very successful in their winter hunt for furs and food. There was no trader at the Agency, so they were looking for permission from the Agent to go to Denver to trade their furs. Ouray was giving strict orders to his Utes that none of them should go into the San Juan Mountains, so they evidently had come up the Gunnison River. It is unknown if they got their permission.

There were many disheartening national, state, and local events that occurred in Colorado in the mid-1870s. For example, late 1872 church records indicate there was an epidemic in Conejos that killed forty-five children that year. From 1872 to 1876, buffalo hunters on the Colorado plains killed four million buffalo for the hides only. This eliminated food, clothing, shelter, and bedding for the few Native Americans left in Colorado (a few Plains Indians, but mainly the Utes) and left the Plains Indians with nowhere to go except reservations. Lafe's mill burned in 1874, a total loss of $16,000; but because of the good economic times in the San Luis Valley, it was quickly rebuilt that same year with better equipment, but at a cost of $27,000. The May 12, 1874, issue of *The Rocky Mountain News* reported the event, noting that "it was the work of torching." The culprit was never found. Lafe hired Daniel Pike Church, an experienced millwright and Civil

War veteran, to rebuild the mill building and install the necessary but most advanced equipment.

Lafe traveled to St. Louis to buy the new mill equipment. While there, he hired Charles S. Lawton, an experienced mill operator, to manage the business. Lawton ran the mill as an employee for five years before becoming Lafe's business partner in the enterprise. Head was not paying much attention to the mill operation, as he was now mainly concerned with his sheep herd. Lawton had come to Trinidad, Colorado, in 1871 from Missouri, and moved to Conejos in 1875; then he went to Denver and Boulder for a short time, and was back in Conejos in 1878, where he again operated the flour mill for Head.

As mentioned, Governor McCook was removed from his Colorado Territorial Governor position the first time in early 1873 for committing fraud and theft, much of it involving the Ute Indians. He had been replaced by Governor Samuel Elbert on April 4, 1873, who himself lasted for only about a year as governor. McCook had stolen goods meant for the Utes and charged the government as much as six times what he paid for some of the food. The investigation into McCook also showed he had diverted thousands of dollars meant for the Utes into his own bank account. James Thompson, McCook's brother-in-law, had also been appointed a Special Agent for the Utes at the Denver Agency, but did nothing to earn his salary. When all this came to light, the citizens of Colorado demanded that McCook be removed. McCook (who was an ex-Army officer) was again removed from office by petition of Colorado citizens but was again later appointed Colorado Governor on June 19, 1874, but he only lasted until March 29, 1875, when he was again removed by petition and John Routt took over until Colorado became a state.

In January 1874, Lafe attended a meeting of Mexican-American War Veterans. He and other such veterans felt they should have a pension like U.S. veterans of other wars. The meeting was held in Denver, and Lafe was the presiding officer at the opening of the convention. His first order of business was to get a list of those present and the details of their service in the war. The group voted to join the National Association of Mexican-American War Veterans and accepted their bylaws and constitution for the local organization. Head was appointed to a committee to bring their request to the attention of the Colorado legislature; and if a resolution to this effect was passed, he was to send it on to the U.S. legislature. The proposed petition mentioned as reasons for the pension the valuable service of those in the war, the tremendous benefits to all United States citizens that were received from the land and minerals acquired in the war, and the fact

CHAPTER 12

that many of the veterans of the war were not only poor, but absolutely destitute. The group asked for a pension of eight dollars a month (about $168 in today's money) for all who had served for more than sixty days during the war. It took thirteen years for the United States Congress to pass the Mexican War Veteran Pension Law; and the pensions were only paid from the day the Pension Act was effective, not from the date a soldier's service ended. To receive a pension a veteran had to be at least sixty-two years of age unless they were disabled, then they could receive the pension at any age. The veteran also had to be honorably discharged.

The Colorado Mexican-American War veterans also agreed to hold annual meetings of their association on the anniversary of the Battle of Chapultepec. That battle occurred in Mexico City on September 13, 1847, when 2,000 U.S. soldiers stormed the castle of that name, which was being

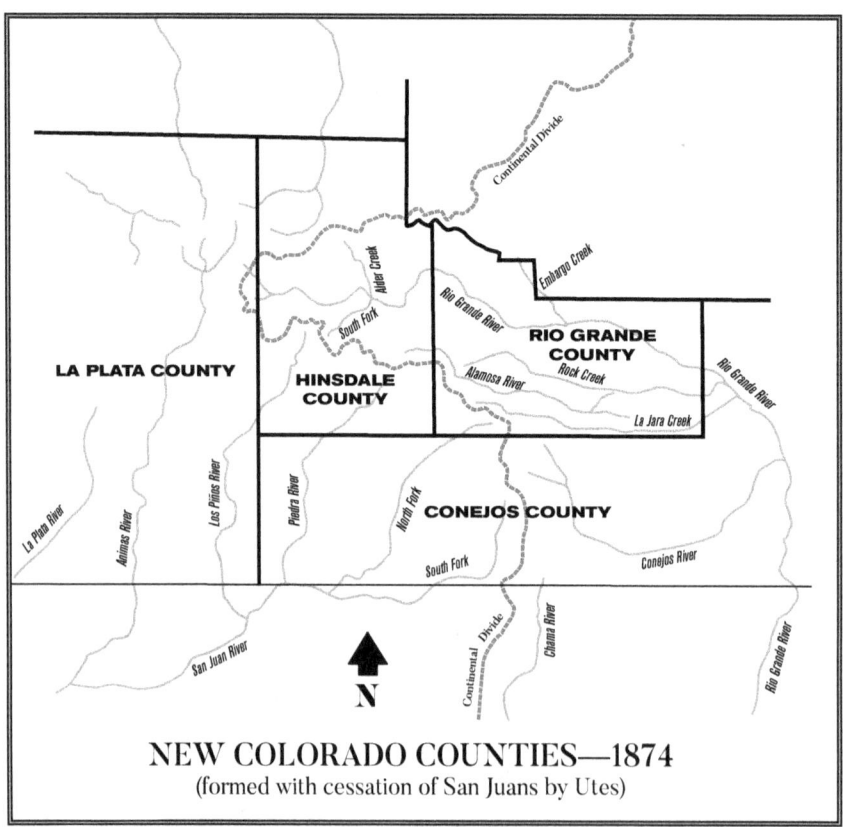

Map showing new counties created in 1874.

Western Reflections Publishing Co. Map.

held by 880 Mexican soldiers. The United States sustained many casualties, but won the battle in only sixty to ninety minutes. Many American soldiers scaled the wall and fought hand to hand with the Mexicans. By nightfall the Americans controlled, not only the fort, but much of Mexico City. It was one of the first battles for the newly created U.S. Marines and the bright red stripe on the pants of marine officers honors those who fell at Chapultepec.

The move of the Indian Agency from Cochetopa Pass to what some called the Los Piños II Agency on the Uncompahgre River had been quickly approved after the Treaty of 1873 was ratified in 1874, as a flood of prospectors began to pass into the San Juan Mountains, many of them over Cochetopa Pass. However, the actual move of the Agency did not start until mid-summer 1875 and was not complete until November of that year. The move included 1,400 head of Ute cattle that had been grazing in Taylor Park.[157] Otto Mears built the first toll road into the San Juans to Lake City in 1875, built another toll road to the new Agency in the Uncompahgre Valley the next year, and got the contract to move the Ute Agency to its Uncompahgre Valley location. He also received the new mail contract to that location and continued to deliver cattle and other rations at inflated prices to the band now called the "Uncompahgre" Utes instead of the Tabeguache. At the same time, the Utes were still doing well with their hunting, perhaps because the prospectors were moving the game out of the mountains, or the hunting was simply better in Western Colorado because it was not overrun by Americans. The Utes were reported to soon have many hides to trade.

Many of the Capote and Mouache became farmers at this time, but the Weeminuche and Jicarilla Apaches refused to do so, and raising cattle at the southern Agency was only somewhat successful. Each Agency had a cattle herd; but the herds were cared for by American cowboys, and the cattle were soon insufficient in number to feed the Utes. The Utes were actually encouraged to chase their cattle like buffalo, so that they "could still get the thrill of the kill." Mears, in the late 1870s, supposedly bought 4,000 head of cattle in the San Luis Valley, transported them to the Uncompahgre Valley, and sold them to the U.S. government at the new Agency on the Uncompahgre at a "thumping profit."[158]

In 1873, Lafe had gone back into politics and won election on October 11, 1873, as a Territorial Senator (Council) from the 11th District (the lower San Luis Valley) of the Colorado Territorial Legislature. He represented the large Conejos County, and his salary as a member of the Council was $1,000 per year. While the Legislature was in session (usually for a few

CHAPTER 12

Utes and Agency employees at the post office of the new Los Piños II Agency on the Uncompahgre River. Note the building is of adobe instead of logs which were used at the first Los Piños Agency.

Author's Collection.

months every two years), members also received $6 a day for meals, lodging, and other expenses. They were allowed $3 for every twenty miles of travel between their residence and the territorial capital, which was now Denver. Lafe rented a room in January and February, 1874, while the Senate met.

On the first Monday in January 1874, Lafe took his seat for the 11th District in the Tenth Session of the Colorado Territory Legislative Assembly. The thirteen members of the Senate opened their meeting at 2 p.m., and after electing officers and picking support staff, adjourned for the day. They met again on Tuesday, and that afternoon the House and the Senate met together. Samuel H. Elbert, Colorado Territorial Governor, delivered the annual opening address. He reported that the Territorial Militia had "only fifty serviceable guns… and a few boxes of cartridges, only one of five of which will explode." In short, the Colorado militia was in poor shape to protect any of Colorado's citizens, and Elbert requested it be brought up to full strength. The militia was also having difficulty securing full enrollment of well-trained and disciplined troops to protect Colorado citizens from Indian outbreaks, to check mob violence, and to enforce civil authority.

The San Juans and A Political Leader Once Again

Another money problem for the Territorial legislature in their Tenth Session was that the Territory had only allocated thirty cents a day for the upkeep of each of the seventy-five convicts housed in the Cañon City Penitentiary, which was built in 1871 and was only meant to hold forty prisoners.

Territorial Governor Elbert also reported he was anxious for the ratification by the U.S. Senate of the new 1873 Ute Treaty (which had already been delayed for months) and the opening up of three million acres of mineral rich Colorado land to mining. The Governor further mentioned that the number of schools in Colorado had increased fifty percent over the previous year and that there was now an average daily attendance of 7,456 students at 180 schools. Railroads were quickly expanding into the Territory, and 624 miles of track had been completed with another 544 miles under construction. The Territory also boasted 1,017 miles of telegraph line. Colorado could be proud of its quick progress. However, Governor Elbert saved his big announcement to near the end of his speech.

> *The time has come when… we can properly apply for admission as a State into the federal union, and I accordingly recommend a memorial to that end* (a "memorial was a written request from the legislature that the Governor take a particular action").[159]

The memorial was immediately made. The first actual bill of this legislature was to address grievances against the Utes, and the second was to establish a military post in southwest Colorado and build Colorado's portion of a military wagon road from the Rio Grande River across the main range to Fort Defiance near today's Gallup, New Mexico. The fort in Colorado was not established until 1878, and was first called "Fort Pagosa Springs," then Camp Lewis, and finally Fort Lewis. The road would certainly have helped Conejos, as it was to run from Fort Garland to Conejos to the Continental Divide and over to the headwaters of the Chama River, then down the Chama to the west of the Jemez Mountains.

Lafe was also a member of the committee that reviewed proposed legislation, and they decided when, if at all, a bill should go to the floor for a vote. His committee made recommendations to amend a bill or to refer it to a certain committee. During the next few days of the legislature, members announced the bills they planned to introduce. Lafe's list included a bill to establish assay offices where gold, silver, and other precious metals and minerals could be valued and a bill to simplify the transfer of real estate and to fix equal filing fees charged by all Colorado County Clerks. On Wednesday,

CHAPTER 12

January 7, 1874, Head gave notice that he would introduce a bill to create a new county out of the southwest portion of Conejos County (eventually this would be La Plata County). He also said he would like to see a new county made somewhere around Del Norte (eventually Rio Grande County).

The Senate (Council) had plenty to do. The Senate Chairman appointed members to committees, and Lafe was assigned to four—the Committee on Incorporation and Railroads; Counties; Federal Relations; and Enrollment (member attendance). He also served on a special committee to recommend an interpreter for the Council. This was needed because several elected members spoke Spanish as their first language and came with varying skills in English.

In late January of 1874, Lafe and George M. Chilicott co-chaired a special committee to find a location for the state capital, as a location needed to be picked before Colorado could officially apply to become a state. A Denver resident had offered ten acres and other incentives. After much discussion, Lafe's committee proposed Pueblo as the site for the capital. Council

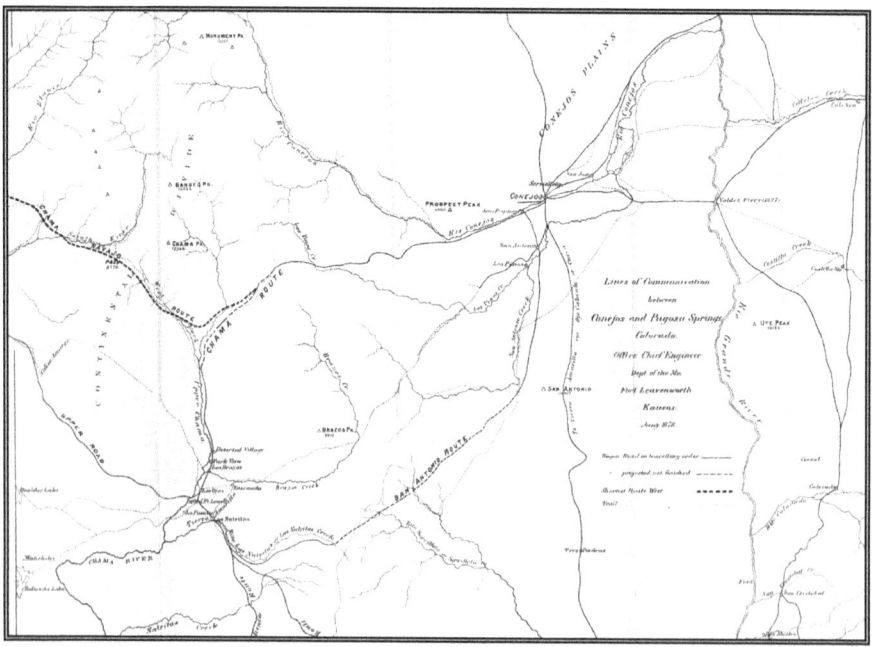

This survey map was prepared in 1878 by the chief engineer at Fort Leavenworth showing two options of the portion of the military road to Arizona from Conejos and from Pagosa Springs (one up the Conejos and the other up the San Antonio).

Center for Southwest Studies, Fort Lewis College.

members debated the merits of both sites and eventually voted 9-4 against the Pueblo location. Lafe was one of the four votes for having Pueblo as the capital, as it was nearer the middle of the State; but the state capital would be built in Denver (the territorial capital for the last seven years), which was a much larger city, but closer to the northern border of Colorado Territory.

While in Denver talking to residents about their town becoming the capital, Lafe attended a conference of the Southern Colorado Stock Growers at the Tremont House. He was elected chairman and the members voted to unite with the Colorado Stock Growers Association and meet with them in Pueblo on the first Monday in June.

The Colorado Territory Council adjourned on February 13, 1874, and Lafe returned to Conejos. Lafe soon faced yet another obligation. Back on December 20, 1873, *The Pueblo Daily Chieftain* had offered a detailed report about "The Las Animas Land Grab." Lafe may have read about it, but would have had no idea that he would become involved in it as a grand juror. Questions had arisen about the operation of the United States Land Office in Pueblo. Special Agent M. B. Robinson was sent from Washington to investigate. His full report appeared in the February 1, 1874 *Pueblo Daily Chieftain*. Robinson found that many people who had filed land claims had not lived on or improved the land as required by law, even though they reported to have done so. In the Land Office at Pueblo, Robinson found the same handwriting on many "Proof of Settlement" forms that were supposedly filed by different homesteaders. He matched these with the writing of Charles A. Cook, a Land Office clerk. An example of the false claims was an eighteen acre parcel that had supposedly been plowed, fenced, and crops cultivated; but Robinson had found none of these improvements or a house when he visited the property. He wrote that the entire section (640 acres) is "unbroken prairie and the only plowing ever done on the whole tract, as the land clearly shows, was the grading of a railroad bed that runs along one side of the property."

Agent Robinson discovered that the clerk, Mr. Cook, had connections to David Moffat, Jr., a Colorado railroad and banking investor; Mr. Carr, president of the Arkansas Valley Railroad; and Jerome B. Chaffey, the territorial delegate to the United States Congress. *The Colorado Daily Chieftain* reported on June 17, 1874:

> At the request of the court, the jurors were selected as nearly as possible from every county in the judicial district. Nine counties are represented on the jury, more than half have (never before been represented in any similar body in session here).

CHAPTER 12

Twenty-three jurors were called from the counties of El Paso, Bent, Fremont, Las Animas, Huerfano, Costilla, the new Rio Grande County, Conejos, and Pueblo. Lafayette Head was the sole juror from Conejos County. On June 24, 1874, the *Chieftain* reported the jury's decision. They issued 132 indictments for perjury, subordination of perjury, fraud, conspiracy, and violations of tax laws.

This was the second grand jury that Lafe had served on during his lifetime. William Parish, Lafe's mill operator, remembered an occasion during a rugged winter a few years earlier when Lafe had been called to serve on a Pueblo Grand Jury. That year the snow was deeper than usual in the southern mountains of Colorado. Lafe started off with a number of men accompanying him. He had six horses hitched to his hack and the other men were leading six more ahead of his hack to break trail. Lafe received word that La Veta and Sangre de Cristo Passes, northeast of Conejos, were both buried in heavy, impassable snow. He decided to go to Del Norte, then go north through the San Luis Valley to Saguache, and then over Poncha Pass. As they moved northward, they found less snow on the ground, so Lafe sent his workers and the extra horses back to Conejos. By the time Lafe had reached Del Norte, he had only Mr. Parish to accompany him.

A little before Lafe and Parish reached Del Norte, darkness settled in, and low clouds hid the moon and stars. They debated whether to continue on or find a place nearby to spend the night; but Mr. Parish soon spotted a small light coming through a stand of trees. They turned toward it and found a little cabin. Lafe knocked on the door, which was opened just enough for the man inside to stick his head out. Lafe asked if they might sleep somewhere out of the cold. "No!" said the man inside. Lafe offered to pay for

Colorado snowstorms can come on quickly in the mountains today, but were even more dangerous to travelers in the 1870s because they had little protection from the cold and usually the roads were quickly not visible.

Clamp, *Echoes From the Rocky Mountains.*

the lodging. The man still refused. "My wife is expecting a child soon," he said, "and I don't want any men coming in here."[160] Parish later recalled that "Head and me went on and spent a cold, miserable night camped outside. Next morning we were covered with snow and nearly frozen. We managed to get through Poncha Pass though and made it to Pueblo." However, that was not the end of Parish's story. Several years later, Lafe was sitting by his fireplace on a blustery cold night, when he heard a knock on the door. A snow-covered man stood shivering in the wind. It was the man who had turned Lafe and Parish away in the blizzard. Lafe did not mention the past event and invited the stranger to come in and warm himself by the fire. Martina served him hot food. After the man was fed, Lafe and his unexpected guest sat by the fire and chatted amicably. The blizzard lasted several days and the man stayed until it was over. One night the man suddenly stood up and slapped his hand to his forehead several times. Then he said that he recognized Lafe. "Where can I get some men to kick me down the road?"[161] he asked. Lafe said that he had recognized the man from the start and that would not be necessary. He said he actually enjoyed the opportunity to offer hospitality to a man who had turned him and Mr. Parish away on that cold night several years earlier.

To add to Lafe's challenges in the summer of 1875, a "plague of grasshoppers" (probably locusts as they are very similar to grasshoppers, but tend to swarm and grasshoppers do not) arrived at his ranch. It was a devastating event. Farmers from all over the West watched helplessly as black clouds of hungry locust descended on their fields and ate their crops. This great plague extended over the entire West and continued off and on until the end of the nineteenth century. The largest swarm sighted during this time was greater than the size of California and had an estimated 12.5 trillion insects. Amazingly the species was extinct by 1902.

Head and Pfeiffer were enjoying their retirement as Indian Agents during the 1870s. Pfeiffer lived in Costilla, as well as having a "stock ranch" near the Rio Grande about ten miles upriver (west) from Del Norte. Pfeiffer and Lafe both went to their friends' Catholic churches when in their home towns; and the three Jesuit Catholic priests assigned to Conejos at the time, plus Pfeiffer and the Heads had many long dinners together and loved to talk and joke until well into the night. In 1875, Pfeiffer announced at one of these dinners that he had married a Del Norte girl, but it was a hoax pulled by Pfeiffer because so many of his friends kept pushing for him to get remarried. Conejos merchants Myers and Stollstimier were usually part of Lafe's group. These last two men left Conejos in 1876, when they bought a ranch west of Pagosa Springs.

CHAPTER 12

Both Pfeiffer and Head kept informed about and were involved with the Native Americans in their areas, even after they were no longer Agents. Both were also frequently consulted by both the military and civilians on Ute Indian matters, and sometimes acted as translators. To some little extent, they took the place of Kit Carson.

CHAPTER THIRTEEN

Colorado Statehood, "The Utes Must Go," and Mormons
(1876-1880)

> *During the transformation from frontier days to modern statehood, from the Mexican-American War to modern Colorado, (Lafayette Head) was a catalyst, whether as a trader, settler, husband, rancher, miller, slave owner, Indian Agent, politician, or a lodge man.*
> Virginia Simmons, *Rabbit Brush Rambler*

President Ulysses S. Grant signed the "Enabling Act for Admission of Colorado as a State" on March 3, 1875. On October 25, 1875, residents of the then territory elected thirty-nine men to write the state constitution at the Constitutional Convention for Colorado. Lafe was one of four men from the "southern" part of the territory elected. He, Agapeta Vigil, Jesus M. Garcia, and Casmiro Barela were the only Spanish-speaking delegates; however, there were also two German-speaking men. Among the thirty-nine delegates were fifteen lawyers, three bankers, and men involved in mining, farming, stock-raising, newspaper publishing, and railroad building. Lafe arrived in Denver in time for the December 20, 1875, opening of the Constitutional Convention. He took a room at the Broadwell House at 16th and Larimer Streets, a three-block walk to the convention site.

Delegates assembled at 2 p.m. in the Odd Fellows Hall in Denver in the basement of the First National Bank Building at 1509 Blake Street. They agreed to take an oath to support the United States Constitution and to faithfully discharge their duties as representatives of the people of Colorado. Then they adjourned until the next day. There were large American flags behind the presiding officer's seat and smaller ones on each side. Every county in Colorado was represented. On Tuesday, the delegates took their oath and elected a President of the Convention. On Wednesday, they elected a Secretary. They also chose a Sergeant-at-Arms with one assistant, a janitor, a page, and an interpreter. There was one urgent need—writing

CHAPTER 13

paper. The convention chairman appointed three men to "devise means of obtaining stationery for the use of the officers and members of the convention." By the end of the day the convention chairman and the chairman of the "Stationery Committee" reported that writing paper had been found for the clerks, and that paper would be provided for the rest of the convention starting the following day.

On Thursday, the members heard the report of the Committee on Rules, which suggested fifty-five rules for the convention. The chairman announced a "Ways and Means Committee" to determine how to finance convention expenses. Travel allowances and daily expenses were also a major concern of the convention members. Lafe was one of the five members appointed to this committee, and they soon announced that there was no money available from the Territory of Colorado to fund the convention. Only eighty-eight cents remained from funds that had been provided previously by the U.S. Congress to the Territorial Legislature in June 1875. The convention quickly passed a resolution that the Colorado Territorial Representative to U.S. Congress should request an immediate appropriation of $25,000 for the convention.

Each member of the convention had four or five committee assignments. In addition to Ways and Means, Lafe was a member of the Committee on the Colorado Executive Department; the Committee on Irrigation, Agriculture and Manufacturing; and the Miscellaneous Committee. With all assignments made, the convention adjourned until January 4, 1876. After the holiday recess, Lafe made a presentation to the convention as Chairman of the Miscellaneous Committee. He offered a proposed Preamble to the Colorado Constitution, which was adopted and remains unchanged today. Lafe also drafted several important parts of the constitution related to agriculture and water rights.

On January 13, the Colorado Constitutional Convention received two petitions asking that women be allowed to vote in the new State of Colorado. Another such petition came a few weeks later. An attempt was made for women's suffrage in Colorado by introducing a clause to the constitution making it obligatory that the first legislature pass a law conferring the elective franchise upon women; which was, however, to be submitted to a vote of the male citizens at the first election thereafter. After much debate, the bill never made it to a vote. Although it did not pass, in 1893 Colorado was one of the first states in the Union to grant women the right to vote, over a quarter of a century before national Women's Suffrage.

When statehood seemed imminent for Colorado, it was proposed that the U.S. Congress be asked to remove all the Utes in Colorado to Indian

Territory in the future Oklahoma. Many of the Plains Indians had already been moved there. Then, when the Battle of the Little Bighorn occurred on June 25, 1876, there was a general cry to get all Indians out of the West. Exactly where they would go was not stated, but it was the favorite political topic of the time. Neither suggestion was considered by the convention.

Lafe requested a one week leave of absence on January 15, but apparently he took two weeks for business back home. On February 5, 1876, Lafe presented a report on behalf of the Miscellaneous Committee, which recommended publication of the final Colorado Constitution in Spanish and German, as well as English. The proposal was adopted.

The U.S. Congress eventually approved more funds for Colorado's Constitutional Convention's expenses. Members received $6 per day for living expenses, so after sixty-five days of meetings, each delegate was paid $390. Congress had guessed that the new constitution would be completed in that amount of time. For meeting time beyond sixty-five days, the men would receive a certificate for expenses "to be paid out of future appropriations made by the State or Territorial Legislature or the National Congress." A travel allowance was also provided—fifteen cents per mile traveled from home to the convention. Lafe received $81 for each 540 miles of roundtrip travel from Conejos to Denver.

On the afternoon of February 28, 1876, Lafe was absent from the convention and, for unknown reasons (but he was probably needed on his ranch), never did return. The Colorado Constitution was completed two weeks later on March 14, 1876. Ten thousand bound copies of the Colorado Constitution were printed in English, as well as 2,000 pamphlet-size copies in Spanish and 1,000 such copies in German. Total expenses of the convention, including allowances for the first sixty-five days, were $23,930.87. Incidental expenses were $2,914.87. This included the cost of lamps, chimneys, and oil for light, plus coal and wood for the meeting room fireplaces and stoves. Absent members could sign the document later in person or by proxy until Election Day.

Colorado's Statehood election took place on June 1, 1876. The vote was 15,443 in favor and 4,039 opposed; however, Colorado did not officially became a state for two more months. It was nicknamed "The Centennial State," as it was established in the year of the 100th birthday of the nation. Colorado political parties held their conventions in July to select candidates for the various offices in the new government, and Colorado newspapers were full of political ads. Denver's *Daily Rocky Mountain News*, July 24, 1876, had a headline ad that proclaimed "Lafayette Head, Southern Colorado's Choice for Governor."

CHAPTER 13

Colorado officially became a state on August 1, 1876, and the first day of the Republican Convention in Pueblo was August 23, 1876. Otto Mears was there for his first and only time as a delegate, and he played a very prominent role at the convention on different committees and helped with the selection of the slate for the party's nominees. John Routt was an obvious candidate for governor, as he had been serving as the last Territorial Governor of Colorado (from March 29, 1876 to August 1, 1876); and Lafayette Head, as a delegate from Conejos, was nominated for both Governor and Lieutenant Governor.

The Pueblo Chieftan of August 23, 1876, announced support for Lafe:

> Hon. Lafayette Head, one of the oldest and most esteemed residents of Southern Colorado, is a candidate for the enviable nomination of governor of the state. We are candid when we affirm as an independent newspaper that the sole hope of success for the Republican Party depends upon this nomination, as year by year the south has been robbed of its rights.
>
> Head is well known here and throughout the state as a gentleman whose character is above reproach. He is true as steel to his convictions of right and wrong, and he is moreover a man who leaves his imprint for good upon any cause which he espouses. He is completely identified with the interests of southern Colorado, being one of the pioneers of the country, and a resident of this county since 1854. Generous to a fault, he has allowed himself to be made a Republican Party slave for the past eighteen years.... We would strongly urge upon the party about to nominate their state officers not to slight this portion of the state, and, as a deserved tribute, to honor Lafayette Head with the nomination of Governor.

Although Martina usually stayed at home when Lafe traveled; on this occasion when he traveled to the Republican Convention in Pueblo, he encouraged her to come along, as the wives of most candidates would be there. The 1876 Colorado Republican Party Convention was too important to miss, so Martina accompanied Lafe to the convention, where she said she enjoyed meeting the delegates and their wives. She apparently bent many an ear promoting her husband's skills and abilities. The Pueblo Daily Chieftain reported on Thursday, August 24, that "Most Southern delegates got in Tuesday evening and spent Wednesday laying plans to head off the common enemy—'the Denver Ring.'" The Denver Ring was a group of corrupt and powerful officials (including even past territorial governors), who through wealth or politics worked behind the scenes illegally for their own profit. Chaffee and Evans evidently belonged in to such a ring at this time. Santa Fe also had a "ring" in New Mexico Territory.

In an afternoon meeting, sixty-three delegates from southern Colorado counties "agreed to present the name of Honorable Lafayette Head for governor." The Colorado Daily Chieftain's editor had made predictions for the outcome of the convention. "If we were going to guess at the successful wrestlers in the political arena, we would guess… S. H. Elbert, governor; Willard Teller, congressman; Lafayette Head, lieutenant governor… but a great deal depends on circumstances."

Campaign poster for Rutherford B. Hayes and W.A. Wheeler for President and Vice President in 1876.

Courtesy U. S. Library of Congress.

A special train arrived in Pueblo from Denver at 6:30 p.m. Wednesday evening, carrying some 200 passengers, including delegates, lobbyists, and a brass band. At 8:45 that evening the convention came to order in Pueblo's courthouse. Delegates found their names posted above their assigned seats. It is telling that *The Daily Chieftain* noted that "this was of great assistance to the presiding officer in recognizing the gentlemen from San Juan, Conejos, and other remote counties." Besides reporters from Pueblo's *The Daily Chieftan, The Daily News, The Denver Tribune, The Las Animas Leader, The Fairplay Sentinel, The Enterprise, Chronicle, The Mountaineer,* and *The Rocky Mountain News* had desks on one side of the room. American flags and banners decorated the walls. One large banner carried pictures of the

CHAPTER 13

Republican candidates for U.S. President and Vice-President—Rutherford B. Hayes and William A. Wheeler. *The Daily Chieftain* noted, "A telegraphic instrument had...been placed in the courtroom near the secretary's desk, and thus the doings of the convention were sent abroad direct to the outside world." The evening meeting was fairly brief. After accounting for the delegates present, making announcements, and giving notice for the schedule on Friday, they adjourned. Delegates, wives, and friends then held a torchlight parade through the streets of Pueblo.

On Friday, nine names were placed in nomination for Governor. Each nomination was followed by speeches extolling the virtues and qualifications of the candidates. The men deemed most likely to be elected as Colorado's first governor were John Routt, B. H. Elbert, Lafayette Head, and George M. Chilicott. In the afternoon, after four rounds of voting by paper ballots, no candidate had enough votes to be elected, and the chairman called for a break until half past seven in the evening.

The delegates returned that evening, talking about a rumored compromise deal. After the chairman called the assembly to order, Lafe rose to speak and withdrew as a candidate for governor. Then Elbert withdrew. Someone made a motion to elect Routt by acclamation, and he was so elected. Routt then asked the assembly to elect Lafe as Lieutenant Governor in the same manner, and Lafe was elected. It was noted that Head had already spent thirty years in Colorado, and that he was a "venerable and able looking man, and made a fine impression on the crowd." Routt made a brief speech, and then Lafe followed and thanked the members for their friendship and pledged to use every honest effort for the success of the eticket. He credited his strength to his friends and closed by saying that he was a much better worker than a talker. The meeting ended at 9 p.m. with a toast: "We will

The plaza of the town of Conejos looked pretty deserted about 1880-1900. From left to right are a blacksmith's shop, carpentry shop, and the post office. Head's house is in the large grove of trees to the left of center and a small part of his mill can be seen behind it. The church is to the right with the school attached behind it and the edge of the courthouse is at the far right.
Courtesy of the Luther Bean Museum, Adams State University, Gift of Gwendolyn Hill, #1975,10.1p.

Lafe house's dominated the residences in Conejos. Only a portion of it is shown here. It was also well landscaped with plenty of cottonwood trees to shade it from the summer sun but which allowed the warmth of the winter sun.
Courtesy of the Luther Bean Museum, Adams State University, Gift of Gwendolyn Hill, #1975.10.1i.

Routt them in the north and Head them off in the south."[162] After Lafe was elected to run as Lieutenant Governor, a little more elaborate slogan was adopted: "In Colorado we shall Routt the enemy in the north and Head him off in the south, and pull down the temple upon him."

The Saturday edition of the *Daily Rocky Mountain News* of August 25, 1876, reported:

> *Mr. Head has lived here so long, and is so well known and so highly regarded, that the fitness of his nomination admits of no question, while many will doubtless regret that he was not given first place on the ticket.*

The Chieftain had correctly predicted the choices for Lieutenant Governor, Treasurer, Auditor, and Congressman, but Routt's nomination for Governor was a surprise to many readers. On Saturday, the members selected candidates for other state offices and adjourned at noon on August 25, 1876. That evening, however, the candidates took a train to Denver, where a large crowd greeted them and held a torchlight parade up 15th Street. They lifted the nominees onto a stage that had been built, while the crowd cheered. Routt made a speech in which he said he went to Pueblo intending to decline if nominated, but that the "high honor of nomination by acclamation" caused him to accept. Lafe also made a few remarks.

The Sunday *Rocky Mountain News* of August 26, 1876 wrote of Lafe: "His name is a tower of strength in the South and Southwest and in his immediate neighborhood it will hardly be known that anyone else is on the ticket." The *Sunday Denver News* of the same date called Lafe, "A gentleman of ripe experience in political affairs."

Of course opposing political parties did their best to paint the Republican candidates in a negative light. *The Colorado Transcript* of Golden, September 20, 1876, offers an example about Lafe. In a column credited to the Democratic Executive Committee, the paper took jabs at several of the Republican candidates and their wives:

> *Some of our Republican exchanges are rather touchy on the subject of Madame Lafayette Head. But they fail to tell us who was nominated at Pueblo, Lafayette or his estimable wife. The majority of delegates voted for the latter—a fact that rebounds to her credit. Outside his wife's influence, Lafayette Head would never have been heard from.... Lafayette Head is trying to show that he amounts to something outside of being the husband of his wife.*

In the October general election, Routt defeated the Democratic candidate for Governor, Bela M. Hughes, 14,154 to 12,316. The votes for Lieutenant Governor were only a little closer. Lafe received 14,191 votes to 13,093 for Democrat Michael Beshoar.

Mears may have had something to do with Head winning the nomination and the election, but it is likely that he only helped and was not **the** reason. Throughout his life Mears liked to sponsor men with whom he was thoroughly familiar, and who he knew he could influence in the legislature. Michael Kaplan, in his book on Otto Mears, wrote a very unfavorable opinion about Lafe:

> *Head in the same manner achieved a high government post. His mentor (Otto Mears) was never one to do something for nothing and consequently never campaigned for anyone unless he received a promise for a payoff after the individual gained office. Head, who was not known for his intelligence or intractability, probably gave in to Mears' demands and was in consequence put on the slate. Another factor which increased the protégé's desirability as a candidate was that he was of Spanish-American descent (sic); and, as he was married to a Spanish-American, would command a large Mexican vote. Consequently, his sponsor probably convinced the other political bosses that it would be in everyone's interest to add Head to the slate.*[163]

Unfortunately Kaplan missed several important points. Mears had political and economic power; but so did Lafe, who was not "of Spanish-American descent" as Kaplan writes. Lafe had been elected to the New Mexico and the Colorado Territorial Legislatures many times before Mears even came to Colorado. There were good reasons that Lafe had great political power among the Mexican-Americans and would well represent the "southern" part of the state, which was composed of more than a quarter of the state's voters. Lafe was a smart man, and he was very well known and liked throughout the state. He was on many Colorado boards and citizen committees. Lafe was the perfect candidate in his own right. He would have been a good addition to any slate. On the other hand, it would be just like Mears to try to take credit for Lafe's election to increase his own political power.

On October 31, 1876, *The Rocky Mountain News* welcomed Lafe with a front page note:

> *Honorable Lafayette Head, the first Lieutenant Governor of Colorado, arrived from the south last evening and has taken*

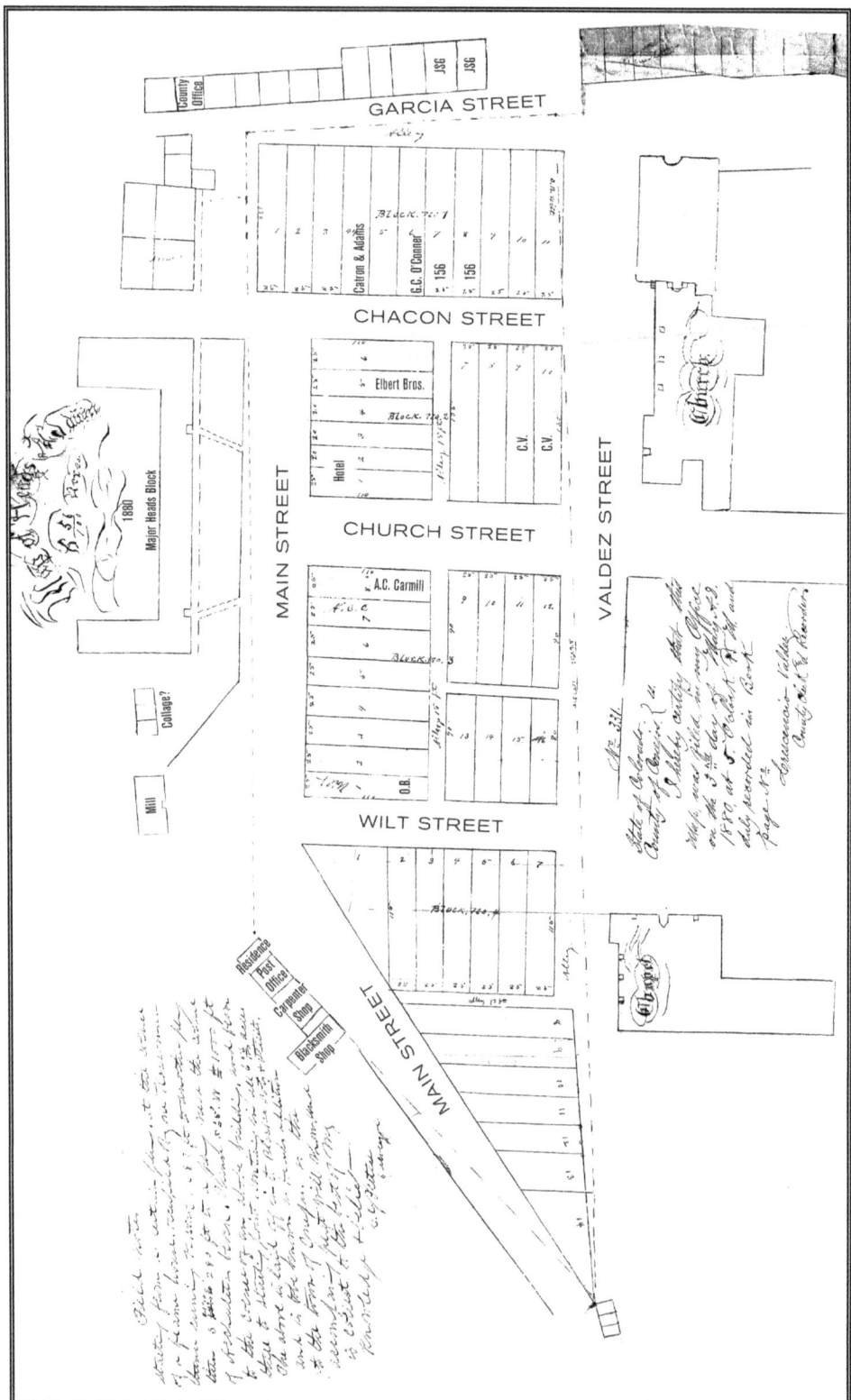

up residence at the Alvord House. He was welcomed to Denver by a host of friends.

The Colorado Legislature met on the first Wednesday in January—but only in odd numbered years. There were twenty-six elected members of the Senate, and they had a lot of work ahead as they established priorities for the new state. All was not business, however. Governor Routt, Lieutenant Governor Head, and other newly elected state officers hosted "A Grand Complimentary Benefit." Denver Mayor Buckingham and the Daniels, Fisher & Company department store joined in funding the event. It was held on the evening of January 16, 1877, and the main attraction was a society play titled "Frou Frou or The Thoughtless Wife." The performance debuted in Denver. Mrs. N. C. Forrester, wife of a Boston actor/theatre manager, played the lead role in the five act play. Afterward, there was a recitation of *Bingen on the Rhine*. Then Sig A. Caspar closed the show with a cornet solo of "Carnival of Venice." It is hard to believe that Lafe would have enjoyed being at the performance. He would probably much rather have been on the front porch of his Conejos home watching his cows graze.

Lafe and the Governor spent much of their time between the general election and Christmas planning their agenda for the coming year. After enjoying the Christmas holiday at home in Conejos, Lafe was back in Denver for the January 3, 1877, opening session of the new Colorado State Legislature. Travel was still challenging as heavy snows blanketed much of the state.

It was not long before the first major issue of the new administration had everyone talking. On January 23, 1877, Southern Colorado's *Pueblo Chieftain* announced "... outrageous salaries proposed to be paid to state officials." The paper reported that Routt, as Territorial Governor, had received a proposed base annual salary from the legislature of $1,800 plus $2,500 for "contingent expenses," $1,200 per year for his duties as ex-officio Commissioner of Indian Affairs for Colorado, and $1,000 for the salary of his private secretary. The U.S. Congress had funded almost $2,000 more than this total when Colorado was a territory; but now the new State of Colorado government would be responsible for the salaries of its elected officials. The January 26 *Chieftain* reported that the Colorado Senate had approved pay rates setting the Governor's salary at $2,500 and

Opposite: This plat of Conejos was drawn in 1880 when Conejos was at its prime. It was probably drawn so lots could be sold when the railroad arrived, as the townspeople did not know yet that Conejos would be skipped and Antonito built.

From Conejos County Clerk's plat files

the Lieutenant Governor's salary at $1,000. Pay for the Governor's private secretary was also set at $1,000. The proposed rate seemed fair, but *The Chieftain* noted "Expect an attempt to modify when these salaries come up for passage."

On February 1, 1877, a conference committee of the Colorado House and Senate settled on the following annual salaries:

> *District and Supreme Court Judges - $3,500*
> *Governor, Secretary of State, Auditor, and Treasurer - $2,000*
> *Attorney General and Superintendent of Public*
> *Instruction - $1,800*
> *Governor's Secretary - $800 plus fees collected*
> *Lieutenant Governor (also Presiding Officer*
> *of the Senate) - $600*

After taking this action, the legislature took several months establishing its rules and procedures. During the first long session, members of the Colorado legislature voted to only be in session for fifty days in the future. They also voted for a four-dollar-a-day housing and food allowance for themselves while in session and fifteen cents a mile for travel from their home district. On March 23, 1877, three days after the first legislature adjourned, *The Daily Rocky Mountain News* reported that "the presiding officer, Honorable Lafayette Head, disappointed many who were prejudiced against him... with his uniform kindness, fairness, and courtesy." After adjournment, Lafe conferred with the Governor and then went back to Conejos.

Head served as Lieutenant Governor and Presiding Officer of the Colorado Senate for only one term ending in January 1879. Lafe chose not to run for reelection, probably because he was anxious to stay at home. The Republicans won again in the 1878 election, so he probably would have been re-elected if he had chosen to run. Instead, the infamous H.A.W. Tabor became the Lieutenant Governor of Colorado. Lafe would be mentioned in 1882 by the *Rocky Mountain News* as a potential candidate for U.S. Senator, but again Lafe chose not to run. He obviously missed his ranch life in the San Luis Valley and wanted to retire from public office. Albert B. Sanford, a reporter for the Alamosa newspaper, visited Lafe's large new home while on a trip through the San Luis Valley in 1877. He described his house as a mammoth residence, with innumerable rooms. It was:

> *...a long, low adobe building with a porch the entire length. Shaded by numerous cottonwoods. The main living rooms were filled with the most interesting furnishings of Mexican*

and Indian workmanship. The floors were carpeted with Navajo and native Mexican blankets and rugs.[164]

Frank Fosset, a visiting travel writer wrote with considerable bias about The Valley in 1879:

> The southern half of San Luis Valley is mainly peopled by Mexicans and their descendants, with a sprinkling of Americans and Europeans. Alamosa, however, is an American town… there is some farming done, and a fair quantity of wheat and other grains are raised.…There are flour mills at Saguache and Conejos.[165]

More than one author has pointed out the obvious racial bias of Fossett's writing. The Americans who had settled in the San Luis Valley did not seem to have this bias, but visitors did and sometimes even today refer to the San Luis Valley locals as "Mexicans" rather than Mexican-Americans or Latinos.

The drilling of artesian wells started in the San Luis Valley in 1877, in addition to there already being hundreds of irrigation ditches. The wells opened up much more dry land in The Valley for agriculture. Thousands of wells were drilled in the late 1800s and early 1900s.

Pfeiffer and Head wrote each other long letters with the news from their areas. Typical are these excerpts from a long letter Head wrote Pfeiffer on June 15, 1878, in which Head was desperately trying to get Pfeiffer to come visit. It gives us a good idea (without corrections) of what now mattered most to Head—his crops, his livestock, and his friends.

> Mr. Fred Myer has been over buying wool went home yesterday will be back tomorrow.…
>
> The surveyors of the Narrow Gauge are now here on their way to Santa Fe and I suppose the Graders have already commenced work with a large force of work hands as they are bound to be at Santa Fe within five months from this time, then we can visit our old time friends on the Rail Road…
>
> There is not many changes since you were here. The Sisters of Loreta (sic) have completed a very large building on the south side of the church and established a good school for girls and also another for boys under 12 years old. Donacion Archuleta married Miss Gallegos of Taos, daughter of Don Lino sold out his interest in store to his father and moved out to Nabajo

CHAPTER 13

Creek to live. Austin married Doña Luez and Florencio Sedalia daughter of Tomas Peña Moritz is still a Bachelor. Major Saladar (sic) is up from his home near Albuquerque looking quite well and says crops are looking well in that country and Don Pablo Garcia is merchandising and doing well.[166]

Transportation continued to improve greatly in Colorado in the 1870s. Because of the rush to the San Juans, Barlow and Sanderson in May or June of 1874 had brought in thirty-eight horses to a station in the San Luis Valley for a daily run from Pueblo to Del Norte. Travel to and from the San Luis Valley was also being greatly upgraded, as the Denver & Rio Grande (D&RG) Railroad spread southward from Denver. The line went from Denver through Pueblo to Walsenburg. In July 1876, the D&RG was at the Town of La Veta, and the railroad was over La Veta Pass by June, 1877. In late June of 1877, the D&RG was at Garland City about six miles short of Fort Garland. The train puffed into the new city and railroad station of Alamosa on the west bank of the river on June 6, 1878. The depot was situated on the west bank of the river and this gave freight and passenger service to both sides of the Rio Grande River in the San Luis Valley. Most of Garland City literally was moved to Alamosa on railroad cars.

The Del Norte *Manifold* on June 19, 1877, noted that the San Juan mines had been almost inaccessible, but many of the trails were being upgraded quickly to good wagon roads because of the arrival of the railroad in Alamosa. One earlier wagon road was through Cañon City, Poncha Pass, and Saguache to Lake City and another was from Pueblo over La Veta Pass to Del Norte, and then to Lake City. Becoming a state had brought new opportunities and obligations for Lafe. He registered the brands he used for his livestock on April 12, 1877, at the Office of the Conejos County Clerk.

For the next three years the railroad remained in Alamosa and was not extended, as the D&RG was having heavy financial problems; but Lafe

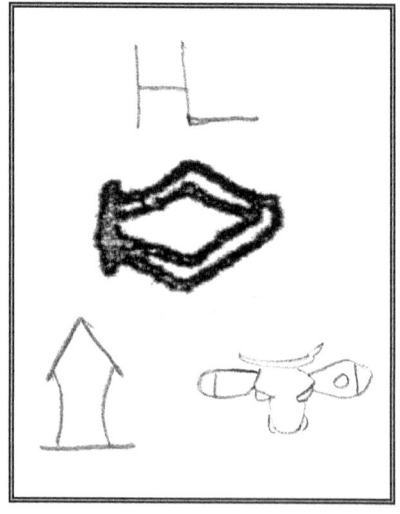

Besides his sheep Lafe had a large enough cattle herd that he registered three of his brands.

Conejos Brand Records.

was only a twenty-nine mile ride from the railroad at Alamosa. As the railroad moved across Colorado, so did true civilization. The Pagosa and Rio Grande Toll Road Company was announced in November 1876. It was a planned toll road from Conejos to the headwaters of the Chama River, then to Pagosa Springs. The distance from Alamosa to Pagosa Springs using the road would be 100 miles.

In 1880, the D&RG Railroad finally extended its line from Alamosa to Española, New Mexico Territory, but with the main route going toward the new town of Durango, Colorado, and on to rich new mines near Silverton, Colorado. The Division Headquarters of the D&RG was established in Alamosa, and a spur to Del Norte was built in 1881. After railroad construction started again, the railroad soon covered the twenty-nine miles to Conejos. However, the station was built one mile south of Conejos in the new D&RG town of Antonio. It was a typical move of the D&RG that they would try to get a small town like Conejos to offer free land and a free depot to the railroad; and if the existing town did not, they would be skipped, and the railroad would instead build a new town a mile or two away so that it could profit from the sale of lots in the new town.

The new town next to Conejos was originally a sheep herder's camp called "San Antonio" or "San Antonio Junction" after the nearby river that was a tributary and joined the Conejos River near the spot. The name was changed to just "Antonio" within two month of the D&RG's arrival and was soon changed again to" Antonito." The initial town was said to be very wild, with saloons and prostitutes; but most of those using these services were probably railroad laborers and the crowd of gamblers and other lawbreakers that normally followed railroad construction. Although the train did not stop in Conejos, the station in Antonito was only one mile away, and a hack that only charged a fare of twenty-five cents ran between the two towns. It was 1890 before the D&RG tied Villa Grove into the northern San Luis Valley system by coming down the east side of the San Luis Valley to Fort Garland from Poncha Pass and then going west to Alamosa. Bancroft wrote in his *History of Colorado* that, until the D&RG reached Conejos in southern Colorado, it was:

> …almost exclusively a Spanish-American or Mexican population, which, while they sent members to the general assembly, (they) maintained little communication with the United States Americans to the north of them.[167]

At Antonio (Antonito) the track split. One branch went south to Española and eventually to Santa Fe. The other was constructed to

CHAPTER 13

Ouray and Chipeta about 1880 when negotiations were going on to move the Utes yet again. Below Ouray's shoulders are black pouches with medicinal herbs prescribed by the Ute medicine man. He was sick and the White man's medicine was not helping, so Chipeta sewed them there.

Author's Collection.

where Durango would eventually be built by the D&RG (replacing the existing town of nearby Animas City) and then on to Silverton.

Although the railroad brought economic prosperity to the San Luis Valley, it also continued to bring scores of land speculators. Many of the settlers in The Valley were poor, uneducated settlers who still were not familiar with the American land laws. In the early 1870s, representatives of land and livestock enterprises using European capital and in alliance sometimes with the "Santa Fe Ring" or the "Denver Ring" made progress towards acquiring New Mexican land grants in what was now Colorado.

Lafe made a trip to Pueblo in late April 1879, and the *Pueblo Chieftain* noted his visit:

> *The Major holds out against old Father Time as well as any man we know. He looks as young now as he did when we first knew him fourteen years ago. He… is a gentleman that enjoys the confidence and respect of the people among whom he lives.*

The 4th Annual Colorado State Business Directory, 1879, shows Head still had a flour mill in Conejos. There were four general merchandise stores, but none were owned by Head. There were the same businesses in the 1880 edition, but this time Head was listed as a wool grower, so it is possible he had sold the mill. However, with the railroad bypassing Conejos, the town was now at its peak.

There was yet another racial group appearing in the San Luis Valley. Many African-American soldiers stayed in the army after the Civil War; and in 1866, Congress had authorized six companies of African-American troops with White officers. Some of these troops were stationed at Fort Lyon in eastern Colorado. Unfortunately, they were often subject to racist activities; but they needed the job, and they did their job well. African-American soldiers did not come to Southwest Colorado until 1875, when "Buffalo Soldiers" of the Ninth Cavalry were moved to the New Mexico Military District, of which Fort Garland was a part. They were stationed at Fort Garland for three and a half years.

The Buffalo soldiers saw little action that first year, but in 1876 they were sent to the La Plata Mountains to help keep the prospectors and Utes apart during the mining rush to far southwest Colorado. They also helped remove settlers from off the Ute reservation in the Uncompahgre Valley in 1876. In May of 1878, five companies went to the Los Piños II Agency in the Uncompahgre Valley to monitor treaty negotiations with the Uncompahgre Utes. Besides their occasional forays, the rest of their time was spent doing repairs on the fort, whitewashing the fort's adobe

Buffalo soliders retreive a wounded comrade.

Frederick Remington drawing "The Rescue of Corporal Scott."

CHAPTER 13

walls, and building a new stockade. One of the buffalo soldiers, Private Francis Redmond, was a school teacher at the fort. The soldiers could do extra duty, including jobs as cooks, hospital orderlies, stable police, or quartermasters, for which they earned a small amount of extra pay. Some worked as guards.

Meanwhile, neither the State nor the Federal government had moved the Utes to outside the State of Colorado, and both were still addressing the "Ute issue." The Southern Ute Agency at today's Ignacio was started in 1877. By the Agreement of Nov. 9, 1878, the Southern Utes "ceded their rights to the Confederated Ute territory except for such lands... as might be allotted to them in severalty,"[168] and the Mouache, Capote, and Weeminuche moved to the Southern Ute Agency that year. In July of 1878, a law was passed that the Tabeguache Utes should be moved further west in the State of Colorado, but the move never happened. Even the Whites were not excited about the potential 1878 move of the Tabeguache, as it was only to far western Colorado, and the Whites were asking that the Tabeguache Utes be moved out of the state. The Southern Utes were also asked to move to the northern part of the Colorado reservation, but all three bands refused. They did, however, agree to a slightly new location of the reservation, but

Ouray wears the same outfit in this picture with Ignacio about 1878. Ouray knew he would die soon of Bright's Disease and had chosen Ignacio of the Southern Utes as Chief of those tribes.

Author's Collection.

Congress did not ratify the agreement. The final outburst of Ute frustration occurred on September 29, 1879.

Prior to a now infamous September 29 attack, Agent Nathan Meeker was having trouble with the Yampa and White River Utes and had requested soldiers to help him control the Utes at the White River Agency. He was bound and determined to turn "his" Utes into progressive, self-sustaining farmers, whether it was by education or force. The Utes were just as determined not to become farmers or doing any work they considered lowly, demeaning, and humiliating. A small group of Utes had even paid a visit to Governor Frederick Pitkin to request that he help stop Meeker from fence-building and plowing up their land. They asked for another Agent, but the anti-Native American governor took no action on any of their requests. To aggravate an already tense situation on both sides, by June of 1879 there were large forest fires burning in Western Colorado that were being blamed on the Utes; and the northern Utes had not received their food supplies, which were being held for past due storage costs in a railroad warehouse in Rawlins, Wyoming.

However the generally permissive attitude toward the Utes was changing. Alfred Meachum, editor of the Native American friendly journal *Council Fires* explained:

> *They were like spoiled children. They had never been subjected nor taught to recognize the authority of an agent. They have been humored, scolded and petted by turns until they were anything but hopeful subjects for civilization.*[169]

The immediate cause of the uprising was that Meeker plowed up part of the Ute horse-racing track to prepare the land for planting crops. This was probably done because Meeker was mad at Ute Johnson for using Agency grain to feed the Ute race horses instead of the Agency work horses. Johnson, husband of Ouray's sister Susan, stopped the plowing by firing warning shots at the team breaking the ground. Then, a few days later, Meeker cornered Johnson and threatened to make him kill his ponies, and the two had a short physical fight. Meeker immediately fired off a letter to Fort Steele in Wyoming requesting troops be sent to protect him and his family. One very ominous sign soon appeared—the White River Ute women and children started moving away from the Agency's building, and within a few days only four of the original ninety-four tepees were in the area of the Agency.

Major T. T. Thornburgh was sent from Wyoming on September 22 with thirty-three supply wagons, three companies of cavalry and one company of infantry (a total of 178 men). They were met by Utes along the way who

CHAPTER 13

requested that they not bring such a large group of soldiers onto the reservation. The Utes suggested Thornburgh and five men come to check out the situation. Thornburgh refused their request and continued his march to the Agency with all of his men and supplies. Then the troops were met by Wilmer Eskridge, an employee at the Agency, and two Utes who said Meeker had suggested a peace council before the large group of soldiers came on the reservation. The Utes said they were worried that what happened at Sand Creek would happen to them, even though the Sand Creek Massacre had happened fifteen years earlier. Thornburgh was warned by the Utes that their people would fight if his army crossed Milk Creek onto their reservation. Thornburgh ignored the warning, and his small army was ambushed by about 100 Utes. Nine soldiers were killed immediately. Then Thornburgh tried a quick charge to get to his supply wagons, and he was killed. The soldiers dug in, and that night, one of the Army scouts was sent for reinforcements.

At this time there were Buffalo soldiers somewhat close-by who had been sent from Fort Garland to Middle Park to check on the wildfires that

Dozens of drawings were later done of the Milk Creek Battle, with some of them, like this, becoming highly unrealistic, in fact perhaps staged after Custer's Last Stand. There were no steep mountains in the area, and the men made a breastwork of their wagons and dead horses in the valley.

Harper's Weekly, November 1, 1879

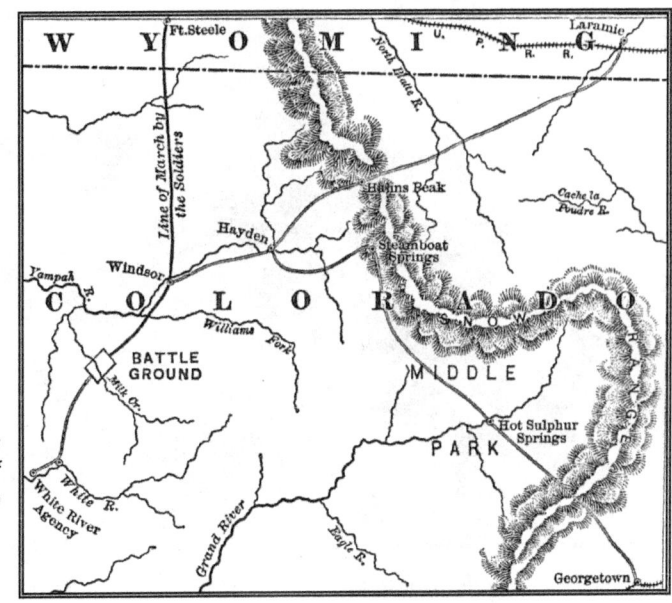

This map, shows the line of march of Thornburg from Ft. Steel Wyoming, the battleground, and the White River Agency.

From *Bancroft's History of Colorado*

had been raging in that area during the summer of 1879, and they were able to quickly respond to Thornburgh's call for help. Captain Payne and his forty-three Buffalo Soldiers arrived the third day of the siege, but there were not enough of them to stop the fight. It was perhaps one of the Buffalo soldiers' finest hours. On October 5, almost 1,000 relief troops arrived at Milk Creek, and a runner arrived from Chief Ouray saying he wanted the fighting stopped immediately. The Utes fled and later said thirty-seven of their men had been killed in the fight. The soldiers had been pinned down for about a week and thirteen soldiers had been killed and forty-three were wounded. During the fighting, Governor Pitkin started near panic among Colorado citizens when he sent a telegraph message throughout the state that read: "Indians off their reservation, seeking to destroy your settlements by fire, are game to be hunted and destroyed like wild beasts."[170] Rumors that the Utes were killing Whites and burning settlements were soon everywhere in the state, all of which were not true.

Pitkin sent the Colorado Guard from Saguache "to bring in all the hostile Ute Indians off the reservation 'dead or alive.'" Pitkin sent out messages that all of Thornburg's officers had been killed when in fact Thornburg himself was the only dead officer. Colorado newspapers wrote that up to 3,000 Utes were involved in the uprising, that Lake City was surrounded, and that a huge encampment of Utes was just north of Cochetopa Pass. Actually most of the White River Utes had scattered for their own safety

CHAPTER 13

Drawing showing the devastation at the Meeker Agency after the soldiers arrived. The building still standing is the smokehouse where the women and children hid until captured.

Harper's Weekly, December 6, 1879.

by this time, and most of Pitkin's fears and threats were centered on the peaceful Tabeguache, who had done absolutely nothing wrong. The Meeker Massacre helped restore the importance of Fort Garland and its garrison, as it was the center of operations for quelling a then greatly feared Ute uprising that never occurred.

It was almost a week after the event that accurate accounts of the Meeker Massacre surfaced. During that time Western Colorado settlers armed themselves with government supplied weapons and prepared to defend their homes and towns. Finally some of the truth was printed as the facts came out that only a few Utes were involved at the White River Agency itself and that Thornburg had perhaps started the fight because he had totally ignored a request by the White River Utes to bring only a small group of soldiers onto the reservation.

After the American women being held captive at the Agency had been released and brought to Ouray's house, matters began to settle down. A council was called to decide how to punish the Ute perpetrators. At their first meeting, which was in Colorado, Ouray said the Utes did not want the Meeker women to testify, personally or second hand, as Native Americans at the time did not consider women's testimony to be reliable (Chipeta was an exception). Chief Douglas had held the Meeker women in his tepee and

Antelope and Puvitz were suspected of killing Meeker. Ouray said it was impossible to try just one or two Utes because all of the White River Utes had been involved. Ouray further asked that the hearing be transferred to Washington for whatever agreement would be made (treaties were no longer being made with Native Americans, only "agreements").

Ouray said, "We believe we cannot obtain a fair trial in Colorado, we believe no justice would be shown."[171] The proposal to bring the Utes to Washington was telegraphed to Secretary of the Interior and Indian Superintendent Carl Schurz, who quickly approved of the action. After much talk and deliberation, Chief of the White River Utes Douglas and eight other White River Utes were taken to Washington, D. C. along with Ouray and Chipeta. The Colorado phase of the investigation ended on its sixth day.

On January 8, 1880, Ouray, Chipeta, Douglas, and the eight White River Utes from the White River Agency left the reservation. A small unit of soldiers escorted them, but the danger this time was from Whites, not other Indian tribes. Their reception in Pueblo was terrible. The depot was extremely crowded by a hostile group of an estimated 2,000 Whites, who jeered and threw rocks, sticks, and coal at the Utes. Some of the Utes were hit by the coal and others were hit by the fists of angry men. They had to skip dinner and hold up in a train car for the night. This time the whole expense of the trip to Washington was to be taken out of the Ute's annuity.

The Utes left Colorado the next day on January 16, 1880, to go to Washington to determine the fate of their people, but only one, Chief Douglas, was officially on the list of attackers the white women had made. Otto Mears went as interpreter. Although the cry was almost unanimous in Colorado that the White River Utes should leave the state, there were some Whites who felt the Tabeguache should be allowed to stay in Colorado, since they had not participated in the Meeker Massacre. However the state-wide cry was "The Utes Must Go." On the way to Washington, Chief Douglas was taken as a prisoner and kept at Fort Leavenworth. He was released one year later after being declared insane.

While in Washington, the Utes always appeared in their best native dress coats of antelope skins adorned with embroidery of many colored beads and porcupine quills. Chipeta was taken on a shopping trip and bought yards of dress material, hose, a skirt, gloves, thread, needles, and buttons at Tunnel, Clark and Company. An interesting example of the government bureaucracy at the time was that it was later determined that nineteen government officials examined and approved the receipts for those items with the process taking over a month. The bill totaled $27.99. Chipeta also

CHAPTER 13

had four dresses and four undergarments made by Mrs. O.M. Roundtree at a cost of $27.00.

Carl Schurz, Secretary of the Interior, said Ouray:

> ...spoke like a man of high order of intelligence and of larger views, who had risen above the prejudices and aversions of his race, and expressed his thoughts in language clear and precise, entirely unburdened by the figures of speech and the superfluidity commonly current in Indian talk.[172]

Although the stated reason for the trip to Washington was to put the Utes believed responsible for the "Meeker Massacre" at the White River Agency on trial, it soon included obtaining an agreement to get the Utes out of Colorado. The agreement stated that no payments of any kind would be made to the White River Utes until the guilty parties of the Agency massacre surrendered, were no longer in the United States, or were dead. The Meeker women would be paid restitution out of the White River band's share of any payments, and all the Ute chiefs agreed to find out who was responsible for the massacre and surrender them to the authorities. The Utes would be paid $10,000 for a school where they could learn to self-support themselves. The Utes were to be paid $50,000 a year forever as payment for their land but to be distributed per capita each year. At the end of twenty-five years that yearly amount could be capitalized and paid in one lump sum. The annual $25,000 payments for the San Juan Mountains would also be continued. The White River Utes agreed to move immediately to a reservation in Utah, but those Utes who already owned land by

"The Utes Must Go" was the cry of every newspaper in Colorado. After the massacre at the White River Agency and Ouray's death they were doomed to such a fate.

Author's Collection.

severalty could keep their land and remain in Colorado. The Southern Utes were to be move to La Plata County, and would be removed to Utah if there was not enough good land in La Plata County for their reservation. The Uncompahgre Utes agreed to move to the Colorado River near the mouth of the Gunnison (today's Grand Junction); and, if not enough good land was found, they agreed to move to Utah. The Utes were also to get $60,000 in cash for past due annuities. They were to settle in severalty (individual ownership, not tribal ownership), and once settled, they would get a house, a wagon, tools, cattle, and community flour mills. Agencies and schools would be continued until the Utes could support themselves. They would also receive cash payments for any improvements made on land being given up by a Ute family or individual.

The Utes had gone to Washington, without any discussion about giving up their land and were simply presented with this proposed agreement; but Ouray refused to discuss the agreement until the younger men of the tribe could also discuss it, so the Utes returned home. Section 2 of the proposed agreement authorized the U.S. President to appoint a commission to present the agreement to the individual Utes for their approval. They had until October 15 to get three-fourths of the Utes to sign. The Commissioners for the U.S. included Otto Mears (who had mixed emotions because, with ratification of this agreement, he would be losing his "cash cow"), George Manypenny, and Alfred Meachum. The Commissioners traveled to Colorado and a council was held at the Los Piños II Agency on the Uncompahgre River. Ouray opened the meeting by explaining his reasons for signing the agreement in Washington. A major hurdle was the payment of $75,000 ($25,000 due yearly under the 1873 treaty; and $50,000 due annually under the 1880 treaty), which the Utes said they had to actually receive before they would sign the agreement (the Utes had learned their lessons well, but too late). The government said they would not pay until the Utes signed the agreement. One hundred forty-five Utes did nevertheless sign at Los Piños within three days.

Meachum stayed at Los Piños II, while the other commissioners went to the Southern Ute Agency to get signatures. On August 24, 1880, Ouray died at the Southern Ute Agency, and many felt that his death would doom the 1880 treaty, but then Chief Kaniache, who always vehemently fought against anything the Whites proposed, was struck dead by lightning and many of the Utes took this as an omen that they should sign the agreement. There were 541 adult Ute males who had now signed; but, nowhere close to the number of signatures needed to reflect three-quarters of the men of the tribe. However, the Americans said that number was greater than

CHAPTER 13

the required three-quarters; even though the Bureau of Indian Affairs had estimated that there were 4,000 adult male Utes, and the number needed to approve the agreement would therefore be 3,000. The agreement originally provided that all of the Utes, except the Tabeguache, would be moved out of Colorado, but the Southern Utes were eventually allowed to stay in southern Colorado, as none of them would sign the agreement, so the number needed was reduced. Congress ratified the agreement on June 15, 1880, before the Commission's signature-gathering task was completed.

There was no hope for the Tabeguache to stay in the area around the San Juans, even though the Tabeguache rightfully insisted they had done nothing wrong and should be allowed to stay. The agreement provided that the Tabeguache were to be removed to the mouth of the Uncompahgre to settle upon agricultural land, near the mouth of the Gunnison River in Colorado and the adjoining Grand (Colorado) River area, some of which is pure desert, but Grand Mesa was one of the Utes' favorite summer spots. However, they were to be moved there only if the Indian Commission approved the site. The Tabeguache were assured they would have a reservation in Colorado "at or adjacent to the 'Grand Valley' (where Grand Junction is today), and that it would be restricted from the Whites.

Most Whites argued that the Meeker Massacre had nullified all previous Ute treaties. As the October 15 deadline approached, the Commissioners realized they had nowhere near number of signatures needed. Many Utes

Ouray and Chipeta in Washington in 1880. Note Ouray's "medicine bag" on his shoulder.

Author's Collection.

were hesitant to sign the agreement because they felt they did not know exactly where they were going under the agreement's wording. It was a valid concern.

It was at this point that Otto Mears started paying the Utes two or three silver dollars each for signing the agreement. By September 11, 1880, he said he had the requisite number of signatures, but in actuality the figure was still not even close. When George Manypenny, the chairman of the commission, found out what Mears had done, he refused to sign the agreement and had Mears charged with bribery. Mears was called to Washington, where he stated the Utes would rather have the two dollars in hard cash than have the government's promise for $50,000 and $25,000 in future years. The charges were dropped against Mears, and he was even reimbursed for the money he supposedly had paid out (about $2,000), which meant he had paid for about 1,000 signatures and still did not have enough signatures to make the agreement valid. The payments to the Utes specified in the agreement still had not arrived by October 15; Whites started moving into the Uncompahgre Valley anyway. On October 21, Meachum slipped away from the Agency with several other white officials. By December 17, 1880, the Utes were complaining that Mears had told them before they signed the agreement that they were not selling the Uncompahgre Valley and they could stay and even take homes there. Mears claimed this statement was a lie, said they had sold their land all the way to the mouth of the Gunnison at today's Grand Junction, but he left the Los Piños II Agency. Commissioner French (there were now five commissioners) complained to Washington that both commissioners Bowman and Mears were belittling the problem:

> *They have no appreciation of this Indian problem, in any of its relations, and apparently care as little for the welfare of the Indians as they do for the barking Coyote.* [173]

Secretary Schurz tried to figure out the mess, but the settlers who had already moved into the valley and filed on land were allowed to stay. Four Utes and Agent William Berry went to Washington where the Utes again explained they thought they were not selling the Uncompahgre Valley. By April 1881, the issue was still not resolved.

Meanwhile, Meachum was charged as an accessory to the murder of Ute Andrew Jackson, but he was released on bond. He then went to pay the White River Utes at the Uintah Reservation in accordance with the agreement, but none of them were there. Finally they arrived at the reservation and 669 White River Utes signed the agreement to move and were paid.

CHAPTER 13

The Utes leaving Colorado near today's Grand Junction.

From Jocknick, *Early Day's on the Western Slope*.

The U.S. officials were getting close to the number of Utes needed to sign the agreement.

The land along the Grand (Colorado) River was still supposed to belong to the Tabeguache Utes, but three of the five Commissioners including Mears decided there was not enough land there of "sufficient quantity" for them to stay, and that the Uncompahgre Utes should be removed altogether from Colorado.

Mears and the other two commissioners siding with him chose a site in the Utah desert, as they said the Utes would not be safe in Colorado. Mears got the contract to build the new Agency and to sell Ouray's farm and the possessions that Chipeta did not want (which he said were most of them because she had decided to move with her people to Utah). Eventually Chipeta received $700 for the sale of her land and the valuable personal property that she and Ouray had been given over the years. Mears obviously had his hand in the proceeds. Mears came to Utah to see the new Agency buildings and Chipeta's new home, which were very basic and obviously did not cost the amount allocated to build them. Chipeta chose to live in a tepee instead of a house. When Mears discovered that the Utes had a plot to kill him for being the vote that caused them to leave Colorado, he escaped on horseback in the middle of the night.

The Tabeguache left Colorado from September 1 through September 7, 1881. As mentioned, the Southern Utes, who were composed of the

Colorado Statehood, "The Utes Must Go," and Mormons

Mouache, Capote, and Weeminuche bands, agreed to a reservation along the southern border of Colorado. The Southern Utes basically stayed where they were, even though it was expected that many more Whites would soon come to southern Colorado because the Town of Durango was being built by the D&RG Railroad (another new "railroad" town that would soon turn nearby Animas City into a ghost town). In an ironic twist, the Indians Rights Association argued that the Southern Utes should become farmers; but that they should not be allowed to live along the New Mexico-Colorado border, as it was becoming a haven for criminals and would be too dangerous for them.

For a short while after the Meeker Massacre it was thought that all the Utes in Colorado might be killed. However, most of the government officials soon realized that it was only a small number of Utes at the White River Agency that had caused the problem. Matters concerning the Southern Utes continued in dispute for years. Bills were presented in Congress in the late 1880s to move the Southern Utes to Utah, but they failed three times. Then the Utah Whites decided they did not want any more Native Americans in Utah, and the Indian Rights movement took up the Southern Ute cause. Five more removal bills failed, but in 1895 a bill did pass that allowed individual Utes to take homesteads and own them in fee simple.[174] This had been provided for in the 1880 treaty agreement, but in this bill the tracts not taken by Utes would be open for purchase by Whites. The Mouache and Capote decided to take this offer, with their Agency remaining at Ignacio; but the always individualistic Weeminuche

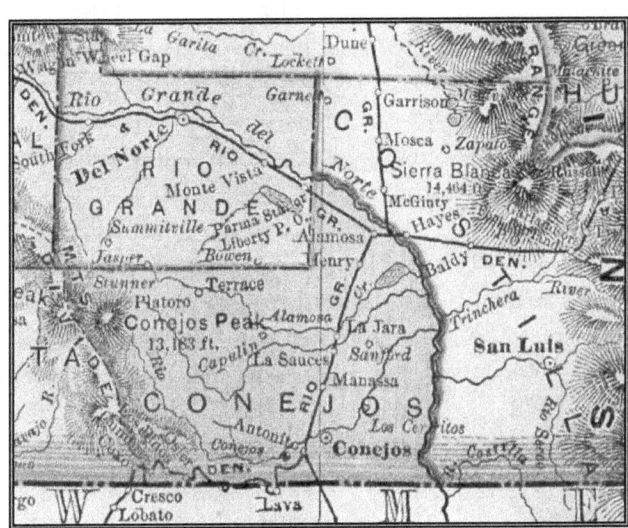

Map showing Platoro, Jasper, and Stunner Mining areas.

Author's Collection.

decided to keep their land in common at would be called the Ute Mountain Agency at Navajo Springs.

All the activity involving Western Colorado's Native American population aside, an increased movement of miners and settlers into the San Luis Valley and surrounding areas in the late 1800s made it an exciting and, for some, a lucrative time. In 1879, several mining discoveries had even been made near the headwaters of the Conejos River. They were reached by a toll road that followed the river the entire way from Conejos. The discoveries were made at spots called Jasper, Stunner, and Loynton at various times, and included silver, gold, and nickel. We do not know if Lafe had any mining interests, but the new mining would certainly have helped businesses in Conejos and Antonito.

The late 1870s also saw a group from the Church of Jesus Christ of Latter Day Saints (usually called "Mormons") led by missionary John Morgan, start a new home in the San Luis Valley in 1877. Seventy-two new converts started from Georgia and Alabama. About fifty people in all arrived in Pueblo on November 24, 1877. They decided to stay the winter in Pueblo and await the building of the D&RG Railroad before going over La Veta Pass and into the San Luis Valley. A few lived in leased homes; but, by December 1, the fifty Mormans had built barracks to winter in Pueblo. The men worked odd jobs around Pueblo that winter, pooled their money, and sent a scouting party to the San Luis Valley in March 1878, with $400 for the land purchase.

Among the first travelers on the new train into the San Luis Valley in the spring of 1878 were four Mormon men looking for a suitable place to establish the Mormon colony. They found the San Luis Valley to be a good place for farming, and the fork of the San Antonio and Conejos Rivers was especially attractive. One of the men, John Stewart, went to Conejos to meet with Lafe and former Territorial Governor A. C. Hunt, who had a ranch in the valley. Stewart was pleased that the two men "accepted the prospect of a Mormon colony... and offered to assist to promote the project."[175] That spring, Lafe was asked by the State Land Board to appraise state land in Conejos County along with A. C. Hunt and José Victor Garcia. The Mormon group was ready to make a purchase on the lower south and east side of the Conejos River. After the appraisal was completed and the land purchased, the group of about fifty Mormon colonists arrived around May 1878.

The Mormons were eager to start building homes, and Lafe came to know the colonists well. He even co-signed a note for Stewart to buy a 120 acre ranch with an adobe house. The purchase price was only $35. The

Mormons soon bought two farms, 160 acres, and a house for $85. Then they bought a yoke of oxen and a plow, very possibly from Lafe, borrowed wagons and tools (mostly from Lafe), and planted crops. They were joined there by a small group that came from Utah in wagons, which settled on a site on the northeast side of the Conejos River. Mormon settler, Soren C. Berthelson, later wrote that the "Mexican people in the valley" were friendly and noted "the kindness shown to the settlers, especially by José Victor Garcia and Lafayette Head."

The newer Mormon converts were mainly from the U.S. southern states, but some of the new arrivals were from Denmark and had first gone to Utah and then come back to the east to the new Mormon settlement of Manassa. The group included brand-new to long-time Mormons and several different theologies within the Mormon Church. Some of the extreme fundamentalist Mormons were called "American Yankee Mormons." The Southern Mormons had not had much luck converting other Southerners, some of whom were downright hostile towards them and had sometimes even made threats of death. A few Mormons in the South were actually murdered, and many in the Southern group wanted to immigrate to the West to escape the danger. Some of the Mormons were poor; some were middle class. The group included eight families—four farmers, two carpenters, one blacksmith, and one grocer. While they were building their homes, they stayed at Los Cerritos.

The 1878 harvest had not been good, so the Mormons had to supplement their food with a Mexican diet. The Utah Mormons were pretty much in charge and were teaching the Mormon doctrine to those who had only recently converted. Many of the Mormons were forced to take paying jobs in 1879 and early 1880 to survive; and many of those worked making railroad ties, even traveling as far as Leadville for work. There were about 145 adults in the group by the beginning of 1880, when they returned to Manassa and dug ditches for irrigation and built fences to keep the open range animals away from their crops. They mostly built log houses instead of the valley's traditional adobe.

The early Mormons at first did not realize that farming in the San Luis Valley was very different than in the Deep South, and they had trouble with their first crops. They needed the Western Mormon leaders in Utah to help them with the local agriculture, as they were not used to the dry Western climate; so a Utah group was sent in the summer of 1878 to help, but many of these were from the Denmark group. Two of the Utah group surveyed Manassa, following the Mormon practice of four lots to each block. Manassa and Ephraim were two Mormon colonies built very close to Conejos.

CHAPTER 13

By 1879, the Mormons had finished the town of Manassa, including homes, a school, and a place of worship. The towns of Ephraim and Richfield were also soon built. Ephraim was settled in 1879 and Richfield in 1881. Although Lafe and other prominent citizens of the valley gave them a good welcome, the church leaders had been assured by the D&RG that the railroad, which at this time was still in Alamosa, would proceed immediately to their town and provide them with railroad transportation. The arrival of the railroad would take another two years.

In November of 1880, Silas Smith came to The Valley and purchased a mill for the group. He had charge over a large Mormon mission area that included lower Utah, Arizona, New Mexico, and southern Colorado. Eventually the Danes in the group moved to Ephraim and Richfield. They continued their Danish ways; and many continued to speak Danish, including while in church. There were, of course, some definite cultural differences between the Danish and American Mormons.

More Mormons came at least twice a year; and by 1890, they had over 5,000 acres under cultivation, and were known in the San Luis Valley as having the "most thorough and productive cultivation." By this time, there were 400 Mormons in the area, and some San Luis Valley locals started rebelling. Some of the earliest Mexican-American arrivals in the valley even tried damming the Conejos River so the Mormons would not have irrigation water; but the Mormons soon destroyed the dams. Bias against the Mormons was unfortunately growing quickly in the entire state.

Although he never again ran for public office, Head did keep his hand in politics. He had been one of six Colorado delegates to the 1880 Republican Convention in Chicago (held June 2 to June 8), which named James A. Garfield as their candidate for President. The delegates included former Governor John L. Routt. The convention met in Chicago's Interstate Exposition building.

Lafe was amazed, as it was a "new-fangled" glass and steel structure, and one of the largest buildings in the nation at the time. Chicago was by then the country's fourth largest city, with over a half million residents. It was an overwhelming place for the entire Colorado delegation. Denver was a tiny town (35,619 population) compared to Chicago. The entire population of the State of Colorado was only a little more than 194,000 in 1880.

CHAPTER FOURTEEN

Piedad, Grandfather, and More Mysteries
(1881-1897)

The Major was an unassuming person, very modest, yet without timidity. He was of that cool character necessary to the accomplishment of just such things as he did accomplish.
   J. H. Thomas, Attorney-at-Law, Antonito, Colorado

A faithful public servant... we especially commend the example of his broad charity and open-handed generosity.
   Santa Fe Daily New Mexican
   March 15, 1897

The Head family celebrated a wedding in 1881. Lafe and Martina's granddaughter, Piedad ("Piety" in Spanish) Cisneros, married William Hill on February 1, 1881, in the St. Augustine Catholic Church in Antonito (formerly Antonio). She was seventeen years old but may have been born in 1860 or 1861 (*The Diary of the Jesuit Brothers*, Vol. 1 states 1864). The couple soon had a son and named the boy "George." There is almost as much confusion about Piedad's life as with that of Martina. This author has not been able to supply an answer to these mysteries, but will relate a few of the many conflicting facts. Frank Hall wrote in 1895:

> *Twenty five years ago, being childless, (1869 or 1870) he (Lafe) adopted a little Mexican girl, then three years old, cared for and educated her at the Sisters' convent in Conejos. Her name was Piedad (piety) Sisneros. She is now 28 years old (making her birthdate in 1866 or 1867) and maintains the Major's fine establishment with exalted grace.*[176]

CHAPTER 14

Piedad was raised by Lafe and Martina and supposedly her father was José Cisneros (the boy the widowed Martina brought into her marriage with Lafe) and who died on June 12, 1867, as a young adult while trying to cross the Rio Grande River.

Lafe, Piedad, and Lafe's grandson George Hill (age 10) posed for this photo later in Lafe's life. He adored the boy who graduated from high school at the time of Lafe's death.

Courtesy of the Luther Bean Museum, Adams State University, Gift of Gwendolyn Hill, #1975.10.1k.

José Sisneros was three years old in the 1850 census, meaning he was born in 1847 (See Chapter 4). Piedad was supposed to have been his child, and if she was born in 1860, José would have fathered a child at age twelve or thirteen.

The 1850 census shows Lafe and Martina married, living in Abiqui, but with no children. Best odds are they were not married, Martina did not want to say so, and she was embarrassed about her child or children or did not want to explain the situation. Another possibility is that Piedad was not José's child and was adopted from the Conejos church at age three. Did Lafe and Martina put her at the church for adoption? Regardless, Piedad was treated as the only living heir of Lafe and inherited his estate when he died. However, he may possibly have had illegitimate children who also should have shared in the estate.[177]

No record has been found of Piedad's mother. Although her father José was said to be from Martina's previous marriage, he could possibly have been Lafe's child, depending on just when Martina and Lafe started living together or married (See Chapter 4). No court or church proceedings have been found for Piedad's adoption, Piedad's birth, or Lafe and Martina's marriage, but that was not unusual for that time and place.

Lafe was getting older (55), when the railroad came to The Valley in the 1880s. It meant good economic growth for San Luis Valley agriculture and ranching, as freight costs were much cheaper and the time was much shorter to get San Luis Valley products to market. The railroad helped businesses in both Conejos and Antonito for a while, but eventually Antonito became the main town. The only detriment to Lafe was that the D&RG Railroad started the town of San Antonio or Antonio (and within months called "Antonito") a mile to the south of Conejos; and the new settlement would soon start taking businesses from Conejos.

The railroad also meant The Valley was no longer isolated. Hubert Bancroft in 1890 wrote that until the Denver and Rio Grande Railroad reached Conejos in 1880, Southern Colorado was:

> ...inhabited almost exclusively (by a) Spanish-American or Mexican population, which, while they sent members to the general assembly, maintained little communication with the United States Americans to the north of them.[178]

Little credit was being given by Bancroft to Lafe's attempts to bring knowledge of the possibilities of the San Luis Valley north to the rest of Colorado or to the fact that central southern Colorado contained nearly a quarter of the population of the State of Colorado in the 1860s and

CHAPTER 14

1870s. However, the new railroad, just like the later automobile and airplane, changed life quickly in the San Luis Valley. The twenty-year lease on Fort Garland's land ended on June 30, 1882; and William Gilpin, who was now a major owner in the Sangre de Cristo Grant, raised the rent from $1 per year to $100 per month. In October, 1882, the Army announced the post was obsolete; and on August 30, 1883, the Army's large American flag in the middle of its plaza was lowered for the last time. Even before the post closed, an inspector in 1879 had suggested the post be allowed to decay. Adobe takes a lot of upkeep, many of the fort's buildings did not get repaired, and water began to seep through the fort's roof and was destroying the fort. On November 30, 1883, Fort Garland was abandoned. The soldiers at the fort were transferred to Fort Lewis at Hesperus near Durango. The Army then paid to have the soldiers who were buried at Fort Garland's cemetery disinterred and moved to Fort Leavenworth. The six square mile tract of land around the fort reverted to the Trinchera Estate, which had bought what was left of the Sangre de Cristo Grant from William Gilpin and his partners.

The "wild and wooly" days of the Old West were gone, and in the 1880s until his death in 1897, Lafe kept busy as did any typical older farmer and rancher almost anywhere in the United States. Lafe visited his mill regularly, attended church and lodge meetings regularly, and always enjoyed visits from friends or strangers. Many of his good friends, however, were dead, and he was living in a new world. He was delighted that his great grandson George Hill (Piedad's child) lived with him some of the time; and when he was there, Lafe spent a great deal of time with the boy.

It had not been until 1877 that the Grand Lodge of the Territory of New Mexico had been formed, and the Montezuma Masonic Lodge then became #1 on November 1, 1880. A demit (a release from a lodge without losing membership in the national organization) was issued to Lafayette Head from Santa Fe Lodge on November 1, 1880, allowing him to transfer to another lodge. Various leaders in Alamosa formed their Masonic Lodge shortly after the town was founded in 1880; and, in 1881, Lafe transferred his membership from the Santa Fe Lodge to the Alamosa Lodge. It was a quick and easy trip (less than an hour by train) from Conejos to Alamosa. He eventually became one of the Chaplains of the Lodge.

Besides Lafe possibly being a Penitente and the possibility of illegitimate children, there is one other mystery that has bothered historians over the years about Lafe's life. It is two photographs showing Lafe in his old age with what has been described as his Masonic uniform with a cross on one sleeve, which recognizes him as a chaplain, and he is wearing or holding a Knights Templar sword. There is a general feeling that a man could not belong to all three—at least at one time. The Knights Templar sword is confusing because there are several organizations over the years that have used that name. The organization was founded in 1119 and was titled "The Poor Knights of Christ and the Temple of Solomon," known for short as the "Knights Templar." Their members took a monk's vow of poverty that all active members lived up to. This first group was actually approved by the Pope.

There was another Knights Templar group that practiced the Gnostic schism of Christianity that Christ was fully human and sired a child with Mary Magdalene. The mission of both groups was to free the Holy Land from Muslim control. Evidently both groups were found guilty of heresy in the fourteenth century. The first group was dedicated to protecting pilgrims going to the Holy Land, as well as protecting the Holy Land itself. This

This photo of Lafe, has caused some controversy and mystery, as he is supposedly is wearing a Masonic uniform and holding a Knights Templar sword (now in the Luther Bean Museum at Adams State University) and was a very strong Roman Catholic. Supposedly you cannot be all three at one time. There is also a chaplain's emblem on his sleeve.

Courtesy of the Luther Bean Museum, Adams State University, Gift of Gwendolyn Hill, #1975.10.1j.

group felt its members had been wrongfully declared to be heretics by King Phillip, because he owed the group a considerable amount of money and felt that by labeling it and its members as heretics, he would get out of paying them back. This group also refused to join King Phillip's secular army and became a secret organization that, unfortunately, was recently confirmed by the Vatican to be heretical.

Lafe was a member of the Knights Templar in Pueblo and the International Order of Odd Fellows (IOOF) at Antonito, Colorado. The IOOF is not affiliated with the Masons, but is very similar in values and symbolism.

It seems very likely that Lafe was a master Mason, a firm Catholic, an Odd Fellow, and a Knights Templar at the same time. His name is inscribed on the Knights Templar sword, although it is possible the sword was just given to him by a Knight and he never joined the organization. One historian writes that Lafe belonged to all three organizations; but that he may have become a Knights Templar in the 1880s when he was no longer a Mason, therefore not belonging to both at the same time. However, the official rolls of the Masons show Lafe was a Mason from when he joined on December 13, 1853, until his death in 1897, with only one short period when he was on a demit. His funeral in the Catholic cemetery in Conejos was noted in the Jesuit diary as being led by the Masons.

Later in the spring of 1881, Lafe received news that his good friend Albert Pfeiffer had died at his ranch near Del Norte. Lafe greatly mourned the loss of his longtime friend, lodge brother, and chess partner. It was the first of a series of difficult losses over the next several years.

The 1885 Census showed the Head household as: "Male Lafe, age sixty; Female M. J. (Martina), fifty-two; Female Piedad Hill, twenty-one; and Male George Hill, no age (and Lafe's great grandson). The census also shows Adelaide, daughter, fourteen; Marcelin, twenty-one, son; Abe Head, fifteen, son; M. Head, twenty-six, son; J. Head, twenty-one, daughter; E. Head, grandson (no age); and Joseph Head, grandson, two. The children over twenty were probably Native American "slaves" still living with Lafe; and the younger children, probably children of his "slaves."

The little settlement on the Conejos River that Lafe and Martina called home had grown into a true town by the time the railroad arrived in 1882. Around the plaza were a bank, a trading post, a mercantile store, a rooming house, saloons, a doctor, and several lawyer offices. It was a thriving town for a few more years; but after the railroad bypassed Conejos and built Antonito, many of the businesses moved to that nearby town. The 1885 state census still counted 365 people living in Conejos. Of these, 315 citizens had been born in either New Mexico or Colorado, including five Cheyenne Indians.

There were thirty-five people from other states and fifteen from other countries. Most of the men listed their occupation as farmers, herders, laborers, or servants; but there were also seven Mexican-American clerks, five priests, five nuns, four blacksmiths, three merchants, two millers, and one each of shoemaker, laundry woman, banker, clergyman, teacher, and the inevitable frontier saloonkeeper rounded out the economy of the town.

Early travel writer Earnest Ingersol wrote in 1885:

> Along Conejos Creek are numerous small Mexican ranches, good enough types of their sort but the town itself has been Americanized until its claim to being a Mexican plaza is about lost.... Annexed to it is an academy for boys, and another for girls, both under the charge of priests and nuns of the Roman Catholic Church. These schools have no counterparts among the Mexicans nearer than Santa Fe, and have a wide reputation. Lacking interest for the tourist, the practical man will learn that Conejos is a very fair business place in certain lines. It is the headquarters of the sheep and cattlemen of the San Luis Park. In sheep I learn that although about 250,000 are sold out of the park annually, fully 500,000 are left.... Through a constant effort to improve the breed by introducing highly bred Merino and Cotswold rams.... Cattle is (sic) less of an industry here because the sheep are so numerous as to consume most of the pasturage.[179]

After about 1887, agricultural pursuits began to dominate the San Luis Valley. The Homestead Act encouraged these pursuits, free land was too much for many settlers to pass up, and agriculture needed much less land than cattle or sheep. Transportation on the Denver and Rio Grande Railroad made it easy to get agricultural products to market.

> ... the agricultural industry began to grow. Land was homesteaded and fenced off and the country up and down the Conejos and Rio Grande became settled; towns began to spring up, stores were more plentiful, and with all these things the stockmen were driven gradually back and forced to keep their stock further up in the hills....
>
> There were no game laws in those days. The antelope were all over the valley in large herds and there were innumerable ducks and plenty of fish. With no laws to protect them soon the antelope were killed off.[180]

CHAPTER 14

By 1886, the western cattle industry was way over-extended. There were an estimated 185,000 sheep in Costilla and Conejos Counties alone and many of them belonged to Lafe. There was trouble between the sheep men and the cattle men in all of Colorado at the time, but in the southern part of San Luis Valley the trouble was considered Anglo racism of the cattlemen in the northern part of the San Luis Valley against the Mexican-American sheepmen in the southern portion of The Valley. Then the harsh winter of 1886-1887, combined with extensive over-grazing, wiped out as much as fifty percent of the cattle herds. The invention of barbed wire in the mid-1870s had helped farmers to inexpensively fence off their land, but it also increased the cost of raising cattle, as ranchers now had to raise, cut, and store hay for the winter in the over-grazed valley. The San Luis Valley cattle boom ended in the late 1880s, after a sharp decline in cattle prices, a hard drought, and several very harsh winters in a row. Lafe went back to raising mostly sheep.

Lafe's family had a lot of deaths in the 1880s. Lafe's good friend Albert Pfieffer died in 1881, then Piedad's first husband William Hill died in 1883, Lafe's mother Margaret Head Arnold (photo above) died in 1887, and his wife Martina died in 1888.

Courtesy of the Luther Bean Museum, Adams State University, Gift of Gwendolyn Hill, #1975.10.1f.

Piedad and her son returned to Lafe's home after her husband William died in 1883, and she took over the management of his household. She decorated the interior of the house very elegantly for the time and took charge of the dinners and entertainment held by Head. However Piedad soon married Alfred Nelson and left Lafe's home again. In 1887, Lafe's mother died. Margaret Head Arnold had lived her last years in California with her youngest son, Jessie Arnold, and his family. Then Lafe's life partner Martina died on November 18, 1888. By best guess she was only fifty-six years old. Lafe arranged for her burial in the Conejos cemetery that she had helped to create. Then Piedad's second husband, Alfred Nelson, died December 14, 1888. It must have been hard to have two husbands and a grandmother die before Piedad was twenty-eight years old. Lafe took

Martina's death hard also, but he remained active with his business, friends, organizations, and particularly his grandchild.

By 1889, Frank Hall wrote that Piedad:

> ...maintains the Major's fine establishment with exalted grace. She has been twice married; the last time to Alfred Nelson, of Swedish birth, the inventor of the famous Nelson knitting machine, from which he acquired a large fortune. He died in Conejos December 14, 1888.[181]

In 1890, the Conejos Board of County Commissioners debated over where to build the new county courthouse, as the old one had burned down. Joseph H. Thomas, a member of the Board, wanted to build it in Antonito. Lafe made an improvised speech to the Commissioners in opposition to the suggestion. It was a speech that Mr. Thomas quoted often in later years. It included, in part, the following:

> When the colony first came here we went all around the edge of this valley and sought for the best place in it for the purpose of establishing a settlement. After having circled the valley we came to Conejos, (or) rather Guadalupe, which is substantially the same place, and we decided Conejos was the finest spot in the valley, and if it was the best place in the valley, it is still the best place for a court house.[182]

In August of 1891, Lafe and Piedad took ten-year-old George to Denver to enroll him in the College of The Sacred Heart. The school accepted boys ages ten and up. Father Personé, who had once served the Catholic Church in Conejos, was president of the school. It was located on fifty acres in the Clear Creek Valley west of the city. Tuition and board was $100 for a five month term. An extra $10 fee covered "washing and mending of linens" for the term. The daily schedule was strict, from "Rising" at 5:30 a.m. to "Retiring" at 9 p.m., six days a week. Parents could visit on Sundays between 1 and 5 p.m.

During George's first years at the school, Piedad stayed in Denver for long periods of time to be close to her young son. Lafe missed them both greatly and visited them in Denver often. Between school terms and over holidays, George returned to Conejos; and when he was older, Piedad remained in Conejos and made only occasional visits to his school, which was evidently okay with George. He graduated from the school (the equivalent of today's high school) in 1897.

CHAPTER 14

The new 1890 Conejos County courthouse was built in Conejos instead of being moved to the larger and faster-growing Antonito, thanks in large part to Lafe's political pressure. The courthouse was built of white sandstone carved into cubes with a "V" shape on one side. It was "a stately and imposing edifice," 42 x 88 feet. The cost was $35,000, and it was occupied for the first time on March 17, 1891.

History was already recording Lafe's many accomplishments and deeds. Frank Hall in his four volumes *History of Colorado* wrote in 1895:

> *Major Head's colony was the only one that succeeded in maintaining a permanent foothold in the San Luis Valley. His influence over this people has almost been supreme and always exerted for whatever he believed to be their best welfare. In the many years he has resided there he has acquired (a) large landed estates. He lives in a large and fine adobe house, which is a veritable palace in its interior furnishings and adornments, the seat of a boundless and refined hospitality. In 1865 (sic—1855) he moved from Guadalupe to more elevated ground on the south side of the Conejos river and there built his present home. Others followed and it soon became a center for trade.*[183]

Lafe was seventy years old in 1895. Conejos was smaller in 1895 than it had been in 1880 or 1885 due to the railroad stopping in Antonito; but Conejos still had the area's biggest and best Catholic private school, a large and beautiful Catholic church, and the county's courthouse. As the years passed, Lafe continued to visit his mill regularly and consult with the operator. In 1893, flour from Head's Mill won the gold medal at the Louisiana Expedition in St. Louis. That flour, called "Royal Cream," also took first prize at the state fair in Colorado. It was a large improvement from his original "Mexican flour."

In early March 1897, Lafe and Piedad made a trip to Denver to visit George. Lafe visited with old friends there and paid a visit to the state capitol building. In the Senate chambers, Lieutenant Governor Jared L. Brush invited Lafe to sit at the "President of the Senate" desk, where he had "wielded the gavel" twenty years before." Later during his stay in Denver, Lafe was taking a walk with ex-Governor Routt through the capital grounds and the capitol building that was still under construction. The effort was evidently too much for the old pioneer. He became ill and retired to his room at the Hotel Albert, where he died two days later at 8 p.m. on March 8, 1897. He was just thirty days short of his seventy-second birthday.

On March 9th, the *Rocky Mountain News* reported that

> hardly a day went by when less than a score of guests sat at dinner with him and the poor were always welcome to his bounty. None of his friends ever came within a hundred miles of his ranch without turning aside to make a visit.

The *Denver Republican* noted that Head left an estate valued at about $50,000 (about a million dollars today), which included his home, a 2,000 acre ranch, sheep and cattle, and a grist mill near Conejos.

The *Rocky Mountain News* on March 10, 1897, noted in an article that Lafe had settled in the San Luis Valley five years before the arrival of the settlers who most people considered to be the first Colorado pioneers, and before the Territory of Colorado was even considered by anyone. It further noted:

> Upon his splendid ranch in the San Luis Valley he lived like one of the ancient patriarchs. He had a cordial welcome for friends and strangers alike, and the poor found in him always a considerate and substantial benefactor.... (His) life illustrates all of the noblest characteristics of the American pioneer.

Lafe's obituary in the *Rocky Mountain News* of March 10, 1897, referred to him as one of the most prominent and picturesque men in southern Colorado.

> His death was announced in the Colorado legislature and the House of Representatives appointed five members to accompany the body to the railroad depot. A committee of Senators was appointed to accompany the body to Conejos and attend the funeral.
>
> He was the friend and companion of Kit Carson, of the elder Bents, of Governor Gilpin, of Dick Wootton, of Maxwell, and of many others whose names are famous in frontier history. He was a man of high principles and official integrity and he leaves behind him a name to be respected and honored.
>
> (Lieutenant) Governor Head was one of the most genial and hospitable of men. Upon his splendid ranch he lived like one of the ancient patriarchs. He had a cordial welcome for friends and strangers alike, and the poor found in him always a friend of the common man. He was a brave, generous, upright, kindly man, who delighted in good deeds and whose life was that of a

CHAPTER 14

> *considerate and substantial benefactor. The changes which he saw going on about him never changed the character that illustrated all of the noblest characteristics of the American pioneer.*

Lafe's Last Will and Testament was dated December 22, 1886, and since Martina had died and his "adopted" son Juan Cisneros had drowned, he left everything to his granddaughter Piedad, as his sole surviving heir. Lafe's Will directed that his body be given for burial to the Alamosa Lodge Number 44 of the Ancient, True, and Accepted Masons. The Catholic Church of Our Lady of Guadalupe at Conejos had no problem with Lafe being buried in the church cemetery or the burial ceremony being performed by the Masons.

Reports described his funeral as "elaborate." A long procession followed the coffin to Our Lady of Guadalupe Cemetery, where Lafayette Head was buried beside Martina. The death of "Raphael Cabeza" was recorded in the *Diary of the Jesuit Residence, 1895-1900* with a notation that his funeral was conducted by the Masons.

After Piedad moved in to Lafe's house, she redecorated lavishly as the original home was evidently decorated in "Western style." This is the living room with Piedad on left and a Mrs. Web on the right and servant at the rear in the dining room. Note Lafe's portrait on the wall.

Courtesy of the Luther Bean Museum, Adams State University, Gift of Gwendolyn Hill, #1975.10.1m.

Piedad, Grandfather, and More Mysteries

Looking into the drawing room from the dining room of the house. It was for relaxation after dinner with rocking chairs and a piano.

Courtesy of the Luthor Bean Museum, Adams State University, Gift of Gwendolyn Hill, #1975.10.1n.

Just a few years before Lafe's death, Piedad had finally settled the estate of her second husband, Alfred Nelson, who had died eight years earlier. Alfred's family owned the Rockford Mitten and Hosiery Company in Illinois. In 1885, Alfred had made improvements to his father's original design of the company's knitting machine and filed a patent for the new design under his own name. At his death his valuable patent belonged to Piedad. Alfred Nelson's family was not pleased that he had married "an Indian maiden (sic) in disregard of his parent's wishes." They were even more upset that she now held the patent on equipment vital to their business. Piedad finally settled with Alfred's family for "a handsome amount" and gave up any further claim to Alfred's patent and estate.

At a meeting of the citizens of Conejos County, held at the Town Hall of Conejos on Thursday, March 11, 1897, the following resolution was unanimously adopted:

> *Whereas Death has removed from our midst the Honorable Lafayette Head, the founder of the Town of Conejos and of Conejos County, a long distinguished resident of Colorado, a member of the territorial council and of the convention that framed the state constitution, and the first lieutenant governor of the state… we mourn a faithful public servant, a most worthy citizen and a man respected and beloved… for his many excellent qualities of mind and heart…. in his dealings with*

CHAPTER 14

> his fellow man the deceased was governed by the universal brotherhood of man....

As mentioned, the new state capitol building in Denver was under construction when Lafe died. As it neared its completion, the Board of Capitol Management decided to select twelve people to be honored with stained glass portraits in the windows of the capitol dome. The Board initially considered seventy-seven nominations, and after many meetings, they had made only three firm selections and twelve people were still finalists for the nine remaining portrait spaces. On December 25, 1899, *The Denver Evening Post* reported:

> The Board of Capitol Management will meet tomorrow for the purpose of selecting the remaining subjects for portraits in the windows of the capitol dome. The probabilities are that no women will be considered and the men who are most favorably spoken of for the remaining nine pictures are: Horace M. Hale, pioneer educator; Otto Mears, the pathfinder of the San Juan; Zebulon Pike and S. S. Long for whom Pike's peak and Long's peak are named; Green Russell, discoverer of gold; Governor Hunt and Lafayette Head; Senator Barela, Senator G. M. Chilicott; General Larimer and Governor Pitkin; Governor John L. Routt.

Lafe was heavily favored in the newspapers to be one of the final nine finalists, but he did not make the difficult final cut. He would no doubt have been supremely honored just to be nominated alongside those individuals who shaped Colorado's most formative years, and most of whom he knew well and could call his friend.

On August 29, 1899, Piedad officially received all property of the Conejos Roller Mill Company along with the books of accounts receivables. There was a credit balance of $6,420.40 and a cash balance of $3,196.61. The mill generated about $19,000 a year profit. She also owned Lafe's house, his ranch land at Conejos, and large herds of cattle and sheep. There were also many remaining loans to collect or be forgiven by Lafe's estate (most made to his friends), and additional claims against the estate to be considered. One of Lafe's sisters contested the will, but later dropped her claim. Lafe's grandson, George Hill, took over managing the Conejos Roller Mill.

Ranch and Range magazine wrote an article on Lafe a few years later that read in part that:

> Lafe knew not the limits of hospitality and seldom was his house free from more than a dozen friends. He built the second oldest grist mill in Colorado in 1870 (sic). His mill went from a couple of rough burrs to an up to date plan sifter roller mill with a capacity of 125 barrels a day. He had an ample warehouse and 50,000 bushel elevator. His mill is still doing very well at this time. Lafe had Mr. Arends as the manager of his mill. Head estate valued at more than $50,000. Mrs. Nelson is "a refined lady of courteous manner, unbounded in her charities and liked by all who have the good fortune to come within reach of her attractive influence. She lives in the house originally built by Major Head but transformed by her into an entirely modern luxuriant furnished residence. (The house) was "built after the old Spanish style, with walls two feet thick, protecting its occupants from winter blasts and the summer suns, and has a frontage of more than 210 feet by 60 feet in depth, and is almost entirely surrounded by a wide porch. Facing the oldest church in the state on one side, the oldest town on another, the second oldest mill on another, this place stands out pre-eminent as an historical spot.... One piece of furniture particularly attracted our attention. It was that of a combined billiards and dining table of richly carved oak and of immense weight.

Forty-three year old Piedad died on August 21, 1904, of an internal hemorrhage a year before Lafe's estate was settled. Her death and her funeral the following day were noted in the *Diarios of the Jesuit Residence*.[184] She was identified in the Diary by her birth name, Piedad Sisneros. The Masons also participated in her funeral, and she was buried in the same plot that already contained Martina's and Lafe's bodies.

Lafe would have relished one particular triumph in his estate settlement, or perhaps it would have made him boiling mad. On July 27, 1905, the executor reported to the court that he had collected on Lafe's 1855 claim for livestock stolen by Ute Indians. After fifty years, the United States government paid $345 on Lafe's original estimated loss of $735. That final settlement allowed closure of the estate of Lafayette Head.

Epilogue

Fort Marcy's walls still remain buried under a grassy knoll near the Santa Fe, New Mexico Plaza. It is now a scenic overlook, but it is all but forgotten, as it is not well advertised. Hopefully at some future date what is left of its walls may be uncovered and perhaps rebuilt. It was, after all, the first U.S. Army fort west of the Mississippi River.

Lafe's large, fine adobe house, one of the nicest in the San Luis Valley, was allowed to fall into ruin and no longer exists.

There was no D&RG Railroad passenger service to Antonito after 1951; but in the late 1960s, when its rails were going to be pulled up, railroad buffs saved the portion of the route between Antonito and Chama, New Mexico, and it is now a well-loved tourist attraction under the name "The Cumbres and Toltec Scenic Railroad." It and the portion of the D&RG Railroad from Durango to Silverton are still running.

After the D&RG came and the Utes were removed it was a very different life in the San Luis Valley, as symbolized in this drawing of the train, a deserted Ute wickiup, and Mt. Sierra Blanca.

From Ingersoll, *Crest of the Continent*.

Epilogue

In 1926, on Ash Wednesday, Our Lady of Guadalupe Church was severely damaged by fire. Only one small corner of the adobe church is now original. The priests' residences were moved to Antonito at that time. The present church was built on the same spot as the old church. The two brick towers were built in 1948, as well as the church being enlarged again. After the fire, there was a discussion about moving the church to Antonito, but it was decided to leave it in Conejos, so it would remain the oldest parish in Colorado.

The Southern Utes have recently begun to rebound economically. The Ute Mountain and Southern Utes have casinos, oil wells, and can hunt game again in Colorado without a license. The Weeminuche rely heavily on their casinos and also allow cultural tours into an extension of Mesa Verde that is on their land.

Fort Garland was abandoned in 1882, but today is a popular tourist attraction. Lafe would have been proud that citizens from Conejos and Costilla Counties, led by a drive by the Masons, formed the Fort Garland Historical Fair Association in May of 1928 for the purpose of preserving the site. The group approached the Colorado Historical Society and the National Park Service without much support, and then they sold shares to locals to keep a purchase option on the property. It was eventually purchased and is now owned by the Colorado State Historical Society.

The San Luis Valley still has a definite "Mexican" atmosphere and an easy going way of life. It is enjoyed by all who travel there. The Conejos River is now known far and wide for its great trout fishing.

In 1901, the Conejos Land Grant was held to be officially null and void by the United States Land Court. It was the only Mexican Land Grant in which the grantees never received any of the land they were seeking. The Court had heard 300 cases over a thirteen year period, of which only 26 were affirmed in full, and only twelve were community grants.

Some of Lafe's personal items, including his Knights Templar sword, are on display in the Luther Bean Museum at Adams State University in Alamosa.

The courthouse that Lafe fought so hard for in his old age burned yet again in 1980, but was rebuilt in its original location as a modern building.

The population of the Town of Conejos continued to decrease after Lafe's death, and in the 2010 census it had fifty-eight citizens, although Conejos County had a population of 8,256. Hopefully its citizens will not let the town disappear as Lafe's house did.

Endnotes

1 Letter in author's possession from Colorado State University Archives, "Lafayette Head Papers."
2 See Ortiz and Reichelt, "History of Rio Arriba County."
3 *Ranch and Range* Magazine, "Mrs. Piedad Nelson."
4 Ibid.
5 *Denver Republican*, Quoted in Martin, *Colorado Hall of Fame*, pg. 1.
6 Swadesh, *Los Primeros Pobladores*, pg. 25.
7 Ibid., pg. 68.
8 Conrad, *Encyclopedia of the History of Missouri*, "Howard and Charlton Counties."
9 Kindall, *Historic Sites and Markers Along the Mormon and Other Great Western Trails.*
10 *History of Northeast Missouri*, "Howard and Charlton Counties."
11 NECROLOGY digital library okstate.edu/chronicles, "Jesse Arnold."
12 Maggofin, *Down the Santa Fe Trail*, pg. 67.
13 Twitchell, *The History of the Military Occupation of the Territory of New Mexico from 1846 to 1851.*
14 Twitchell, *The Conquest of Santa Fe*, pg. 35.
15 Ibid., pg. 31.
16 Ellis, Editor, *New Mexico Historical Documents*, pg. 4.
17 Lavender, *Bent's Fort*, pg. 274.
18 Horgan, *Lamy of Santa Fe*, pg. 117 and "Churches in Santa Fe 1846," New Mexico Genealogical Society (nm.org): The five churches were Our Lady of Guadalupe, St. Joseph, San Isidro, Our Lady of Light (military chapel), Old San Miguel (oldest church in the U.S. established 1610).
19 Horgan, *Lamy of Santa Fe*, pg. 123.
20 Gregg, *Commerce on the Prairies*, pg. 143.
21 Richardson, *Beyond the Mississippi*, pg. 254.
22 Ibid., pg. 254.
23 Ibid., pg. 254.
24 Ibid., pg. 253.
25 Price, *The Official Report of the Conquest of California and New Mexico*, pgs. 223-231.
26 Ibid.
27 Lafe's Interview with *Field and Range* about the Mexican-American War.
28 *Field and Range*, "Lafayette Head, Reminiscences" 1887-1888 Edition.
29 Bloom, *New Mexico Viewed by Anglo-Americans 1846-49*, pgs. 165-178.
30 Monihan, *The Book of the American West.*
31 Ruxton, *Adventures in Mexico and the Rocky Mountains*, pgs. 208-209.
32 Prucha, *American Indian Treaties: The History of a Political Anomaly*, pg. 257.
33 Kappler, "Treaty with the Utahs, 1849," *U.S. Indian Affairs, Laws and Treaties*, Vol. 2, pgs. 585-587.
34 Linton, Editor, "The Southern Ute of Colorado," Opler, *Acculturation in Seven American Indian Tribes*, pg. 178.

Endnotes

35 Delaney, *The Southern Utes*, pg. 40.
36 Langston, *A History of Masonry in New Mexico 1877-1977*, pgs. 173-174.
37 Michael Steck Collection, Center for Southwest Studies, University of New Mexico, Box 149.
38 *Congressional Globe*, 32 U.S. Congress, 2nd Session, 1852.
39 Thomas, *From Fort Massachusetts to the Rio Grande*, pg. 76.
40 Stoller and Steele, Editors, *Diary of the Jesuit Residence of Our Lady of Guadalupe Parish, Conejos, Colorado*, says it was the Sevelitta near Ojo Caliente.
41 Gregg, *Commerce on the Prairies*, pgs. 137-144.
42 Taylor, *Colorado South of the Border*, pg. 49.
43 Stoller and Steele, Editors, *Diary of the Jesuit Residence of Our Lady of Guadalupe Parish, Conejos, Colorado*, pg. xxii.
44 Merriweather, *Annual Report to the Bureau of Indian Affairs*, National Archives, Washington, D.C., pg. 169.
45 Gunnison and Beckwith, *Reports of Exploration and Surveys to Ascertain the Most Practicable and Economic Route for a Railroad from the Mississippi River to the Pacific Ocean*, Vol.2, pg. 56.
46 Ibid., Vol. 3, pg. 13.
47 Gregg, *Commerce on the Prairie*, pgs. 145-151.
48 Ibid., pgs. 160-161.
49 Letter from Head to Carson dated May 24, 1854, Brigham Young University Archives.
50 Merriweather, *Annual Report to the Bureau of Indian Affairs, Sept. 1, 1854*, National Archives, Washington, D.C.
51 Letter from J.H. Thomas, Antonito lawyer, to D. W. Working, Original in Colorado State University Archives, Lafayette Head Folder 22.
52 Thomas, *From Fort Massachusetts to the Rio Grande*, pg. 108.
53 Ibid., pg. 109.
54 Carson to Merriweather letter, Bureau of Indian Affairs records, Washington, D.C.
55 Lekson, New Mexico State Historical Society, "Fort Pueblo Massacre."
56 Flint, "Biography of St. Vrain," New Mexico.org.
57 Indian Agent Correspondence, Ute National Archives, Washington, D.C.
58 Firstpeople.us/Treaty with the Utah 1849.
59 Carson, *Kit Carson's Own Story of His Life*, pg. 122.
60 Simmons, *San Luis Valley*, pg. 96.
61 Phil Carson, *Ft. Garland*, pg. 42.
62 Dunlay, *Kit Carson and the Indians*, pg. 212.
63 Survey notes of A.P. Wilbar, Deputy Survey General of New Mexico, March 1858.
64 *Rocky Mountain News*, September 3, 1859.
65 Ibid.
66 Oldham, *Albert H. Pfeiffer*, pg. 46.
67 Ibid., pg. 48.
68 Decker, *The Utes Must Go*, pg. 50.
69 J.M. Francisco papers [Box 55, Colorado State University Archives].

70 Oldham, *Albert H. Pfeiffer*, pg. 51.
71 Laura C. Manson White, "Pagosa Springs, Colorado," *Colorado Magazine*, May 1932.
72 Oldham, *Alfred H. Pfeiffer*, pg. 63.
73 Taken from Griswald, *A Century of Cities*, pgs. 85-86.
74 Phil Carson, *Fort Garland Museum*, pg. 42.
75 Thomas, "Don Miguel Antonio Otero and the New Mexico Notch."
76 Bureau of Indian Affairs Records, Washington D.C Microfilm 234, Roll 197.
77 Dunlay, *Kit Carson and the Indians*, pg. 216.
78 Linton, Editor, "The Southern Ute of Colorado," Opler, *Acculturation in Seven American Indian Tribes*, pg. 179.
79 Bauer, Ozment, and Willard, *Colorado Post Offices*, 1859-1989.
80 McClellan, *This is Our Land, Vol. 1*, pgs. 370-371.
81 Bureau of Indian Affairs Records, Washington, D. C.
82 Ibid.
83 Found in Herman Viola's research notes for *Diplomats in Buckskin*, Smithsonian Museum.
84 Downing, "With the Ute Peace Delegation of 1863," pg. 194.
85 *St Joseph Herald* quoted in Smith, *Ouray Chief of the Utes*, pg. 59.
86 Downing, "With the Ute Peace Delegation of 1863," pg. 196.
87 Ibid., pg. 196.
88 Ibid., pg. 203.
89 "Mrs. Piedad Nelson," *Ranch and Range Magazine*.
90 Downing, "With the Ute Peace Delegation of 1863," pg. 203.
91 Ibid., pg. 202.
92 Leonard, "John Nicolay in Colorado," pg. 47.
93 Simmons, *The Ute Indians of Utah, Colorado and New Mexico*, pg. 119.
94 Downing, "With the Ute Peace Delegation of 1863," pg. 203.
95 Smith, *Ouray, Chief of the Utes*, pgs. 64-65.
96 Alexander Cummings to Commissioner D.N. Cooley October 10, 1866, "Report of the Secretary of Interior, Washington: Government Printing Office, 1866."
97 Rockwell, *The Utes A Forgotten People*, pg. 89.
98 Bancroft, *Speeches, Correspondence and Political Papers of Carl Schurtz*, pg. 142.
99 Bangert, "Uncompahgre Statesman," pg. 15.
100 Downing, "With the Ute Peace Delegation of 1863," pg. 201.
101 Petition at Colorado State Archives, "Lafayette Head."
102 Gomez, *Manifest Destiny*, pgs. 108-109.
103 Ellis, *New Mexico Historic Documents*, pg. 15.
104 Dunlay, *Kit Carson & The Indians*, pg. 203.
105 Gilpin, *Report of the Superintendent of Indian Affairs, 1862*, pg. 209.
106 Sanchez, "Survivors of Captivity, Genealogies of Known Captive Indians in Southern Colorado, 1860-1880," March 2014.
107 Carson, Phil, *Fort Garland Museum*, pg. 45.

108 Ibid., pg. 46.
109 Dunlay, *Kit Carson and the Indians*, pg. 376.
110 Carson, Phil, *Fort Carson Museum*, pg. 46.
111 Dunlay, *Kit Carson and the Indians*, pg. 381.
112 See Taylor, "Kaniache," pg. 293
113 Smith, *Ouray, Chief of the Utes*, pg. 68.
114 Ibid., pg. 68.
115 Dunlay, *Kit Carson and the Indians*, pg. 377.
116 Simmons, *The Ute Indian of Utah, Colorado, and New Mexico*, pg. 129.
117 Martin, Editor, *Frontier Eyewitness*, pg. 7.
118 Ancestry.com, "John Lawrence-Father of Saguache."
119 Martin, *Frontier Eyewitness*, pg. 175.
120 Simmons, "When Opportunity Knocked on Saguache's Door," *Colorado Central Magazine*, May 2000.
121 Pueblo, Colorado *Chieftain*, October 8, 1868.
122 See Oldham, *Albert H. Pfeiffer*, pgs. 165-169 for list of chiefs who did sign.
123 Oldham, *Albert H. Pfeiffer*, pg. 169.
124 Ibid., pgs. 165-169.
125 *Indian Affairs, Laws and Treaties*, Vol. 2, Article 5, "Treaty with the Ute, 1868."
126 Simmons, "When Opportunity Knocked on Saguache's Door," *Colorado Central Magazine*, May 2000.
127 Simmons, *The Ute Indians of Utah, Colorado, and New Mexico*, pg. 134.
128 Ibid., pg. 135.
129 *Papers of Andrew Johnson*, Vol. II, April-August 1868.
130 Martin, *Frontier Eyewitness*, pg. 62, June 2, 1871.
131 *Taos County Probate Book*, B-3, pg. 28.
132 *Our Lady of Guadalupe Book of Baptismal Records*, Book 1, pg. 11.
133 Stoller and Steele, editors, *Diary of the Jesuit Residence of Ouray Lady of Guadalupe Parish, Conejos, Colorado, Diary 1*, pg. 2.
134 Ibid., pg. 1.
135 Ibid., pg. 180.
136 Ibid., pgs.78-79.
137 Simmons, *San Jan Valley Historian*, Vol XXIV #4, 1992, "The Penitentes."
138 The secondary source comes from the book *Los Hermanos Penitentes* quoting from *The Penitente Brothers*, by Lorayne Ann Horka-Follick, Ph.D. Western Lore Press, 1969, pg. 133 who in turn is quoting an article from the *Albuquerque Review* of April 6, 1878.
139 See also *Diary of the Jesuit Residence of Our Lady of Guadalupe Parish, Conejos, Colorado, Diary I*, footnote 62, pgs. 35-36.
140 Swadesh, *Los Primeros Pobladores*, pg. 78.
141 Archuleta, *Land of the Penitentes, Land of Tradition*, pg. 70.
142 Swadesh, *Los Primeros Pobladores*, pg. 74 .
143 Simmons, *San Jan Valley Historian*, Vol XXIV #4, 1992, "The Penitentes," pg. 24.
144 Archuleta, *Land of the Penitentes, Land of Tradition*.

145 Swadesh, *Los Primeros Pobladores*, pg. 8.
146 Simmons, *The San Luis Valley*, pg. 215.
147 Simmons, "When Opportunity Knocked on Saguache's Door," *Colorado Central Magazine*, May 2000.
148 Ibid.
149 Smith, *Ouray, Chief of the Utes*, pg. 57.
150 Dunlay, *Kit Carson and the Indians*, pg. 375.
151 Hafen, "Efforts to Recover the Stolen Son of Chief Ouray," pgs. 55-56.
152 Ibid., pgs. 53-62.
153 The Ute Tribal Council, *Ute System of Government*, pg. 9.
154 Jocknick, *Early Days on the Western Slope of Colorado*, pg. 365.
155 Lavender, *The Big Divide*, pg. 99.
156 Ibid.
157 See Athearn, *Frontier in Transition*, Chapter 5.
158 Lavender, *The Big Divide*, pg. 100.
159 Senate Proceedings of 10th Colorado Legislature.
160 CWA Interview Collection, Colorado State Historical Society, "Alamosa, Conejos, and Costilla Counties," pamphlet 349, Doc. 1-49.
161 Ibid.
162 *Daily Rocky Mountain News*, August 24, 1876.
163 Kaplan, *Otto Mears*, pg. 22.
164 Sanford, "Recollections of a Trip to the San Luis Valley, 1877."
165 Fossett, *Colorado*, pg. 187.
166 Oldham, *Albert H. Pfeiffer*, pgs. 234-235.
167 Bancroft, *History of Colorado*, pgs. 592-593.
168 Linton, Editor, "The Southern Ute of Colorado," Opler, *Acculturation in Seven American Indian Tribes*, pg. 80.
169 Behrens, "The Utes Must Go – With Dignity," pgs. 47-48.
170 Smith, *Ouray, Chief of the Utes*, pg. 164.
171 McLellan, *This is Our Land*, Vol. II, pgs. 513-514.
172 Smith, *Ouray, Chief of the Utes*, pg. 176.
173 Behrens, "The Utes Must Go – With Dignity," pg. 55.
174 See Daniels, Helen Sloan, *The Utes of Southwest Colorado* for more details.
175 Echohawk, "Struggling to Find Zion: Mormans in Colorado's San Luis Valley."
176 Hall, *History of Colorado, Vol. IV*, pg. 94.
177 Allegedly, Lafe had several illegitimate children by different women. The stories came to co-author Cynthia Becker through emails connected with her genealogical resource. However, it is unknown if Becker received solid enough information to put the details in this book.
178 Bancroft, *History of Colorado*, pgs. 592-593.
179 Ingersoll, *Crest of the Continent*, pg. 79.
180 McDermoth, Genevieve E., "'Billy' Adams, Colorado's Cowboy Governor," Daughters of the American Revolution, *Pioneers of the San Juan Country, Vol.III*, pg. 24.

Endnotes

181 Hall, *History of Colorado, Vol. IV*, pg. 94.
182 Letter from J. H. Thomas to D. W. Working, February 7, 1925, at Colorado State University Archives, Folder 22.
183 Hall, *History of Colorado, Vol IV*, pg. 93.
184 Stoller and Steele, Editors, *Diary of the Jesuit Residence of Our Lady of Guadalupe Parish, Conejos, Colorado, Vol. VII*, pg. 55.

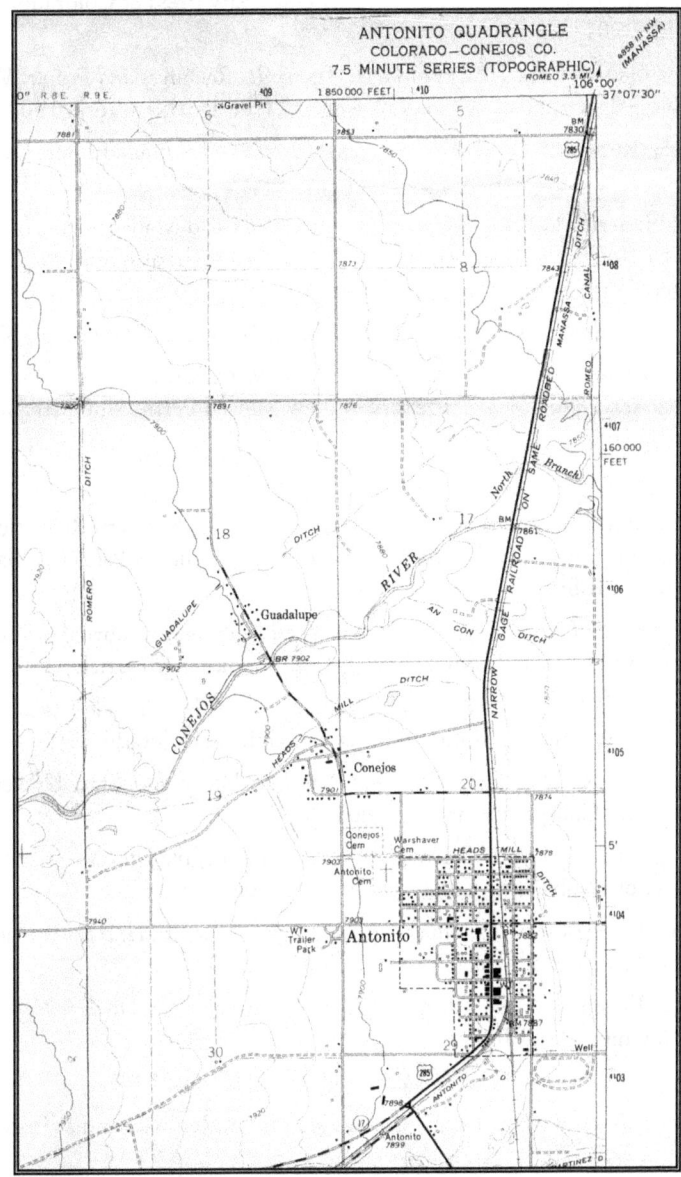

Antonito is now much bigger than either Guadalupe or Conejos.
U S. G. S. Map Antonito Quadrangle Colorado–Conejos County.

Bibliography

BOOKS

Aldama, Arturo, Editor, *Enduring Legacies*, University Press of Colorado, Boulder, 2011.

Anderson, George B., *A History of New Mexico: Its Resources and People*, Vol. II, Pacific States Publishing Co., Los Angeles, Chicago, New York, 1907.

Archuletta, Ruben E., *Land of the Penitentes, Land of Tradition*, El Jefe, Pueblo West, CO 2003.

Athearn, Frederick J., *Land of Contrasts*, Bureau of Land Management, Denver, 1984. (Note: http://www.nps.gov/history/online_books/blm/co/17/contents.htm contains book with page numbers.

Bailey, L. R., *Indian Slave Trade in the Southwest*, Tower Publications, 1966.

Ball, Larry, *Desert Lawmen: The High Sheriffs of New Mexico and Arizona Territories, 1846-1912*, University of New Mexico Press, Albuquerque, 2011.

Bancroft, Frederick, *Speeches, Correspondence and Political Papers of Carl Schurz*, Reprint, March 2012.

Bancroft, Hubert Howe, *History of Colorado*, Reprint by Western Reflections Publishing Co. from *The Works of Hubert Howe Bancroft Vol XVII*, San Francisco, 1889.

Bangert, Buckley, *Uncompahgre Statesman, The Life of Ouray*, Journal of the Western Slope, Vol. 1, No. 2, Spring 1986 (book-length article).

Bauer, William H.; Ozment, James L.; Willard, John H.; *Colorado Post Offices, 1859-1989*, Colorado Railroad Museum, Golden, Colorado, 1990.

Baumann, Paul R., *Dry Land and Water: San Luis Valley, CO*, State University of New York, College at Oneonta, 2001.

Becker, Cynthia and Smith, P. David, *Chipeta: Queen of the Utes*, Western Reflections Publishing Co., Lake City, CO, 2003.

Bergerson, Peter, Editor, *The Papers of Andrew Johnson, Vol. II, April-August 1868*, University of Texas Press, Austin, Texas, 1997.

Beuvanger, Eugene H., *The Rise of the Centennial State: Colorado Territory 1861-1874*, University of Illinois, 2007.

Brandes, Don, *Military Posts of Colorado*, Old Army Press, 1973.

Brown, Dee, *Bury My Heart at Wounded Knee*, Holt, Reinhart and Winston, New York, 1970.

Burdett, Charles, *The Life of Kit Carson, The Great White Hunter and Guide*, Porter and Coates, Philadelphia, 1869.

Bibliography

Carson, Kit, *Kit Carson's Own Story of His Life*, Reprint by The Narrative Press,, Santa Barbara, CA, 2001.

Carson, Phil, *Ft. Garland Museum, A Capsule History and Guide*, Colorado Historical Society, Denver, 2005.

Clamp, John W., *Echoes From the Rocky Mountains*, The National Book Company, Chicago, 1888.

Congressional Record, *A Century of Lawmaking for a New Nation: U. S. Congressional Documents and Debates, 1774-1875*.

Conrad and Company, *Encyclopedia of the History of Missouri*, The Southern History Company, New York, 1901.

Cutts, J.M., *The Conquest of California and New Mexico*, Carey and Hart, Philadelphia, 1847.

Daniels, Helen Sloan, *The Ute Indians of Southwest Colorado*, Western Reflections Publishing Co. Lake City, Colo., 2008.

Daughters of the American Revolution, *Pioneers of the San Juan Country*, self-published.

de Onis, Jose', editor, *The Hispanic Contribution to the State of Colorado*, Westview Publishing Co., Boulder, Colorado, 1976.

Decker, Peter R., *The Utes Must Go!*, Fulcrum Press, Golden, Colorado, 2004.

Delaney, Robert, *The Southern Ute People*, Indian Tribal Series, Phoenix, 1974.

Dill, R. G., *Political Campaigns of Colorado*, The Arapaho Publishing Co., 1895.

Dunlay, Tom, *Kit Carson and the Indians*, University of Nebraska Press, Lincoln, NE, 2000.

EchoHawk, Dana Rae. *Struggling to Find Zion: Mormon's in Colorado's San Luis Valley*, University of Denver, Master's Thesis.

Ellis, Richard N., Editor, *New Mexico Historical Documents*, University of New Mexico Press, Albuquerque, 1975.

Everett, Derek R., *Creating the American West: Boundaries and Borderlands*, University of Oklahoma Press, 2012.

Feril, William Columbus, *Sketches of Colorado*, Vol. 1, Forgotten Books Reprint, 1911.

Fossett, Frank, *Colorado: Its Gold and Silver Mines*, Self-Published, New York, 1879.

Fowler, Dan, *A Laboratory for Anthropology*, University of New Mexico Press, Albuquerque, 2000.

Fuller, Timothy, Editor, *Diary of the Jesuit Residence of Our Lady of Guadalupe parish, Conejos, Colorado, 1871-December 1875 (Vol. 1)*, The Colorado Studies, Number 19, Colorado College, Colorado Springs, Colorado, 1982.

Gallegos, Phillip, "Religious Architecture in Colorado's San Luis Valley," See *Enduring Legacies*.

Gomez, Laura E., *Manifest Destinies, The Making of the Mexican-American Race*, University Press, New York, 2007.

Gregg, Josiah, *Commerce on the Prairies*, Applewood Books, Reprint of 1851 book.

Griswold, Don and Jean, *A Century of Colorado Cities*, Self-published, Denver, 1958.

Gunnison, Captain John W. and Beckwith, Lt. E. G., *Report of Explorations and Surveys to Ascertain the Most Practical and Economic Route for a Railroad From the Mississippi River to the Pacific Ocean in 1853-54*, U. S. Government Printing Office, (12 Volumes) 1855-1861.

Hafen, LeRoy and Hafen, Ann W., *The Colorado Story*, The Old West Publishing Company, Denver, CO, 1953.

Hafen, LeRoy and Hafen, Ann W., *The Old Spanish Trail*, University of Nebraska Press, 1933 (Reprint).

Hall, Frank. *History of the State of Colorado*, Vols. I-IV, The Blake Printing Company, 1889-1895.

Harlan, George, *Postmarks and Places*, Self-Published, 1976.

Harris, Michael D., *History of Missouri and Illinois Territories, 1808-1815* (online).

Heap, Gwinn Harris, *A Central Route to the Pacific*, Lipcott, Graneo and Co., Philadelphia, 1854.

Hensel, Donald Wayne, *A History of the Colorado Constitution in the Nineteenth Century*, Thesis, University of Colorado Department of History, 1957.

History of Boone County, Missouri, Western Historical Company, 1882.

Horgan, Paul, *Lamy of Santa Fe*, The Noonday Press, New York, 1975.

Horka-Follick, Lorayne Ann, Ph.D., *Los Hermanos Pententes*. Westernlore Press, 1968.

Houck, Louis, *History of Missouri, Vol. III, Howard, Boone and Charlton Counties*, O. P. Williams and Co., 1883 Counties (http://files.usgwarchives.net/special/afas/volume5/no4.txt).

Howlett, Rev. W. J., *Life of the Right Reverend Joseph P. Machebuef, D. D.*, Franklin Press, Pueblo, CO, 1908. (Available online).

Illustrated History of Southern California, The Lewis Publishing Company, Chicago, 1890 (article on Jesse H. Arnold, Lafayette Head's half-brother).

Ingersoll, Ernest, *Crest of the Continent*, R.R. Donnelly and Son, Chicago, 1885.

Jefferson, James; Delaney, Robert; Thompson, George, *The Southern Utes, A Tribal History*, Southern Ute tribe, Ignacio, Colorado, 1972.

Jocknick, Sidney, *Early Days on the Western Slope of Colorado*, The Carson-Harper Co., 1913, Reprinted by Western Reflections Publishing Co.

Kaplan, Michael, *Otto Mears, Paradoxical Pathfinder*, San Juan County Book Co., Silverton, Colorado, 1982.

Kappler, Charles, *U. S. Indian Affairs, Laws and Treaties*, Government Printing Office, Washington, D.C., 1903.

Kessler, *North Branch of the Old Spanish Trail*, Adobe Village Press, 1995.

Kindall, Stanley, *Historic Sites and Markers Along the Mormon Trail and Other Great Western Trails*, University of Illinois, Chicago, 1988.

Langston, La Moine, *A History of Masonry* in New Mexico, Hall-Poorbaugh Press, 1977.

Lantis, Dr. David W., Doctoral Thesis, *The San Luis Valley, Colorado – Subsequent Rural Occupation in an Inter-Montane Basin*, 1950 (unpublished).

Lavender, David, *Bent's Fort*, Harper and Row, Garden City, New York, 1954.

Lavender, David, *The Big Divide*, Doubleday & Company, New York, 1949.

Lavender, David, *The Rockies*, Harper & Row, 1968.

Macomb, Captain J. M., Topographical Engineer and J. S. Newberry, Geologist, *From Santa Fe to the Junction of the Grand and Green Rivers*, U.S. Government Printing Office, Washington, 1876.

Magoffin, Susan Shelby, *Down the Santa Fe Trail, The Diary of Susan Shelby Maggofin*, University of Nebraska, Lincoln, 1962 (also Bison Books 1982).

Martin, Bernice, Editor, *Frontier Eyewitness, Diary of John Lawrence, 1867-1908*, Saguache County Museum, 2011.

McClellan, Val. J., *This Is Our Land*, Volumes I & II, Vantage Press, New York, 1977.

Mead, Frances Harvey, *Conejos County*, Century One Press, 1984.

Monihan, Jay, *Book of the American West*, Julian Messner, New York, 1963.

Myers, Joan and Simmons, Mark, *Along the Santa Fe Trail*, University of New Mexico Press, 1986.

Nosserman, Allen, *Many More Mountains, Vol. 1*, Sundance Books, Denver, 1989.

O'Rourke, Paul M., *Frontier in Transition*, Bureau of Land Management Cultural Series No. 10, 1980.

Oldham, Ann, *Albert Pfeiffer: Indian Agent, Soldier, and Mountain Man*, Self-published, 2003.

Opler, Marvin, "The Southern Ute Indians of Colorado," in *Acculturation in Seven American Indian Tribes*, R. Appleton-Century Company, New York, 1940. (book length).

Perrin, William Henry, Editor, *History of Cass County, Illinois*, O.L. Baskin & Co. Historical Publishers, Chicago, 1882.

Price, *Official Report of the Conquest of California and New Mexico*.

Probst, Nell Brown, *A Forgotten People: A History of the South Platte Trail*, Pruett Publishing, Boulder, CO, 1979.

Prucha, Francis Paul, *American Indian Treaties: The History of a Political Anomaly*, University of California Press, 1997.

Richardson, Albert D., *Beyond the Mississippi, From the Great River to the Great Ocean: Life and Adventure on the Prairie, Mountains and Pacific Coast*, American Publishing Co., Hartford, Conn., 1867.

Roberts, Dan, *The Story of the Centennial State*, Eagle Tail Press, Grand Junction, Colorado, 1973.

Rockwell, *The Utes, A Forgotten People*, Reprint of 1956 book by Western Reflections Publishing Co., Montrose, Colorado, 1998.

Russell, Marion, *Land of Enchantment: Along the Santa Fe Trail*, University of New Mexico Press, Albuquerque, 1997.

Ruxton, George, *Adventures in Mexico and the Rocky Mountains*, John Murray, London, 1847.

Saunders, William, Unpublished manuscript regarding Utes and Billy the Kid, Copy in possession of P. David Smith.

Simmons, Virginia McConnell, *The San Luis Valley, Land of the Six-Arm Cross*, Second Edition, University of Colorado Press, Niwot, Colorado, 1999.

Simmons, Virginia McConnell, *The Ute Indians of Utah, Colorado, and New Mexico*, University Press of Colorado, 2000.

Smiley, Jerome, *Semi History of Colorado*, Vol. II, The Lewis Publishing Co., 1913, Also Ouray County website, "Otto Mears."

Smith, P. David, *Ouray, Chief of the Utes*, Wayfinder Press, Ridgway, Colorado, 1986.

Stoller, Marianne L. Ph.D and Thomas J. Steele, S.J., Ph.D., Editotrs and Annotators, *Diaries of the Jesuit Residence of Our Lady of Guadalupe Parish Conejos, Colorado, December 1871-December 1875*, The Colorado College Studies, Number Nineteen, 1982.

Swadesh, Francis Leon, *Los Primeros Pobladores, Hispanic Americans of the Ute Frontier*, University of Notre Dame Press, Notre Dame, 1974.

Taylor, Ralph C., *Colorado: South of the Border*, Sage Books, Denver, 1963.

Thomas, D. B., *From Fort Massachusetts to the Rio Grande*, self-published, Washington, D.C. 2002.

Twitchell, Ralph Emerson, *The History of the Military Occupation of the Territory of New Mexico From 1846 to 1851*, Rio Grande Press, 1909.

Twitchell, Ralph Emerson, *Leading Facts of New Mexican History* (2 Vols.), The Torch Press, Cedar Rapids, Iowa, 1911.

Twitchell, Ralph Emerson, *The Conquest Santa Fe, 1846,* Historical Society of New Mexico, 1921.

Ubaholde, Carl; Benson, Maxine; Smith, Duane, *A Colorado History, Third Edition,* Pruett Publishing Company, Boulder, Colorado, 1972.

Van Ness, John R. and Christine M., Editors, *Spanish and Mexican Land Grants in New Mexico and Colorado,* Colorado Humanities Project, Malcomb Ebright, Publisher, 1980.

Viola, Herman J., *Diplomats in Buckskin,* University of Oklahoma Press, Revised Edition, 1995.

Weigle, *Brothers of Light, Brothers of Blood,* Ancients City Press, 1988.

Wetherington, Ronald K., *Ceran St. Vrain, American Frontier Entrepreneur,* Sunstone Press, Santa Fe, 2012.

Wilkinson, James, *History of Colorado,* Unigraphic, 1901.

Wilkinson, James, *History of Denver, The Denver Times,* The Times-Sun Publishers, Denver, 1901.

Williams, Walter, *History of Northeast Missouri (3 Vols.),* Lewis Publishing Co., Chicago, 1913.

ARTICLES, PHAMPLETS, AND NEWSPAPERS
(Note—Many newspapers are identified in the text itself)

Barnum, Thomas J., "Notes from Del Norte," *Daily Rocky Mountain News* (Denver), June 26, 1877.

Behrens, Jo Leo, "The Utes Must Go – With Dignity, - Alfred B. Meacham's Role on Colorado's Ute Commission, 1880-1881," *Colorado Historical Society's Essays and Monographs,* Number 14, 1994.

Bloom, John P., "New Mexico Viewed by Anglo Americans, 1848," *New Mexico Historical Review,* 1959.

Bond, Anne Wainstein, "Buffalo Soldiers," *Colorado Heritage,* spring 1996. (However the entire issue (six articles) is on Buffalo Soldiers).

Colorado State Historical Society, *Biographical Portraits of Territorial Legislative Council,* Denver, August, 1980.

Corbett, Thomas B., *Legislative Manual Colorado,* 1877.

Crowther, Edward R., "Southern Saints in the San Luis Valley," *The San Luis Valley Historian,* Vol XXXV, No. 3, 2003.

Daves, Doyle, "Lafayette Head," *Wagon Tracks,* Vol. 30, Issue 3, Article 1 (Magazine of the Santa Fe Trail Association), 2016.

Downing, Finis, "With the Peace Delegation of 1863: Across the Plains and at Conejos,"

The Colorado Magazine, State of Colorado Historical Society Vol. 22, No. 5, September, 1945.

General Laws and Joint Resolutions, Memorials and Private Acts at the Third Assembly of the Legislative Assembly of the Territory of Colorado, begun at Golden City on the 1st day of February, 1864, Adjourned to Denver on the 4th day of February; Published by Authority by Byers & Denver Daily, Printers – *Rocky Mountain News* office, 1864.

Gilliford, Andrew, "The Truth Behind a Frontier Myth in Pagosa Springs," *The Durango Herald*, June 10, 2017.

Hafen, Ann, "Efforts to Recover Chief Ouray's Stolen Son," *Colorado Magazine*, Vol. 16. No. 2, 1939.

Head, Lafayette, "Reminiscence (of the Pueblo Revolt)" *Field and Farm Magazine*, 1887-1888 Edition.

Lekson, Stephen H., "Fort Pueblo Massacre," New Mexico History.org.

Leonard, Stephen J., "John Nicolay in Colorado," Colorado Historical Society, *Essays and Monographs in Colorado History*, Number 11, 1990.

Leyendecker, Liston E., Editor, "Hiram Bennett, Pioneer, Frontier Lawyer, Politician," Colorado Historical Society *Monograph* No. 2, 1988.

Martin, Mary and Gene, *Colorado's Hall of Fame*, Little London Press, Colorado Springs, CO, 1974.

McClellan, Ella, "History of the Sacred Heart Church," D.A.R., *Pioneers of the San Juan Country*, Vol. 4.

McDermoth, Genevieve E., "Billy Adams, Colorado's Cowboy Governor," Daughters of the American Revolution, *Pioneers of the San Juan Country*, Vol. 3.

McGrath, Mike, Information on Piedad and John Nelson, personal interview by Cynthia Becker, 8/4/14.

McMenomy, "Our Lady of Guadalupe at Conejos, Colorado,", *Colorado Magazine* #17, 1940.

Newspapers are cited in footnotes, but include *Denver Republican, Durango Herald, New York World, St. Joseph Herald, Daily Rocky Mountain News, Colorado Daily Chieftain.*

Ortiz, Raymond and Reichett, Lauren R., "History of Rio Arriba County," (www.rio-arriba.org/places).

Parkhill, Forbes, "Colorado's First Survey," Historical Society of Colorado, *The Colorado Magazine*, Vol. XXXIII, July 1956.

Portrait & Biographical Record of the State of Colorado, Chapman Publishing Co.

Ranch and Range Magazine, August, 1900, "Mrs. Piedad Nelson."

Romero-Oak, Judy, "Padre Martinez," *Spirit, The Magazine of the Rocky Mountain Southwest*, Spring/Summer 1995.

Rose, Ernie, "The Utahs of the Rocky Mountains, 1833-1835," *Montrose Daily Press*, 1968.

San Luis Valley Historian, misc. issues, including Vol. 1 #1 and #21, Vol. 2 #2, Vol. 5 #1, Vol 6 #s 1 and 2, Vol. 8 #2, Vol. 8 #2, Vol. 17 #2, Vol 20 #3, Vol. 23 #3, Vol. 25 #4, Vol. 26 #4, Vol. 27 # 1, Vol. 29 #4, Vol. 30 #3.

Sanchez, Virginia, "Survivors of Captivity" - Known Captive Indians in Southwest Colorado, 1860-1880 (can be ordered in Somos Primos. com.), March 2014.

Sanford, Albert B., "Recollections of A Trip to the San Luis Valley, 1877," *Colorado Magazine*, Vol. X, #5, September, 1933.

Scott, Glen, Pamphlet accompanying *Historic Trail Map of Trinidad 1x2 Degree*, usgs.gov/map/1275.report.pdf.

Secrest, Clark, "The Bloody Espinozas, *Colorado Heritage*, Colorado Historical Society, Autumn, 2000.

Simmons, Virginia, "Lafayette Head, Conejos Luminary," "Rabbitbrush Rambler," *Valley Courier*, April 21, 2008.

Simmons, Virginia, Uncle Lafe (4 parts), "Rabbitbrush Rambler," *Valley Courier*, 1/15/13, 1/22/13, 1/29/13, and 2/5/13.

Simmons, Virginia, "The Penitente," *San Luis Valley Historian*, Vol. XXIV, No. 4, 1992 (entire issue).

Simmons, Virginia, "When Opportunity Knocked On Saguache's Door," *Colorado Central Magazine*, May, 2000.

Strauter, "100 Years in Colorado's Oldest Parish."

Taylor, Morris F., "Action at Fort Massachusetts: The Indian Campaign of 1855," *Colorado Magazine*, Vol. 42, 1965.

Taylor, Morris F., "Kaniache," *Colorado Magazine*, XLIII/4, 1966.

Thompson. Mark, "Don Miguel Antonio Otero and the New Mexico Notch," *New Mexico Bar Bulletin*, Vol. 50, February 9, 2011.

Uintah-Ouray Ute Tribe (no individual author given), "The Ute System of Government," Salt Lake City, 1977.

Ute Tribal Council, *The Ute System of Government*, Self-Published. n.d.

Veregge, Nina, "Tranformation of Spanish Urban Landscape in the American Southwest," *Journal of the Southwest*, Vol.35, No. 4. Winter, 1993.

White, Laura C., "Pagosa Springs," *Colorado Magazine*, May, 1932.

ELECTRONIC MEDIA

Abel, Annie Heloise, Editor, "Journal of John Ward" in *Indian Affairs in New Mexico Under the Administration of William Carr Lane*, University of New Mexico, http://ejournal.unm.edu.

Aker, Marlin, "The San Luis Valley Land Grants," published in Huerfanocounty/sanluis.html.

Ancestry.com., Inventory of County Archives of Colorado, Conejos County, "Historical Sketch of Conejos County."

Ancestry.com., okmurray/stories/deputy-marshall, see also "John Lawrence, Father of Saguache" and "Taos, New Mexico Revolt."

"Andrew Johnson," www.ipl.org/div/potus/ajohnson.htm.

"Battle of Chapultepec," Wikipedia. org.

Boone's Lick Trace or Booneslick Road," waymaking.com.

Bureau of Engraving and Printing, http://www.moneyfactory.gov.

Census Records, http://www.census/state of colorado.pdf.

Census Records of United States, http://www.census/us.

Churches in Santa Fe, 1846, New Mexico Geneological Society (nmgs.org.).

Enright, Malcom, "Genizaros," New Mexico History.org.

Firstpeople.us/ "Treaties With Utah, 1849."

Flint, Richard and Shirley Cushing, "Biography of Ceran St. Vrain", newmexicohistory.com.

Flint, Richard and Shirley Cushing Flint, "Cimarron Cut Off of the Santa Fe Trail, newmexicohistory.org.

"Jesse Arnold," NECROLOGY, digital library okstate.edu, chronicles.

Langston, LaMorine, "History of Masonry in New Mexico," 1917 http://montezumalodge.org/history.htm.

Legends of America, www.legendsofamerica.com . Articles on Santa Fe Trail and Taos Rebellion.

Lekson, Stephen, "Ft. Pueblo Massacre," New Mexico History.org.

Library of Congress, *A Century of Lawmaking for a New Nation: U.S Congressional Documents and Debates, 1774-1873.* https://memory.loc.gov/amen/amlaw/.

Missouri Digital Heritage, http://www.sos.mo.gov//mdh.

Montezuma Masonic Lodge, www.montzumalodge.org/history.

NECROLOGY digital library, okstate.edu, chronicles, "Jesse Arnold." and "Lafayette Head."

New Mexico History.org, "Stephen Watts Kearney."

Bibliography

New Mexico Office of the State Historian, http://www.newmexicohistory.org.

New Mexico Office of the State Historian, "Pueblo de Abiqui."

New Mexico Office of the State Historian, "Taos Revolt."

Official Website of State of Missouri, http://www.sos.mo.gov/archives/history/history.asp.

Ortiz, Raymond and Reichelt, Lauren, "History of Rio Arriba County," www.rio-arriba.org.

"Republican Convention, 1880, http:en.wikipidedia.org.

Simmons, Marc, *Trail Dust*, "Army Engineer Wrote 1846 Report on New Mexico," *Santa Fe New Mexican* website, September 12, 2014.

"St. Joe, Missouri," website.

Thompson, Mark, "Lafayette Head," New Mexico History.org.

Ward, John, *Journal of John Ward*, edited by Annie Heloise, University of New Mexico, http://ejournal.unm.edu.

MISCELLANEOUS

Adams State University, Luther Bean Museum Archives— Photos and other materials.

CWA Workers, Interviews Collection, "Alamosa, Conejos, and Costilla Counties," 1933-1934, Pamphlet 349, Colorado Historical Society, Box 1-49.

Colorado Revised Statutes, Colorado Constitution, Schedule of Drafters.

Brigham Young University Archives, Vault MSS513; Christopher Carson Collection, 1854-1867; 19th Century Western and Mormon America; L. Thomas Perry Special Collections, Harold B. Lee Library, Brigham Young University; also J. M. Francisco Papers.

Catalog of the College of the Sacred Heart, 1888-1889.

Colorado Division of Water Records, Denver, Colorado.

Colorado Territory Legislative Assembly, Council Journal #10, 1874.

Colorado State Business Directory, 1878.

Colorado State University Archives, misc. including letter from Angelina Hill, letter from J. H. Thomas, J. M. Francisco papers, letter from J. H. Thomas to D.W. Working, Petition to Remove Lafayette Head.

Congressional Globe, 32nd U. S. Congress, 2nd Session, 1852.

Cummings, Alexander to Commissioner D.N. Cooley, October 10, 1866, "Report of the Secretary of Interior, Washington, Government Printing Office, 1866.

Enlistment Rolls, 2nd Auditor's Office, Treasury Department, 2nd Reg't, Missouri Mounted Volunteers (also known as "Riflemen"), Mexican War, (Col.

Sterling Price) document #384: Head, Lafayette, Private, age 21, Capt. S. H. McMillan's Co. D, Enrolled July 6, 1846 at Columbia, Missouri (for period of twelve months), Mustered into Service August 5, 1846 at Ft. Ft. Leavenworth; Muster roll September 17, 1847 "Discharged at Santa Fe by expiration of term of service, August 5, 1847.

General Laws and Joint Resolutions, Memorials and Private Acts Passed at the Third Session of the Legislative Assembly of the Territory of Colorado, 1864.

Gilpin, *Annual Report to Bureau of Indian Affairs,* 1862, National Archives, Washington.

Indian Affairs, Laws and Treaties, Vol. 2, Treaty with the Utes, 1868.

J.M. Francisco Papers (Box 55), Colorado State University Collections, Letter from Evangeline Hill to D. W. Working of Ft. Collins.

Laws of the Territory of New Mexico, 1859.

Merriweather, David, *Annual Report to the Bureau of Indian Affairs,* 1854, National Archives, Washington.

Missouri State Archives.

National Archive Records Administration NARA microfilm 234, Roll 550, Indian Agent Appointments.

NARA, microfilm 234, Roll 197, William Gilpin statement.

"Official Listing of Prizes for "Farinaceous products and their derivatives," Louisiana Purchase Exposition Documents, Missouri Historical Museum, Library and Research Center, St. Louis, Missouri.

Our Lady of Guadalupe, Book of Baptisms, Vol. 1.

Proceedings of the Constitutional Convention held in Denver, Colorado, December 20, 1875 to Frame a Constitution for the State of Colorado, Published by the Authority of Timothy O'Conner, Secretary of State, Denver, Colorado, The Smith-Brooks Press, State Printers, 1907.

Regis University Library Manifest, "Lafayette Head,." Field and Range, Reminiscences, 1887-1888."

Rich, William Gillette, "Memo Book No. 4," Rich Collection, Henry E. Huntington Library, San Marrino, CA.

Schurz, Carl: Carl Schurz Memorial Committee, Speeches, Correspondence, and Political Papers.

Steck, Michael Collection, Center for Southwest Studies, University of New Mexico, CSWR MSS134, Box 1, folder 6, digital collection, www.econtent. unm.edu, Four letters regarding reassignment of Steck and Lafayette Head being appointed Indian Agent for the Jicarilla Apache.

Taos County Records.

Thomas, J. H., Letter in Head Folder, Colorado State University Archives.

Ute Indian Agency Correspondence Files, National Archives, Washington, D.C.

Ute Indian Files, National Archives.

Viola, Herman, research notes for *Diplomats in Buckskin*, National Anthropological Archives, accessed by permission of Mr. Viola.

Wilbar, A. P., Original Survey Fields Notes, March 1858, U.S. Land Office, U.S. Customs House, Denver, Colorado.

Working, D. W., (Author of Colorado Agriculture, 1876-1926. Letter to J. H. Thomas, copy in author's possession.

Lafayette and Martina's graves are inside this fence at the Conejos Cemetery (about 1/4 mile south of the church). Piedad was added to the obelisk, but there is no sign of her grave at the spot.

Author's Collection.

Index

Abiqui, NM   3, 41, 58-62, 64-66, 106, 146
Acamuchnes (Ute)   177
Acequios   110
Adams, General Charles   169, 254-259, 261
Adams-Onís Treaty   28
Agriculture (San Luis Valley)   251, 309, 313
Alamosa, CO   201, 288, 289
Albert, Lt. James   46
Alexander, Captain A.J.   200, 202, 203
"American Yankee" Mormons   304
"American" Flour   117, 185, 249
Andrew Jackson (Ute)   301
Animas City   302
Animas River   133
Ankatosh (Antkatosh) (Ute)   160, 215, 217
Antelope (Ute)   296
Antero (Ute)   261
Antonio, CO   289
Antonito, CO   289, 307, 312, 315, 322
Apache   160, 192
Apache Canyon   37
Apache, Mescalero   130
Arapaho   137, 165, 186, 228, 259, 260
Archuleta, Col. Diego   36, 118
Archuleta, Ruben   244, 245
Aristo, Gen. Mariano   30
Arkansas River Valley   126, 189, 204
Armijo, Don Manuel   3, 36, 37
Armijo, Don Miguel   60
Army of the West   30, 33, 54, 55
Arnold, David Lafayette   189
Arnold, Jesse   25, 189, 314
Arnold, John   25
Arnold, Margaret Head   314
Arnold, Mary   189

Arnold, Price   19
Arny, W.F.   157, 256
Arriba County Sheriff (Head)   3, 66, 76
Arriba County, NM   68
Autobees, Charles   50, 116, 118

Baca, Marcelino   100, 101
Baker, Charles   125, 133, 134, 136, 142, 149
Baker's Park   133, 249
Baker's Toll Road   134-136, 149, 174
Bancroft, Hubert   309
Barela, Casmiro   275
Barlow and Sanderson Stage   288
Barnum, P.T.   162, 217
Barnum, Thomas   150
Beale, Lt. Edward F.   75
Becknell, William   18, 20, 22
Beckwith, Lt. E.G.   89
Bennet, Hiram   139, 154, 156, 214-217
Bent, Charles   38, 39, 44, 49, 50
Bent, Ignacia   50
Bent, William   49
Bent's Fort   31-33, 35
Benton, Senator Thomas Hart   29
Berry, Agent William   301
Berthelson, Soren C.   304
Bias, Racial   287
Black Hawk (Ute)   175, 176
Black Kettle   187
Blackmore, William   264
Blake, Major George   74
Board of Capitol Management   320
Board of Indian Affairs   253
Board of Trade of Southern Colorado   227
Boggs, Mrs. Thomas   50, 218

342

Index

Boggsville 218
Boone, Albert C. 216, 217
Boone, Daniel 18, 19, 22
Boone, Daniel Morgan 18, 19, 22, 25
Boone's Lick Trace 20-22
Bosque Redondo 174, 215
Boulder, CO 188, 265
Brands, Cattle 288
Bridges 149
Brunot, Felix 256-260
Brush, Jared 216
Buffalo 264
Buffalo Soldiers 291, 293, 294
Burgoin, Captain 52
Burials, In church floor 236
Byers, William 134

Cabeza, Raphael (*see* name Head, Lafayette)
Cabeza, Rita 195
Calhoun, James 62-65
California Gulch (Leadville) 126, 147
Camp Lewis 269
Camp Weld 143
Canaby, Col. Edward 143
Cañon City Penitentiary 269
Capital City, CO 270
Capote (Ute Individual) 217
Capote Utes 221, 262, 267, 291, 303
Captain Jack 217
Carleton, Brigadier General James 98, 174
Carr, William 70, 271
Carson, Adaline 26
Carson, Josepha 50, 218, 219
Carson, Juan 194
Carson, Kit 2, 6, 25, 26, 39, 40, 66, 70, 98, 99 102, 105, 108, 112, 113, 118, 119, 122, 123, 125, 130-133, 141, 142, 146, 147, 152, 156, 161, 174, 175, 185, 186, 188, 191-204, 212, 214, 216, 218, 219, 220
Carson, Lindsey 18, 25

Carson, Maria Josepha Jaramillo 211
Casador (Ute) 199
Catholism (prejudice) 13, 48, 49, 312
Cattle 251-253, 263, 287, 289, 309, 313, 314
Cavalry 30, 31
Census-1850 309
Census-1860 247
Census-1870 247
Census-1885 312
"Centennial State" 277
Chacon (Ute) 76, 77
Chaffe, Jerome 258, 271
Chama River 288
Chama River Valley 59-61
Chapman, Captain 106
Chapultec 267
Chavez, General José Maria 92
Cheyenne Indians 127, 154, 165, 186, 202, 260, 312
Cheyenne, WY 258
Chicago, IL 306
Chilicott, George M. 217, 270, 280
Chipeta 193, 290, 297, 302
Chivington, Col. John M. 166, 167
Church, Daniel Pike 269
Cimarron Agency 228, 263
Cimarron, NM 146
Cinche (*see* Quinche) (Ute)
Cisneros, José Cresincio 212, 308
Cisneros, Martina (*see* Head, Martina)
Cisneros, Piedad (*see* Sisneros, Piedad)
Civil Rights Act of 1866 192, 195
Civil War 129, 132, 137, 140, 142, 143, 159, 164, 165, 169, 186
"Civilization" 247
Clark, John and Clarence 159
Clear Creek Diggings 121
Cochetopa Agency (*see* Los Piños I Agency) 222
Cochetopa Pass 103, 105, 221, 223, 224
College of the Sacred Heart 215
Collins, James 118, 119, 123, 124, 128

343

Colorado (Ute)   171
Colorado Agricultural Society   153
Colorado Capitol Building   10
Colorado City   142, 204, 218
"Colorado Clique"   224
Colorado Constitutional Convention   275-277
Colorado Counties   139, 140
Colorado Militia   176, 268
Colorado Springs, CO   188
Colorado Statehood Election   277
Colorado Stockgrowers Association   271
Colorado Territorial House   139
Colorado Territorial Senate   7, 267, 268, 270
Colorado Territorial Volunteers   142, 144, 186
Colorow (Ute)   189
Comanche Indians   157, 165, 202
Conejos Camp   303
Conejos County   140, 151, 190, 247, 268
Conejos County Commissioners   315
Conejos Courthouse   315, 323
Conejos Land Grants (1833 and 1844)   60, 67, 82-84, 93-96, 98, 264, 323
Conejos River   84, 93-97, 110, 112, 120, 121, 140, 151, 231, 233, 264, 303, 304, 306, 312, 313
Conejos Town Hall   319
Conejos Ute Agency   159, 166, 184, 189, 213
Conejos, CO   4, 6, 8, 97, 113, 123, 133, 134, 145, 146, 151, 164, 167, 169, 171, 172, 180, 189, 191, 210, 228, 231, 241, 247, 241, 249, 251, 263, 264, 268, 280, 281, 305, 306, 315, 316, 323
Conell, Sister Ophelia   241
Confederates   154
Conrad, Charles M.   73
Continental Divide   219
Cook, Charles   271

Cooke, Captain Phillip St. George   35, 36, 40
Costilla County   140
Costilla, CO   74, 81, 273
Cotoan (Ouray's son)   257, 259, 260
Cowboys   252
Cree, T.R.   258
Cumbres and Toltec Scenic Railroad   322
Cummings, Alexander   179, 196, 201, 204
Cummings, Major General John Pope   196
Curtis, U.M.   216, 217
Cutler, Ben   157

Daigre, Henry   149
Daniels (Arapaho Agent)   259
Darley, Rev. Alexander   243, 244
Davis, Jefferson   140
Denver & Rio Grande Railroad (D&RG)   247, 288, 289, 302, 304, 309, 322
Del Norte Mine   251
Del Norte, CO   150, 212, 250, 264, 272, 312
Diary of the Jesuit Residence of Our Lady of Guadalupe Parish, Conejos, CO   237-239, 318, 321
"Denver Ring"   168, 278, 279, 290
De Courtney, Lt. James   35, 36
Denver, CO   188, 228, 241, 265, 268, 271, 275, 315
Denver Ute Agency   225, 255
Denver Catholic Diocese   230
"Denver Treaty"   155
Dole, William   154, 157, 163, 173
"Don Raphael"   96
"Dona Cabeza"   96
Doniphan, Col. A.W.   31, 39 42
Douglas, Stephen   138
Douglas (Ute)   296, 297
Downing, Eliza   164, 165, 172

Index

Downing, Finis   164-167, 171, 172, 175, 180
Downing, John   184
Downing, Lucy   164-167
Dragoons   30
Durango, CO   288
Denominations (Indian Assigned)   253

Eaton, E.A.   157
Edwards, Gov. John C.   30
El Cedro Redondo   93, 94
El Emundo, Battle of   52
El Llanito   93
Elbert, Gov. Samuel   224, 265, 268, 269
Enabling Act for the Admission of Colorado as a State   275
Ephraim, CO   305
Epidemic (Conejos)   264
Eskridge, Wilmer   293
Esmond, John   249, 250
Espinosa, Felix   169, 170
Espinosa, José   170
Espinosa, Vivian   169-170
Evans, Gov. John   152, 155, 156, 168, 170, 173, 177, 186-191, 221, 223

Fauntleroy, Col. T.T.   103, 107, 174
Fede, Father Lorenzo   238, 239
Ferries   148-150
59'ers Pioneer Association   126
Fillmore, President Millard   70
Flour (*see* Mill)
Fort Craig, NM   143
Fort Defiance, NM   269
Fort Garland, CO   115-118, 136, 142-145, 149, 150, 169-172, 184, 186, 198-204, 212, 218, 241, 255, 257, 288, 291, 295, 323
Fort Lewis, CO   241, 310
Fort Lyons, CO   142, 187, 218
Fort Marcy, NM   42-44, 47, 73

Fort Massachusetts, CO   74, 75, 88, 89, 98, 103, 104, 107, 112, 115, 116
Fort Pagosa Springs, CO   269
Fort Union, NM   73, 144, 149, 176, 196, 204
Fort Pueblo Massacre   100-102
Fort Stevens, CO   200
Fort Steele, WY   295
Fossett, Frank   287
Four Corners   199
Franciscans   234, 235, 242
Francisco, John M.   127, 149, 150, 235
Fremont, John   26, 40, 106
French, J. Carey   249
Franklin, MO   20, 21, 25, 26
Feast of Our Lady of Guadalupe (December 12)   235, 240

Gabriel, Don José   240
Gallegos, Julian   83, 84
Garcia, Jesus M.   275
Garcia, José Victor   304
Garland City   288
Garland, John   115
Gasparri, Donald   241
Genizaros   60
Gilbert, A.H.   157
Gilpin, Gov. William   31, 41, 42, 123, 132, 133, 140, 142, 143, 145, 152, 153, 310
Glorietta Pass   144
Godfrey (Godfroy), William   159, 164, 166, 177, 209, 215, 217, 223, 225
Godfrey, Mrs.   225
Golden City Convention   152
Golden, CO   142
Gonzales, Sister Vinceta   241
Governor (Lafe running for)   277-280
Grand Mesa   299
Grand River   299, 302
Grand River Utes   168
Grand Valley   300

Grant, President Ulysses 221, 224, 258, 275
Great Basin 192
Gregg, Josiah 45, 79, 90, 91
Greiner, John 67, 69-71
Grouley 160
Guadalupe County 140
Guadalupe Land Grant (*see* Conejos Land Grant)
Guadalupe, CO 93, 95, 114, 171, 172, 184, 231, 233, 264, 315
Guero (Ute) 160
Gunnison River 299
Gunnison, Capt. John W. 89

Haffin, Leroy 201
Hall, Frank 315, 316
Hannibal & St. Joe Railroad 165
Harris, E.R. 190
Hay, John 173
Hays, President Rutherford B. 279
Head, Alfred R. 16, 17, 22, 23
Head, Bartena Gray 5, 23, 25
Head, Eliza Jane Downing 5, 23-25
Head, Lafayette (name-*see* also Cabeza, Raphael) vii, 57
Head, Margaret 5, 22-25, 127
Head, Martina (Sisneros) vii, 3, 8, 57, 62, 63, 96, 113, 114, 180, 181, 191, 193, 194, 196, 212, 213, 239, 240, 278, 282, 309, 314
Head, Miguel 196
Head, Raphael (Also *see* Cabeza, Raphael) 63
Head, Rita 196
Head, William 16, 19-22
Head's Fort (Fort Head) 20, 22
Heard, John 22
Hildago, Don José Miguel 234
Hill, Evangeline 95
Hill, George (William) 308, 310, 313, 316, 320
Hill, William 307, 311
Home Forts 18-20

Homestead Act 153, 251
House (Head's First) 113
House (Head's Second) 171, 250, 280, 281, 286, 318, 319
Howard County, MO 18, 20, 25
Hungry/Starving Utes 186, 199, 208, 213, 221
Hunt, Gov. Alexander 210, 215-217, 223, 224, 255, 304

Idaho Territory (Colorado) 137
Ignacio 292
Immigrants 48
Indian Affair Section of the Department of Interior 252, 254, 256-258
Indian Agencies (General) 250
Indian Agent Head 147, 180, 208, 227
Indian Agents (generally) 70-72, 119, 120, 123-125, 168, 169
Indian Captives 190
Indian Peace Commission 220
Indian Rights Association 302, 303
Ingersol, Ernest 313
International Order of Odd Fellows (I.O.O.F.) 66, 312
Irrigation 110-112

Jackson, William Henry 256
Jacques, José Maria 84, 93-95, 148, 264
Jefferson Territory 125, 126, 137
Jesuit Society of Jesus 211
Jesuits 234, 242, 243
Jicarilla Apache 56, 59, 65, 69, 70-73, 76, 77, 92, 93, 99, 100, 102, 103, 105, 107, 108, 118, 119, 146, 157, 175, 188, 189, 199, 200, 228, 267
Jicarilla Apache Indian Agency 146
Jocknick, Sidney 254, 261
Johnson, Miles 133

346

Index

Johnson, President Andrew 186, 190, 192, 216, 219, 220
José Maria (Ute) 160, 215
Julesburg, CO 166, 188

Kaniache (Ute) 104-107, 118, 160, 197, 199-204, 215, 217, 255, 258, 299
Kanosh (Ute) 261
Kaplan, Michael 283
Kearney, Gen. Stephen Watts 30-44
Kearney's Code 38
Kellogg, Edward M. 216
Kerber Creek 208
Kern, Dr. Benjamin 106
Kiowa Indians 118, 127, 157
Knights Templar 311, 312

La Cañada, Battle of 51, 52
La Loma 133, 149, 150, 249
La Plata County 270
La Veta Pass 288, 304
Lake City, CO 247, 267
Lake Fork of the Gunnison River 133
Lamy, Bishop Juan Baptiste 4, 118, 230-236, 242, 244, 245
Land Grant Court 264
Land Grants (Mexican) 29, 41, 61, 82, 85, 87
Land Ownership (Ute concept of) 176
Land Speculation 264
Las Animas Land Grab 271
Las Cerritos 85
Las Vegas, NM 35, 36
Lavender, David 262
Law of the Indies 111
Lawrence, John 208-211, 215, 216, 223, 229
Lawton, Charles 265
Leone, Father Alexander 237
Lieutenant Governor of Colorado (Lafayette Head) 71, 244, 279, 280, 282, 283, 285
Lincoln, President Abraham 140, 161, 162, 172
Little Annie Mine 251
Livestock 288
Lobato, Pedro 255
Locusts 210, 211, 273
"Long Walk" 131, 175, 215
Los Piños Creek (Central San Luis Valley) 224
Los Piños Creek (Cochetopa Pass) 223-226
Los Piños Creek (Southern-near today's Durango) 221, 223, 224
Los Piños I Agency 223-229, 255-259, 264
Los Piños II Agency 267, 268, 291, 299, 301
Loynton 303
Lueder, Herman 261
Luther Bean Museum 323

Machebuef, Bishop Joseph 232, 233, 235-238, 241, 245
Macomb, Capt. J.M. 121
Madison, Capt. George 154
Magoffin, James 33, 36, 38
Magoffin, Susan 33
Mahoney, Sister Mary 241
Mansfield, Brevet Col. Joseph 88, 89
Manypenny, George 299, 300
Margaretta Lode 251
Marquis de Lafayette 23
Martinez Land Grant 85
Martinez, Antonio 82
Martinez, Barbara 239
Martinez, Father José 234-237, 242
Martinez, José 82, 85
Martinez, Martina (*see* Sisneros, Martina) 82, 85, 93
Martinez, Seldon 82, 85
Masons 4, 65, 66, 243, 310, 312, 318, 321
Maxwell Agency 146, 255

Maxwell Land Grant 85, 109, 225
Maxwell, Lucian 131
McCook (Ute) 256
McCook, Gen. Edward M. 169, 223-225, 265
Meachum, Alfred 293, 299, 301
Mears, Otto 10, 184-186, 207-211, 215, 216, 221-223, 228, 250, 255, 257-262, 267,276, 283, 299-302
Medicine Lodge Treaty 204
Meeker Massacre 292-297, 300, 302
Meeker Women 297
Meeker, Nathan 292, 293, 296
Merriweather, Gov. David 71, 76, 86, 87, 92, 99, 146
Messervy, William 102
Mexican Bar 121
"Mexican Flour" 115, 117
Mexican-American Prejudice 14
Mexican-American War 2, 3, 27-49, 54
Mexican-American War Veterans 265-267
Miles, John D. 259
Milk Creek 293, 294
Mill (Jacques) 114, 115
Mill (Lafe) 114, 115, 147, 151, 172, 227, 238, 252, 265, 290 316, 320
Minerals and Mineral Belt 125, 247, 249
Miners' Code 249
Mining Act of 1872 249
Mission San Geronimo de Taos 52, 53
Missouri 16-27
Missouri Mounted Volunteers 31, 32, 40-44, 50-54
Moffat Jr., David 271
Montaño, Father F. S. 230, 231, 234, 235
Montezuma Masonic Lodge 65, 66
Montoya, Pablo 50, 52
Mora, Battle of 52
Morada 245
Mormon Battalion 31, 32, 40

Mormons (in San Luis Valley) 303-306
Mouache Ute Agency 146
Mouache Utes 71, 73, 99, 100, 105, 107, 108, 118, 158, 174, 179, 188, 197, 204, 212, 221, 228, 255, 262, 263, 267, 291, 303
Muchuchop (Ute) 177
Myers and Stolistimier 273

Navajo 41, 46, 64, 82, 118, 127-129, 136, 174, 175, 194, 215
Navajo Captives 190
Nelson, Alfred 314, 315, 319
Nelson, Piedad 321
Nevava (Ute) 147, 178
New Franklin, MO 21
New Mexico Counties (1850) 69
New Mexico Mounted Volunteers 4, 102, 103, 108, 118
New Mexico Notch 138, 139
New Mexico Territorial Legislature 4, 66, 67, 115, 126, 235
New Rocheport, MO 19
New York City 217
Nicaagot (Nicaagut) (Ute) 160, 215
Nicolay, John 162, 173, 175-177
North Branch Old Spanish Trail 81
Northern Utes 188
Novavetuquaret (Ute) 177

Oakes, Daniel C. 213-219, 223
Obituary (Lafe) 316, 317, 319, 320
"Old Bill" Williams 106
Old Spanish Trail 58, 59, 61, 80, 81, 122
Oldham, Ann 130
Otero, Don Miguel 137, 138
Our Lady of Guadalupe Chapel 95
Our Lady of Guadalupe Church 4, 114, 193, 195, 230-242, 318, 323
Ouray, Chief 6, 105, 125, 148, 151, 152, 156, 159-162, 167, 176-178,

193, 201-204, 208, 209, 215-221, 223, 228, 250, 254-261, 292-299

Paant (Ute) 160, 215
Pabusat (Pahbusat) (Ute) 159, 160, 215
Pagosa and Rio Grande Toll Road 288
Pagosa Hot Springs 122, 129-131, 274
Pagosa Springs, CO 288
Parish, William 272, 273
Penitente Brotherhood 234, 235, 242-246, 269
Perleta, NM 145
Personé, Father Salvadore 236-238, 241, 315
Petition to Remove Head as Indian Agent 182, 183
Pfeiffer, Albert 66, 102, 118-121, 127-133, 141, 149, 185, 198, 200, 212, 218, 219, 241, 254, 273, 274, 287, 312, 314
Piah (Ute) 160, 215, 217
Piedad (*see* Cisneros, Head, Hill, Martinez, Nelson, & Sisneros) 213, 308, 309, 315-318
Pike's Stockade 94
Pikes Peak Region 121, 122
Pitkin, Gov. Frederick 292
Plains Indians 61, 106, 107, 118, 126, 137, 166, 167, 179, 187-189, 204, 215, 264, 277
Polk, President James K. 27, 29, 30, 38, 39, 54
Poncha Pass 104, 272
Pope Pius IX 232
Posthof, F.W. 159
Postmaster 151
Powder Face (Arapaho) 260
Preamble to Colorado Constitution 276
Price, Col. Sterling 31, 33, 34, 40, 42, 50-55

Prospectors 251
Pueblo Grand Jury 272
Pueblo Indians 45
Pueblo Revolt 3, 49-54
Pueblo, CO 271, 297, 304
Puuwich (Pubwich) (Ute) 159, 160
Puvitz (Ute) 296

Quinche (Cinche) (Ute) 148, 158-160, 177, 193

Racism 314
Railroads 269, 287, 310, 313
Range Law (Spanish) 252
Redman, Francis 29
Reese, Dempsey 249
Republican Convention 278, 306
Reservation 163-199, 201, 204, 217, 219, 220, 262
Reynolds, James 154
Rich, William Gillette 243
Richardson, Albert 46-48
Richfield County 303
Rio Abajo 69
Rio Arriba 59, 67, 69, 70
Rio Arriba Bridge Company 147
Rio Grande County 270
Rio Grande Gorge 78, 79
Rio Grande River 78, 110, 130, 148-150, 213, 270, 308
Rio Grande Southern Railroad 250
Roads 149, 270, 288
Robinson, Special Agent M.B. 271
Rolly, Rev. Miguel 235, 236
Romero, Thomasito 50
Routt, Gov. John (Territorial and State) 265, 278, 288, 306, 316
Ruff, Lt. Col. C.F. 31
"Rush to the Rockies" 121, 125
Russell Brothers 121
Russell, Marian 114
Russell, Nathan 208
Ruxton, George F. 56

349

Sacred Heart Academy 241
Saguache 207, 208, 210, 211, 221-223, 225, 228
Saguache County 211
Saguache River 40, 220, 223, 249
Salazar, Fr. Ramon 239
Salazar, Pedro 67
Salazar, Sabino 240
San Acacio 81
San Antonio Mountains 80
San Antonio River 233
San Juan Mountains 12, 41, 42, 62, 80, 89,
San Juan River 263
San Luis (Town) 74, 81
San Pedro 81
Sand Creek Massacre 186, 187, 189, 293
Sandoval, San Pedro 81
Sangre de Cristo Camp 153, 264, 310
Sangre de Cristo Mountains 80, 121, 138, 310
Sangre de Cristo Pass 184
Santa Fe Ring 264, 279, 290
Santa Fe Trail (Cimarron Cutoff) 31, 40
Santa Fe Trail (Mountain Branch) 31, 40, 91
Santa Fe, NM 37, 38, 43-48, 54, 58, 230
Sapatchi 177
Sawatch Range 80
Sawnwatsewich (Sawaich) 177, 217
Schools 269, 315
Schurz, Carl 161, 178, 296
Seldon, José 82
Servillita 63, 67-69, 75, 78, 92-96
Shavano 157, 158, 160, 189, 198, 202
Shawashe Yet 177
Sheep 113, 314
Sherman, Gov. William 201
Sierra Blanca 322
Silverton Railroad 250
Simmons, Virginia 205, 221
Simon Turley's Mill 50

Sioux 258
Sisneros, José 63, 213, 309
Sisneros, Martina (see Head, Martina)
Sisneros, Piedad vii, 9, 63, 213, 307, 309, 321
Sisters of Loretto 241
Sisters of the Order of Mercy 241
Slaves (Native American) 192-196
Smith, Silas 305
Society of Colorado Pioneers 126, 153
Southern Colorado Stock Growers 271
"Southern Mormons" 304
Southern Ute Agency 224, 227, 262, 291, 299, 302
Southern Utes 221, 223, 263, 298, 303, 323
Spanish Peaks 200
Special or Sub-Indian Agents (see Indian Agents)
Speer, Lt. Calvin 225, 227
St. Joseph, MO 160, 164, 165
St. Vrain, Col. Ceran 52, 66, 71, 102, 103, 107
Statehood (Colorado) 269
Steck, Michael 70, 175, 177
Stevens, John 304
Stockton, Gen. George Robert 40
Stunner 303
Summitville 239, 249, 250
Suruipe (Ute) 215, 217
Susan (Ute) 293
Swadesh, Frances Leon 94

Tabby (Ute) 261
Tabeguache Agency 145, 146, 150, 151, 208, 223, 225
Tabeguache Utes 71, 94, 108, 118, 119, 122, 123, 125, 144, 157, 161, 176, 178, 179, 188, 189, 197, 198, 204, 221, 223, 224, 229, 267, 291, 295, 297, 300
Taos Indian Agency 64, 69, 146

Index

Taos Lightning 50
Taos Uprising (*see* Pueblo Revolt)
Taos Valley 78
Taos, Battle of 52, 53
Taos, NM 3, 35, 122, 140, 146
Tappan, Col. Samuel 170, 176, 194
Taylor, General Zachery 30
Telegraph Lines 269
Territory, Colorado 136-140
Territory, New Mexico 58, 66-68, 115
Texas 29, 30, 55
Thomas, J. H. 95, 225, 315
Thompson, James E. 255, 265
Thornburg, Maj. T.T. 293-295
Tiben, Bishop John Henry 230
Tierra Amarillo Land Grant 235
Tierra Blanca (Ute) 100, 101, 103, 104
Tobin, Tom 116, 170, 171
Trader (Lafe) 62
Transportation 313
Trask, Jabez Nelson 229, 253, 254
Traveler's Insurance Company 263
Treaty of 1846 (Ute) 41
Treaty, Denver 155
Treaty, Utes, 1844 Governor Martinez Conflict 61
Treaty of 1849 (Calhoun Treaty) (Ute) 64, 65, 69, 106
Treaty of 1863 (Tabeguache Treaty) 155, 179-181, 201
Treaty of 1866 (Ute) 203
Treaty of 1868 (Kit Carson) 213-221, 249, 255
Treaty of 1873 259-261, 267, 269
Treaty of 1880 298-303
Treaty of Guadalupe-Hidalgo 12, 54-56, 77, 84, 85, 137, 192
Trinidad 91, 265
Trujillo, Anatansio 85, 94
Tupuepa 60
Tupuwaat 59, 60

U.S. Land Grant Court 86
U.S. Mail 267
U.S. Marshal (Head) 3, 65, 67, 76
U.S. Preemption Act of 1841 91, 93, 153
Uintah Reservation 302
Uintah Utes 168, 205, 213, 215, 221, 298
"Uncle Lafe" 96
Uncompahgre Agency 267, 268
Uncompahgre River 267, 299
Uncompahgre Utes 267, 268, 291
Uncompahgre Valley 250, 258, 301
Uncowratgut 177
Unitarian 253
Ussel, Rev. P. Gabriel 231, 232
Utah 302
Ute Agent (Lafe) 4, 6, 67, 69-71, 141, 145
Ute Bands in Colorado 70, 71
Ute Commission (on Removal of Utes) 299-301
Ute Delegation to Washington (1863 Treaty) 165
Ute Indian Prejudice 13
Ute Mountain Agency 303
Ute War of 1855 102-105, 107, 108
Utes, 1844 Governor Martinez Conflict 61

Valasquez, Don Jesus 97, 232
Valdez, Don Celedonio 240, 264
Valdez, Juan Baptiste 115
Valdez, Stanley 82
Valverde, Battle of 144
Vasquez, Celedonio 235
Vasquez, Juan 235
Vhilcoot, George M. 216
Vigil, Agapeta 273
Vigil, Don Aciano 53
Vigil, Juan (New Mexico Governor) 37, 38
Vigil, Rev. Joseph Miguel 233, 234
Villa Grove 208
Viola, Herman 168

⌘ 351 ⌘

Waanibe (Singing Bird)   26
Walker, W.R.   202
Walsen, Fred   208
War of 1812   17
Waro (Ute)   215, 217
Washington City   157, 164, 167, 169, 176
Washington D.C.   216, 261, 297, 298, 300
Washington, Col. John   63
Weeminuche Utes   163, 176, 212, 221, 262, 291
Weightman, Richard   12
Wells   287
Wheaton, Theodore D.   243
Wheeler, Lt. George   237
Wheeler, William A.   279
White River Utes   213, 221, 259, 292, 293, 295, 296, 298
Whitley, Lt. J. H.   58
Whitley, Simon   175, 177
Wightman Gulch   249
Wightman, James   249
Wilbar, A.P.   120, 121
Will (Lafe's)   317, 318
Willock, Lt. Col.   50
Wilson, Tassie   44
Women's National Peace Commission   220
Women's Suffrage   276
Wooton, Dick   100
Workman, D.W.   95

Yampa Utes   213, 221, 292
Yupuswaat

Maps

San Luis Valley Today 15
Missouri Territory-1812 17
US-Mexico-1830 20
Boone's Lick Trace 21
U.S., Mexico, and Texas 27
Santa Fe 39
Battle of La Cañada 51
U.S. States and Territories 68
Fort Massachusetts Plan 75
Old Spanish Trail 81
Mexican Land Grants 83
Fort Garland and Trails 116
Fort Garland Plan 117
U.S. Confederate States 128

Colorado's Original Thirteen Counties 135
New Mexico Notch 138
Western San Juans 141
Confederate Invasion of New Mexico 144
San Luis Valley ca. 1870 207
San Luis Valley and Eastern San Juans 248
New Colorado Counties ca. 1874 266
Military Road Options 270
Conejos Town Plat 284
Meeker Massacre Vicinity 295
Mining Map (Conejos) 303

www.ingramcontent.com/pod-product-compliance
Lightning Source LLC
Chambersburg PA
CBHW050550170426
43201CB00011B/1642